Twin Star Exorcists

ONMYOJI

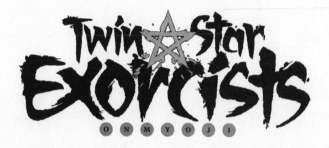

Twin ★ Star Exorcists

O N M Y O J I

8

STORY & ART

YOSHIAKI SUKENO

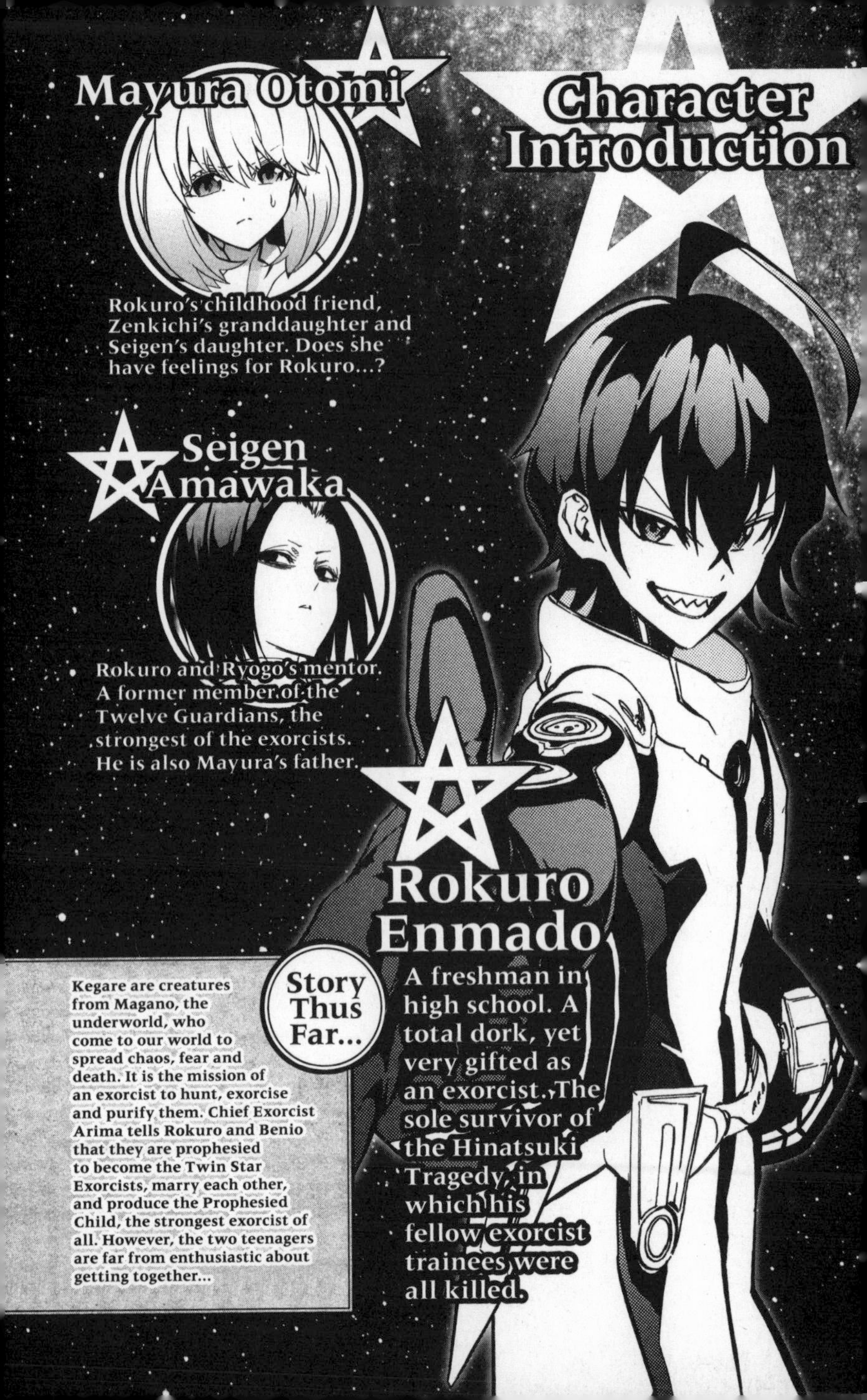
Character Introduction
Mayura Otomi
Rokuro's childhood friend, Zenkichi's granddaughter and Seigen's daughter. Does she have feelings for Rokuro...?
Seigen Amawaka
Rokuro and Ryogo's mentor. A former member of the Twelve Guardians, the strongest of the exorcists. He is also Mayura's father.
Rokuro Enmado
A freshman in high school. A total dork, yet very gifted as an exorcist. The sole survivor of the Hinatsuki Tragedy, in which his fellow exorcist trainees were all killed.
Story Thus Far...
Kegare are creatures from Magano, the underworld, who come to our world to spread chaos, fear and death. It is the mission of an exorcist to hunt, exorcise and purify them. Chief Exorcist Arima tells Rokuro and Benio that they are prophesied to become the Twin Star Exorcists, marry each other, and produce the Prophesied Child, the strongest exorcist of all. However, the two teenagers are far from enthusiastic about getting together...

Sayo Ikaruga

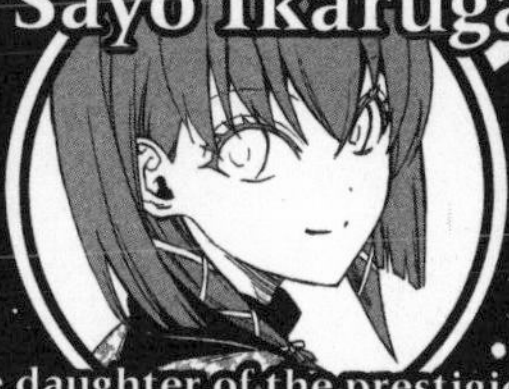

The daughter of the prestigious Ikaruga family from Tsuchimikado Island. She grew up with Shimon like real siblings. Her Spiritual Guardian is Kuzu no Ha.

Shimon Ikaruga

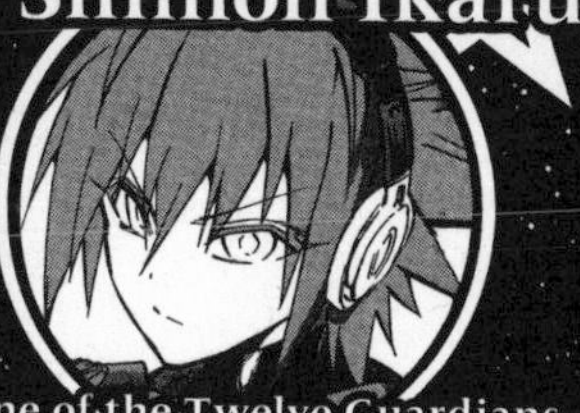

One of the Twelve Guardians, he holds the title of Suzaku. He has deep respect for his mentor, Seigen.

Hijirimaru

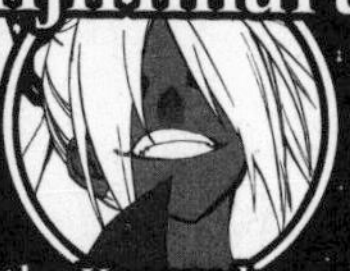

One of the Kegare known as the Basara. He is after Sayo for her strong spiritual power.

Higano

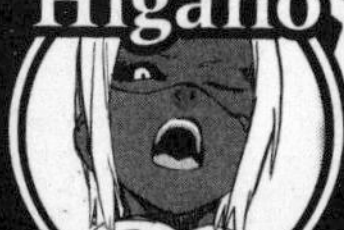

One of the Basara with a totally opposite personality to Hijirimaru. He is always calm and composed.

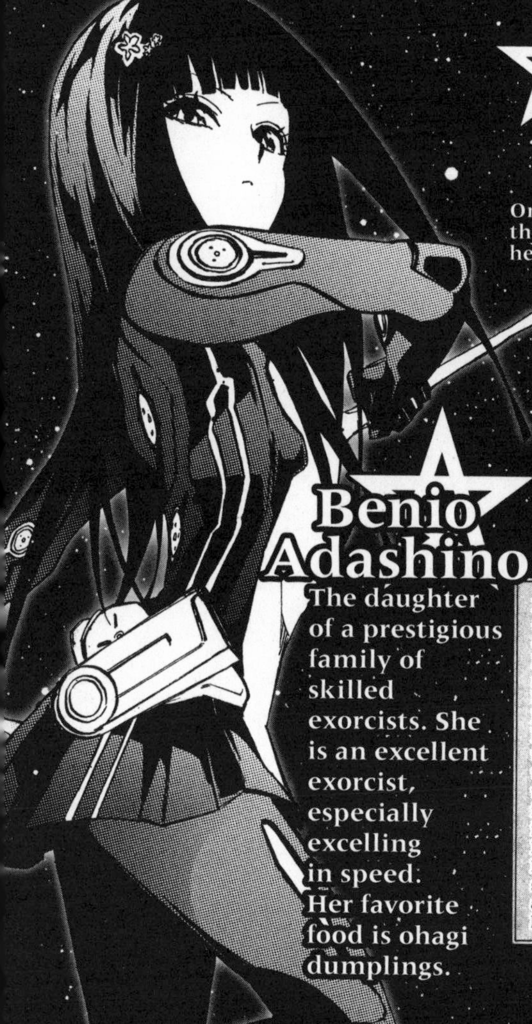

Benio Adashino

The daughter of a prestigious family of skilled exorcists. She is an excellent exorcist, especially excelling in speed. Her favorite food is ohagi dumplings.

Benio's twin brother, presumed dead after he massacred his fellow exorcist trainees, reappears in Magano and attempts to kill his sister and Rokuro. After a fierce battle, the two manage to ward him off and are determined to head to Tsuchimikado Island, the front line of battle against the Kegare. After two years of training, Rokuro is tested by Sayo in the Ascertainment Ritual and is successfully qualified to go. But then Sayo is kidnapped by a Basara, a powerful Kegare who can speak. Now Rokuro, Benio, Shimon and even new exorcist Mayura have headed off to rescue her...!

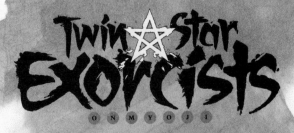

Twin Star Exorcists

ONMYOJI

EXORCISMS

8

ONMYOJI have worked for the Imperial Court since the Heian era. In addition to exorcising evil spirits, as civil servants they performed a variety of roles, including advising nobles by foretelling the future, creating the calendar, observing the movements of the stars, measuring time...

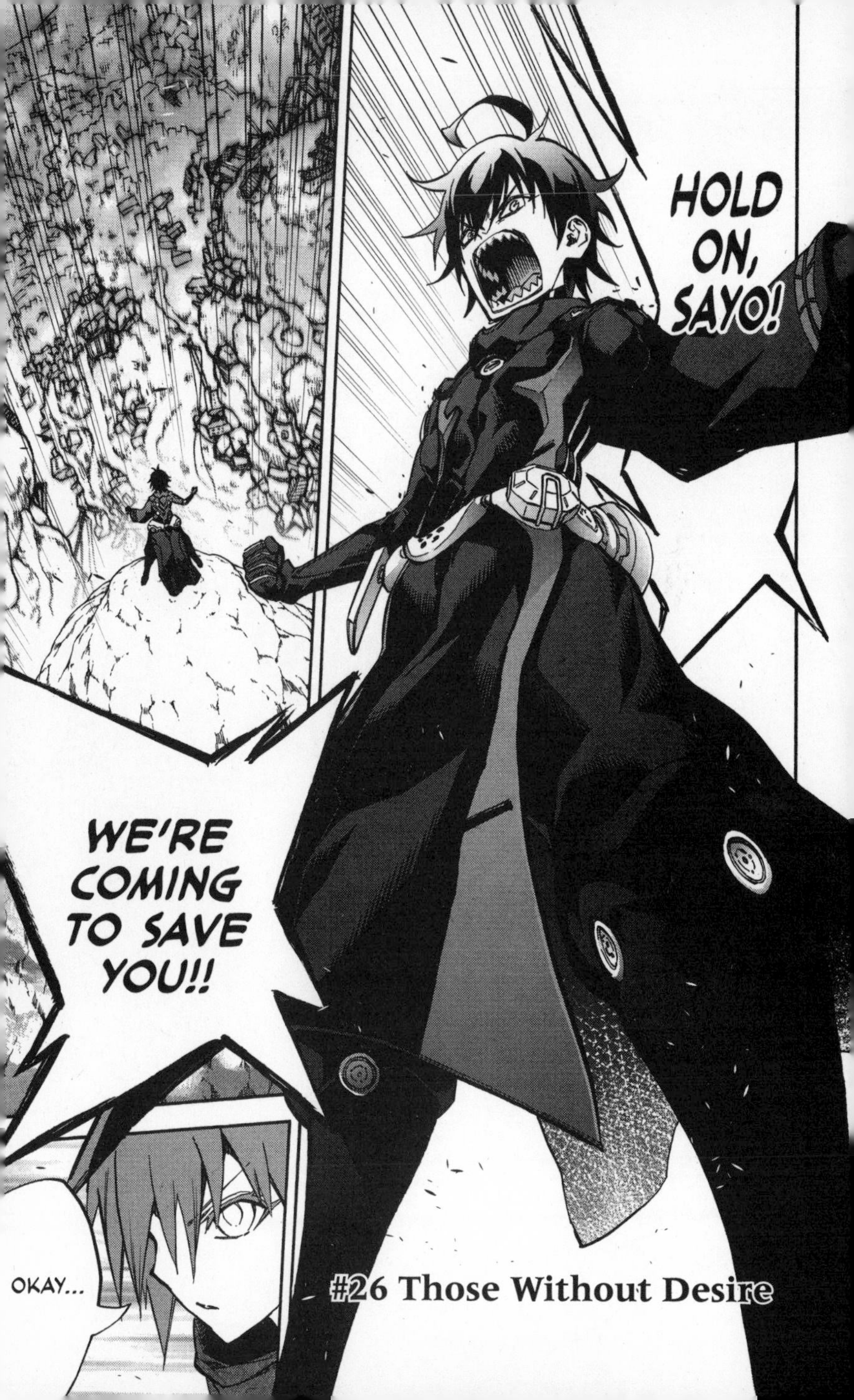
HOLD ON, SAYO!
WE'RE COMING TO SAVE YOU!!
#26 Those Without Desire
OKAY...

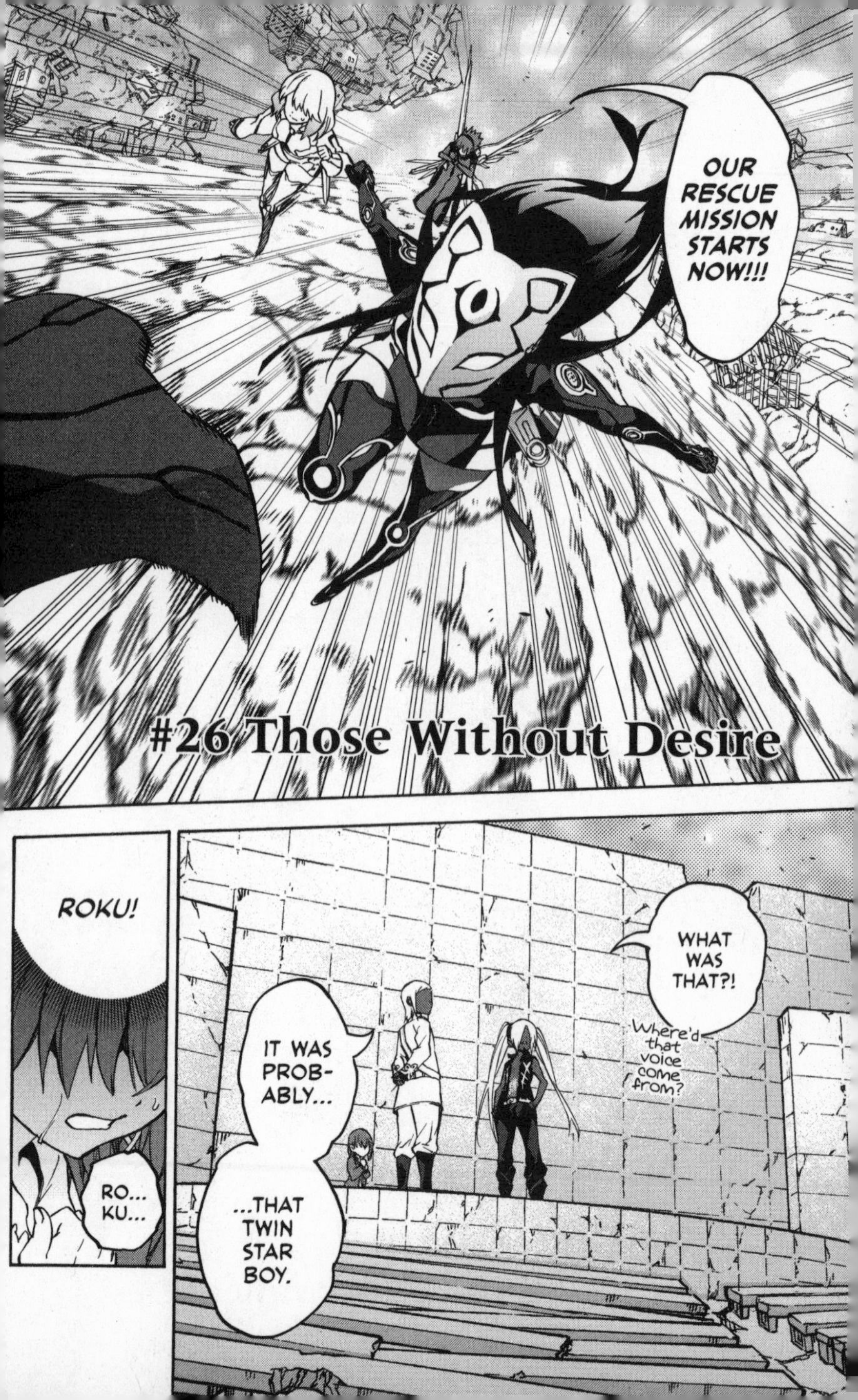
OUR RESCUE MISSION STARTS NOW!!!
#26 Those Without Desire
WHAT WAS THAT?!
Where'd that voice come from?
IT WAS PROB-ABLY...
...THAT TWIN STAR BOY.
ROKU!
RO... KU...

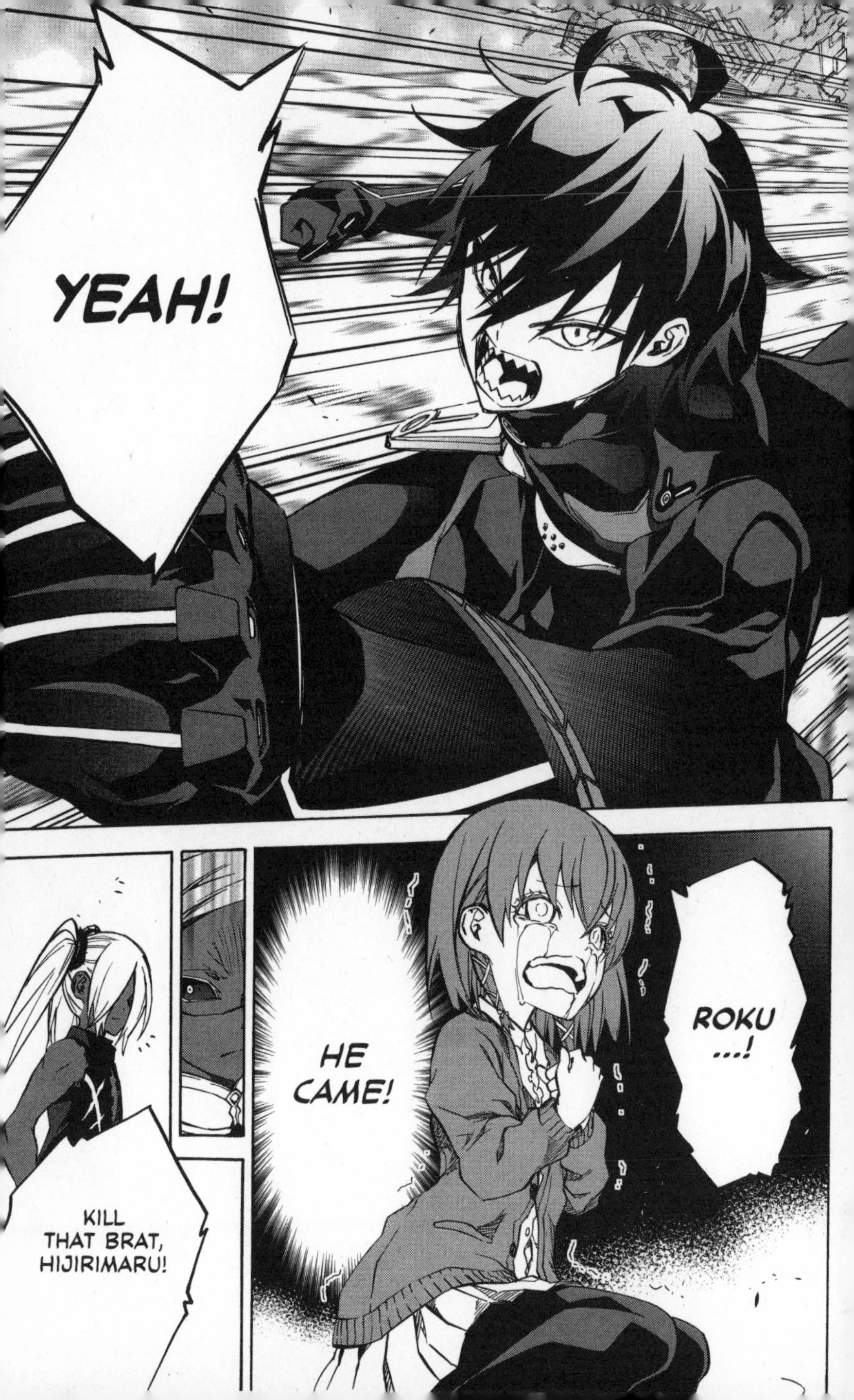
YEAH!
ROKU ...!
HE CAME!
KILL THAT BRAT, HIJIRIMARU!

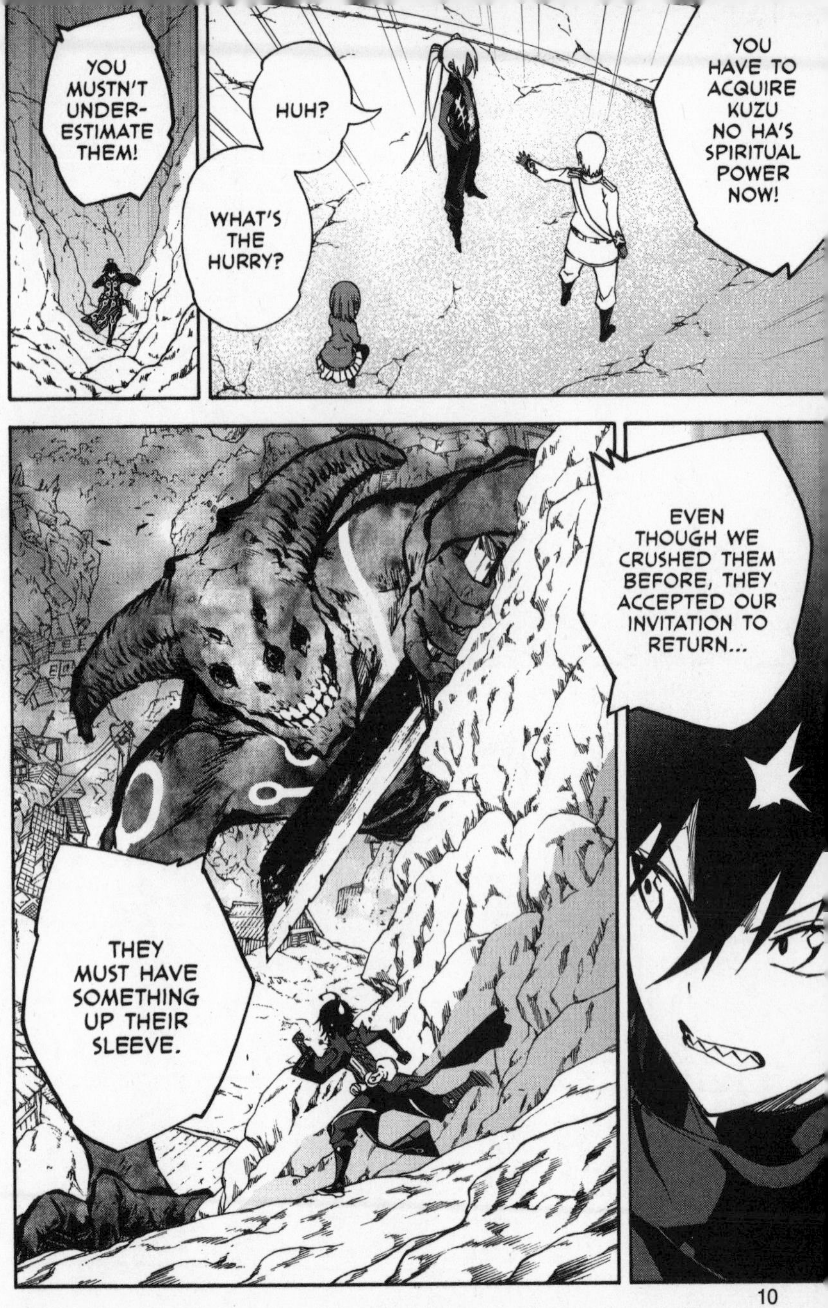
YOU HAVE TO ACQUIRE KUZU NO HA'S SPIRITUAL POWER NOW!
HUH?
WHAT'S THE HURRY?
YOU MUSTN'T UNDER-ESTIMATE THEM!
EVEN THOUGH WE CRUSHED THEM BEFORE, THEY ACCEPTED OUR INVITATION TO RETURN...
THEY MUST HAVE SOMETHING UP THEIR SLEEVE.

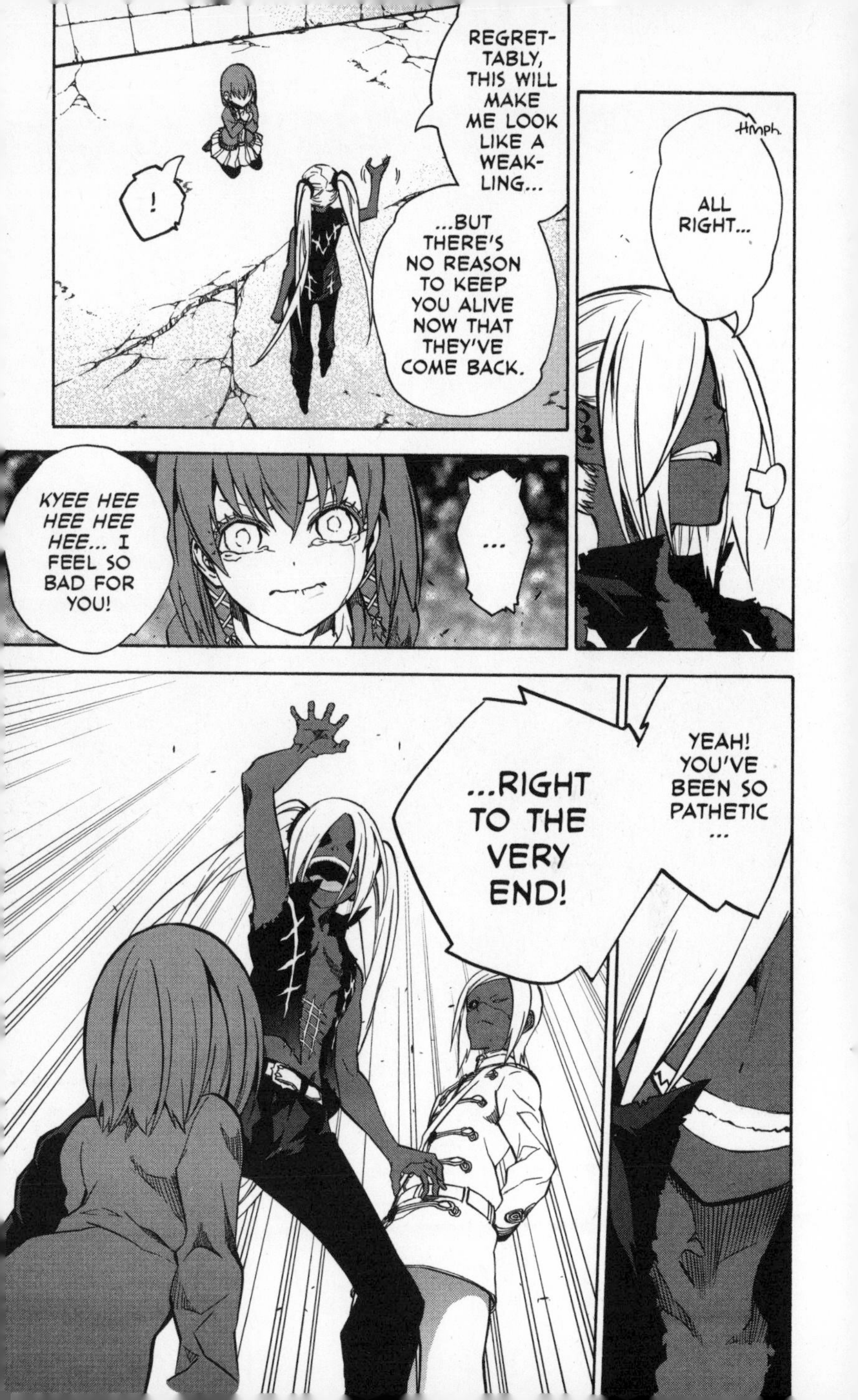
REGRET-TABLY, THIS WILL MAKE ME LOOK LIKE A WEAK-LING...
...BUT THERE'S NO REASON TO KEEP YOU ALIVE NOW THAT THEY'VE COME BACK.
!
Hmph.
ALL RIGHT...
...
KYEE HEE HEE HEE HEE... I FEEL SO BAD FOR YOU!
YEAH! YOU'VE BEEN SO PATHETIC ...
...RIGHT TO THE VERY END!

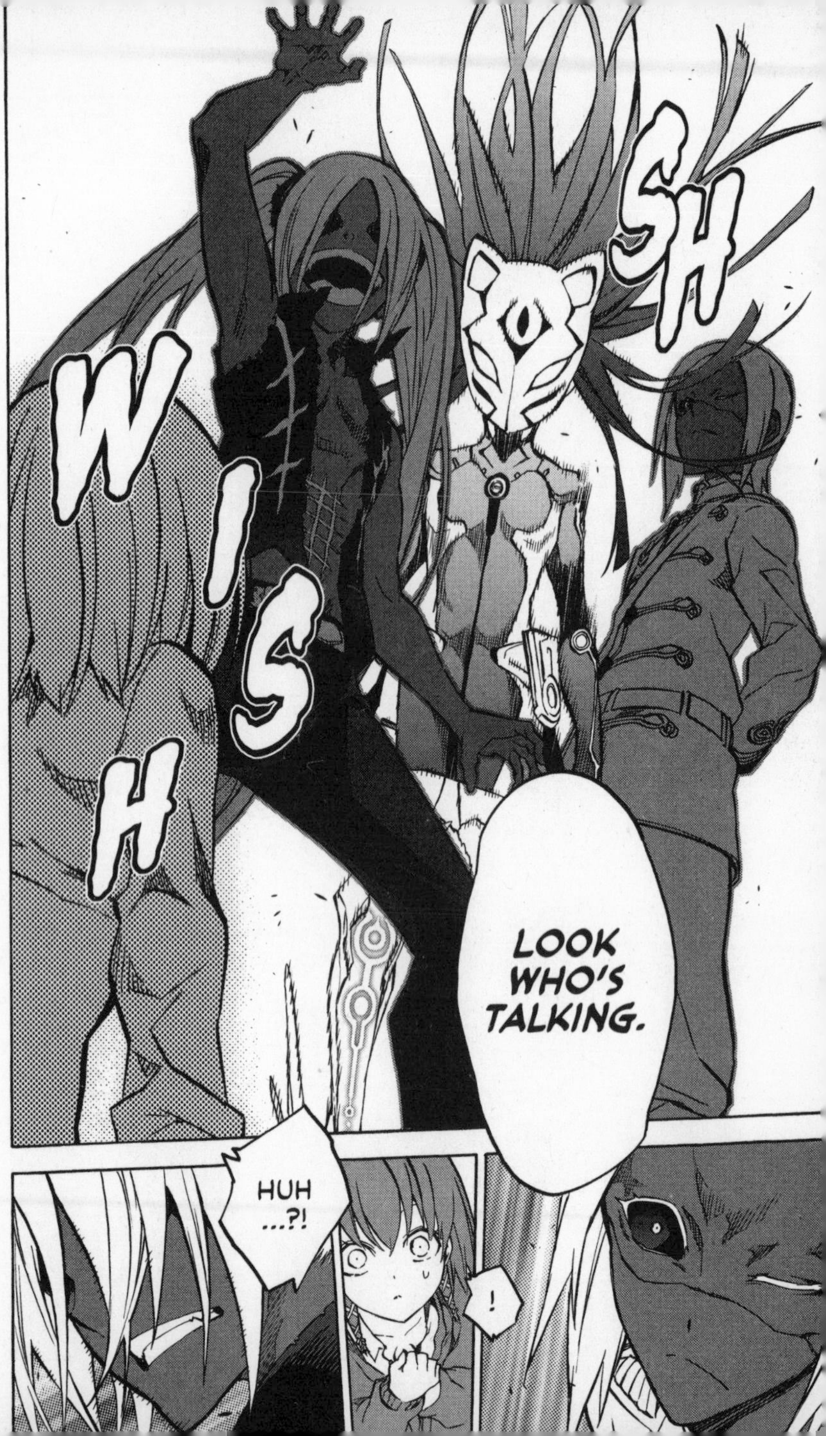
SH
WISH
LOOK WHO'S TALKING.
HUH ...?!
!

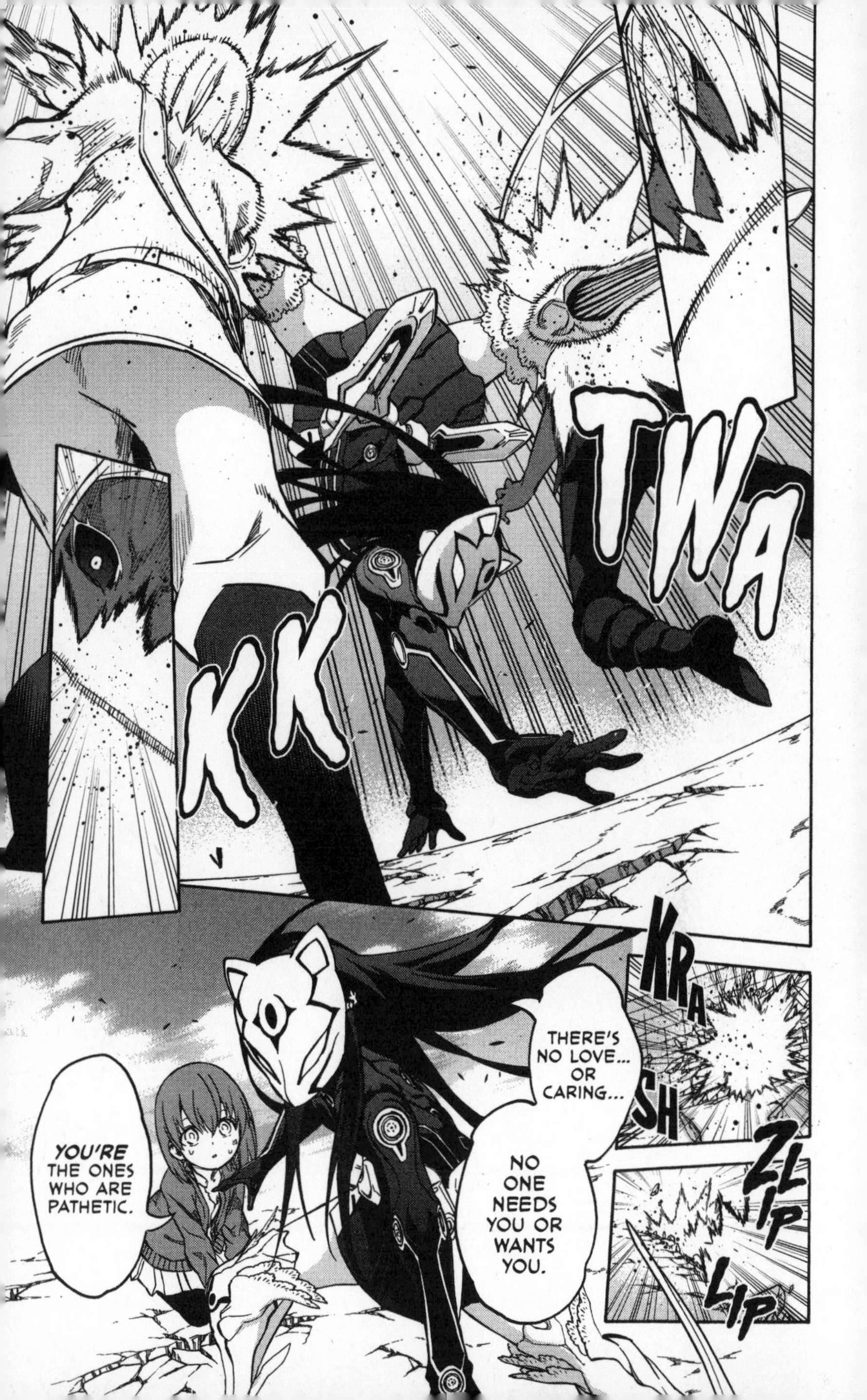
TWA
KK
KRASH
ZLIP
LIP
THERE'S NO LOVE... OR CARING...
NO ONE NEEDS YOU OR WANTS YOU.
YOU'RE THE ONES WHO ARE PATHETIC.

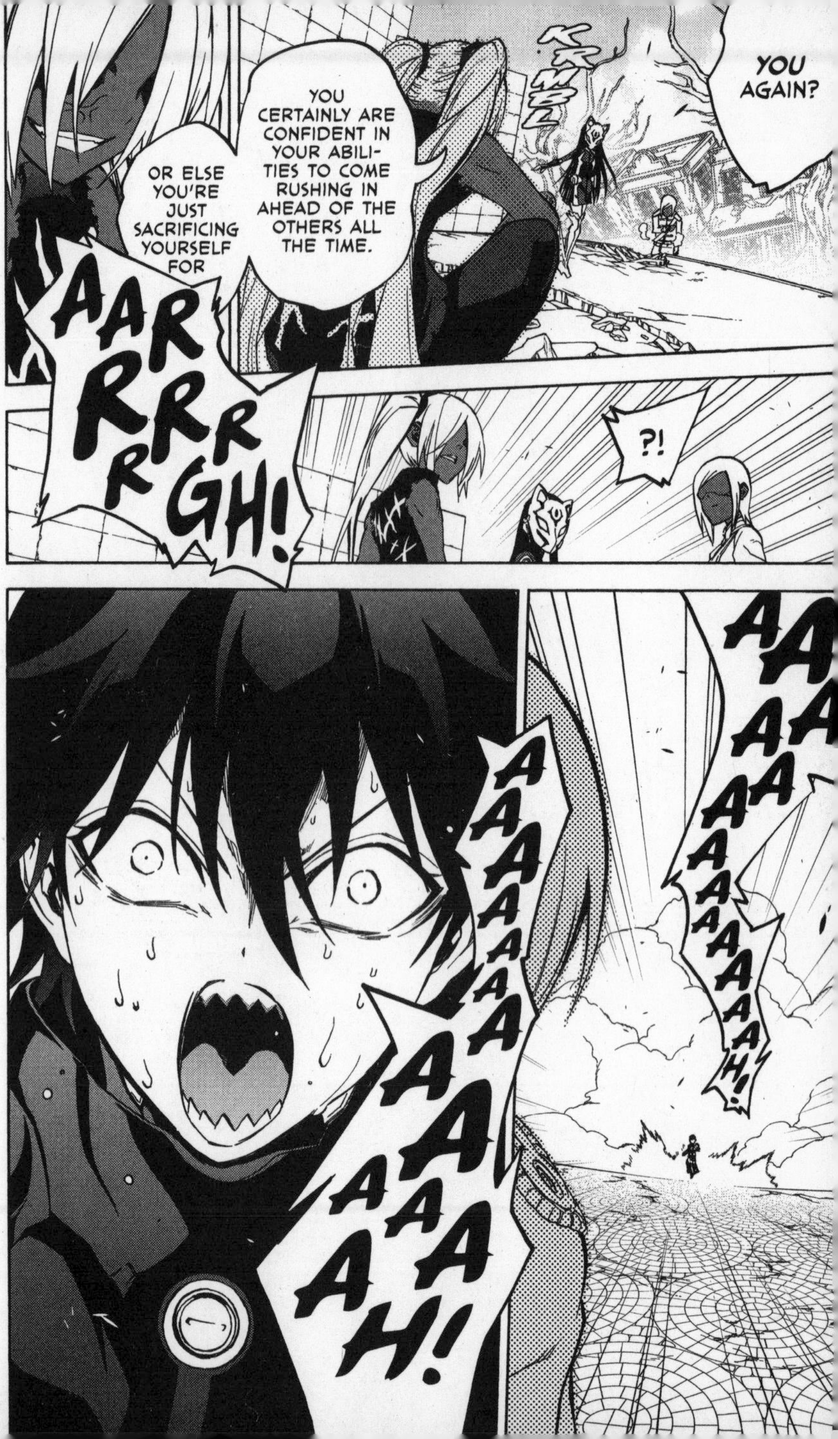
YOU AGAIN?
KRMBL
YOU CERTAINLY ARE CONFIDENT IN YOUR ABILITIES TO COME RUSHING IN AHEAD OF THE OTHERS ALL THE TIME.
OR ELSE YOU'RE JUST SACRIFICING YOURSELF FOR
AARRRRRGH!
?!
AAAAAAAAAAAAAAAAAAH!
AAAAAAAAAAAAAAAAAAAH!

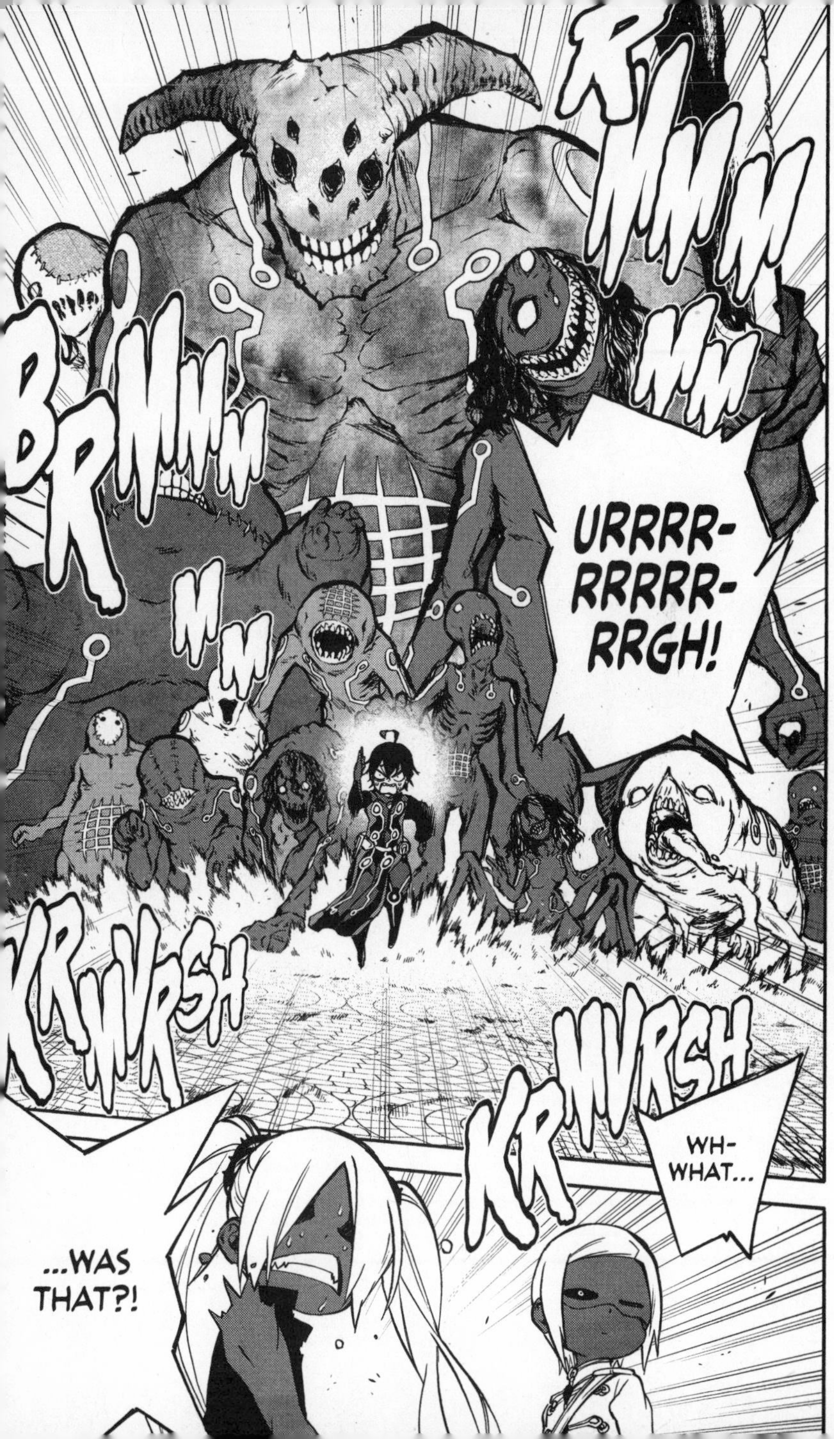
RMMMM MM
BRMMMM MMM
URRRR-RRRRR-RRGH!
KRMVRSH
KRMVRSH
WH-WHAT...
...WAS THAT?!

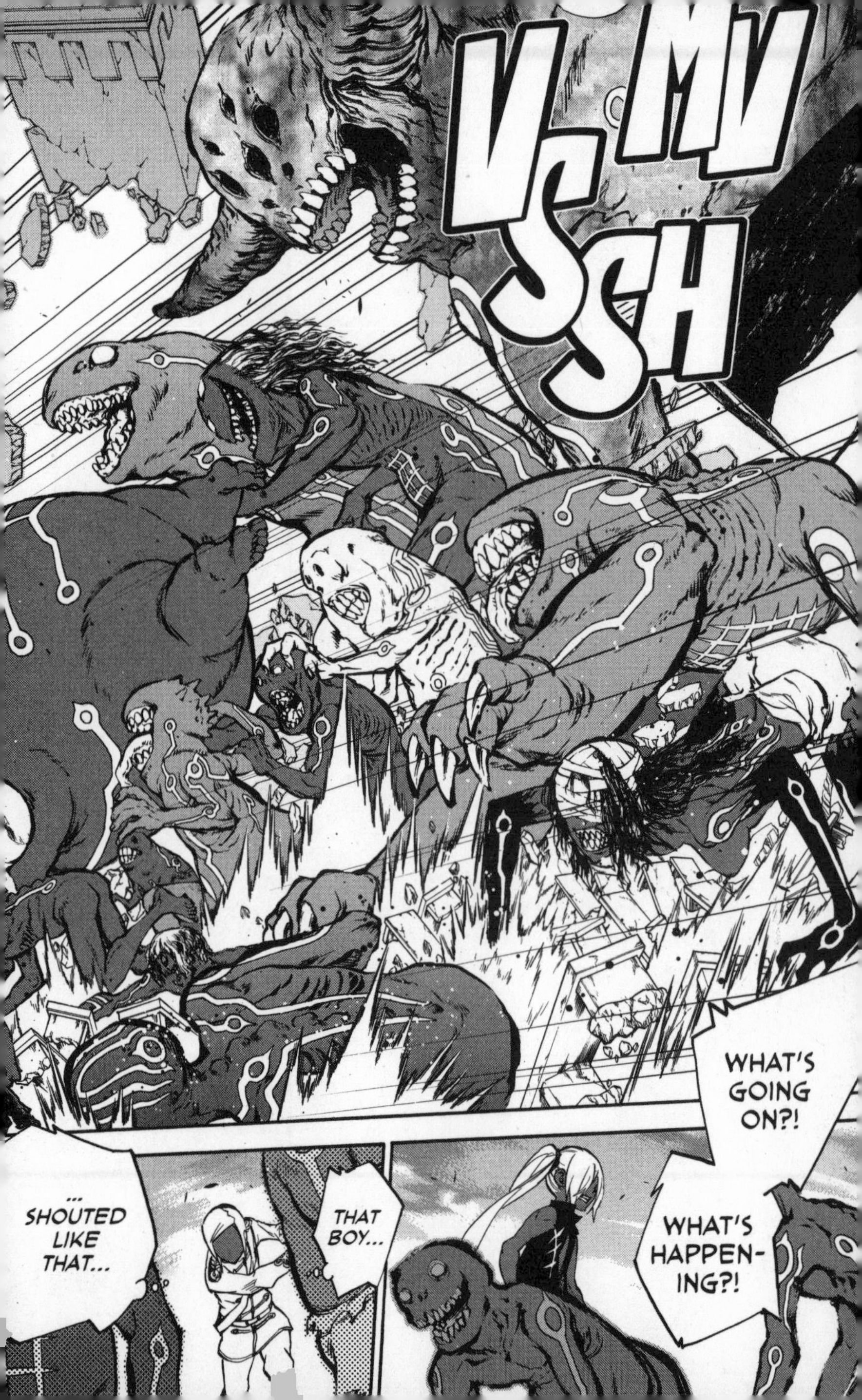
V MV
SH
WHAT'S GOING ON?!
WHAT'S HAPPEN-ING?!
THAT BOY...
...SHOUTED LIKE THAT...

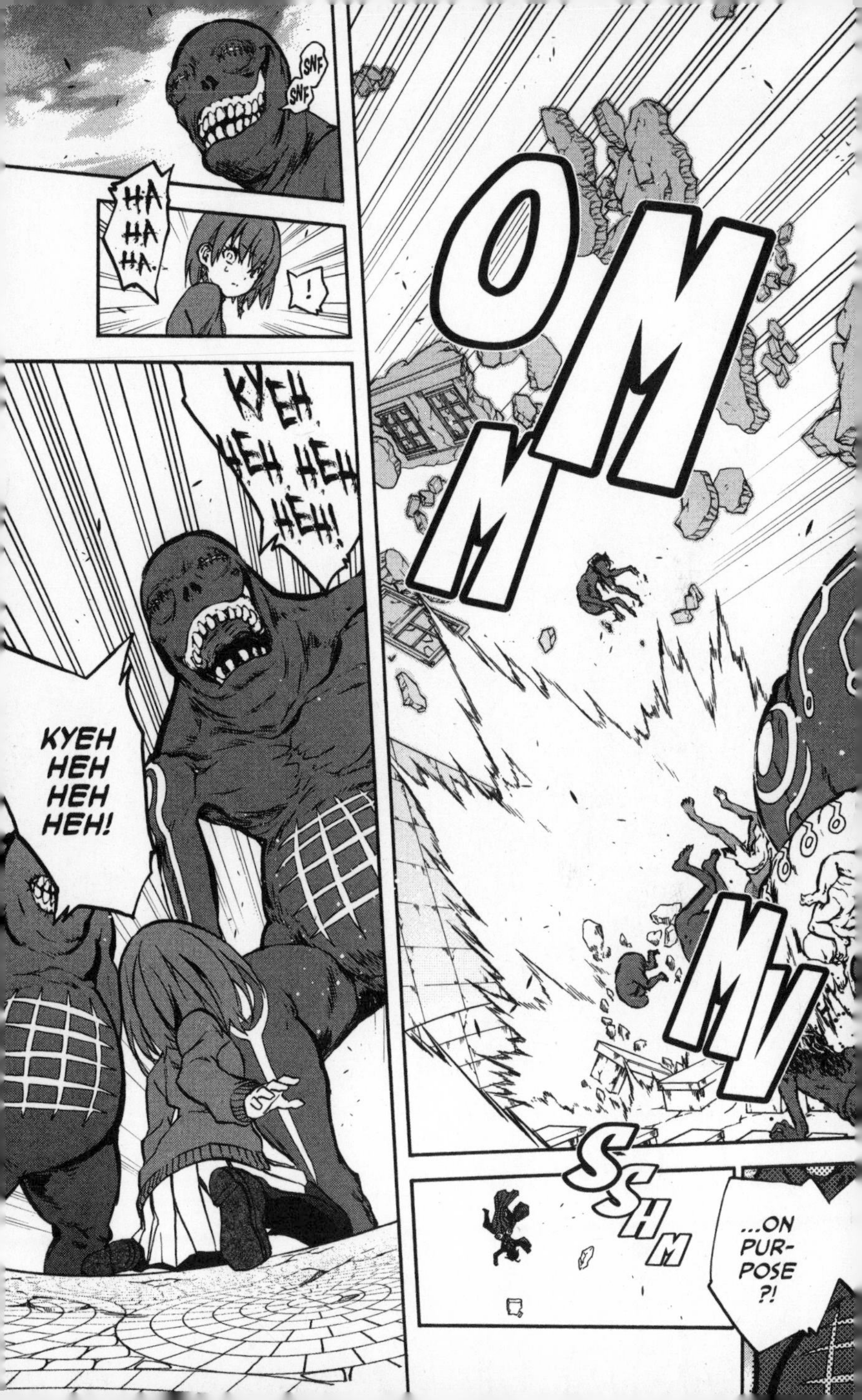

OMMM
MMM
SSHM
...ON PUR-POSE?!
SNF SNF
HA HA HA.
!
KYEH HEH HEH HEH!
KYEH HEH HEH HEH!

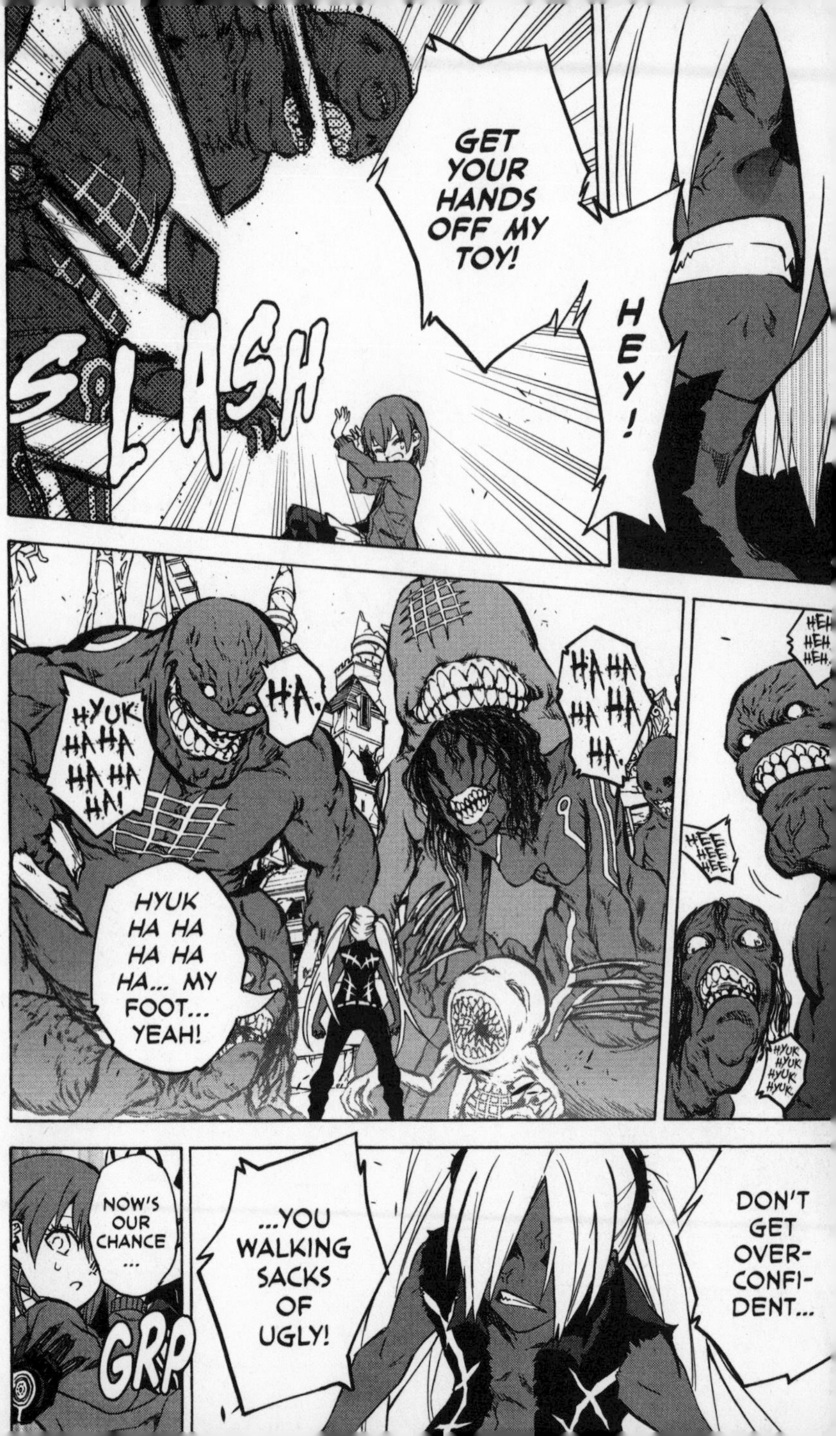
HEY!
GET YOUR HANDS OFF MY TOY!
SLASH
HEH HEH HEH HEH...
HEE HEE HEE HEE
HYUK HYUK HYUK HYUK
HA HA HA HA HA.
HA.
HYUK HA HA HA HA HA!
HYUK HA HA HA HA HA... MY FOOT... YEAH!
DON'T GET OVER-CONFIDENT...
...YOU WALKING SACKS OF UGLY!
NOW'S OUR CHANCE...
GRP

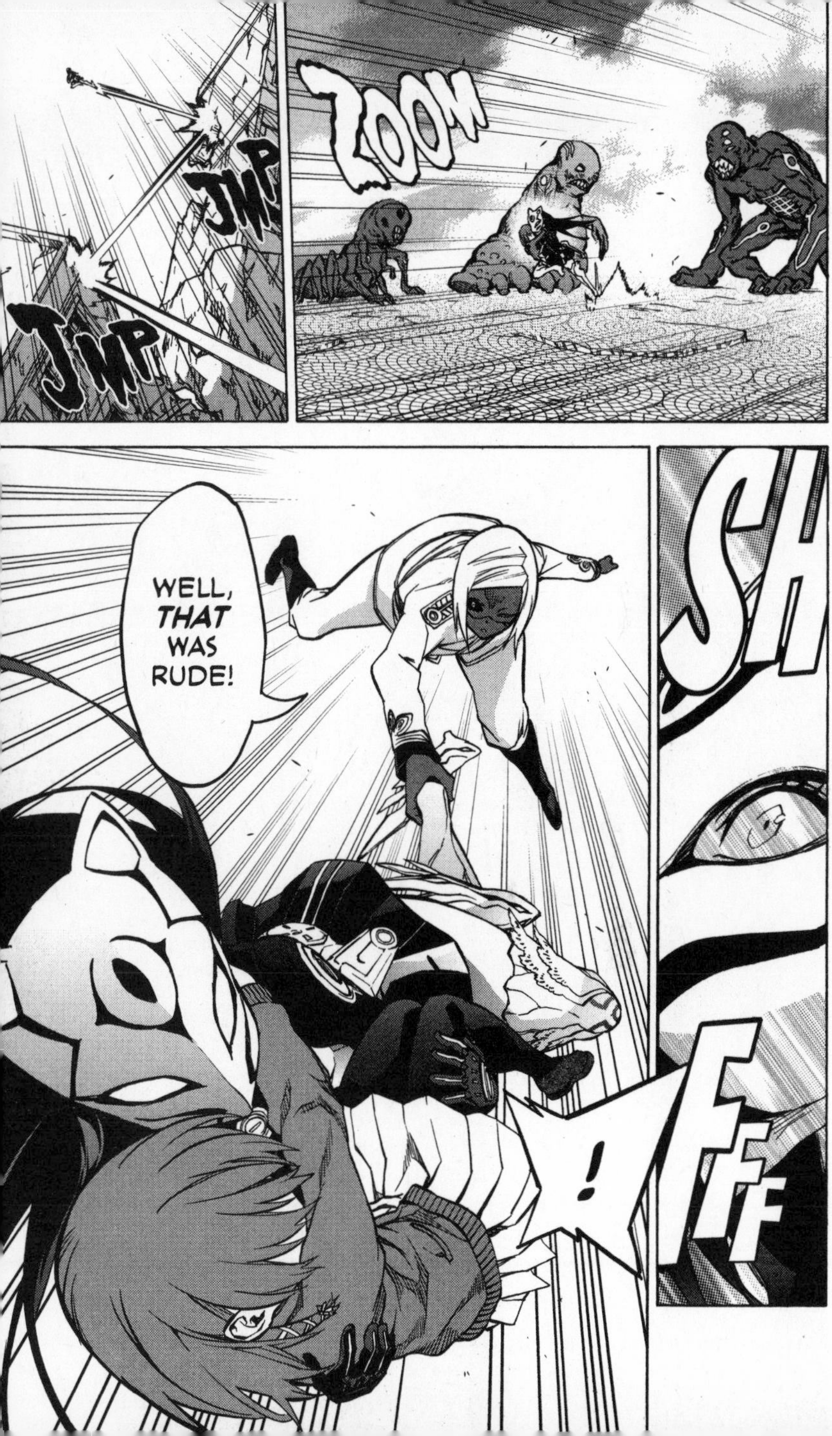
ZOOM
JMP
JMP
SH
WELL, *THAT* WAS RUDE!
!
FFF

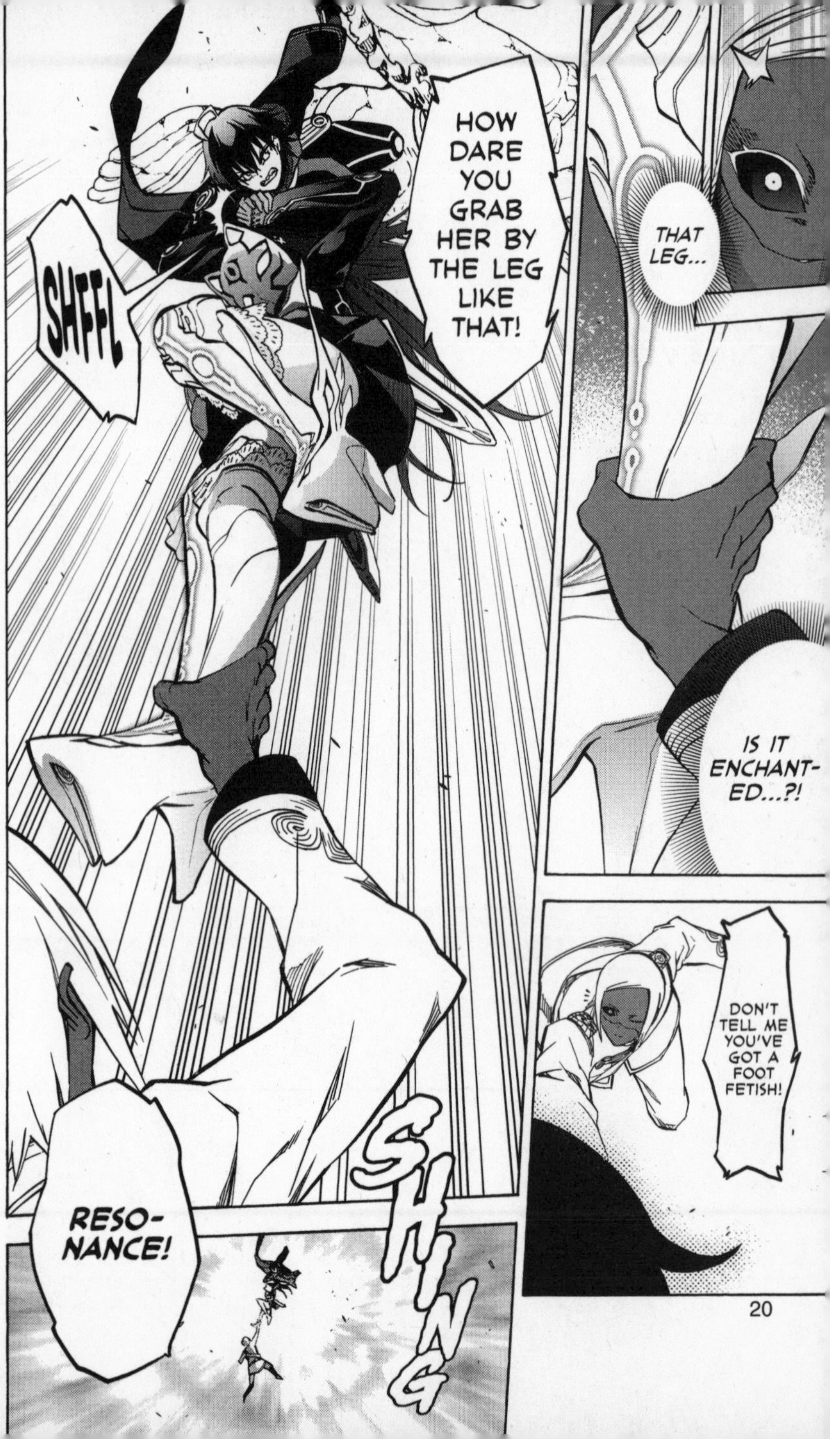
THAT LEG...
IS IT ENCHANTED...?!
DON'T TELL ME YOU'VE GOT A FOOT FETISH!
HOW DARE YOU GRAB HER BY THE LEG LIKE THAT!
SHFFL
RESONANCE!
SHING

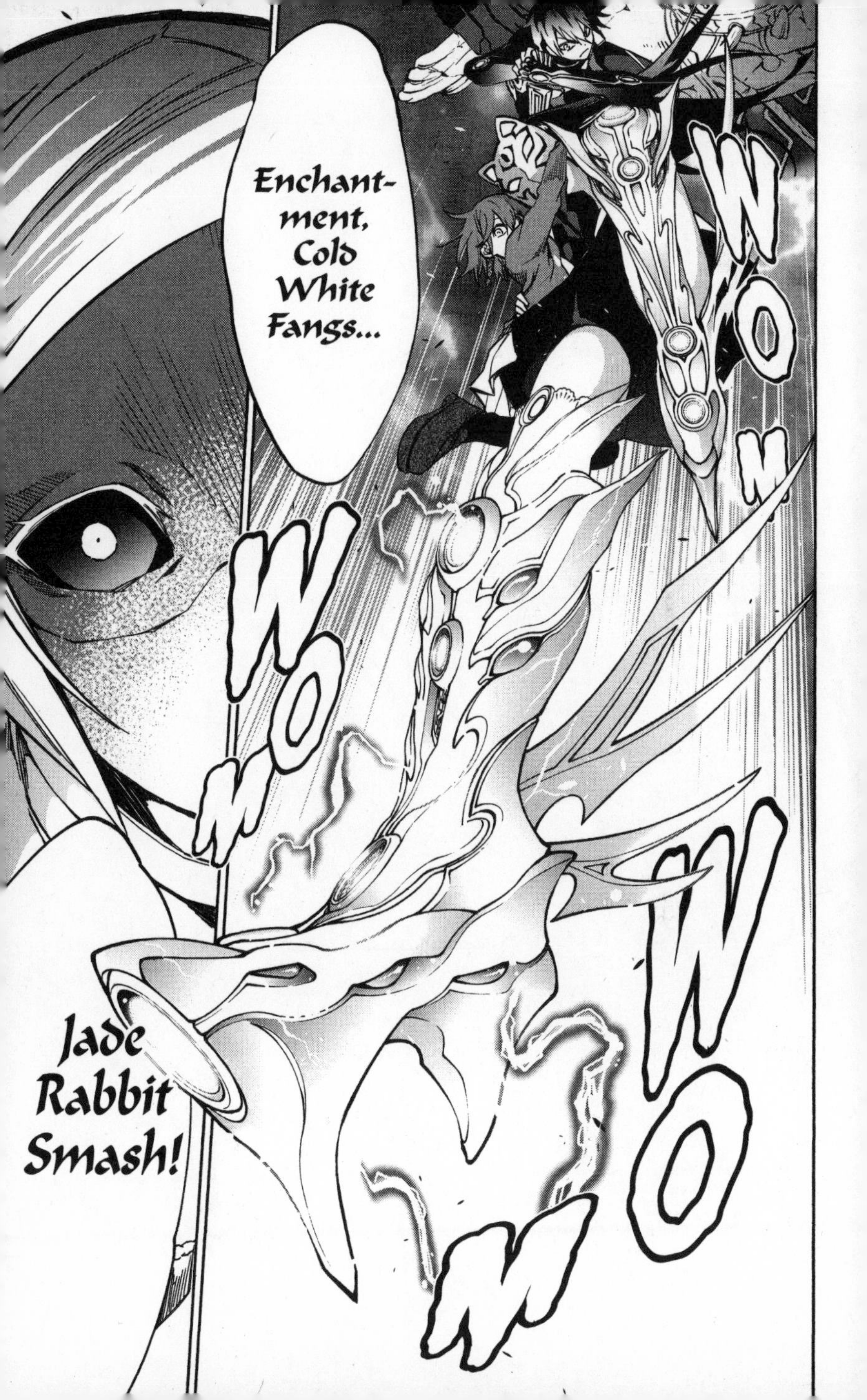
Enchantment, Cold White Fangs...
WOM
WOM
WOM
Jade Rabbit Smash!

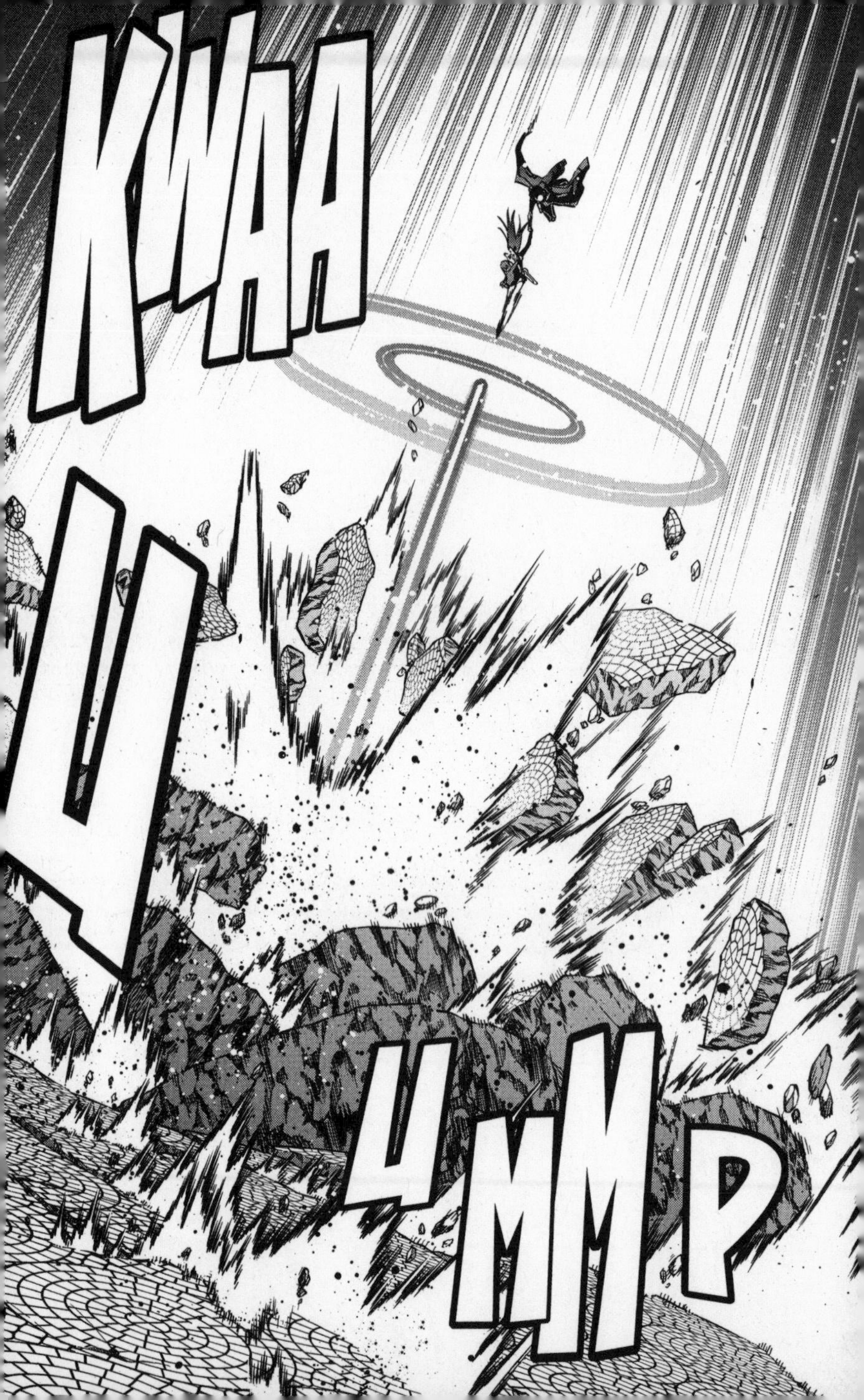
K'WAA
THUMMP

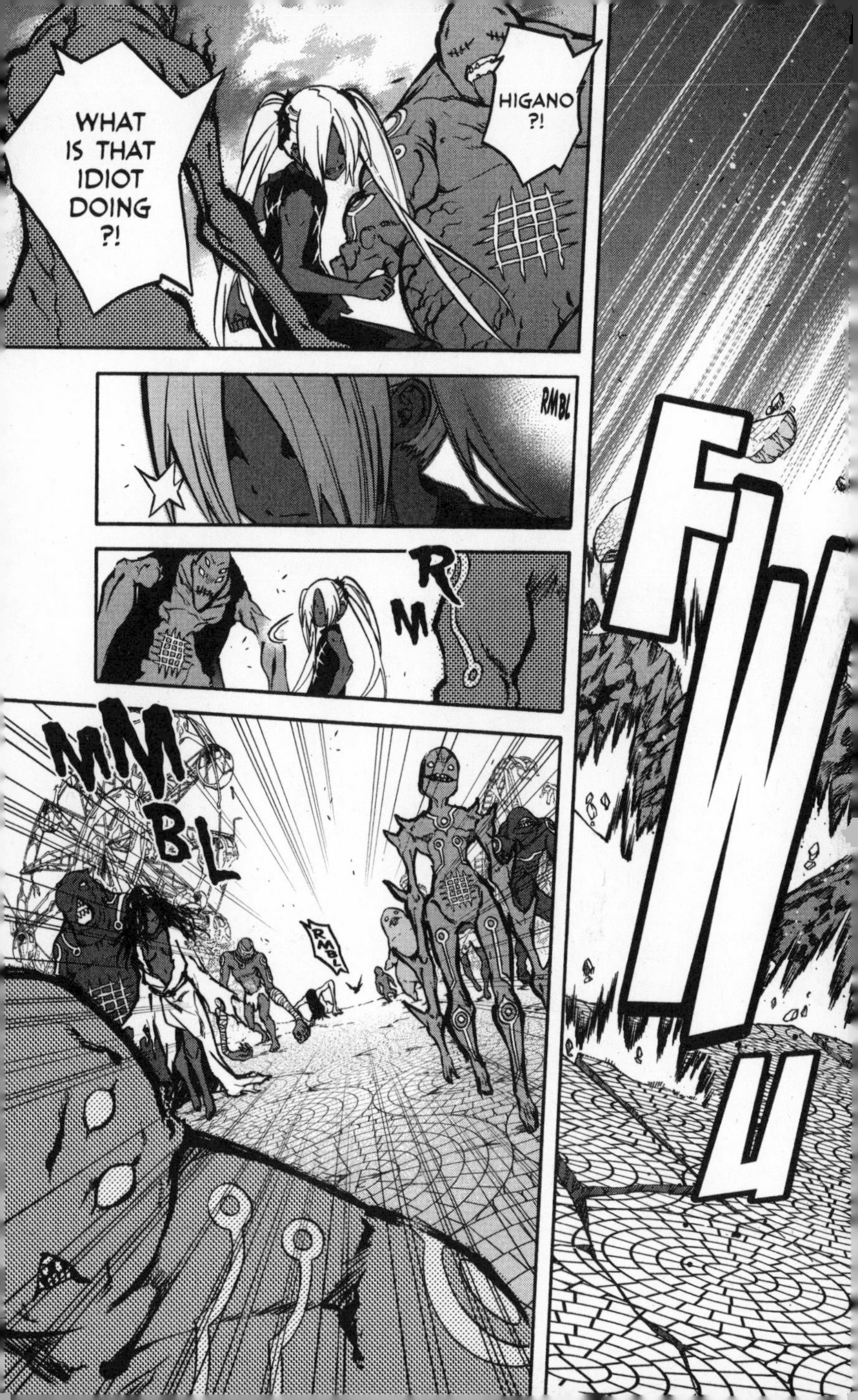
FWU
HIGANO ?!
WHAT IS THAT IDIOT DOING ?!
RMBL
RM
MMBL
RMBL

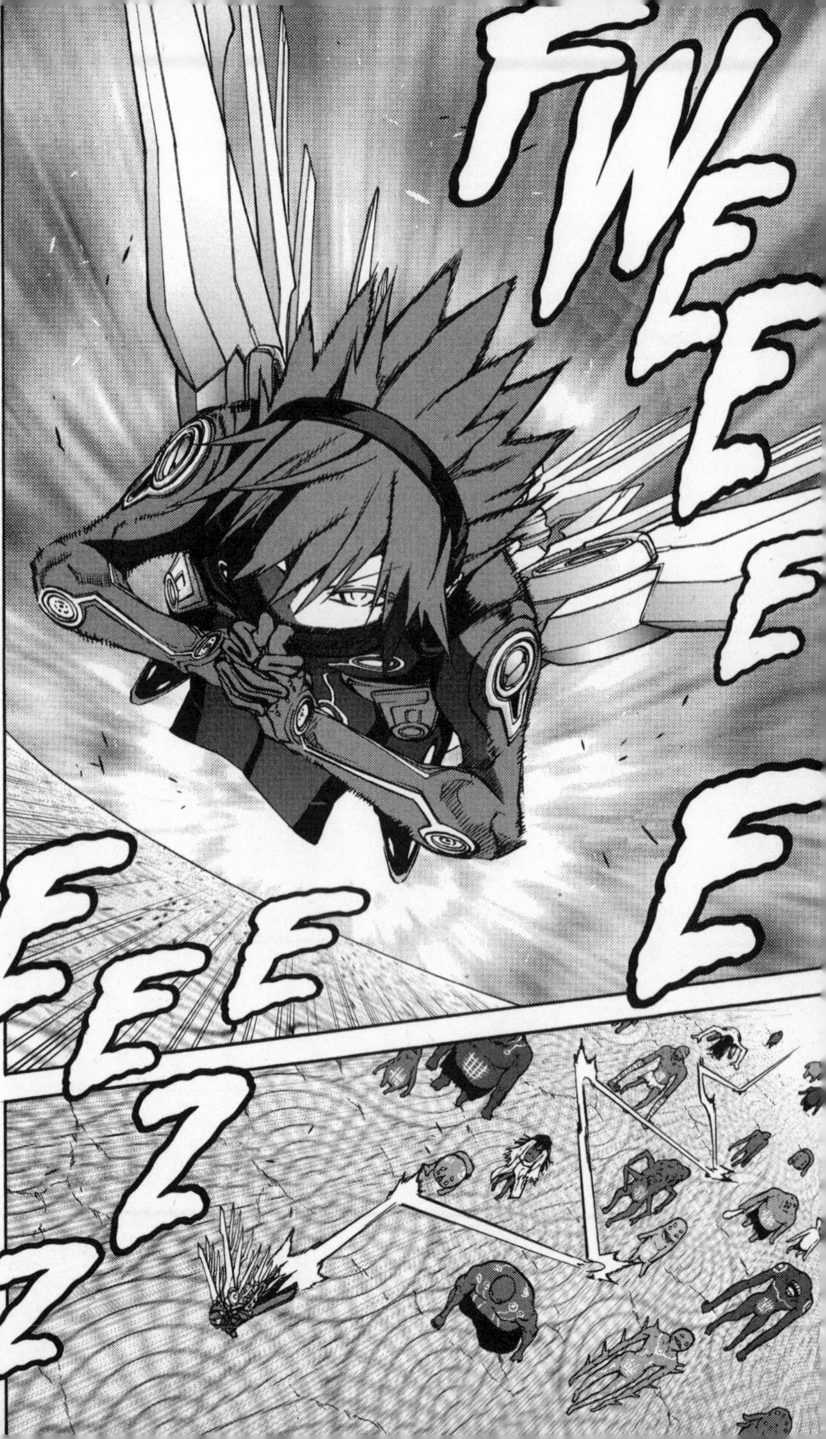
FWEEEEEEEZZ

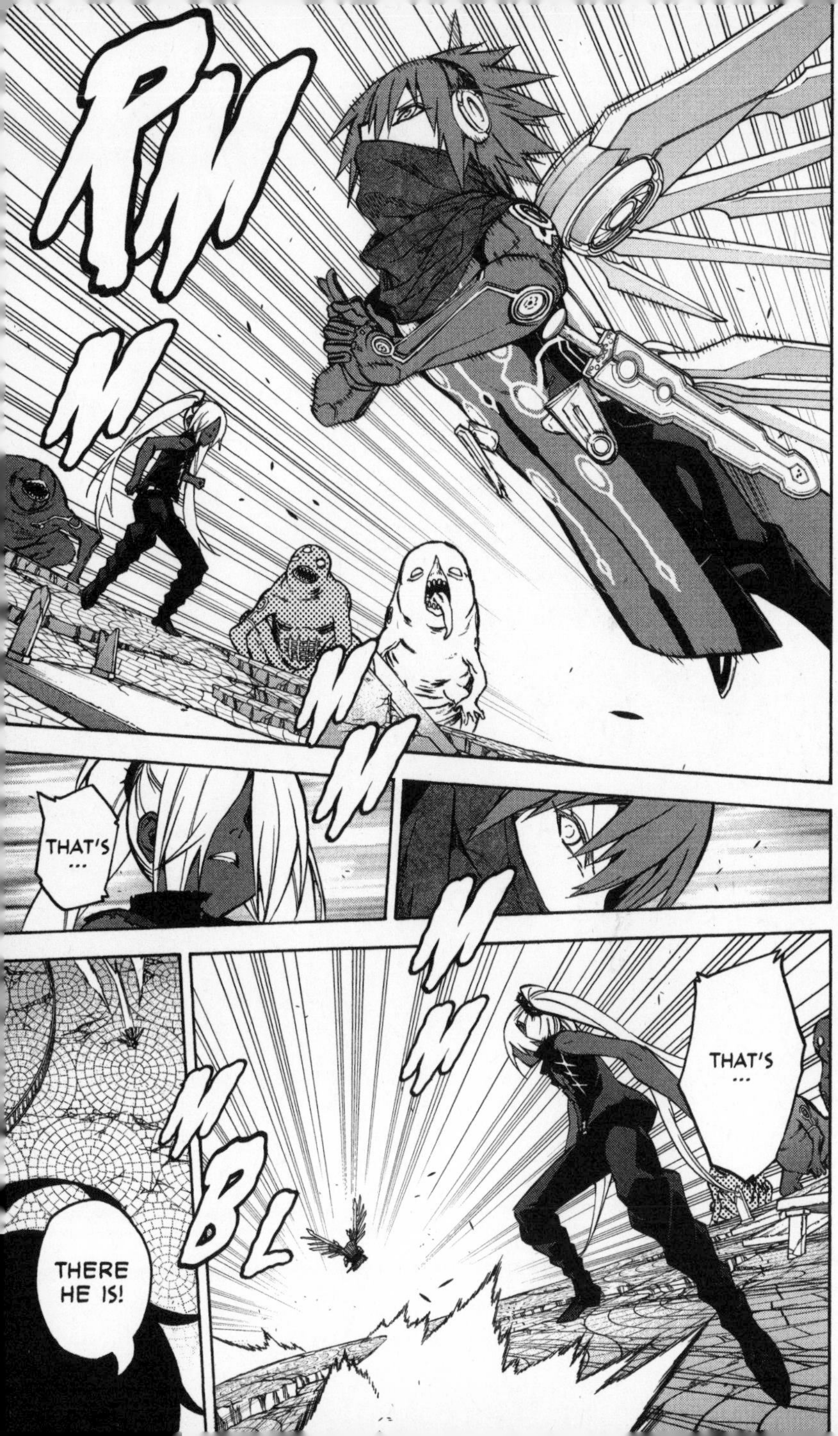
RUMMMMMMBL
THAT'S ...
THAT'S ...
THERE HE IS!

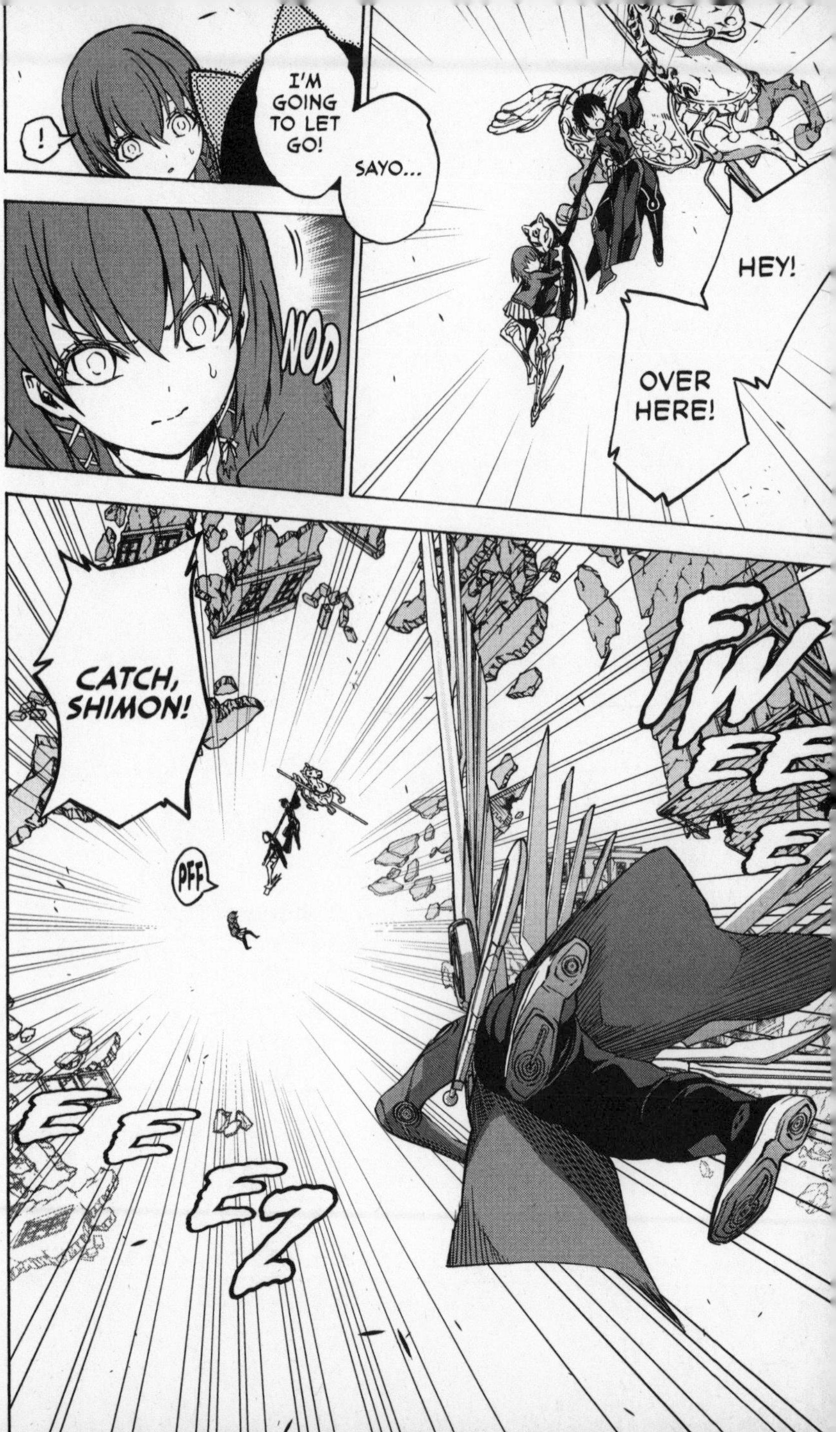
HEY!
OVER HERE!
SAYO...
I'M GOING TO LET GO!
!
NOD
FWEEEEEEEZ
CATCH, SHIMON!
PFF

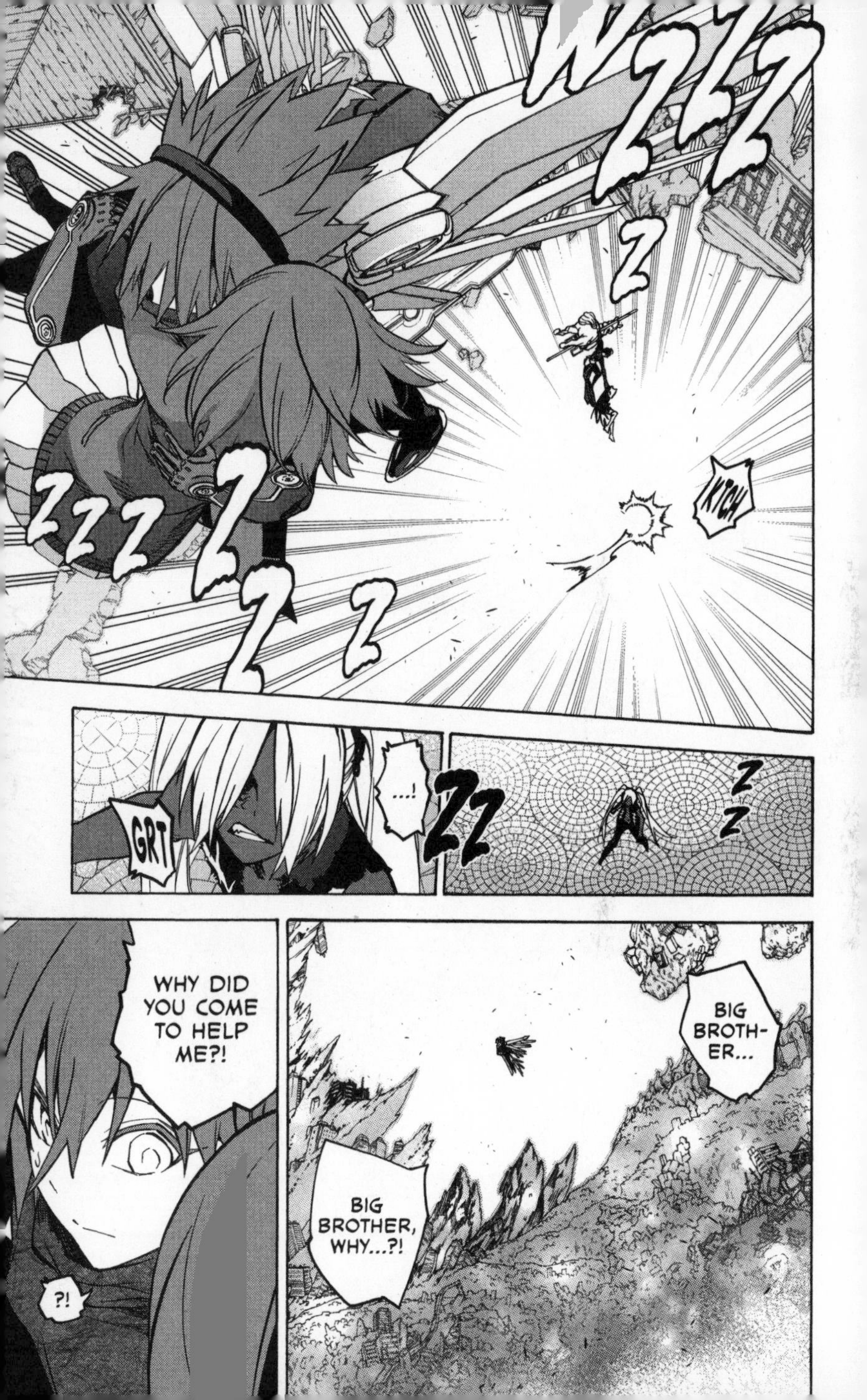
WZZZ
Z
KICH
ZZZZ
Z
Z
Z
Z
Z
...!
ZZ
GRT
BIG BROTH-ER...
BIG BROTHER, WHY...?!
WHY DID YOU COME TO HELP ME?!
?!

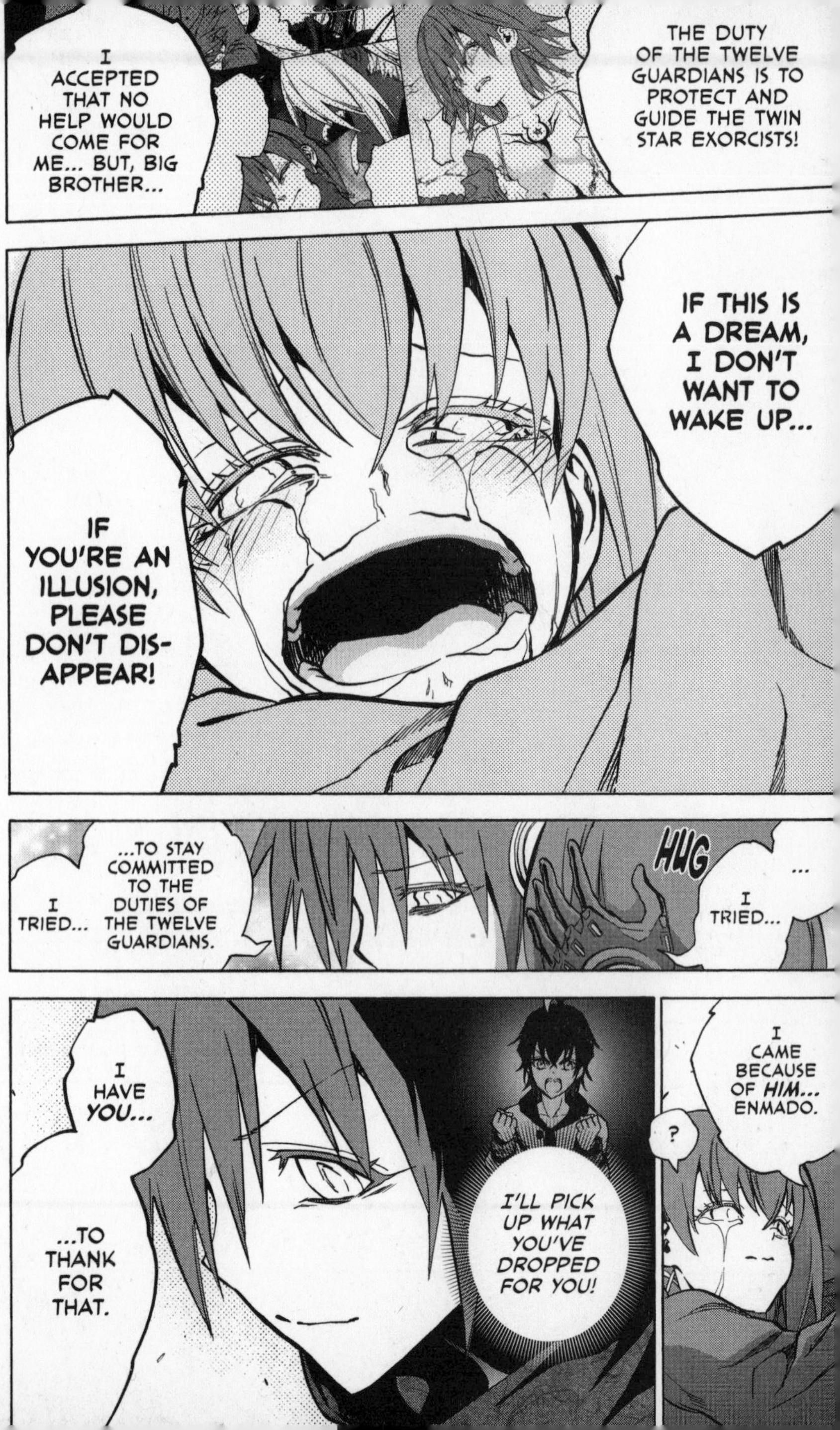
THE DUTY OF THE TWELVE GUARDIANS IS TO PROTECT AND GUIDE THE TWIN STAR EXORCISTS!
I ACCEPTED THAT NO HELP WOULD COME FOR ME... BUT, BIG BROTHER...
IF THIS IS A DREAM, I DON'T WANT TO WAKE UP...
IF YOU'RE AN ILLUSION, PLEASE DON'T DIS-APPEAR!
...
I TRIED...
HUG
I TRIED...
...TO STAY COMMITTED TO THE DUTIES OF THE TWELVE GUARDIANS.
I CAME BECAUSE OF *HIM*... ENMADO.
?
I'LL PICK UP WHAT YOU'VE DROPPED FOR YOU!
I HAVE *YOU*...
...TO THANK FOR THAT.

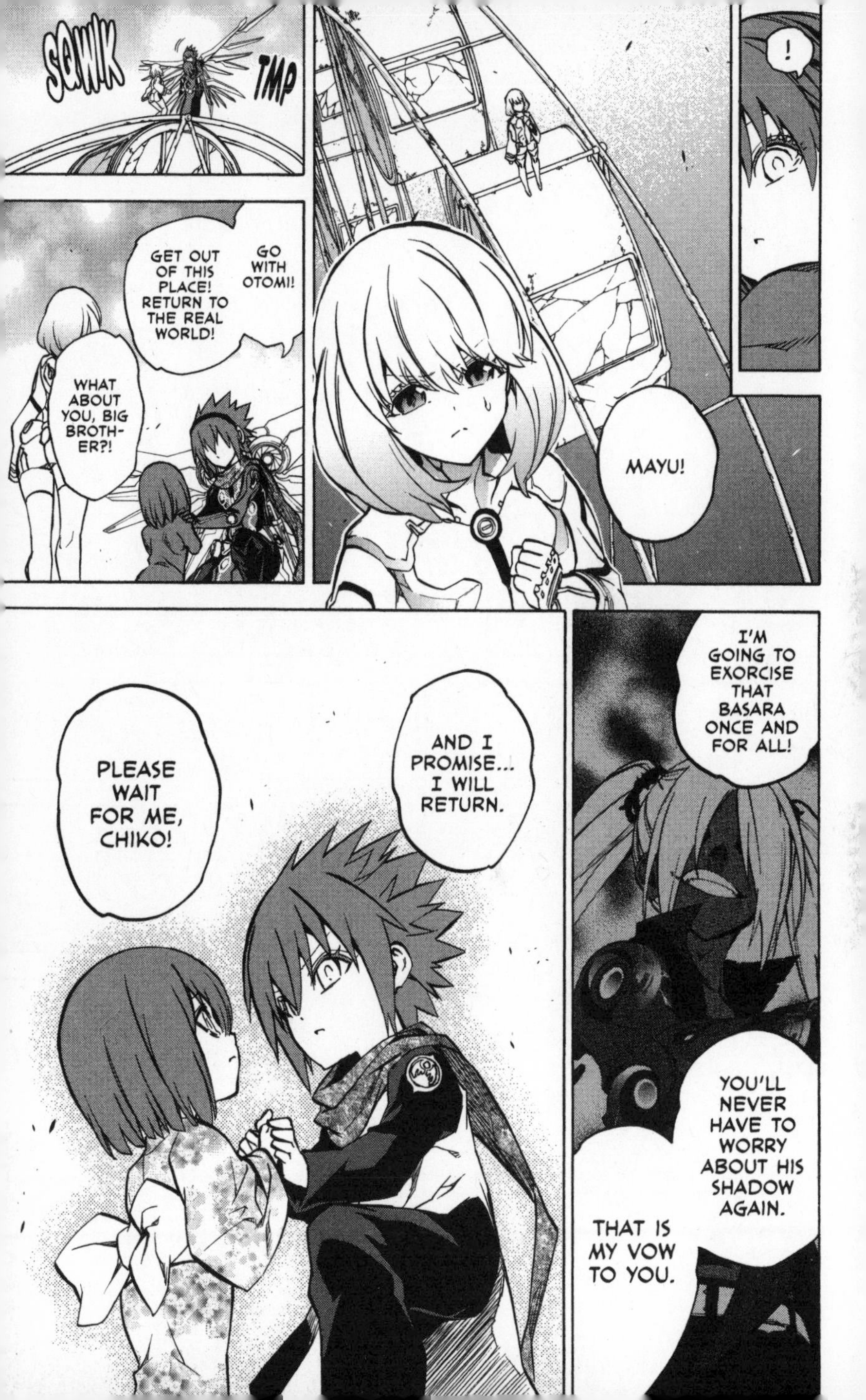
!
MAYU!
SQWIK
TMP
GO WITH OTOMI!
GET OUT OF THIS PLACE! RETURN TO THE REAL WORLD!
WHAT ABOUT YOU, BIG BROTHER?!
I'M GOING TO EXORCISE THAT BASARA ONCE AND FOR ALL!
YOU'LL NEVER HAVE TO WORRY ABOUT HIS SHADOW AGAIN.
THAT IS MY VOW TO YOU.
AND I PROMISE... I WILL RETURN.
PLEASE WAIT FOR ME, CHIKO!

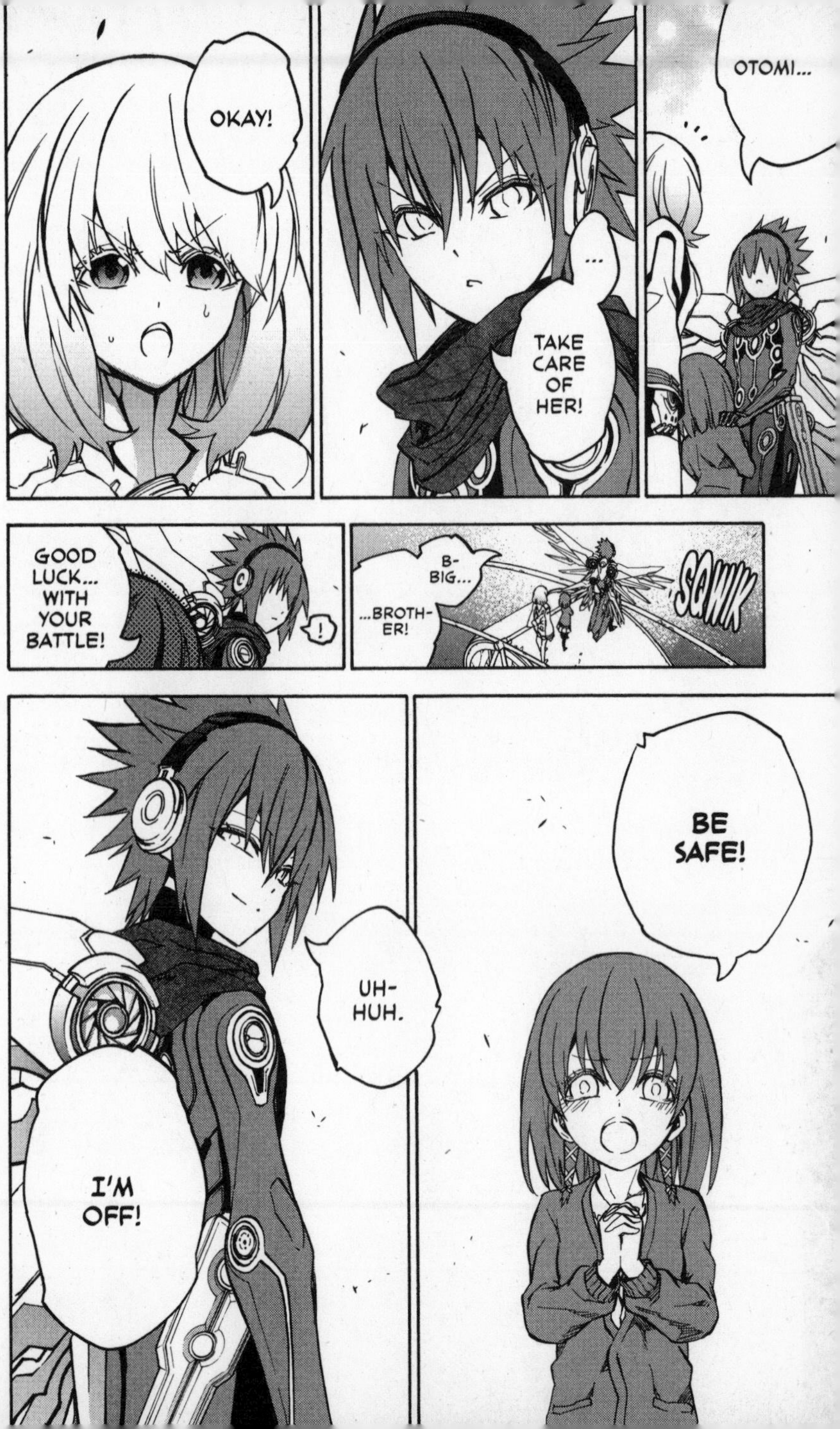
OTOMI...
...
...
TAKE CARE OF HER!
OKAY!
B- BIG... ...BROTH- ER!
SQWIK
GOOD LUCK... WITH YOUR BATTLE!
!
BE SAFE!
UH- HUH.
I'M OFF!

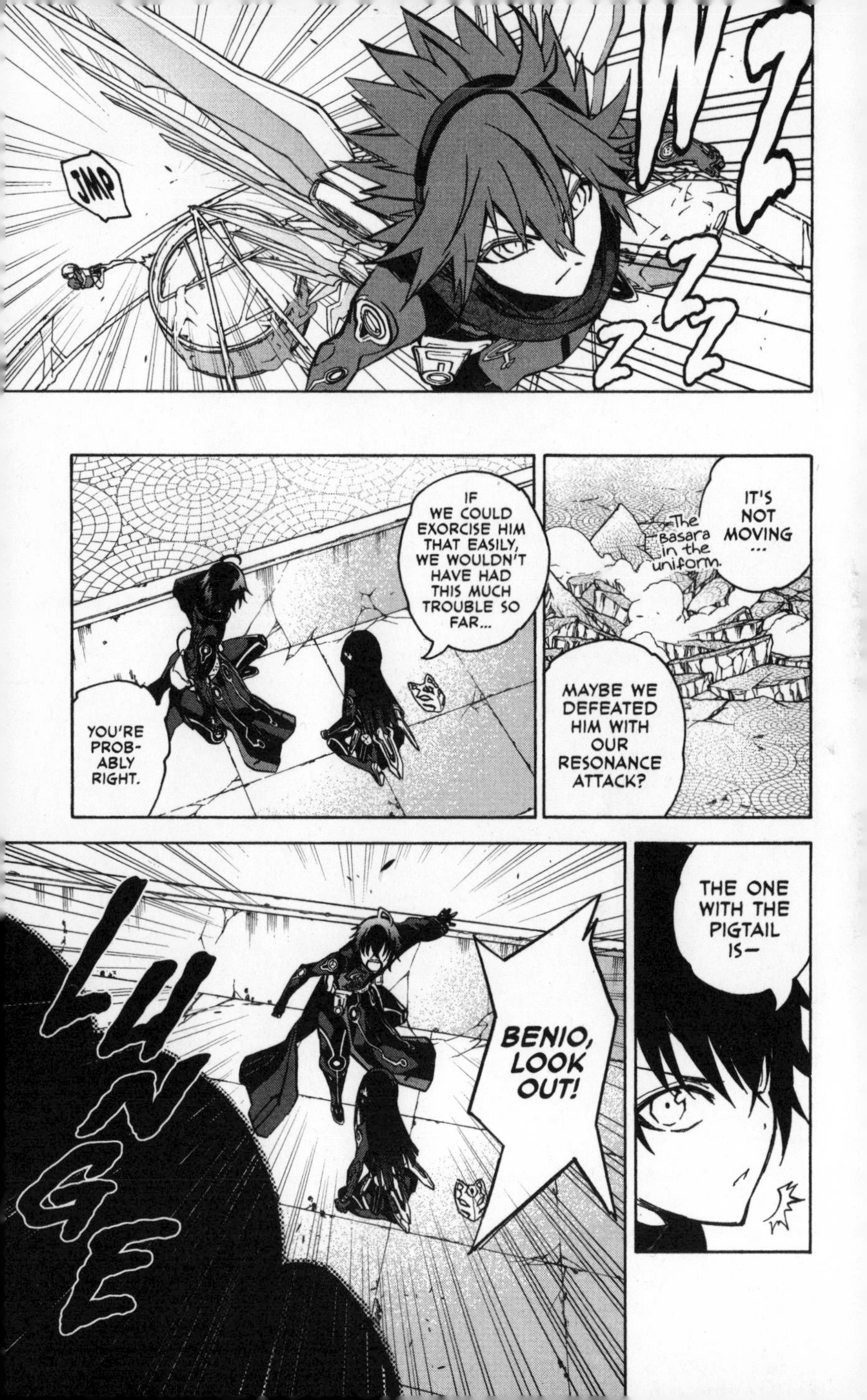
JMP
WZZZZ
IT'S NOT MOVING ...
The Basara in the uniform.
MAYBE WE DEFEATED HIM WITH OUR RESONANCE ATTACK?
IF WE COULD EXORCISE HIM THAT EASILY, WE WOULDN'T HAVE HAD THIS MUCH TROUBLE SO FAR...
YOU'RE PROBABLY RIGHT.
THE ONE WITH THE PIGTAIL IS—
BENIO, LOOK OUT!
LUNGE

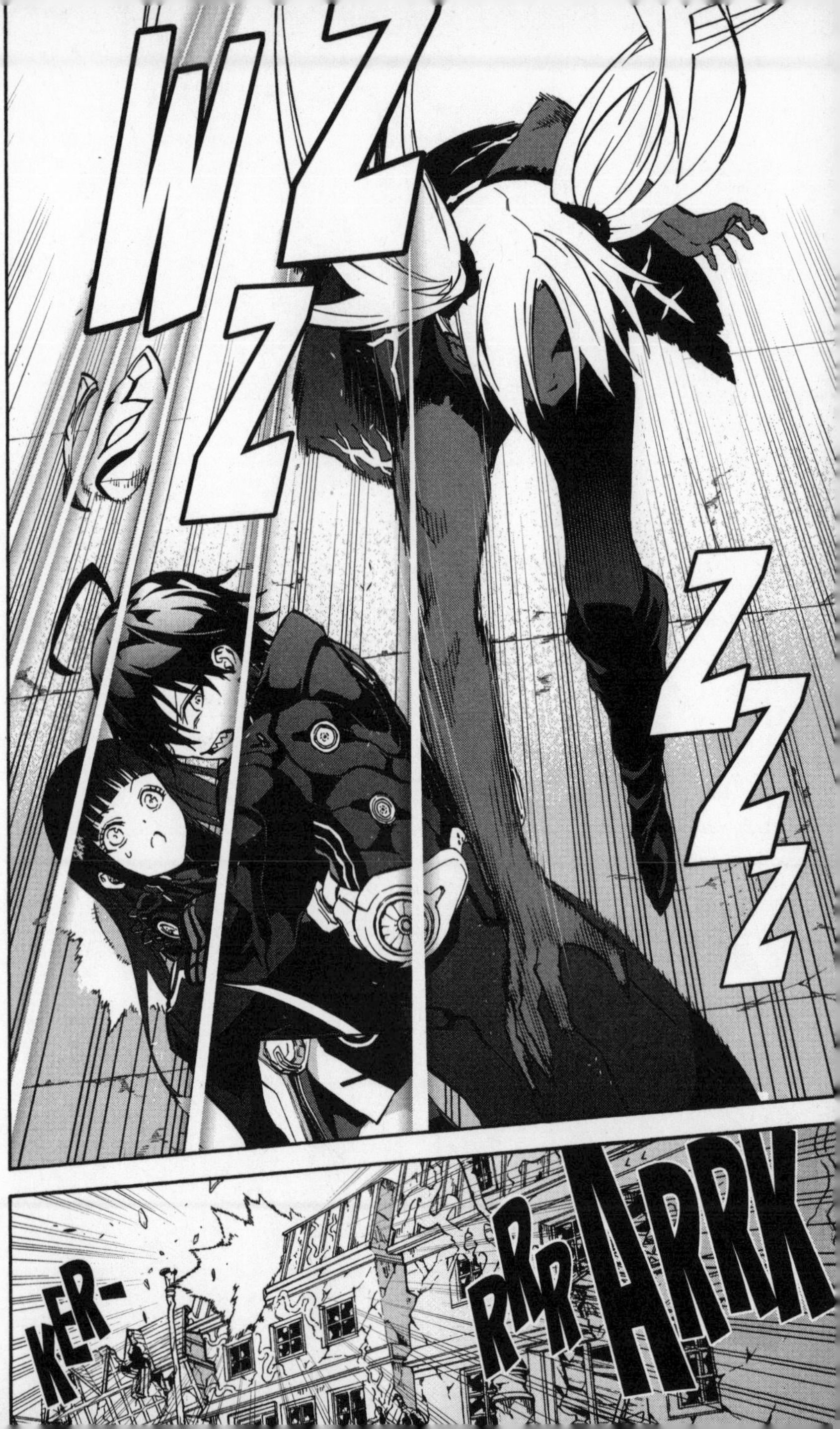
WZZ
ZZZZ
KER-
RRRAHRRK

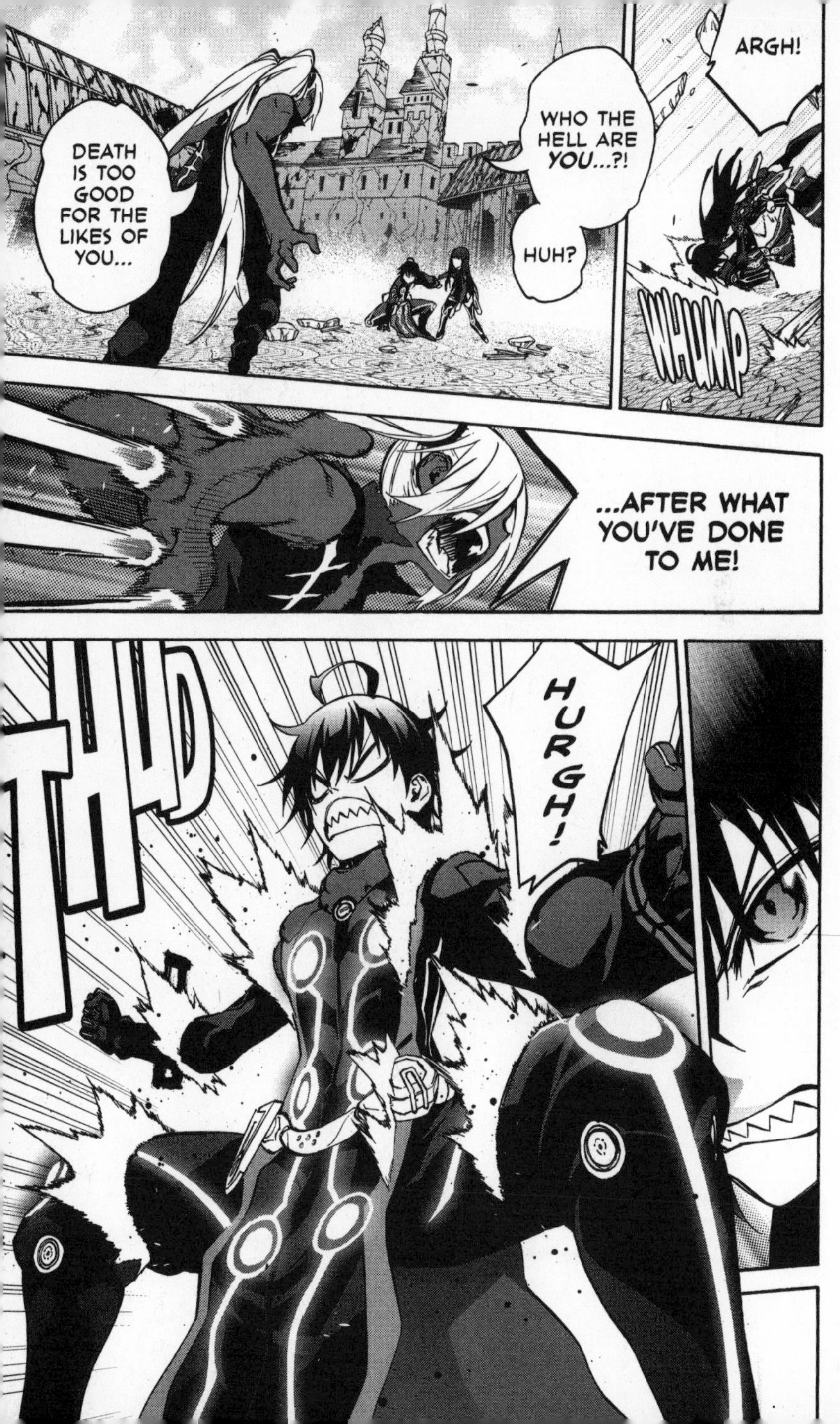
ARGH!
WHUMP
WHO THE HELL ARE YOU...?!
HUH?
DEATH IS TOO GOOD FOR THE LIKES OF YOU...
...AFTER WHAT YOU'VE DONE TO ME!
HURGH!
THUD

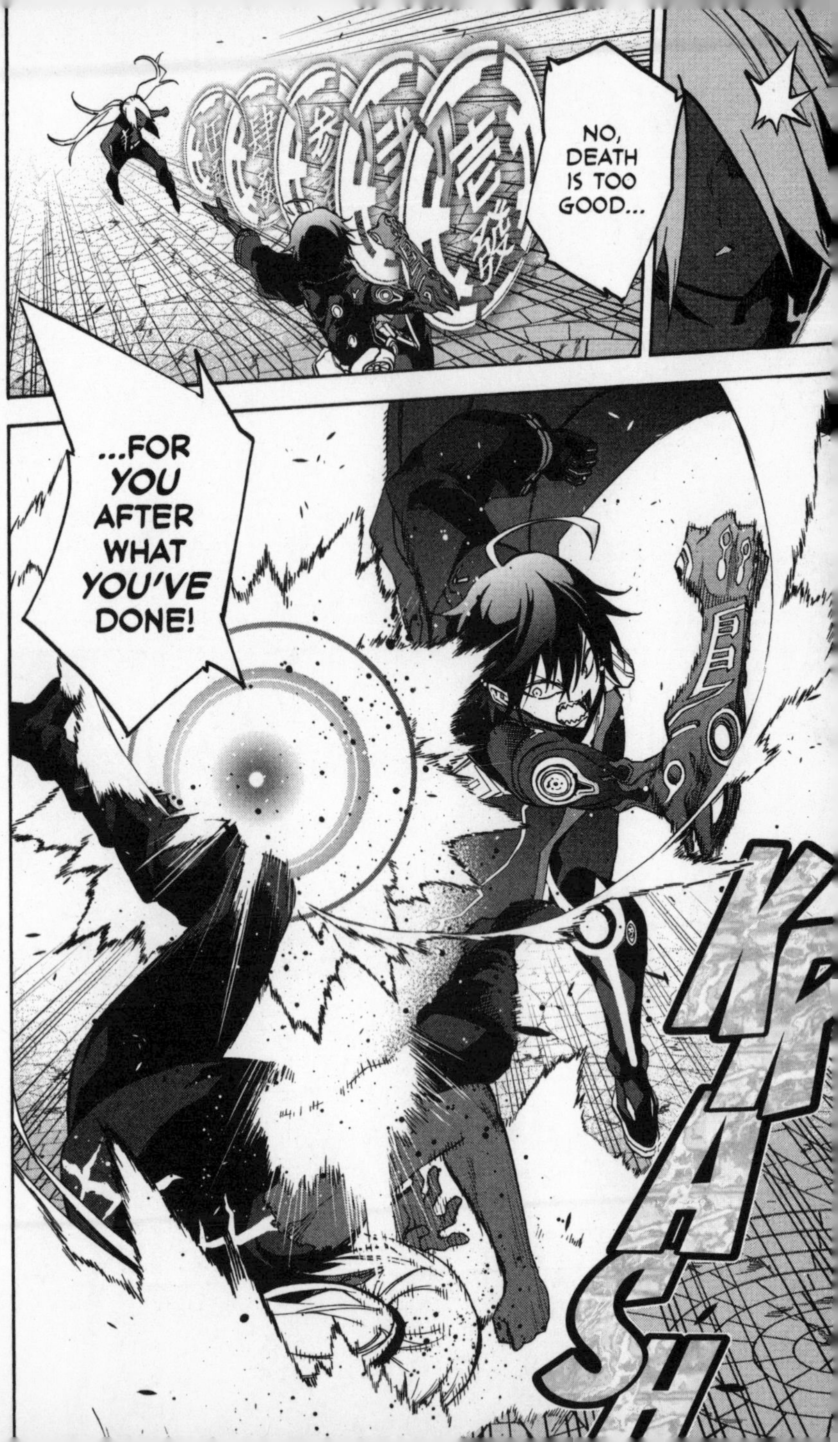
NO, DEATH IS TOO GOOD...
...FOR *YOU* AFTER WHAT *YOU'VE* DONE!

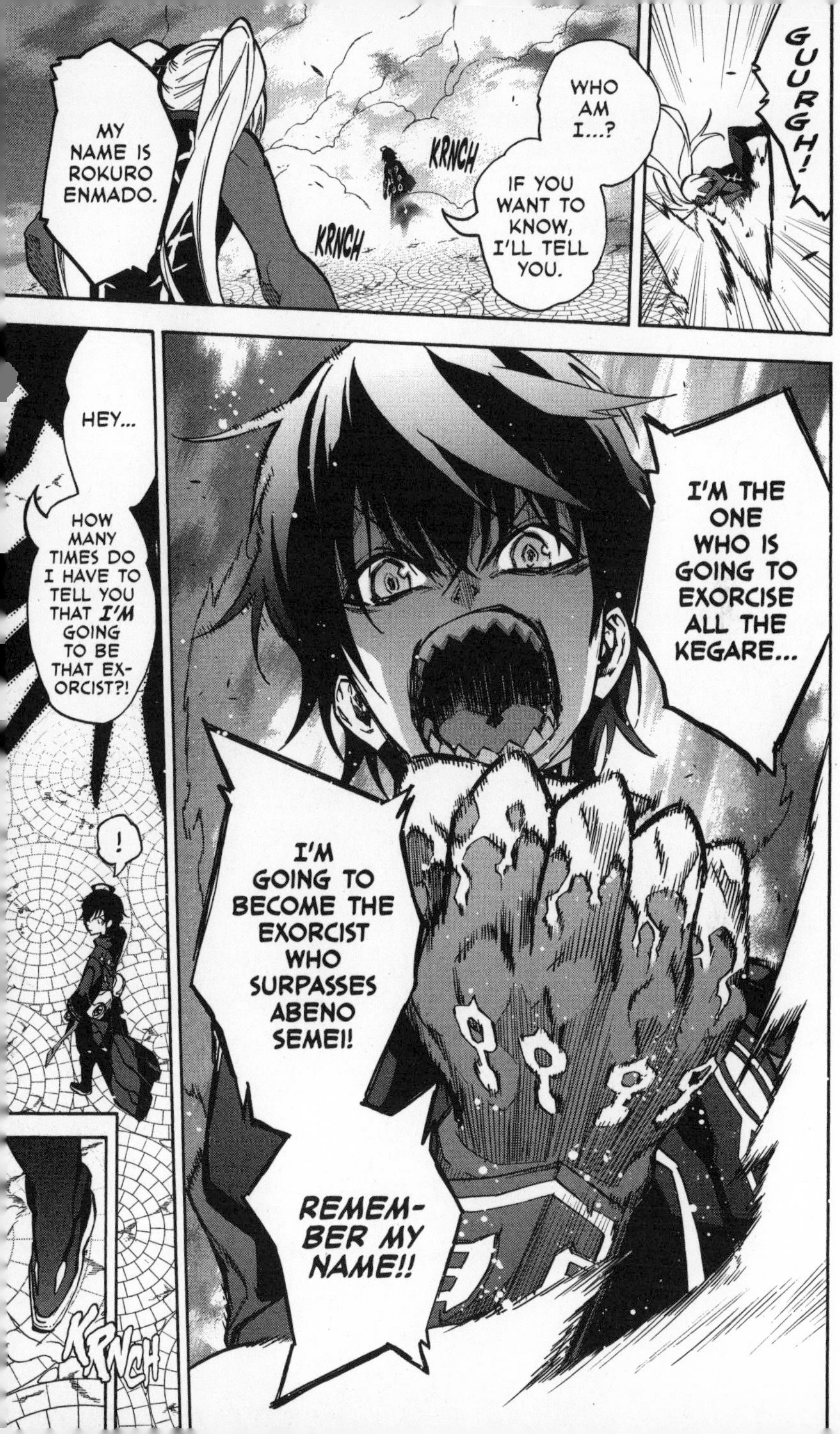
GUURGH!
WHO AM I...?
IF YOU WANT TO KNOW, I'LL TELL YOU.
KRNCH
KRNCH
MY NAME IS ROKURO ENMADO.
I'M THE ONE WHO IS GOING TO EXORCISE ALL THE KEGARE...
I'M GOING TO BECOME THE EXORCIST WHO SURPASSES ABENO SEMEI!
REMEMBER MY NAME!!
HEY...
HOW MANY TIMES DO I HAVE TO TELL YOU THAT *I'M* GOING TO BE THAT EXORCIST?!
!
KRNCH

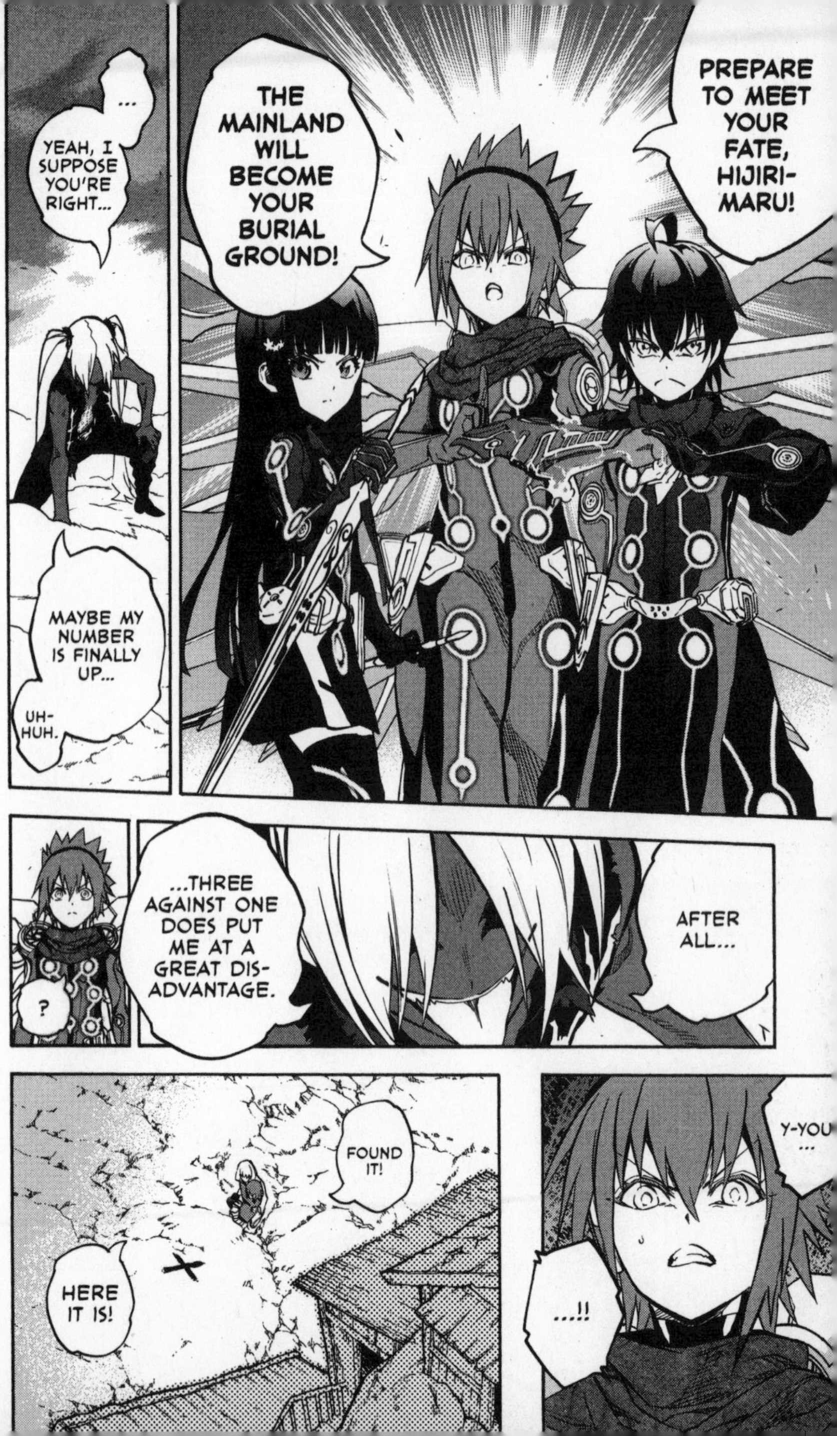
PREPARE TO MEET YOUR FATE, HIJIRI-MARU!
THE MAINLAND WILL BECOME YOUR BURIAL GROUND!
...
YEAH, I SUPPOSE YOU'RE RIGHT...
MAYBE MY NUMBER IS FINALLY UP...
UH-HUH.
AFTER ALL...
...THREE AGAINST ONE DOES PUT ME AT A GREAT DIS-ADVANTAGE.
?
Y-YOU ...
...!!
FOUND IT!
HERE IT IS!

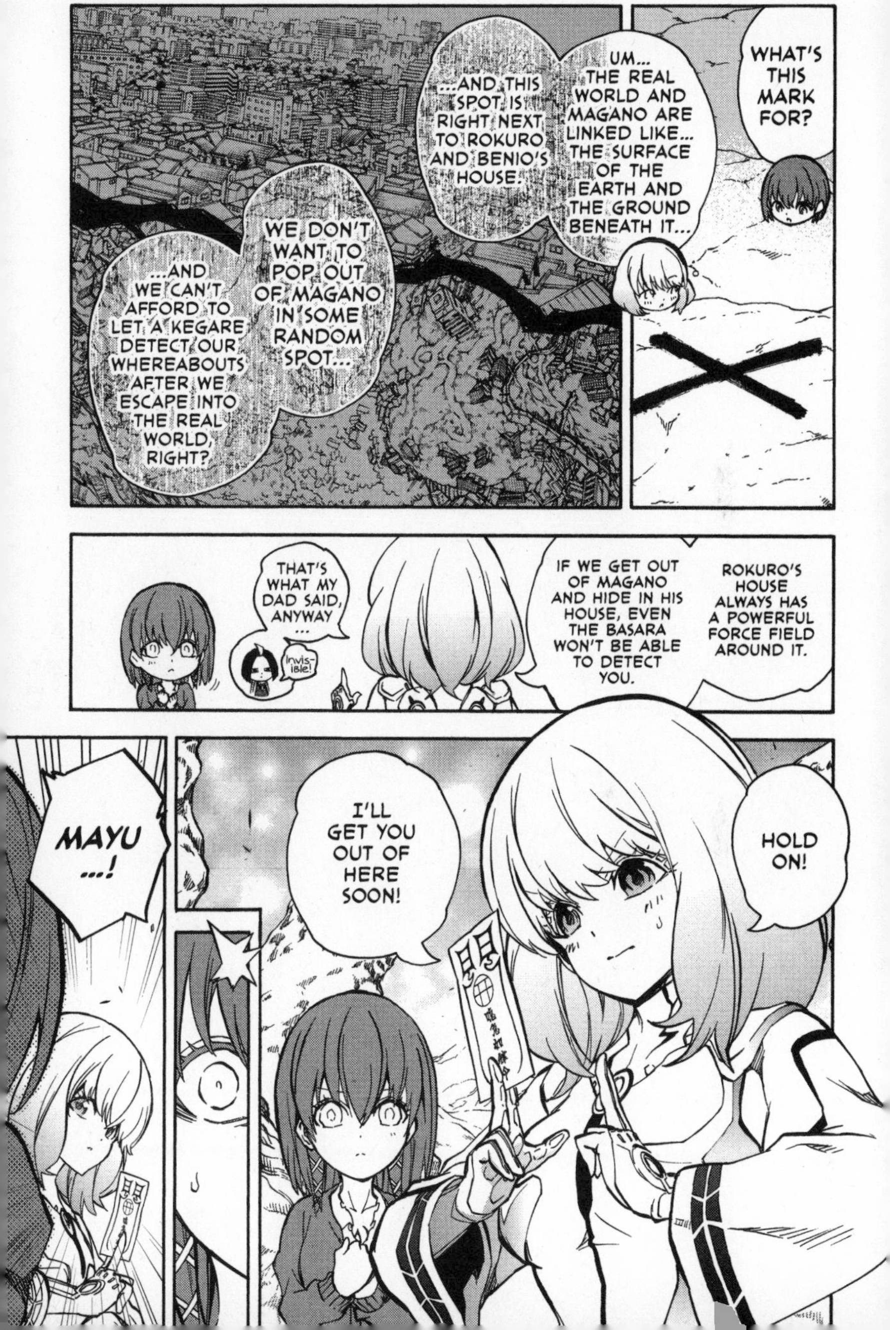
WHAT'S THIS MARK FOR?
UM... THE REAL WORLD AND MAGANO ARE LINKED LIKE... THE SURFACE OF THE EARTH AND THE GROUND BENEATH IT...
...AND THIS SPOT IS RIGHT NEXT TO ROKURO AND BENIO'S HOUSE.
WE DON'T WANT TO POP OUT OF MAGANO IN SOME RANDOM SPOT...
...AND WE CAN'T AFFORD TO LET A KEGARE DETECT OUR WHEREABOUTS AFTER WE ESCAPE INTO THE REAL WORLD, RIGHT?
ROKURO'S HOUSE ALWAYS HAS A POWERFUL FORCE FIELD AROUND IT.
IF WE GET OUT OF MAGANO AND HIDE IN HIS HOUSE, EVEN THE BASARA WON'T BE ABLE TO DETECT YOU.
THAT'S WHAT MY DAD SAID, ANYWAY...
Invis-ible!
HOLD ON!
I'LL GET YOU OUT OF HERE SOON!
MAYU...!

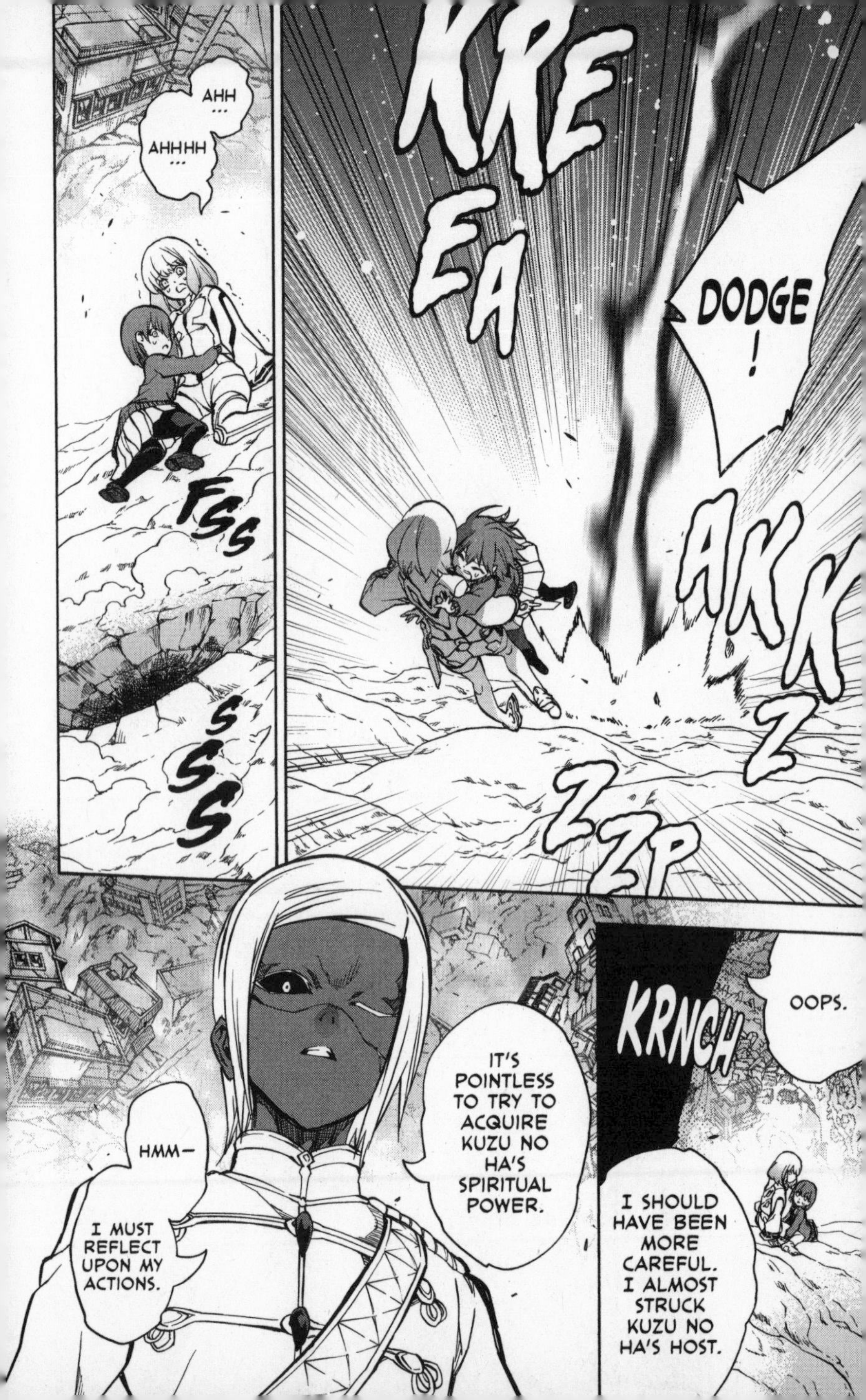

KREEA
DODGE!
AKKZ
ZZP
AHH...
AHHHH...
FSS
SSSS
KRNCH
OOPS.
I SHOULD HAVE BEEN MORE CAREFUL. I ALMOST STRUCK KUZU NO HA'S HOST.
IT'S POINTLESS TO TRY TO ACQUIRE KUZU NO HA'S SPIRITUAL POWER.
HMM—
I MUST REFLECT UPON MY ACTIONS.

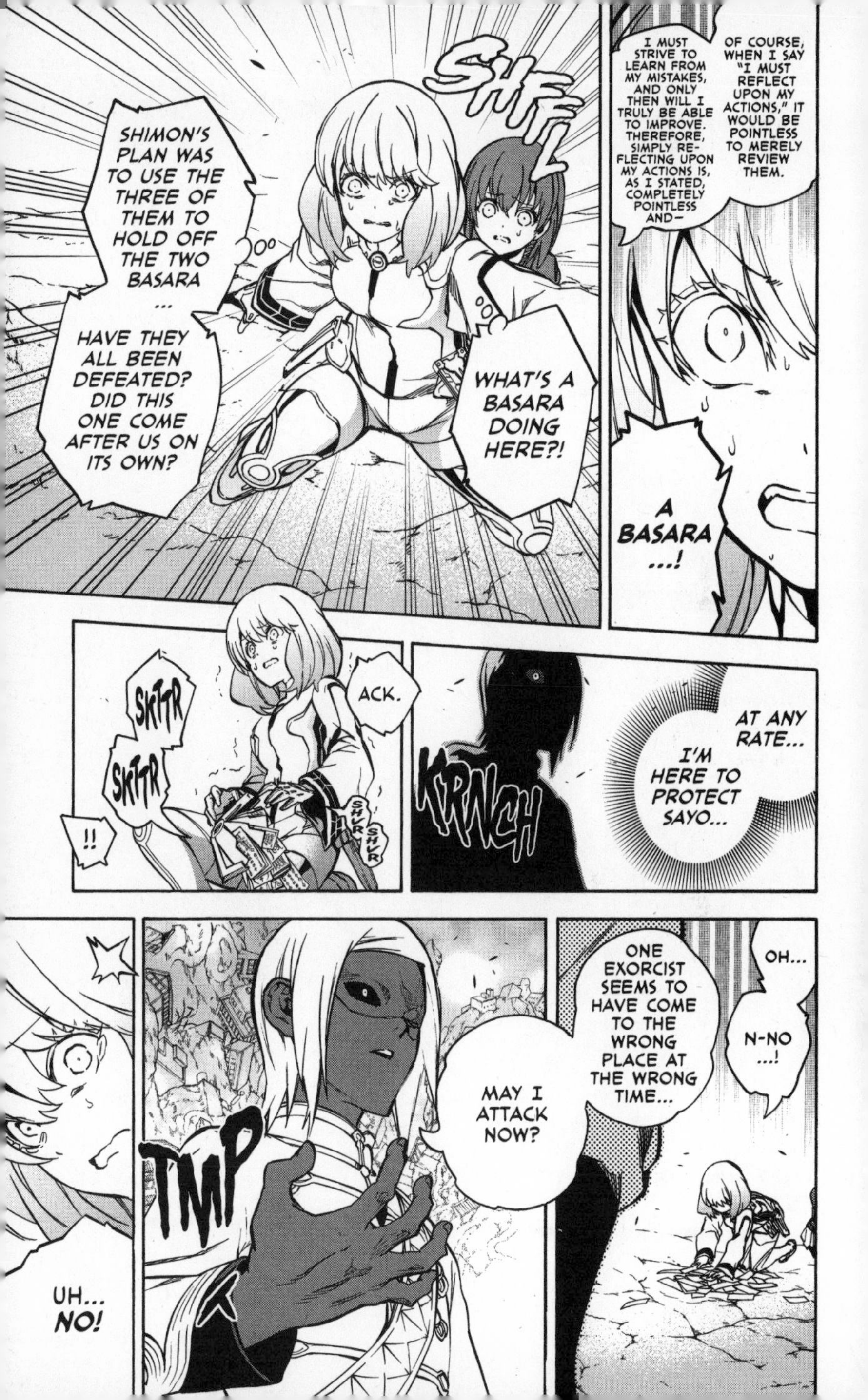

OF COURSE, WHEN I SAY "I MUST REFLECT UPON MY ACTIONS," IT WOULD BE POINTLESS TO MERELY REVIEW THEM.
I MUST STRIVE TO LEARN FROM MY MISTAKES, AND ONLY THEN WILL I TRULY BE ABLE TO IMPROVE. THEREFORE, SIMPLY RE-FLECTING UPON MY ACTIONS IS, AS I STATED, COMPLETELY POINTLESS AND—
A BASARA...!
SHFL
WHAT'S A BASARA DOING HERE?!
SHIMON'S PLAN WAS TO USE THE THREE OF THEM TO HOLD OFF THE TWO BASARA...
HAVE THEY ALL BEEN DEFEATED? DID THIS ONE COME AFTER US ON ITS OWN?
AT ANY RATE... I'M HERE TO PROTECT SAYO...
KRNCH
ACK.
SKTTR
SKTTR
SHVR
SHVR
!!
OH...
N-NO ...!
ONE EXORCIST SEEMS TO HAVE COME TO THE WRONG PLACE AT THE WRONG TIME...
MAY I ATTACK NOW?
TMP
UH... NO!

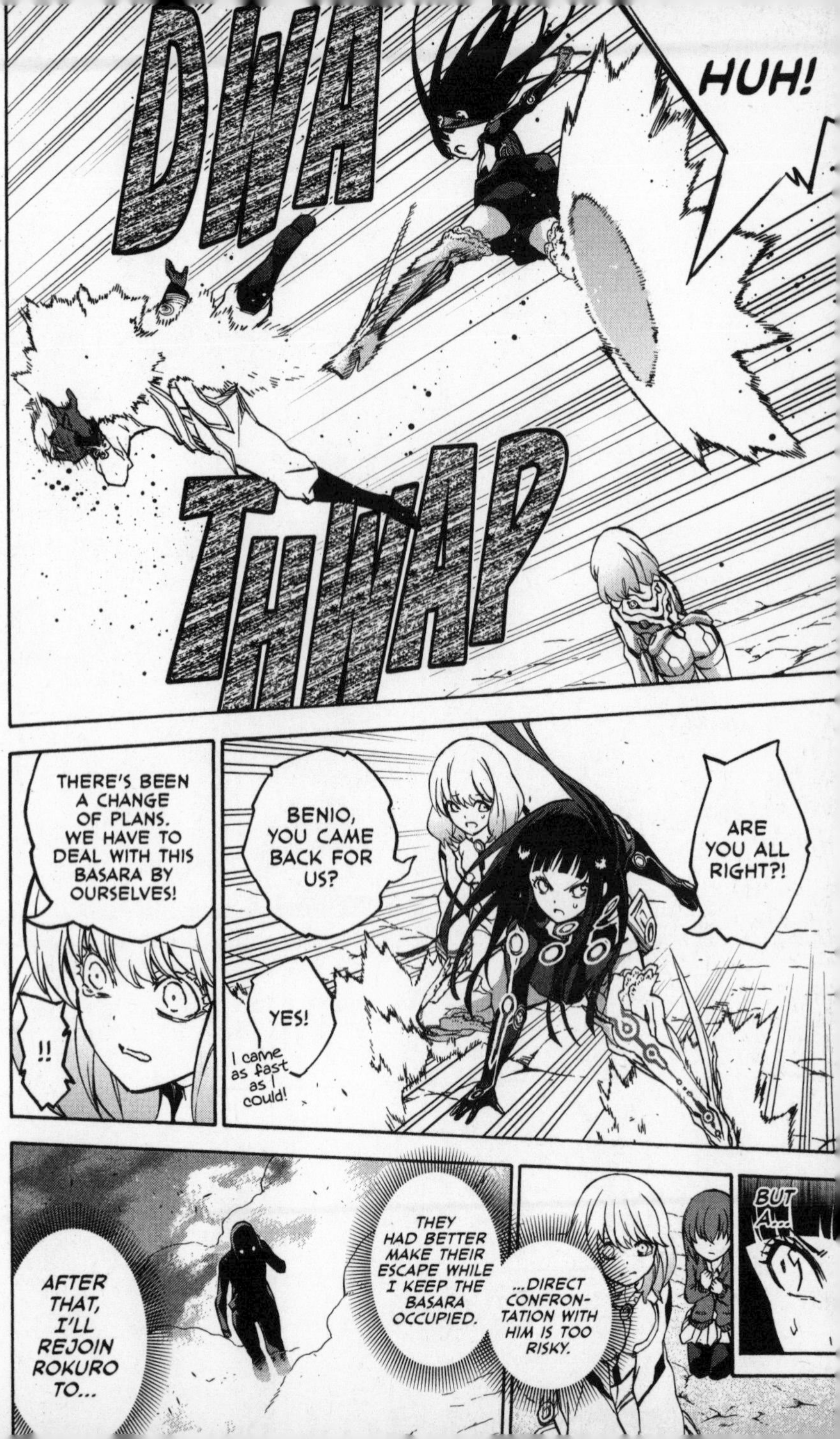
HUH!
DWA
THWAP
ARE YOU ALL RIGHT?!
BENIO, YOU CAME BACK FOR US?
YES!
I came as fast as I could!
THERE'S BEEN A CHANGE OF PLANS. WE HAVE TO DEAL WITH THIS BASARA BY OURSELVES!
!!
BUT A...
...DIRECT CONFRONTATION WITH HIM IS TOO RISKY.
THEY HAD BETTER MAKE THEIR ESCAPE WHILE I KEEP THE BASARA OCCUPIED.
AFTER THAT, I'LL REJOIN ROKURO TO...

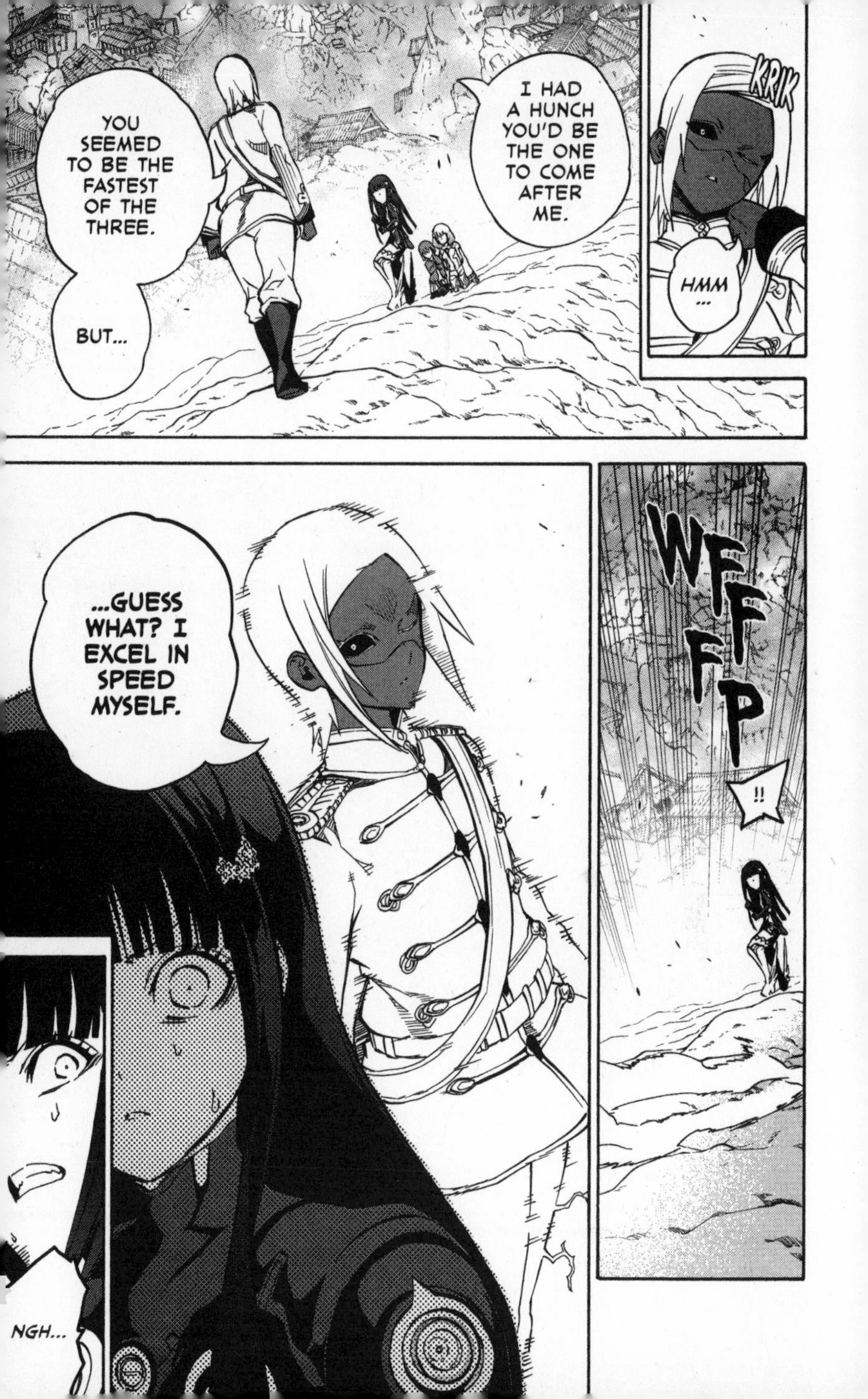
KRIK
HMM...
I HAD A HUNCH YOU'D BE THE ONE TO COME AFTER ME.
YOU SEEMED TO BE THE FASTEST OF THE THREE.
BUT...
WFFFP
!!
...GUESS WHAT? I EXCEL IN SPEED MYSELF.
NGH...

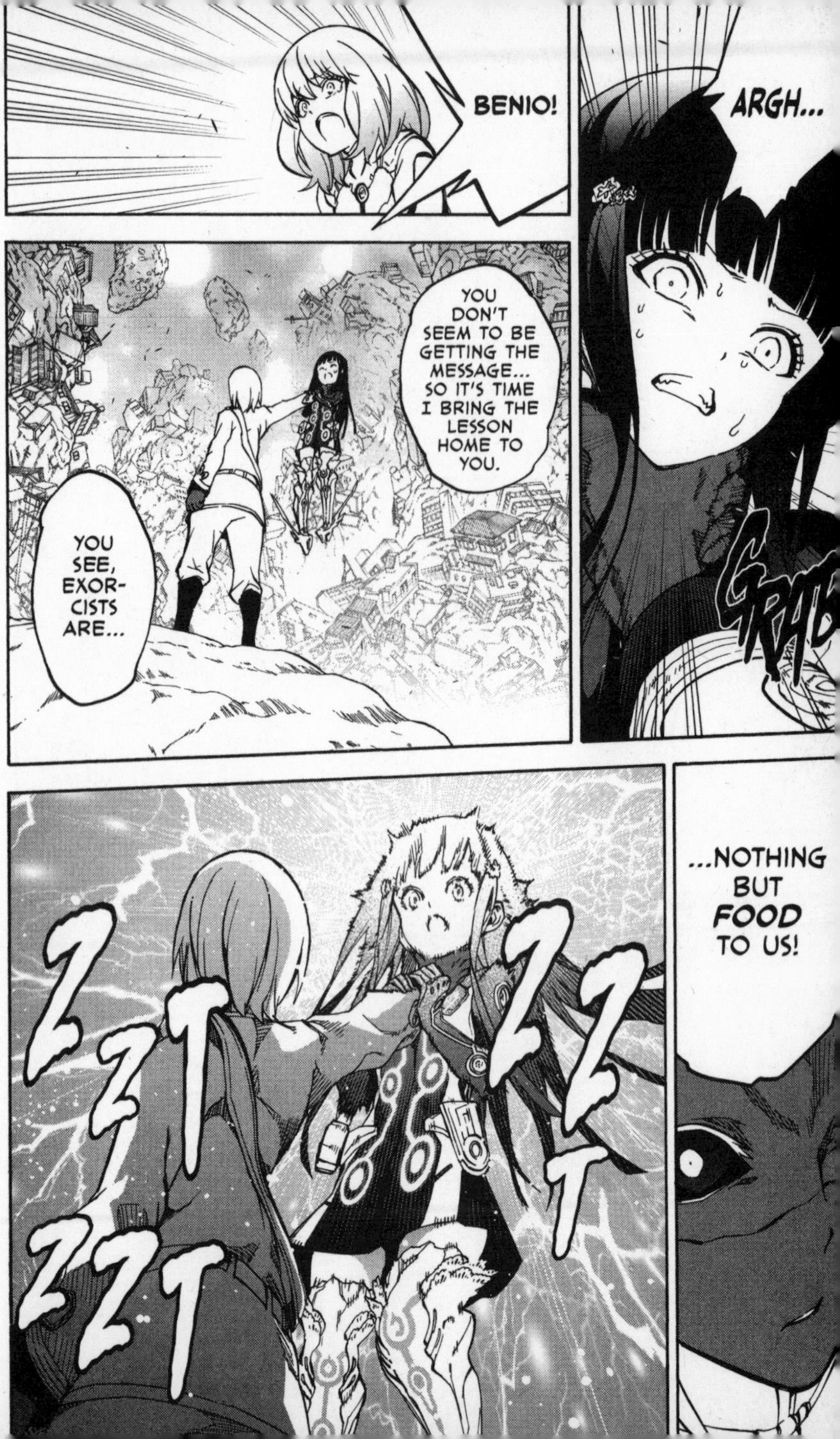
ARGH...
GRAB
BENIO!
YOU DON'T SEEM TO BE GETTING THE MESSAGE... SO IT'S TIME I BRING THE LESSON HOME TO YOU.
YOU SEE, EXOR-CISTS ARE...
...NOTHING BUT FOOD TO US!
ZZZT
ZZZT
ZZZT

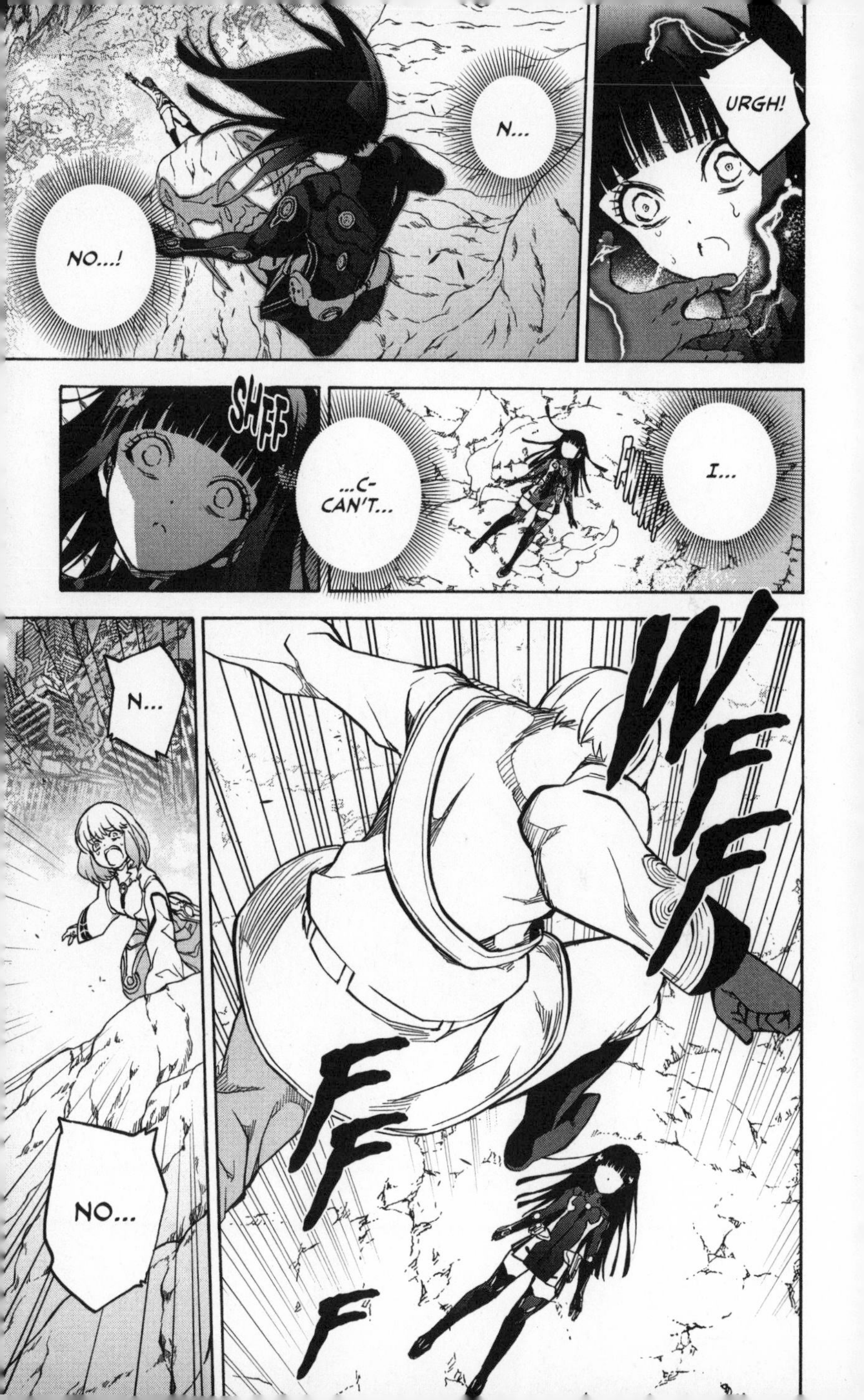
URGH!
N...
NO...!
I...
...C-
CAN'T...
SHFF
WFFFFF
N...
NO...

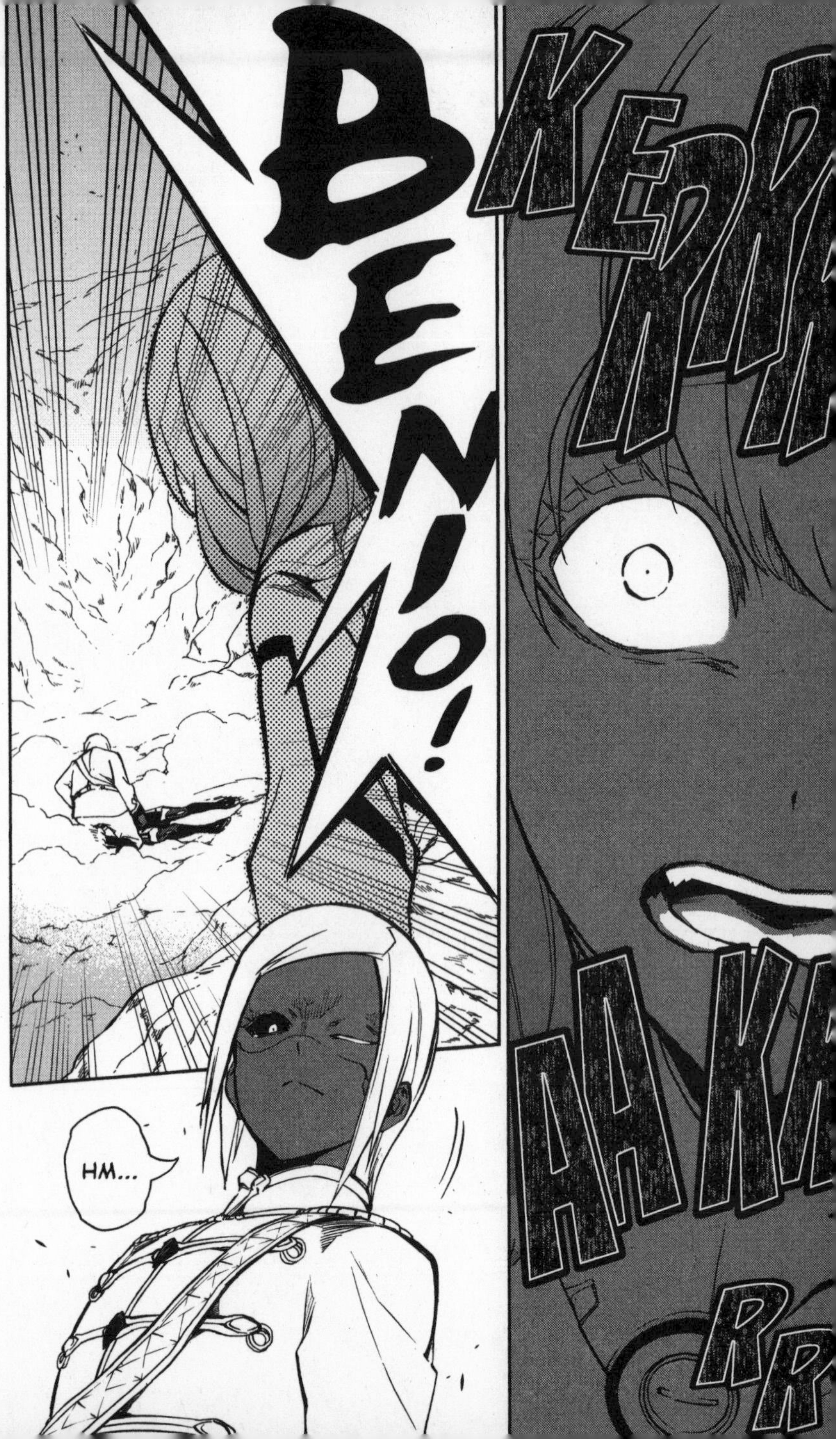

BENIO!
HM...

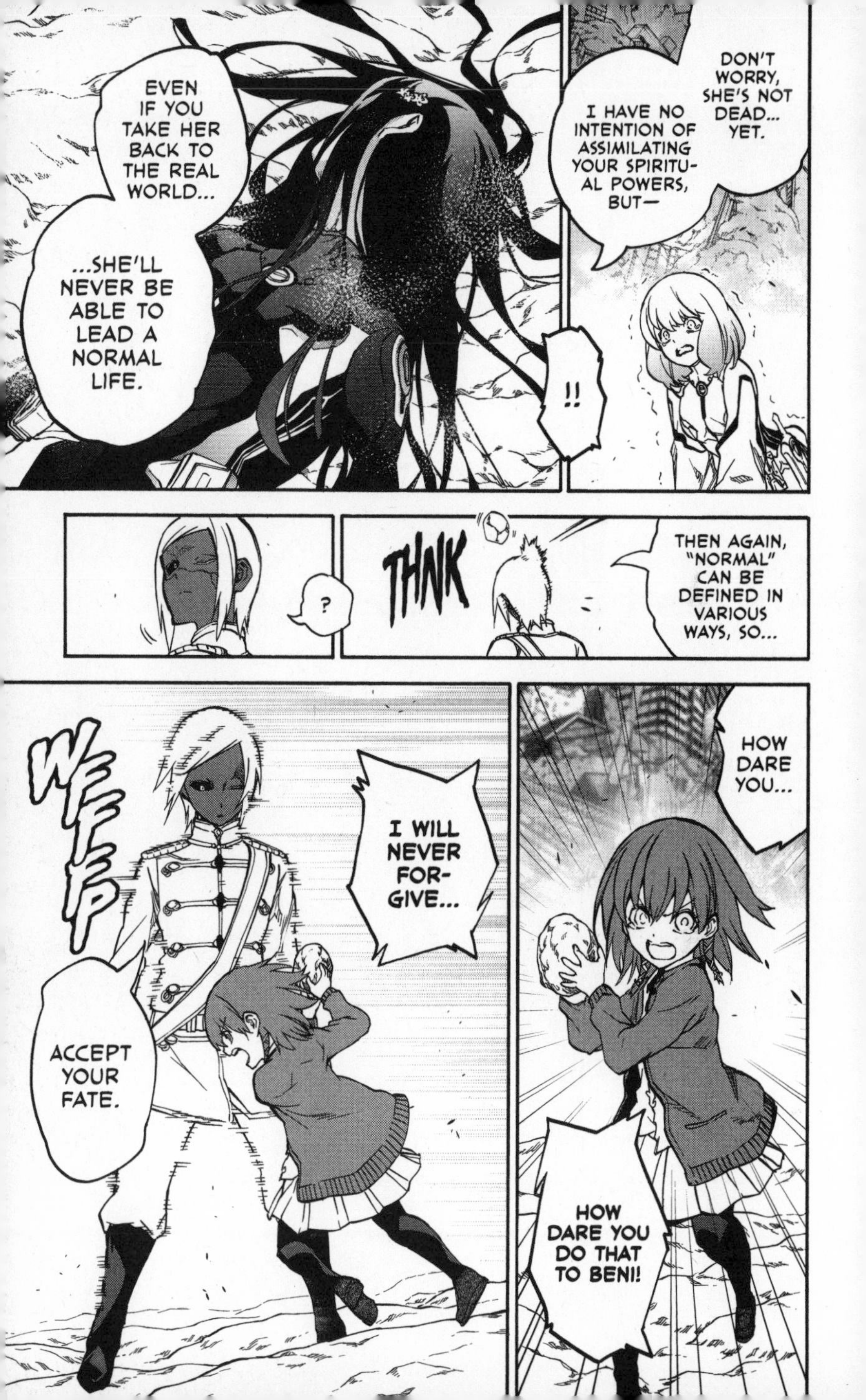
DON'T WORRY, SHE'S NOT DEAD... YET.
I HAVE NO INTENTION OF ASSIMILATING YOUR SPIRITUAL POWERS, BUT—
!!
EVEN IF YOU TAKE HER BACK TO THE REAL WORLD...
...SHE'LL NEVER BE ABLE TO LEAD A NORMAL LIFE.
THEN AGAIN, "NORMAL" CAN BE DEFINED IN VARIOUS WAYS, SO...
THNK
?
HOW DARE YOU...
HOW DARE YOU DO THAT TO BENI!
I WILL NEVER FORGIVE...
ACCEPT YOUR FATE.

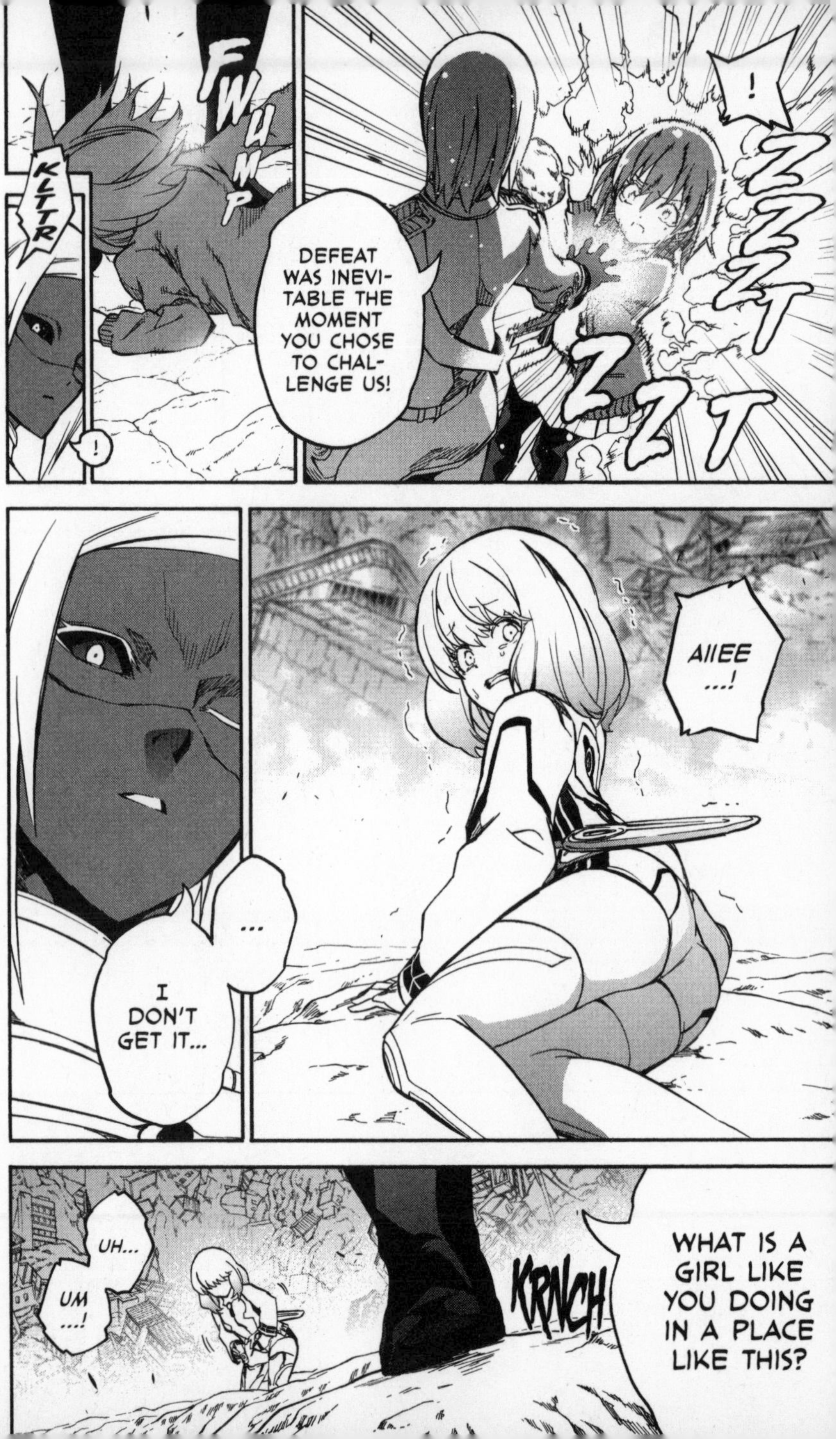
!
ZZZZT
ZZT
DEFEAT WAS INEVITABLE THE MOMENT YOU CHOSE TO CHALLENGE US!
FWUMP
KLTTR
!
AIIEE ...!
...
I DON'T GET IT...
WHAT IS A GIRL LIKE YOU DOING IN A PLACE LIKE THIS?
KRNCH
UH...
UM ...!

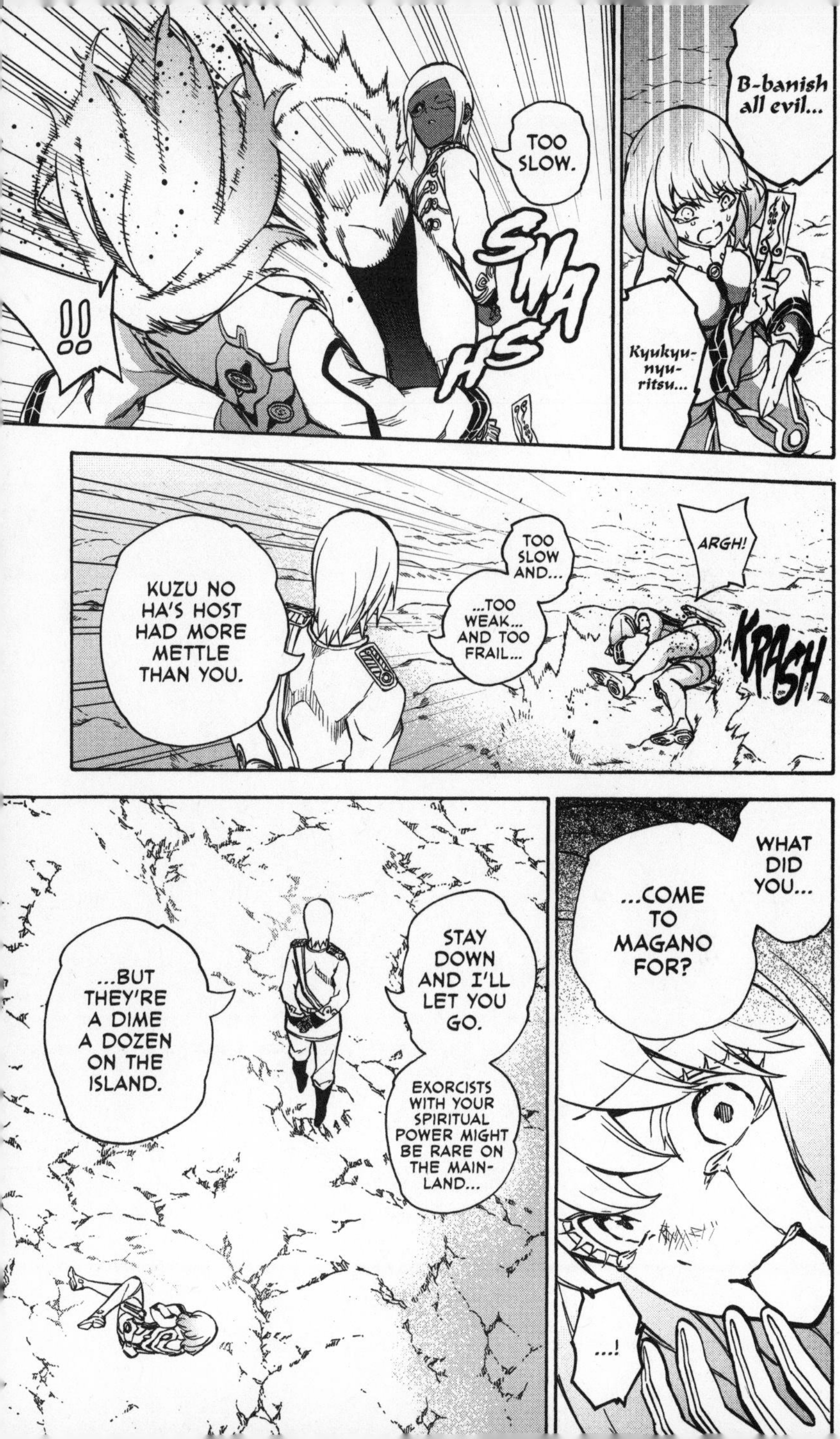
B-banish all evil...
Kyukyu-nyu-ritsu...
TOO SLOW.
SMASH
!!
ARGH!
KRASH
TOO SLOW AND...
...TOO WEAK... AND TOO FRAIL...
KUZU NO HA'S HOST HAD MORE METTLE THAN YOU.
WHAT DID YOU...
...COME TO MAGANO FOR?
...!
STAY DOWN AND I'LL LET YOU GO.
EXORCISTS WITH YOUR SPIRITUAL POWER MIGHT BE RARE ON THE MAIN-LAND...
...BUT THEY'RE A DIME A DOZEN ON THE ISLAND.

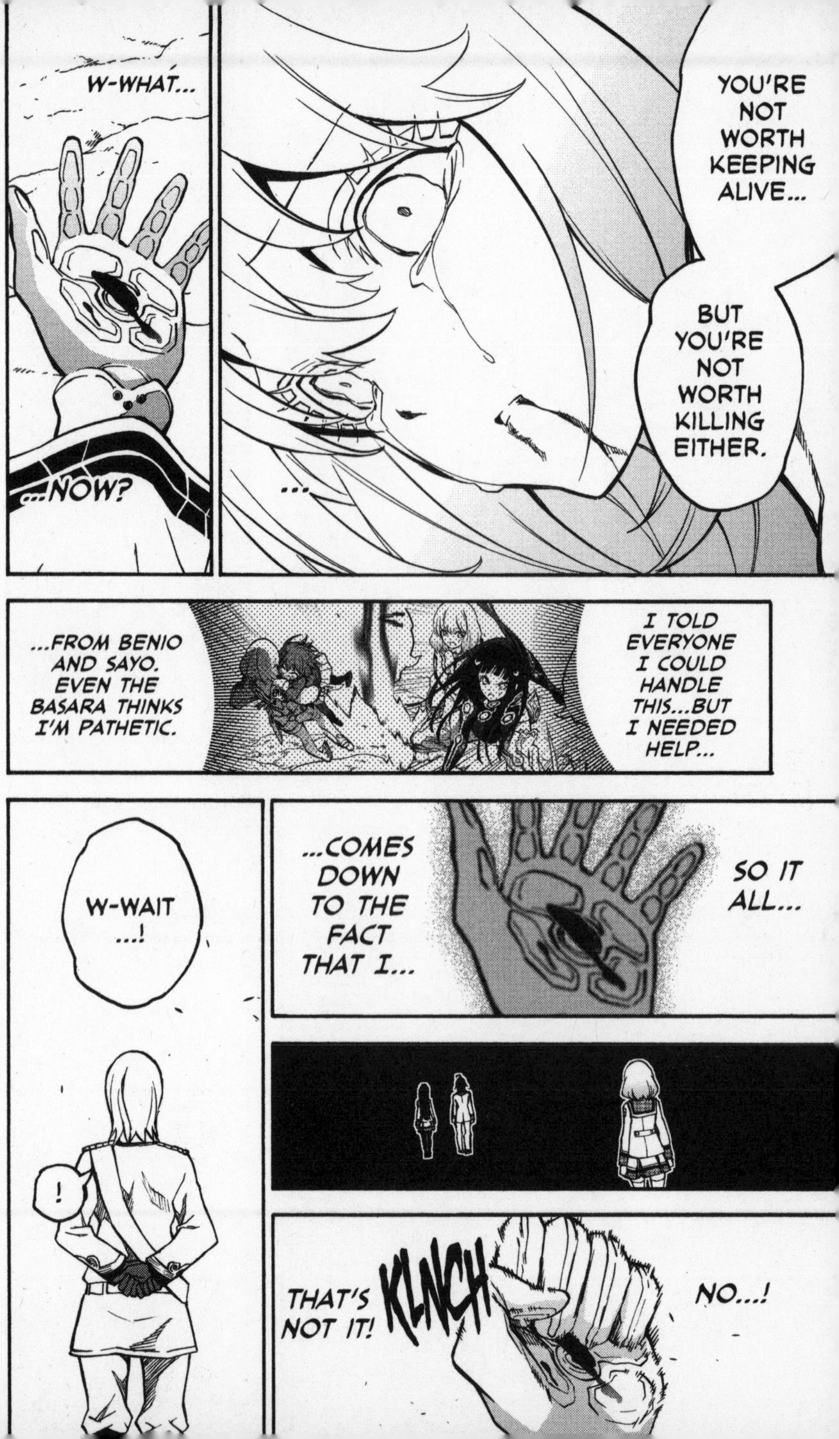
YOU'RE NOT WORTH KEEPING ALIVE...
BUT YOU'RE NOT WORTH KILLING EITHER.
...
W-WHAT...
...NOW?
I TOLD EVERYONE I COULD HANDLE THIS...BUT I NEEDED HELP...
...FROM BENIO AND SAYO. EVEN THE BASARA THINKS I'M PATHETIC.
SO IT ALL...
...COMES DOWN TO THE FACT THAT I...
NO...!
KLNCH
THAT'S NOT IT!
W-WAIT ...!
!

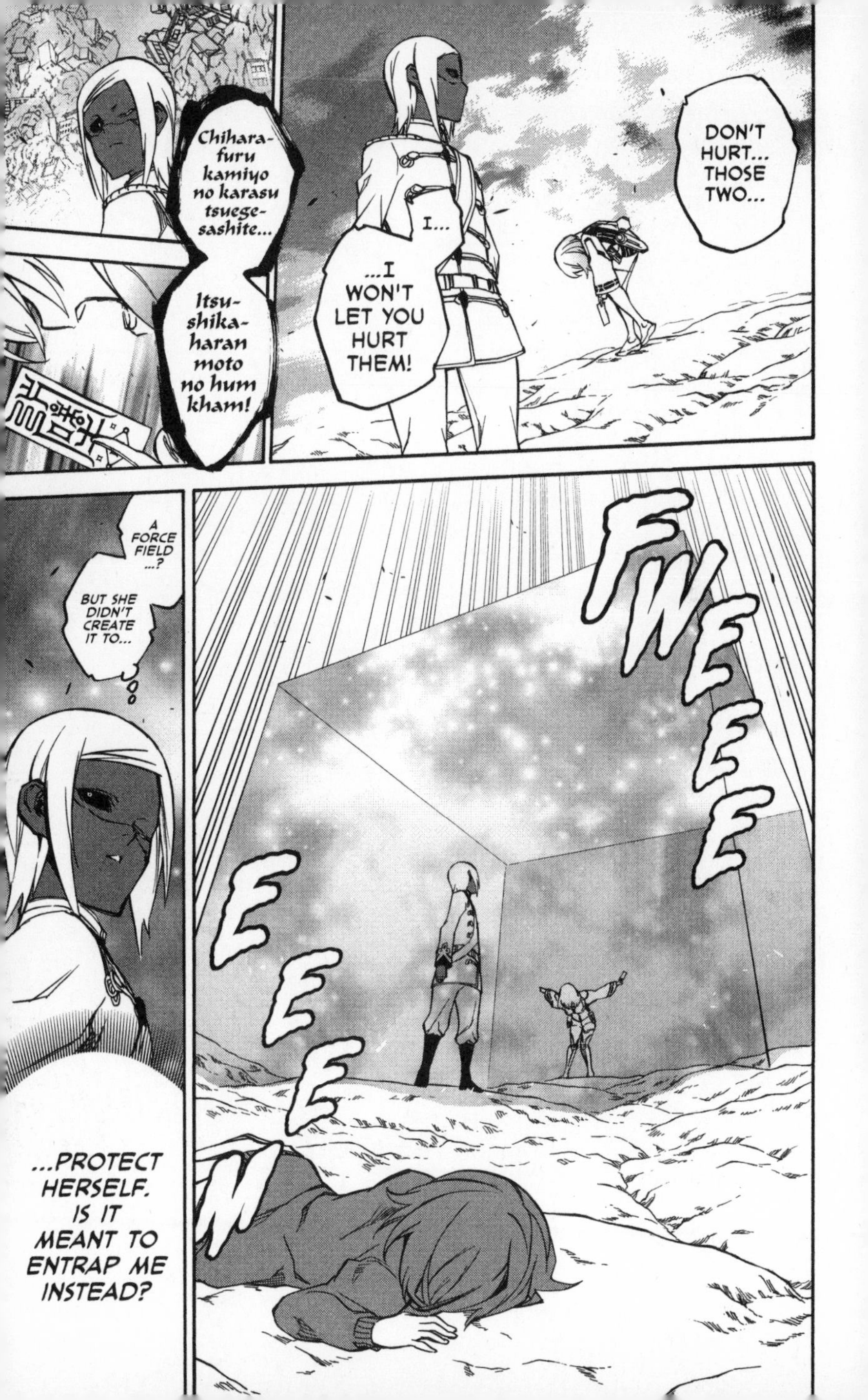
DON'T HURT... THOSE TWO...
I...
...I WON'T LET YOU HURT THEM!
Chihara-furu kamiyo no karasu tsuege-sashite...
Itsu-shika-haran moto no hum kham!
FWEEEEEEEM
A FORCE FIELD ...?
BUT SHE DIDN'T CREATE IT TO...
...PROTECT HERSELF. IS IT MEANT TO ENTRAP ME INSTEAD?

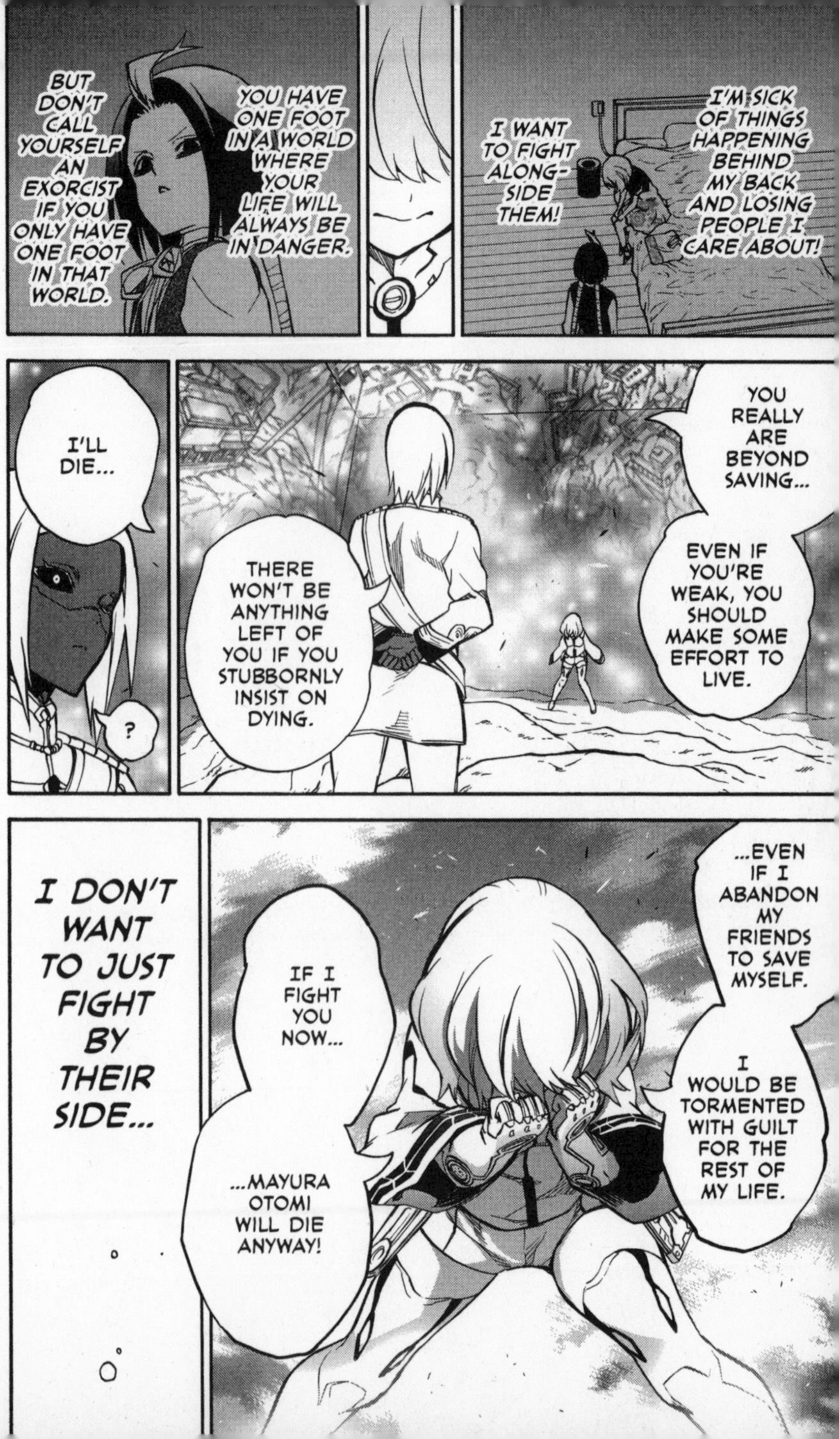
I'M SICK OF THINGS HAPPENING BEHIND MY BACK AND LOSING PEOPLE I CARE ABOUT!
I WANT TO FIGHT ALONG-SIDE THEM!
YOU HAVE ONE FOOT IN A WORLD WHERE YOUR LIFE WILL ALWAYS BE IN DANGER.
BUT DON'T CALL YOURSELF AN EXORCIST IF YOU ONLY HAVE ONE FOOT IN THAT WORLD.
YOU REALLY ARE BEYOND SAVING...
EVEN IF YOU'RE WEAK, YOU SHOULD MAKE SOME EFFORT TO LIVE.
THERE WON'T BE ANYTHING LEFT OF YOU IF YOU STUBBORNLY INSIST ON DYING.
I'LL DIE...
?
...EVEN IF I ABANDON MY FRIENDS TO SAVE MYSELF.
I WOULD BE TORMENTED WITH GUILT FOR THE REST OF MY LIFE.
IF I FIGHT YOU NOW...
...MAYURA OTOMI WILL DIE ANYWAY!
I DON'T WANT TO JUST FIGHT BY THEIR SIDE...

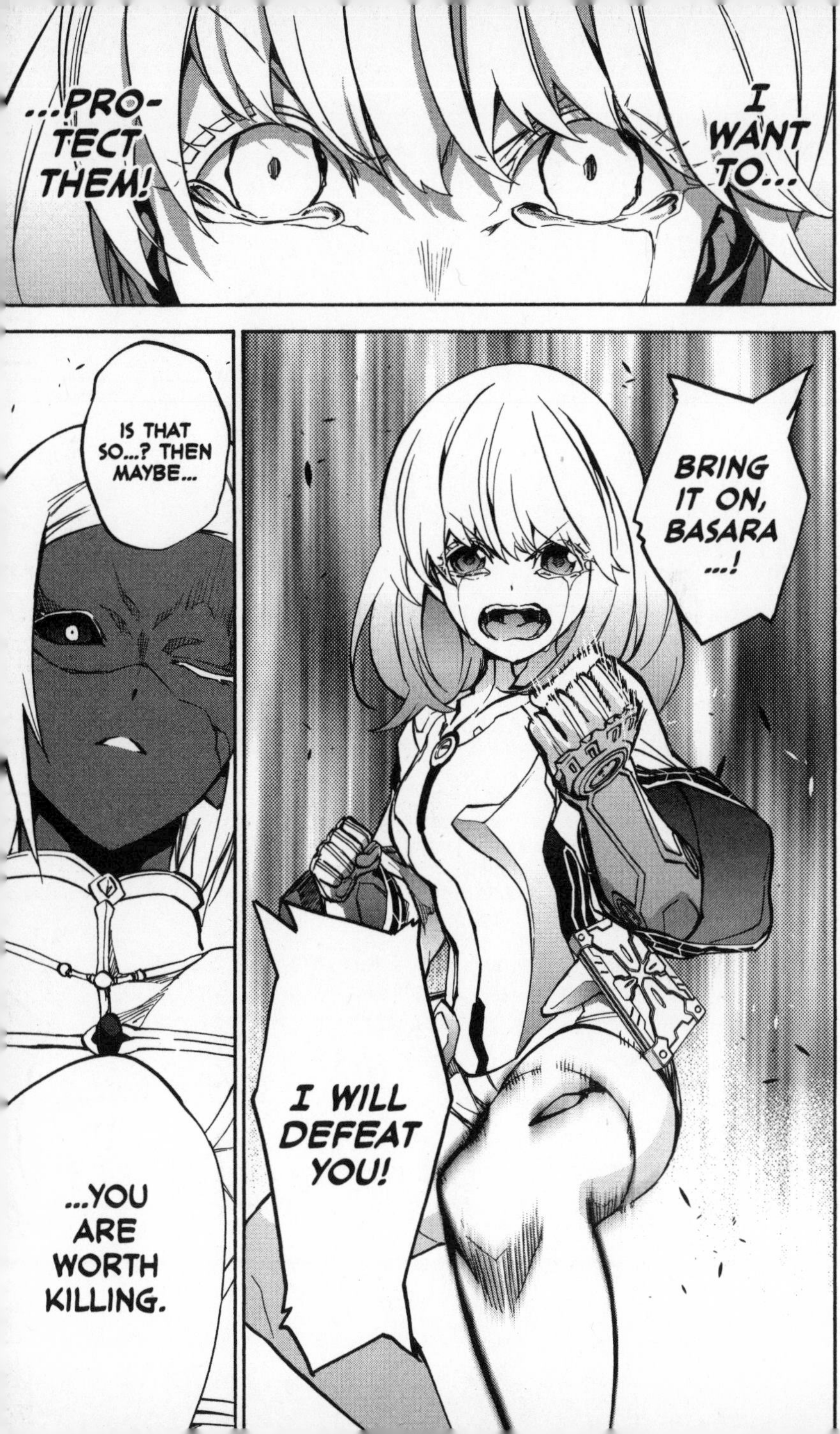
I WANT TO...
...PROTECT THEM!
BRING IT ON, BASARA...!
I WILL DEFEAT YOU!
IS THAT SO...? THEN MAYBE...
...YOU ARE WORTH KILLING.

Column ⑯ Doman

In the previous volume, I introduced the pentagram Seiman, which the exorcists use to ward off evil. This is the Doman, an equally renowned symbol to ward off evil. It consists of four vertical and five horizontal crisscrossing lines.

This originally came from the Kuji Technique (the "Rin Pyo Tou Sha Kai Jin Retsu Zai Zen" chant) which was used in Shugendo, the Way of the Mountain Priest. And like the Seiman, this too is said to have the power to ward off and banish evil. But for the moment, it is used to symbolize the bad guys in this series, since it is carved onto the bodies of Kegare.

The name Doman is derived from a certain famous exorcist, but I'll slowly reveal that in the manga.

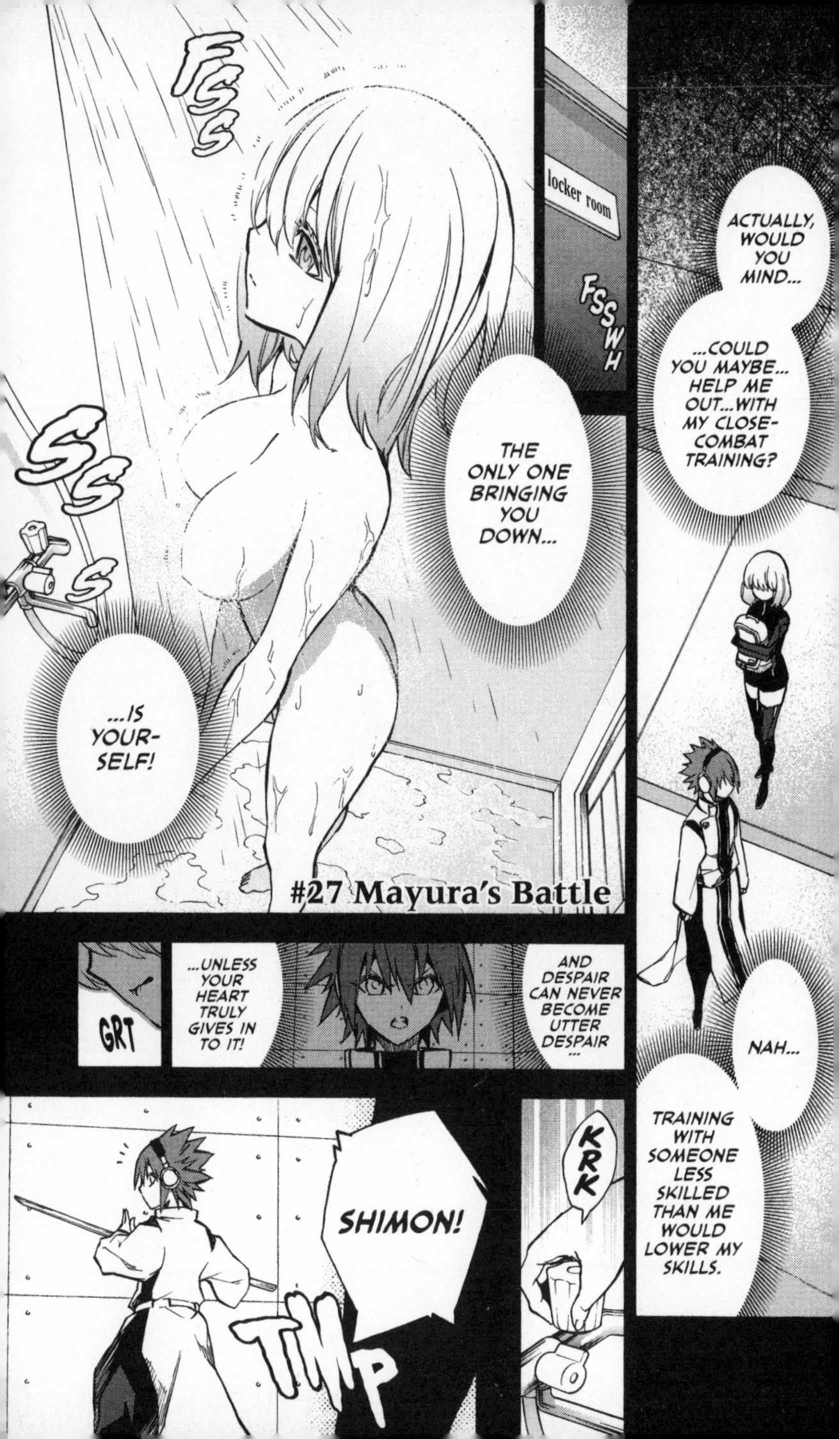
ACTUALLY, WOULD YOU MIND...
...COULD YOU MAYBE... HELP ME OUT...WITH MY CLOSE-COMBAT TRAINING?
NAH...
TRAINING WITH SOMEONE LESS SKILLED THAN ME WOULD LOWER MY SKILLS.
locker room
FSSWH
FSS
THE ONLY ONE BRINGING YOU DOWN...
SSS
...IS YOURSELF!
#27 Mayura's Battle
AND DESPAIR CAN NEVER BECOME UTTER DESPAIR...
...UNLESS YOUR HEART TRULY GIVES IN TO IT!
GRT
KRK
SHIMON!
TMP

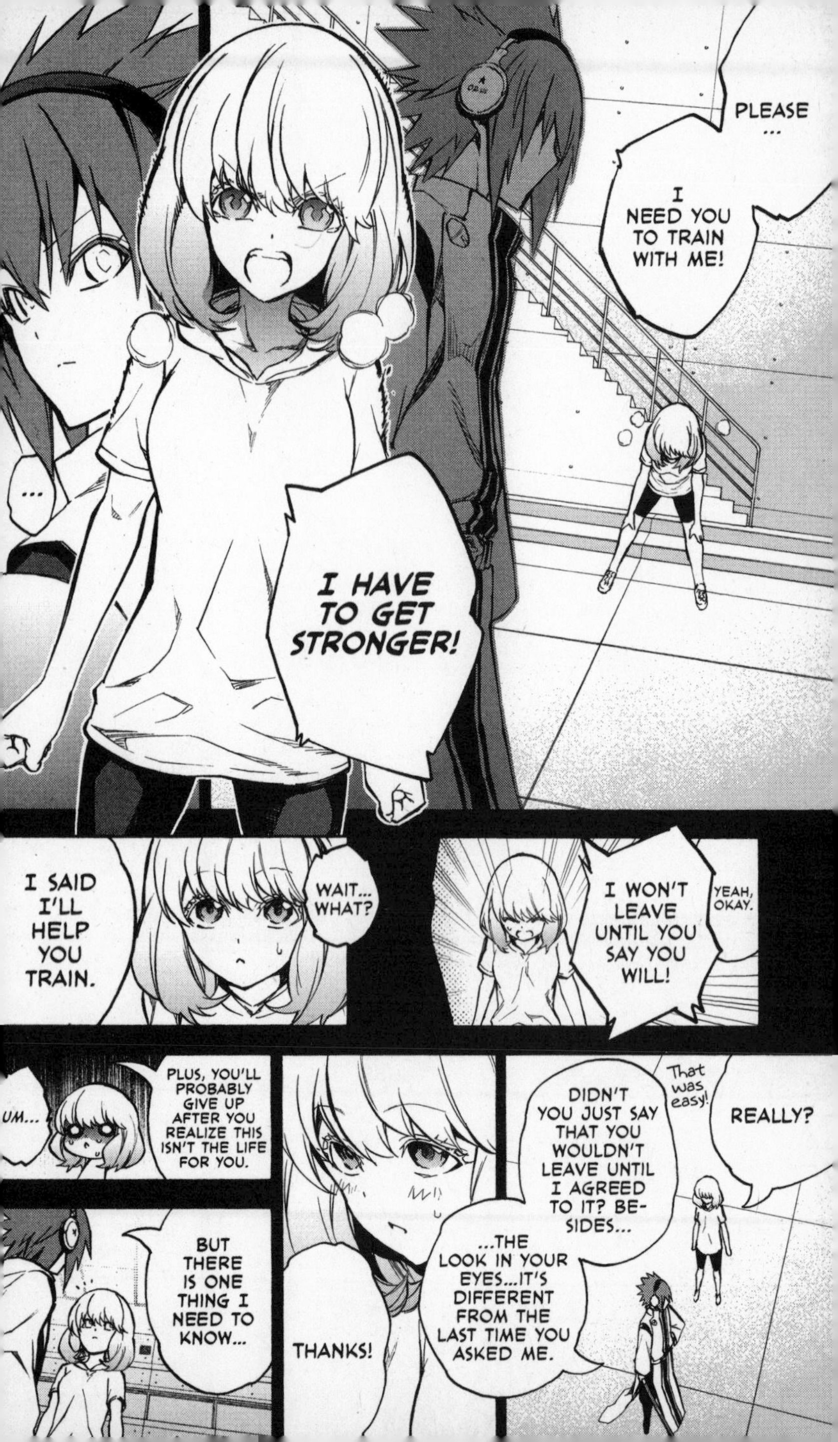
PLEASE...
I NEED YOU TO TRAIN WITH ME!
I HAVE TO GET STRONGER!
...
I WON'T LEAVE UNTIL YOU SAY YOU WILL!
YEAH, OKAY.
WAIT... WHAT?
I SAID I'LL HELP YOU TRAIN.
REALLY?
That was easy!
DIDN'T YOU JUST SAY THAT YOU WOULDN'T LEAVE UNTIL I AGREED TO IT? BE-SIDES...
...THE LOOK IN YOUR EYES...IT'S DIFFERENT FROM THE LAST TIME YOU ASKED ME.
THANKS!
UM...
PLUS, YOU'LL PROBABLY GIVE UP AFTER YOU REALIZE THIS ISN'T THE LIFE FOR YOU.
BUT THERE IS ONE THING I NEED TO KNOW...

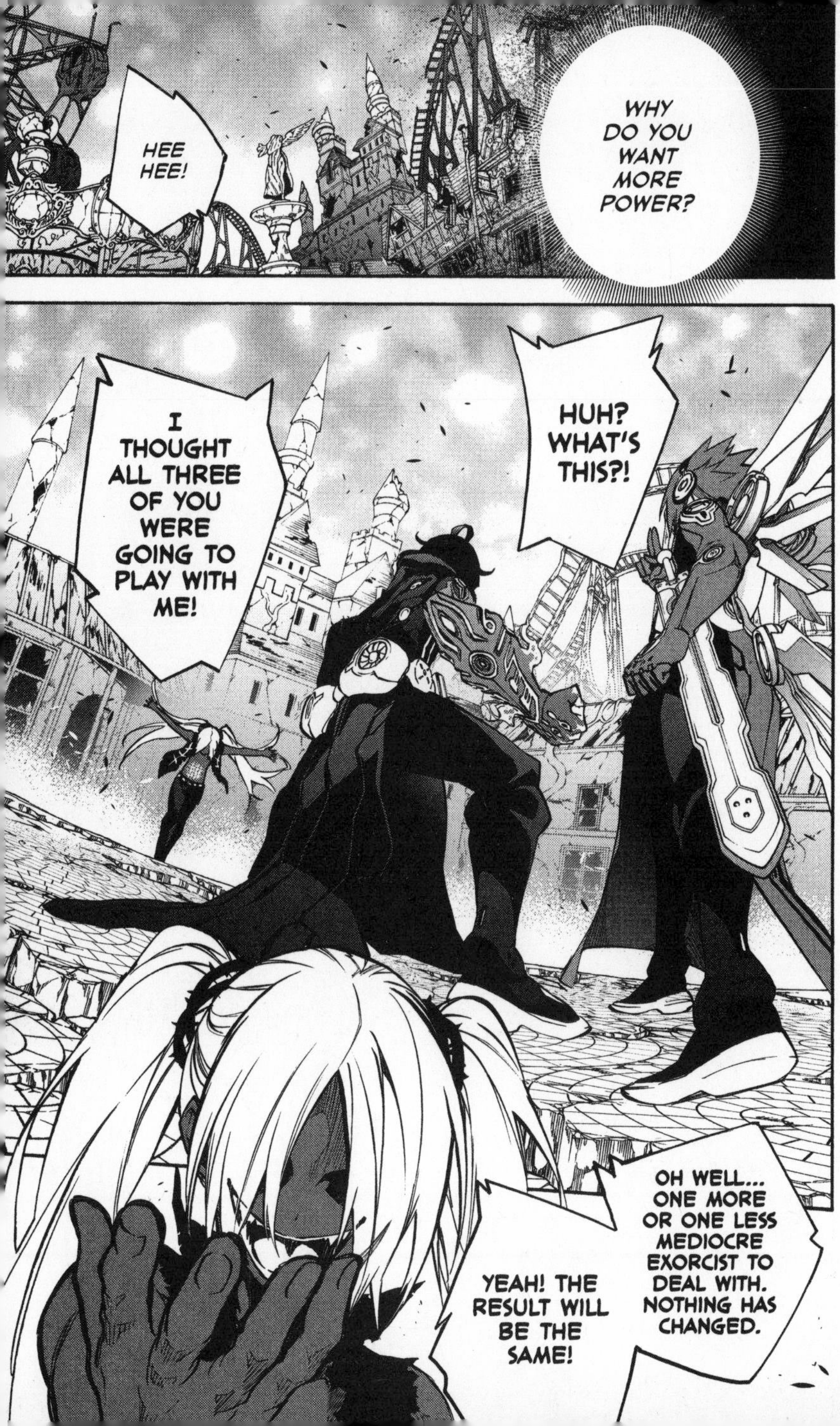
WHY DO YOU WANT MORE POWER?
HEE HEE!
HUH? WHAT'S THIS?!
I THOUGHT ALL THREE OF YOU WERE GOING TO PLAY WITH ME!
OH WELL... ONE MORE OR ONE LESS MEDIOCRE EXORCIST TO DEAL WITH. NOTHING HAS CHANGED.
YEAH! THE RESULT WILL BE THE SAME!

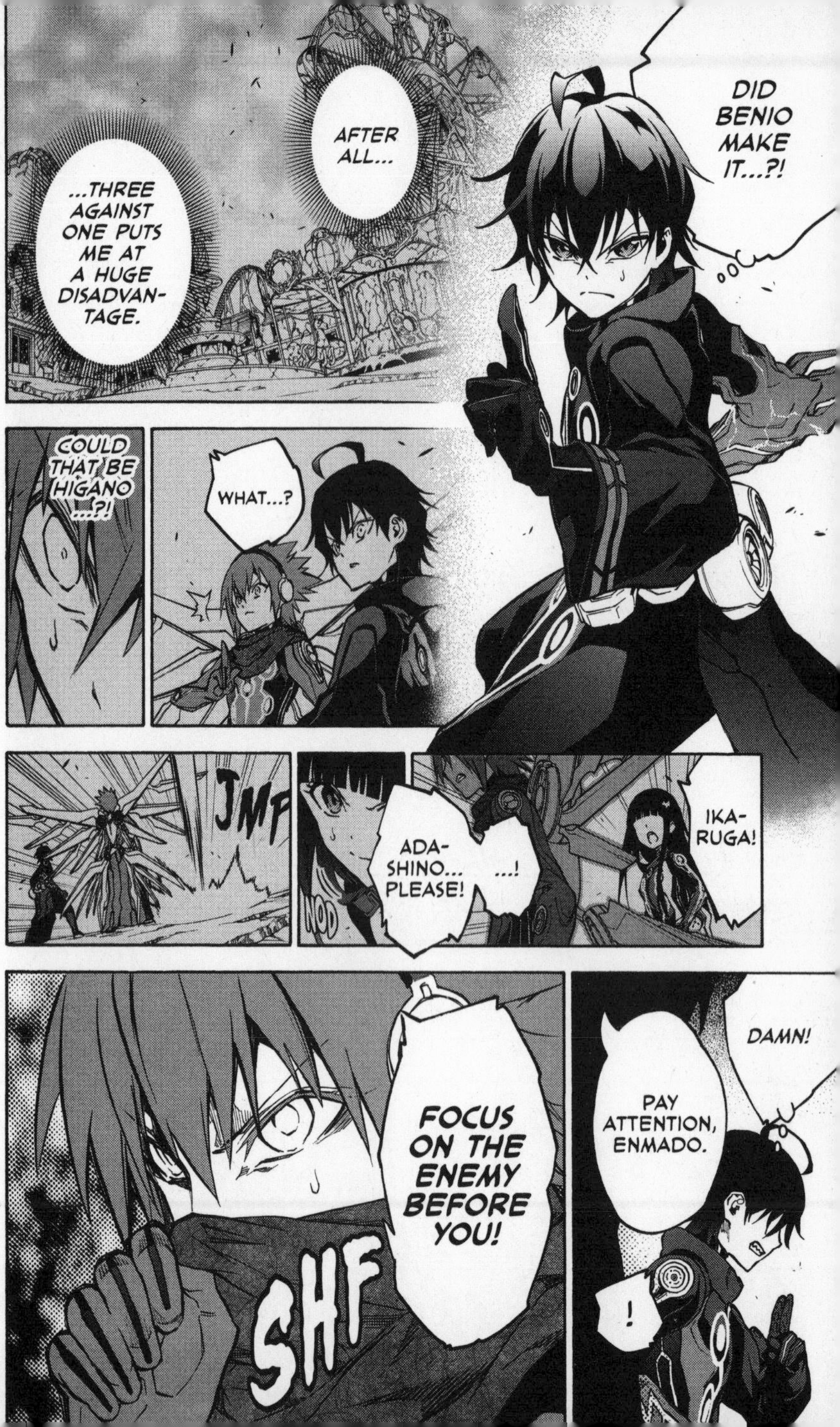
DID BENIO MAKE IT...?!
AFTER ALL...
...THREE AGAINST ONE PUTS ME AT A HUGE DISADVANTAGE.
WHAT...?
COULD THAT BE HIGANO ...?!
IKARUGA!
...!
ADA-SHINO... PLEASE!
NOD
JMF
DAMN!
PAY ATTENTION, ENMADO.
!
FOCUS ON THE ENEMY BEFORE YOU!
SHF

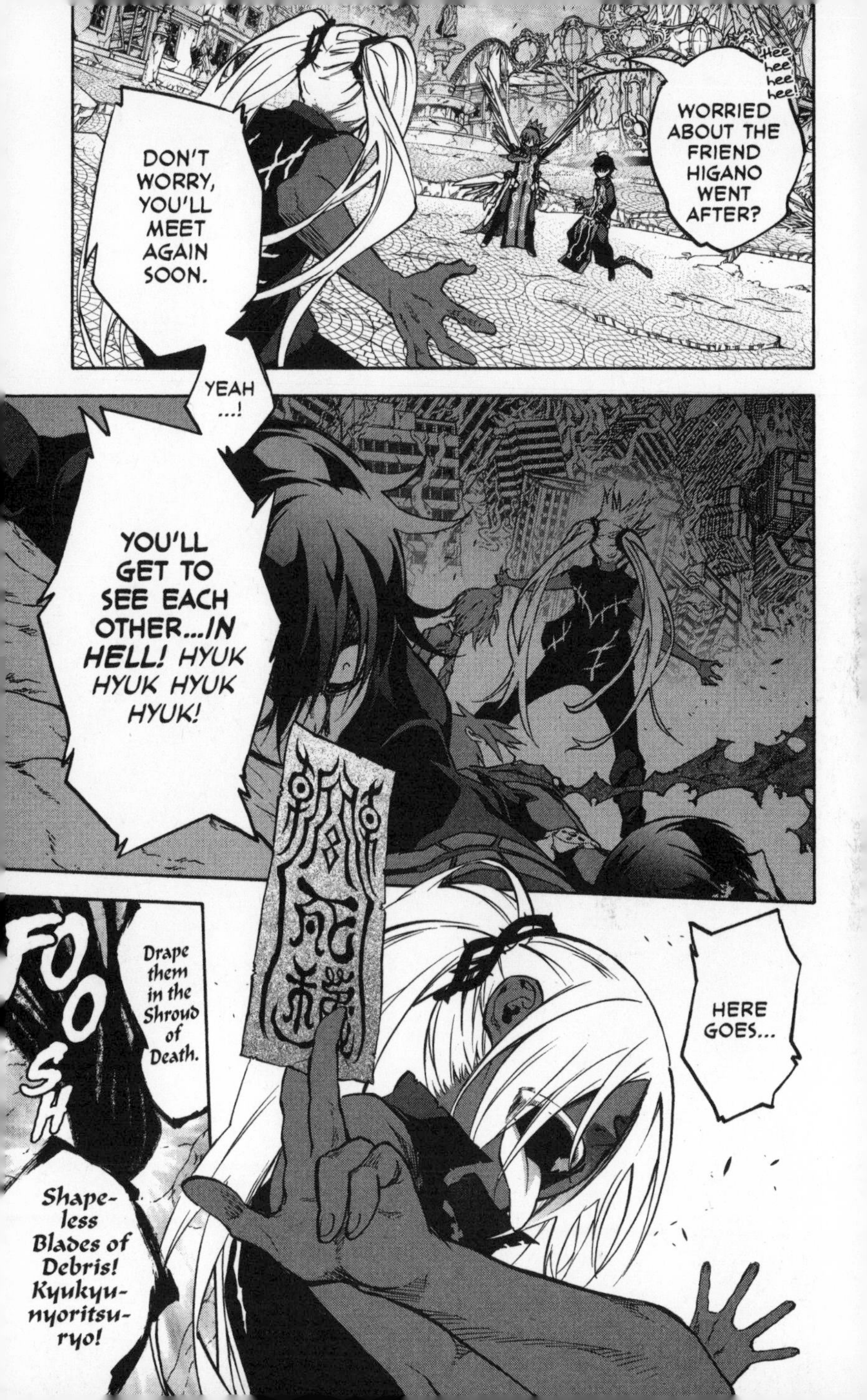
Hee hee hee hee!
WORRIED ABOUT THE FRIEND HIGANO WENT AFTER?
DON'T WORRY, YOU'LL MEET AGAIN SOON.
YEAH ...!
YOU'LL GET TO SEE EACH OTHER...*IN HELL!* HYUK HYUK HYUK HYUK!
HERE GOES...
Drape them in the Shroud of Death.
FOOSH
Shape-less Blades of Debris! Kyukyu-nyoritsu-ryo!

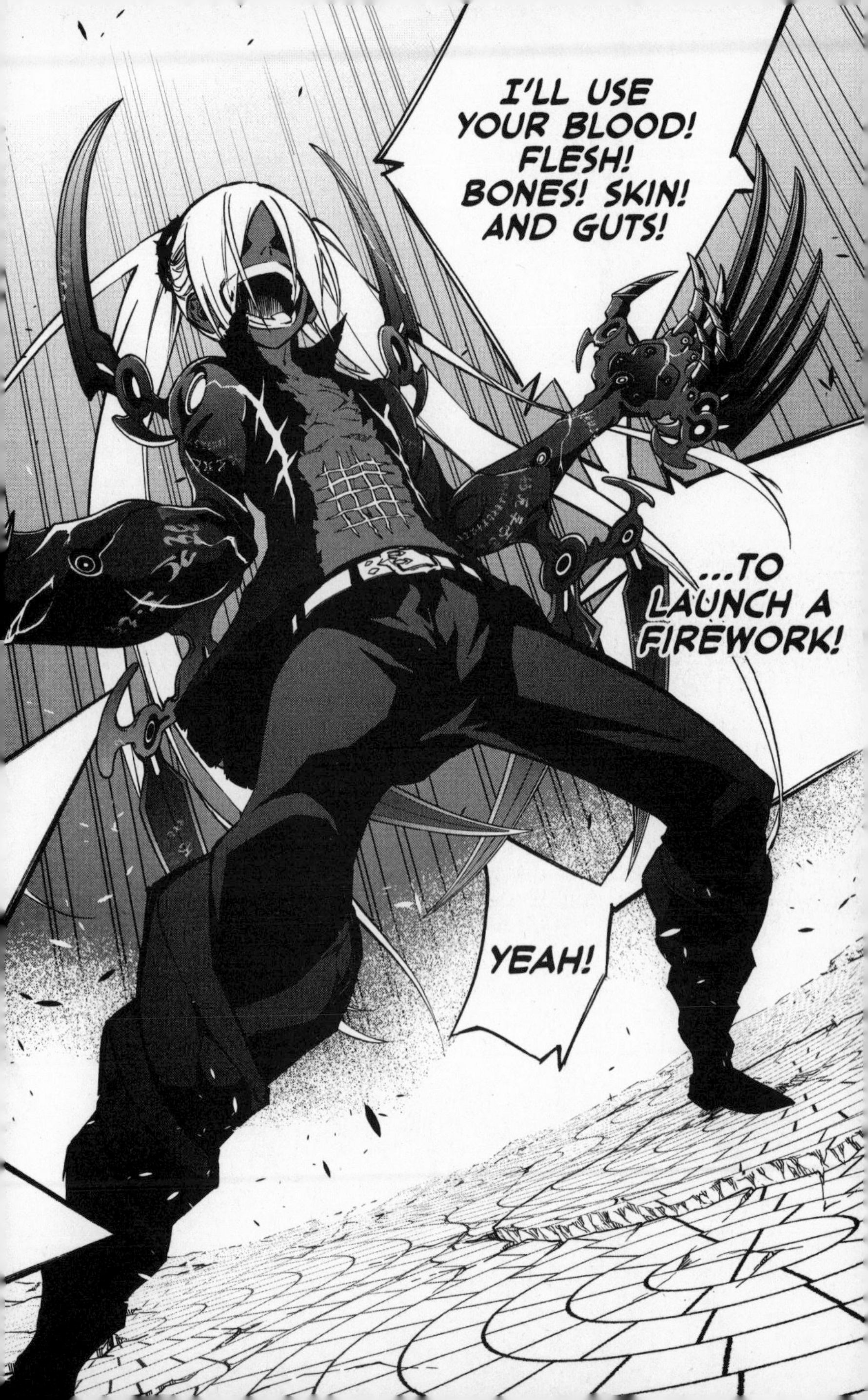
I'LL USE YOUR BLOOD! FLESH! BONES! SKIN! AND GUTS!
...TO LAUNCH A FIREWORK!
YEAH!

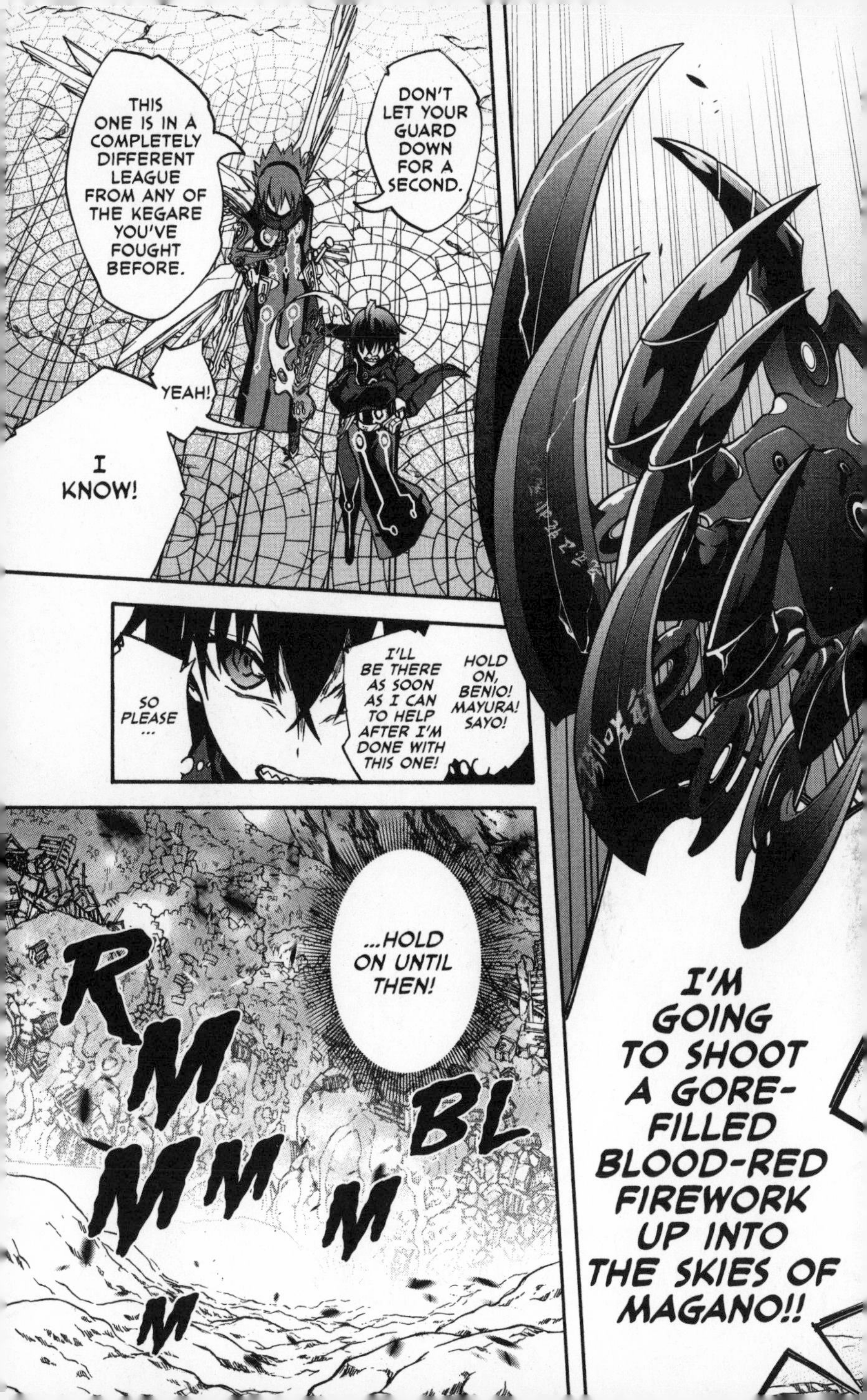
I'M GOING TO SHOOT A GORE-FILLED BLOOD-RED FIREWORK UP INTO THE SKIES OF MAGANO!!
DON'T LET YOUR GUARD DOWN FOR A SECOND.
THIS ONE IS IN A COMPLETELY DIFFERENT LEAGUE FROM ANY OF THE KEGARE YOU'VE FOUGHT BEFORE.
YEAH!
I KNOW!
HOLD ON, BENIO! MAYURA! SAYO!
I'LL BE THERE AS SOON AS I CAN TO HELP AFTER I'M DONE WITH THIS ONE!
SO PLEASE ...
...HOLD ON UNTIL THEN!
RMMMMMBLMM

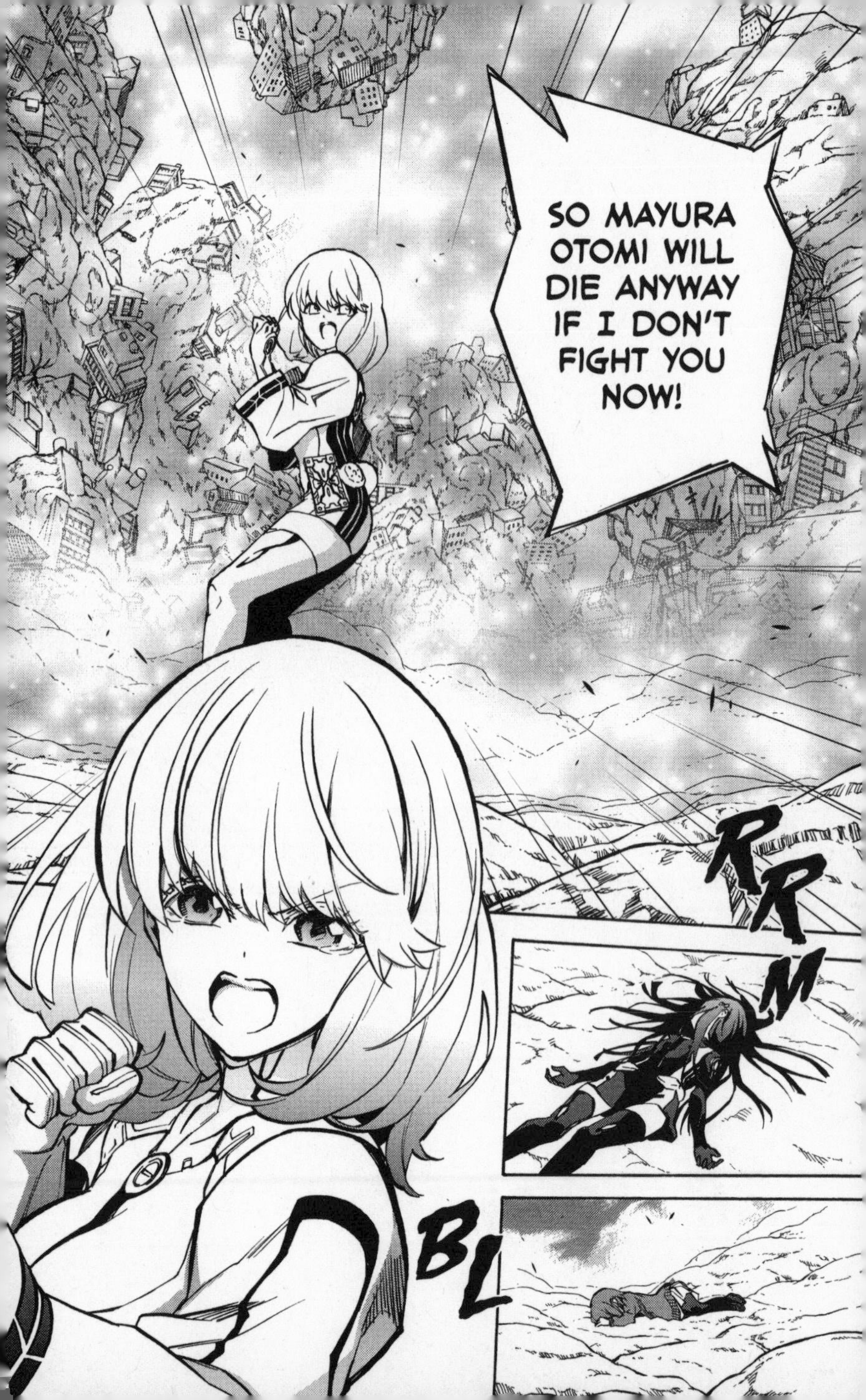
SO MAYURA OTOMI WILL DIE ANYWAY IF I DON'T FIGHT YOU NOW!
RRM
BL

#27 Mayura's Battle

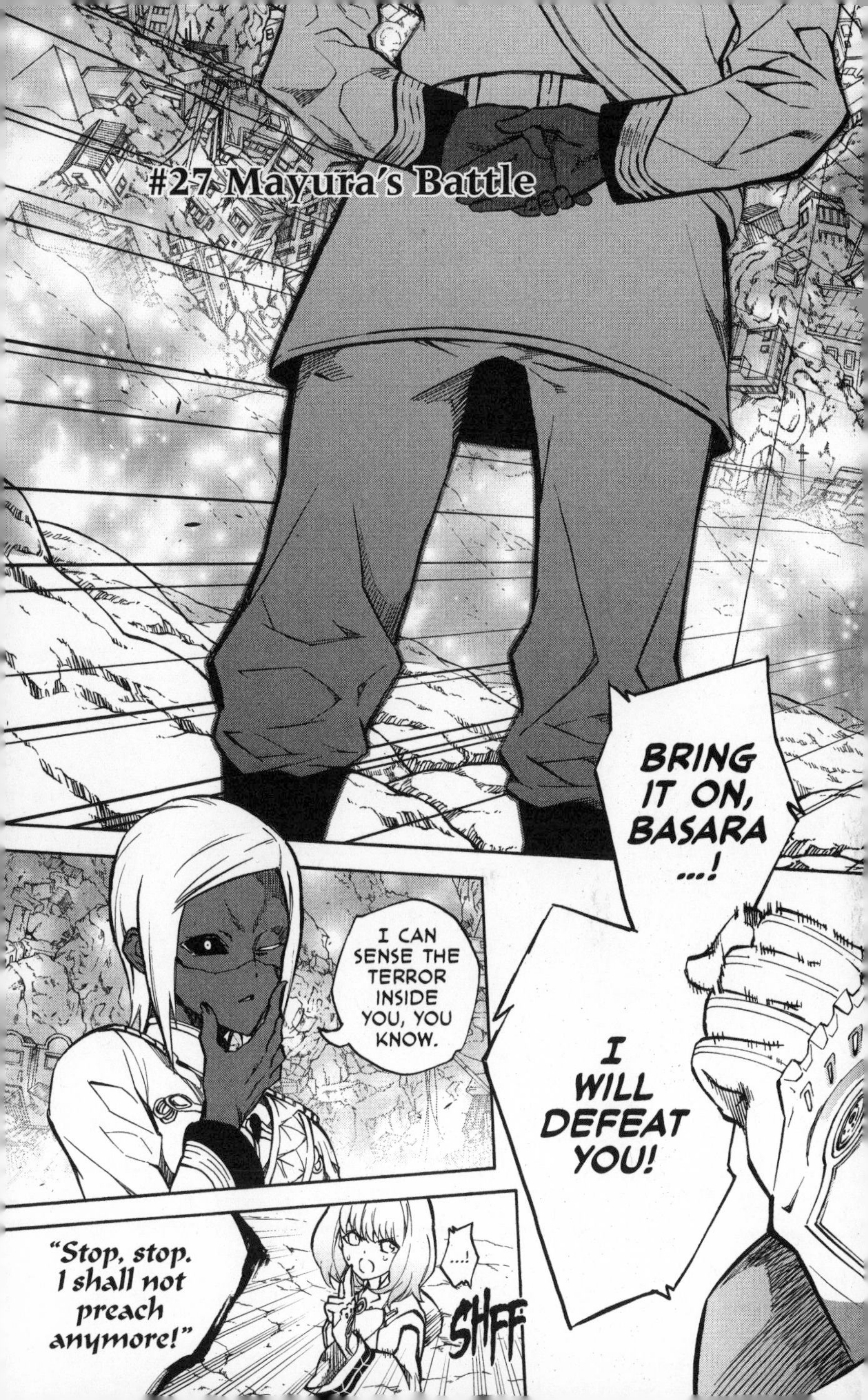
BRING IT ON, BASARA ...!
I WILL DEFEAT YOU!
I CAN SENSE THE TERROR INSIDE YOU, YOU KNOW.
"Stop, stop. I shall not preach anymore!"
...!
SHFF

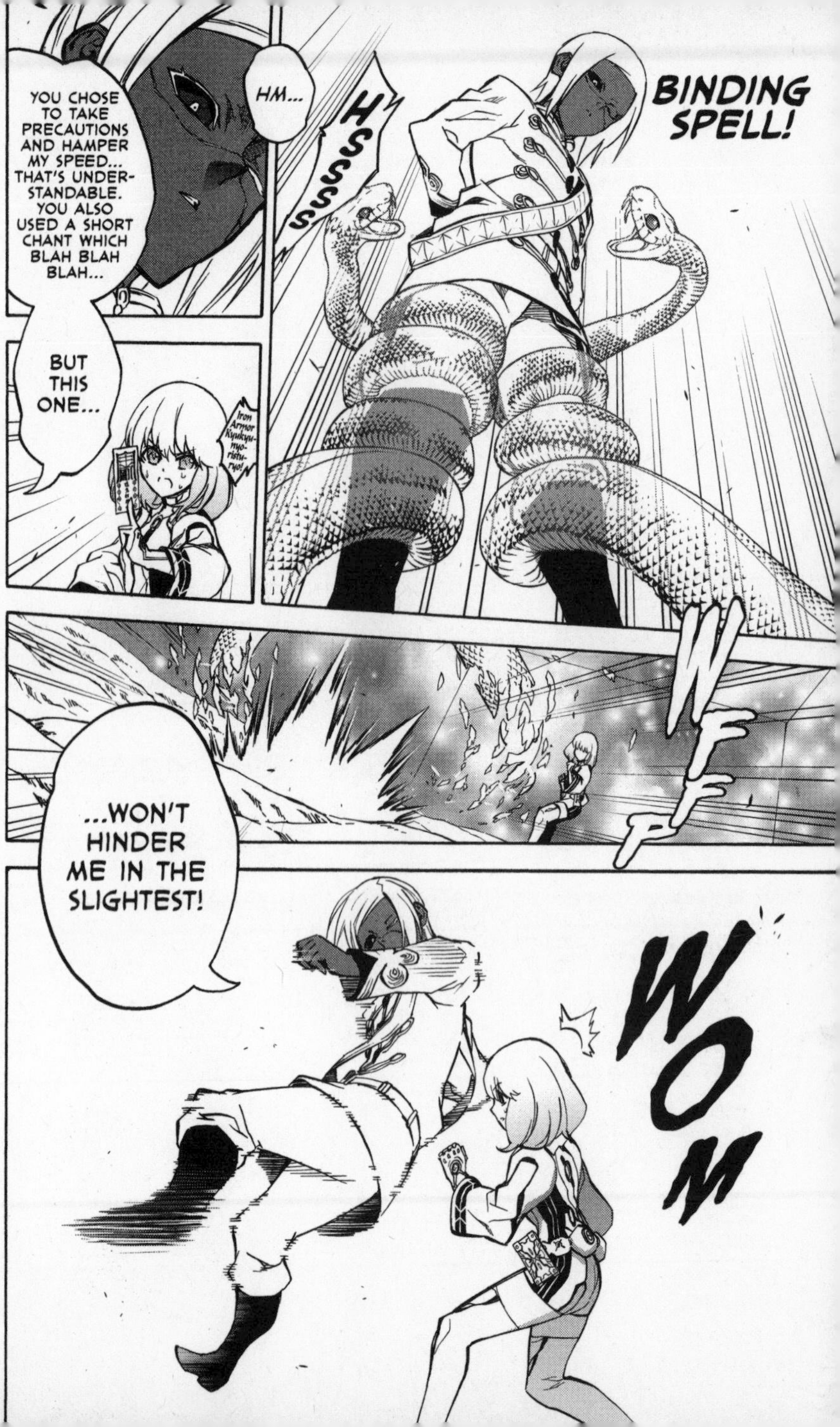
BINDING SPELL!
HSSSSS
HM...
YOU CHOSE TO TAKE PRECAUTIONS AND HAMPER MY SPEED... THAT'S UNDER-STANDABLE. YOU ALSO USED A SHORT CHANT WHICH BLAH BLAH BLAH...
BUT THIS ONE...
Iron Armor Kyukyu-nyo-ristu-ryo!
...WON'T HINDER ME IN THE SLIGHTEST!
WOM

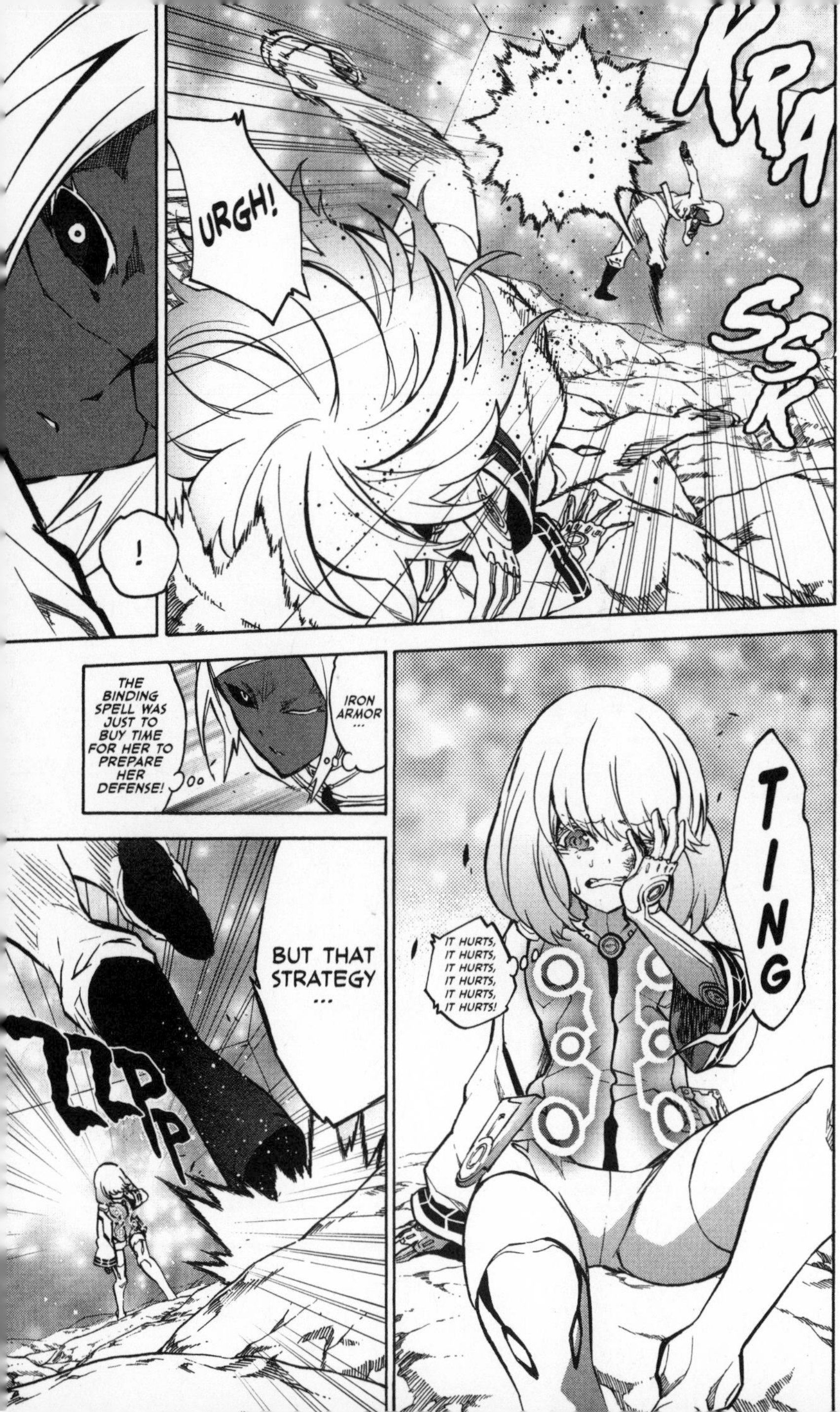
KRA
URGH!
SSK
!
TING
IT HURTS, IT HURTS, IT HURTS, IT HURTS, IT HURTS, IT HURTS!
IRON ARMOR ...
THE BINDING SPELL WAS JUST TO BUY TIME FOR HER TO PREPARE HER DEFENSE!
BUT THAT STRATEGY ...
ZZIP

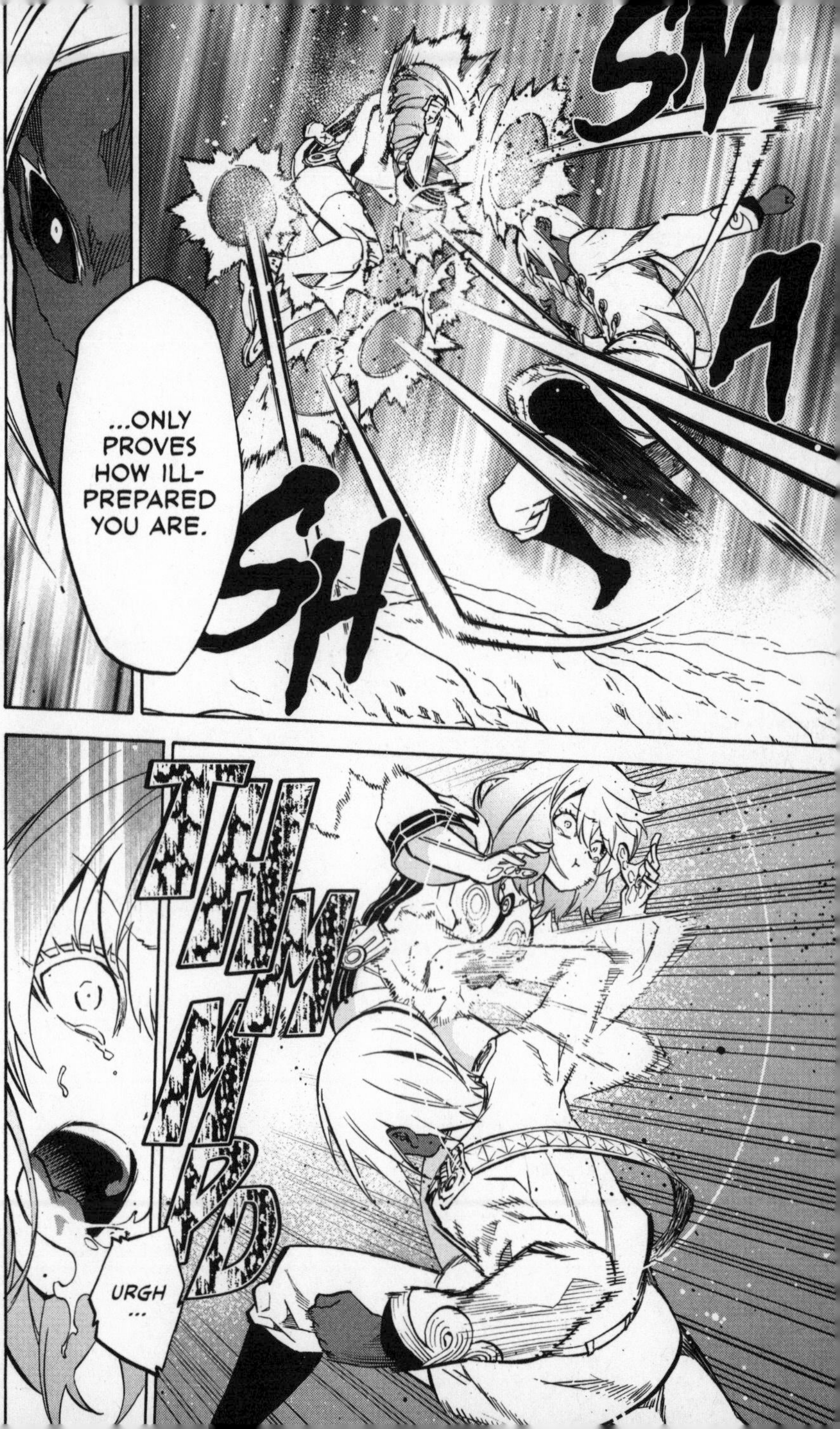
SMASH
...ONLY PROVES HOW ILL-PREPARED YOU ARE.
URGH ...

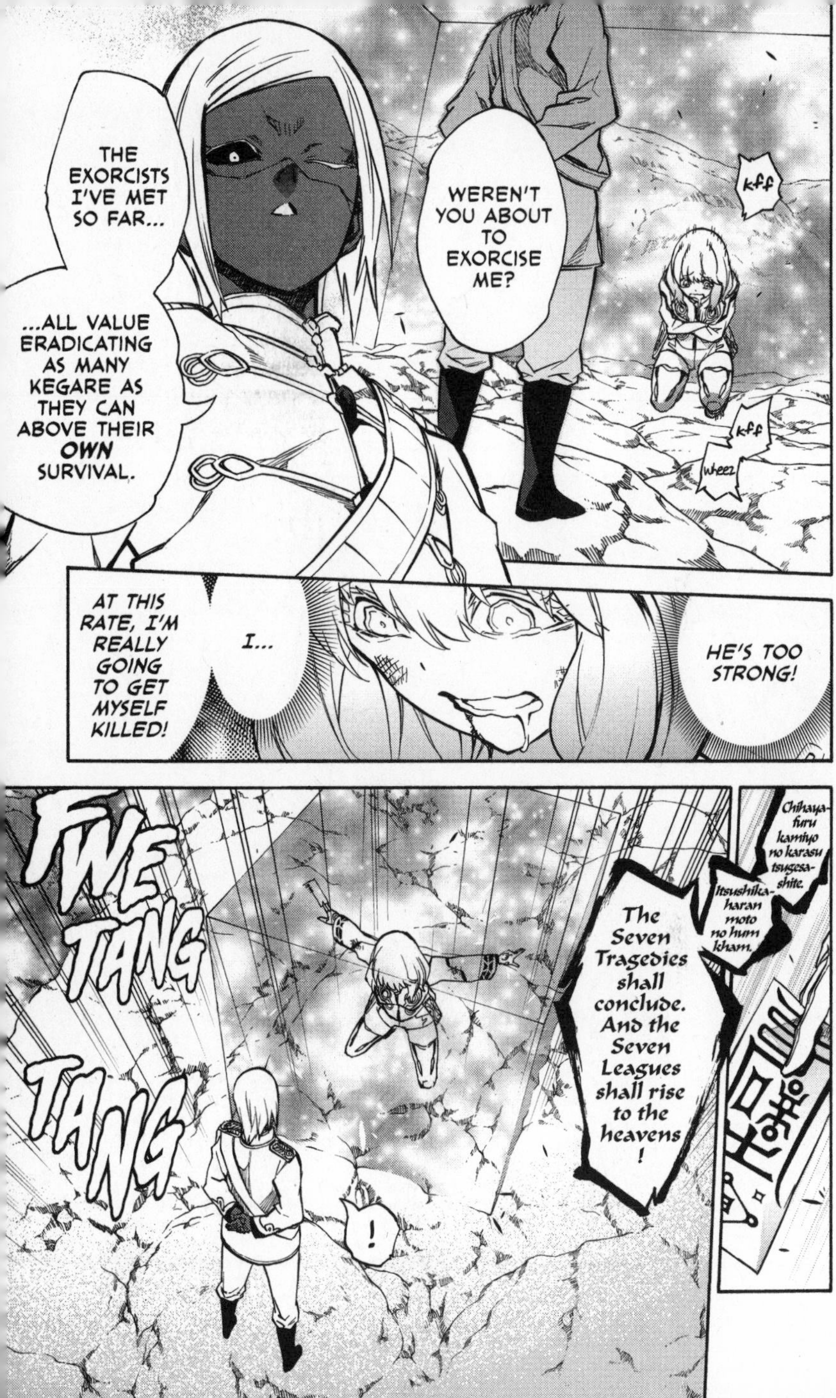
kff
WEREN'T YOU ABOUT TO EXORCISE ME?
kff
wheez
THE EXORCISTS I'VE MET SO FAR...
...ALL VALUE ERADICATING AS MANY KEGARE AS THEY CAN ABOVE THEIR OWN SURVIVAL.
HE'S TOO STRONG!
I...
AT THIS RATE, I'M REALLY GOING TO GET MYSELF KILLED!
Chihaya-furu kamiyo no karasu tsugesashite.
Itsushika-haran moto no hum kham.
The Seven Tragedies shall conclude. And the Seven Leagues shall rise to the heavens!
!
FWE TANG
TANG

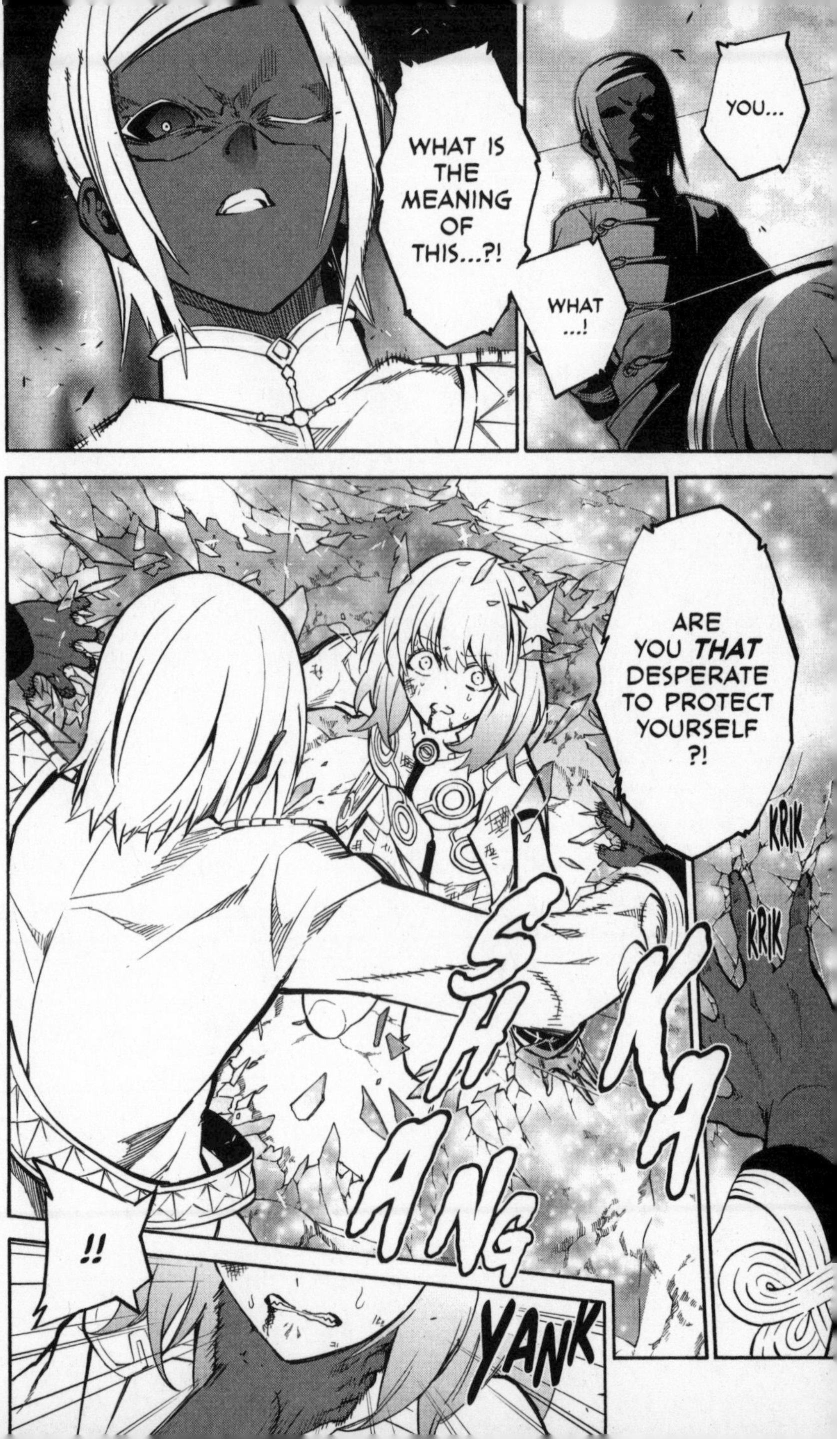
YOU...
WHAT ...!
WHAT IS THE MEANING OF THIS...?!
ARE YOU *THAT* DESPERATE TO PROTECT YOURSELF ?!
KRIK
KRIK
SHKAANG
!!
YANK

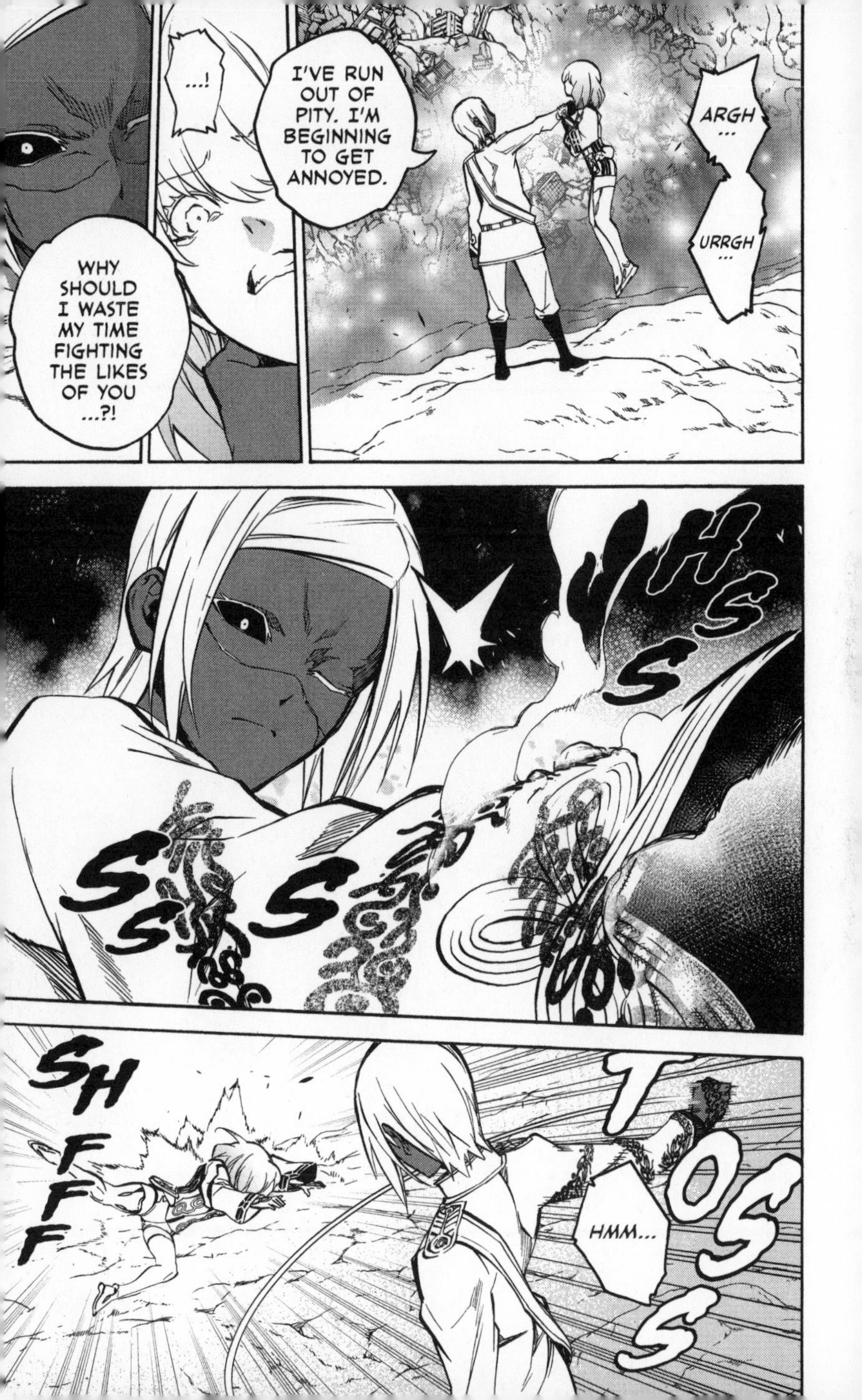
ARGH...
URRGH...
I'VE RUN OUT OF PITY. I'M BEGINNING TO GET ANNOYED.
...!
WHY SHOULD I WASTE MY TIME FIGHTING THE LIKES OF YOU ...?!
HSSS
SSSS
TOSSS
HMM...
SHFFF

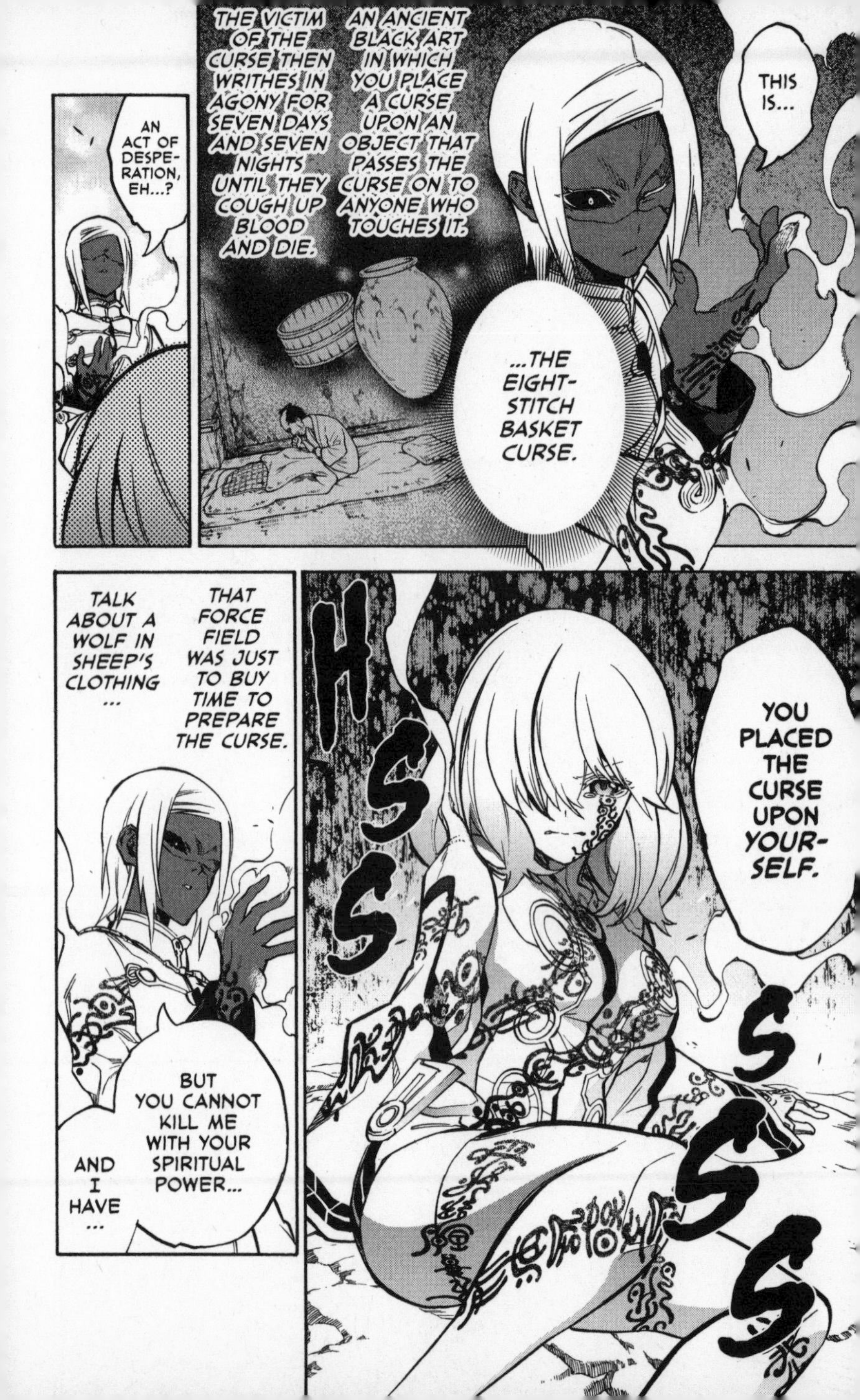
THIS IS...
...THE EIGHT-STITCH BASKET CURSE.
AN ANCIENT BLACK ART IN WHICH YOU PLACE A CURSE UPON AN OBJECT THAT PASSES THE CURSE ON TO ANYONE WHO TOUCHES IT.
THE VICTIM OF THE CURSE THEN WRITHES IN AGONY FOR SEVEN DAYS AND SEVEN NIGHTS UNTIL THEY COUGH UP BLOOD AND DIE.
AN ACT OF DESPERATION, EH...?
HSS
YOU PLACED THE CURSE UPON YOURSELF.
SSSS
THAT FORCE FIELD WAS JUST TO BUY TIME TO PREPARE THE CURSE.
TALK ABOUT A WOLF IN SHEEP'S CLOTHING...
BUT YOU CANNOT KILL ME WITH YOUR SPIRITUAL POWER...
AND I HAVE...

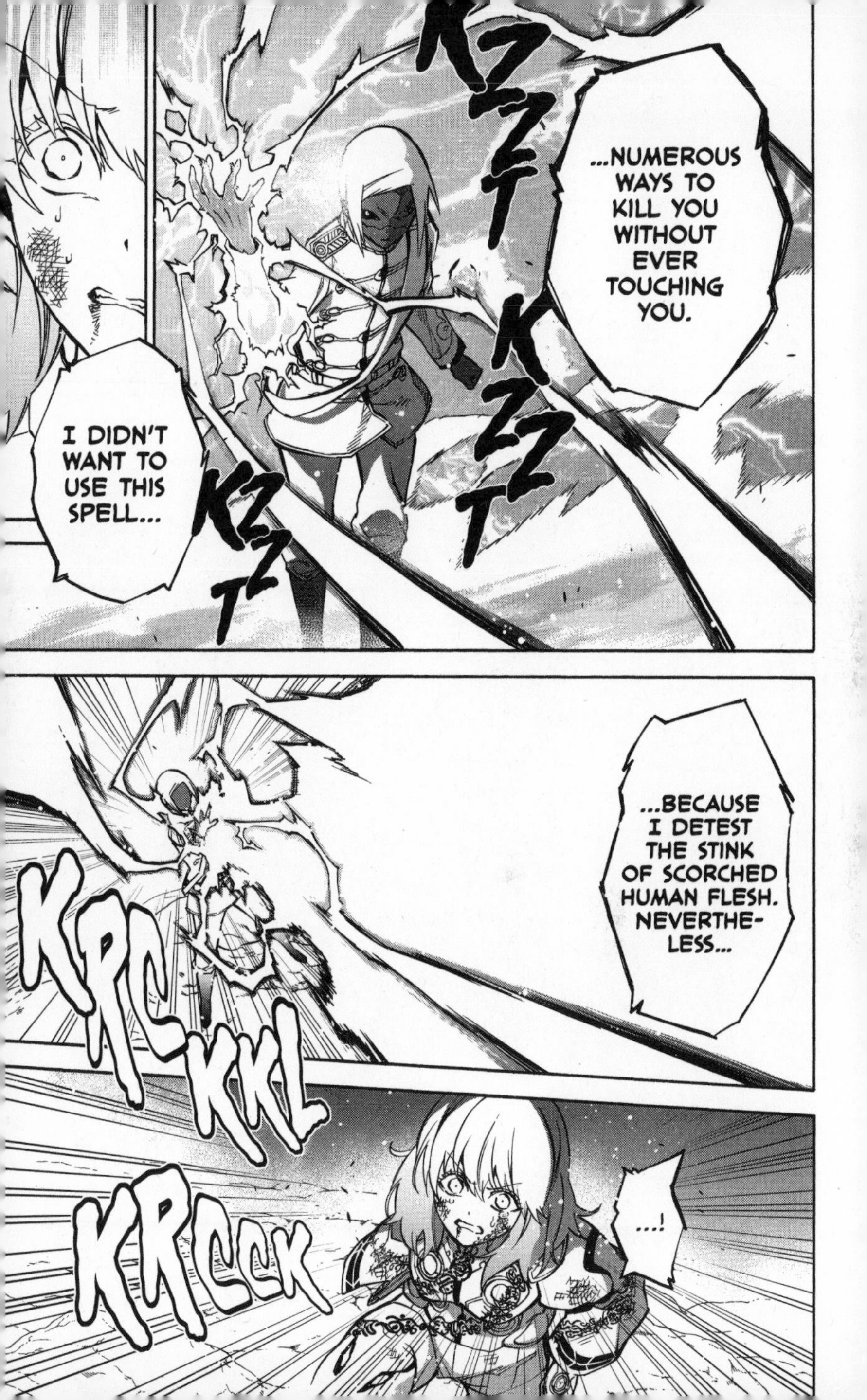
...NUMEROUS WAYS TO KILL YOU WITHOUT EVER TOUCHING YOU.
KZZZT
KZZT
KZZT
I DIDN'T WANT TO USE THIS SPELL...
...BECAUSE I DETEST THE STINK OF SCORCHED HUMAN FLESH. NEVERTHE-LESS...
KPCKKL
...!
KRCCK

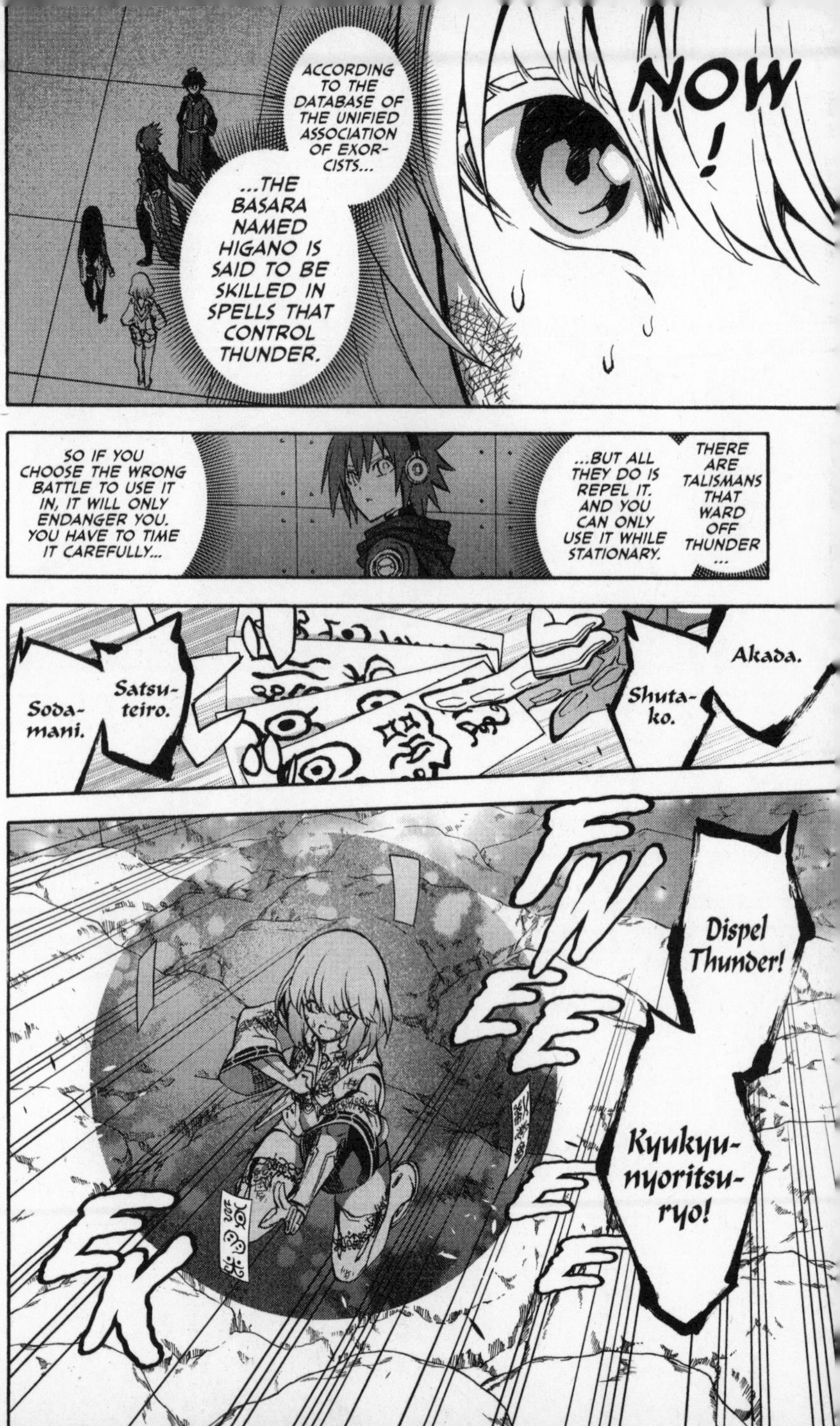
NOW!
ACCORDING TO THE DATABASE OF THE UNIFIED ASSOCIATION OF EXORCISTS...
...THE BASARA NAMED HIGANO IS SAID TO BE SKILLED IN SPELLS THAT CONTROL THUNDER.
THERE ARE TALISMANS THAT WARD OFF THUNDER...
...BUT ALL THEY DO IS REPEL IT. AND YOU CAN ONLY USE IT WHILE STATIONARY.
SO IF YOU CHOOSE THE WRONG BATTLE TO USE IT IN, IT WILL ONLY ENDANGER YOU. YOU HAVE TO TIME IT CAREFULLY...
Akada.
Shuta-ko.
Satsu-teiro.
Soda-mani.
Dispel Thunder!
Kyukyu-nyoritsu-ryo!
FWEEEEEK

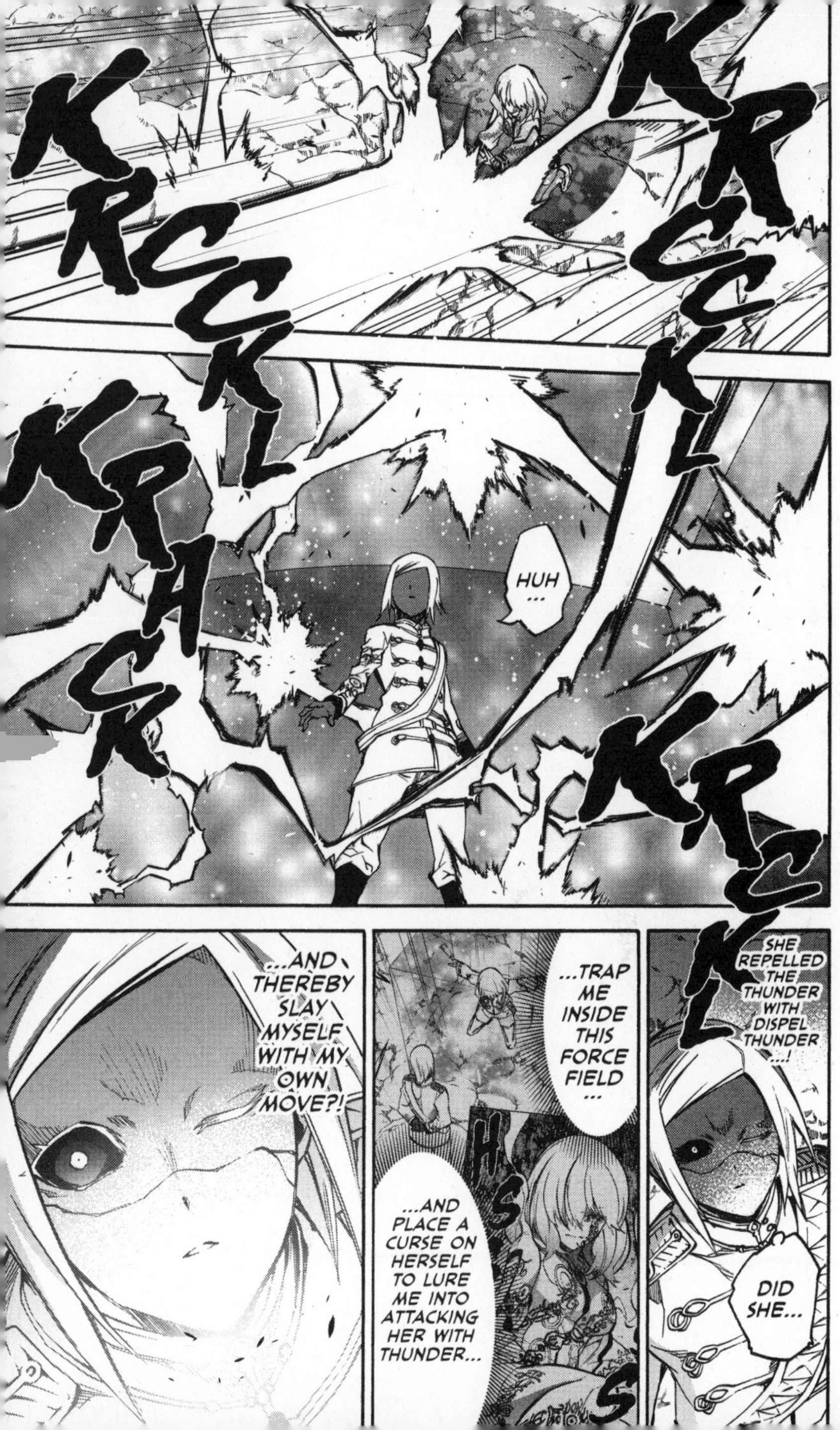
KRCKL
KRCKL
HUH...
KRACK
KRCKL
SHE REPELLED THE THUNDER WITH DISPEL THUNDER...!
DID SHE...
...TRAP ME INSIDE THIS FORCE FIELD...
...AND PLACE A CURSE ON HERSELF TO LURE ME INTO ATTACKING HER WITH THUNDER...
HSS
...AND THEREBY SLAY MYSELF WITH MY OWN MOVE?!

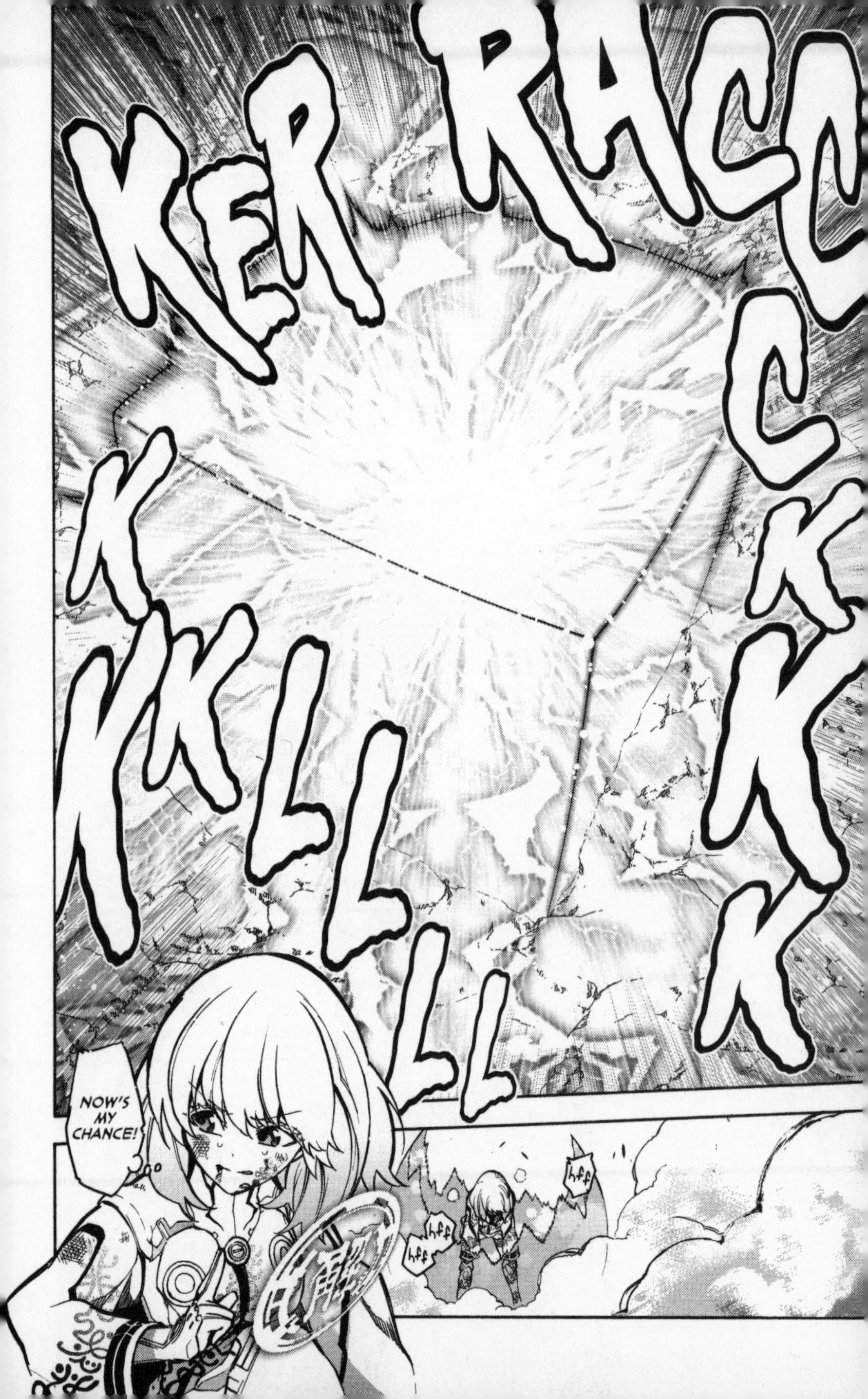
KERRACCCKKK
KKKLLLL
hff
hff
hff
NOW'S MY CHANCE!

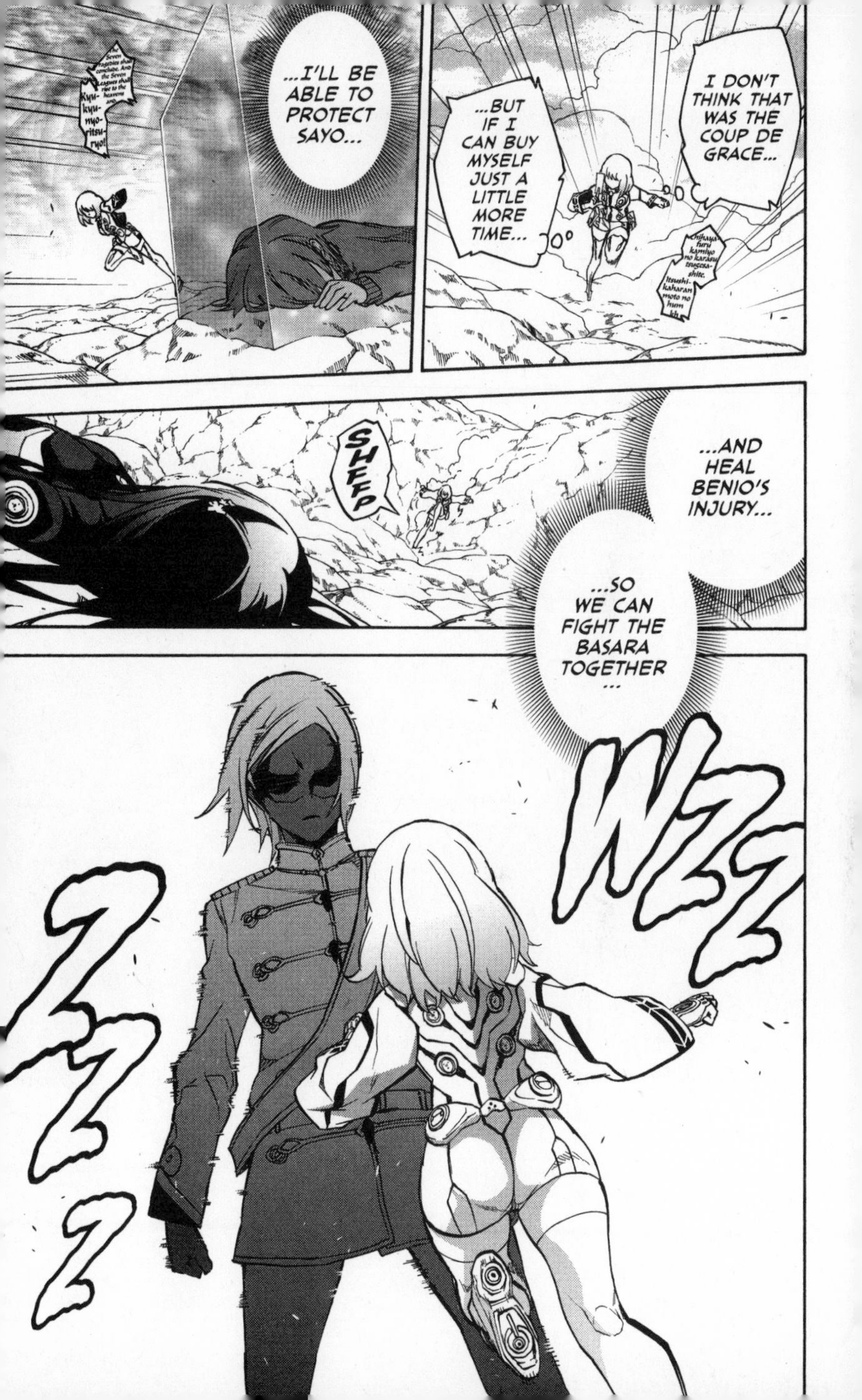
I DON'T THINK THAT WAS THE COUP DE GRACE...
...BUT IF I CAN BUY MYSELF JUST A LITTLE MORE TIME...
Chihaya furu kamiyo no karasu tsugesa-shite. Itsushi-kaharan moto no hum kh
...I'LL BE ABLE TO PROTECT SAYO...
The Seven Tragedies shall conclude. And the Seven Leagues shall rise to the heavens and...
Kyu-kyu-nyo-ritsu-ryo!
...AND HEAL BENIO'S INJURY...
...SO WE CAN FIGHT THE BASARA TOGETHER...
SHFFP
WZZ
ZZZZ

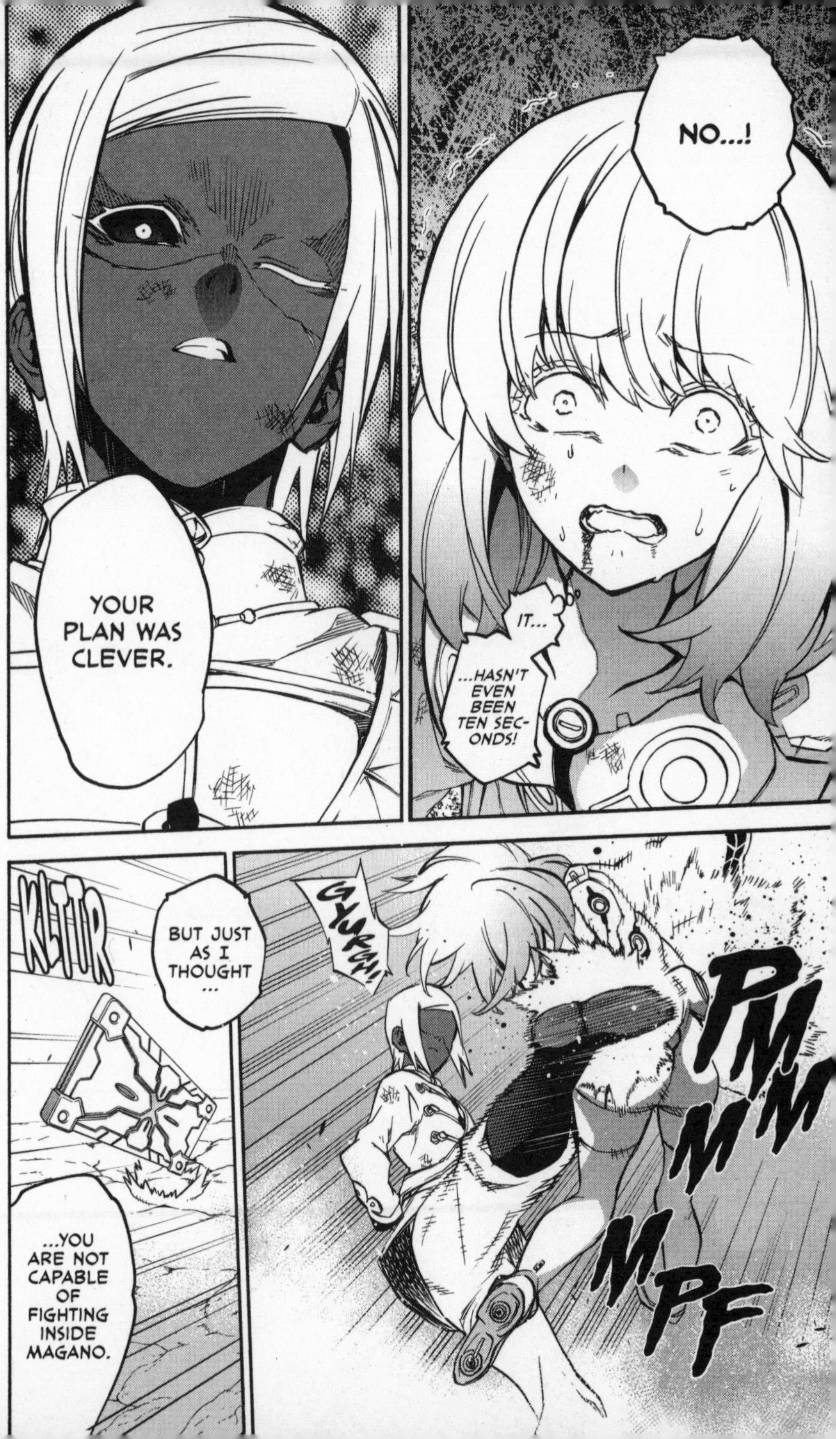

NO...!
IT...
...HASN'T EVEN BEEN TEN SECONDS!
YOUR PLAN WAS CLEVER.
GYURCH!
PMMMMPF
BUT JUST AS I THOUGHT...
KLTTR
...YOU ARE NOT CAPABLE OF FIGHTING INSIDE MAGANO.

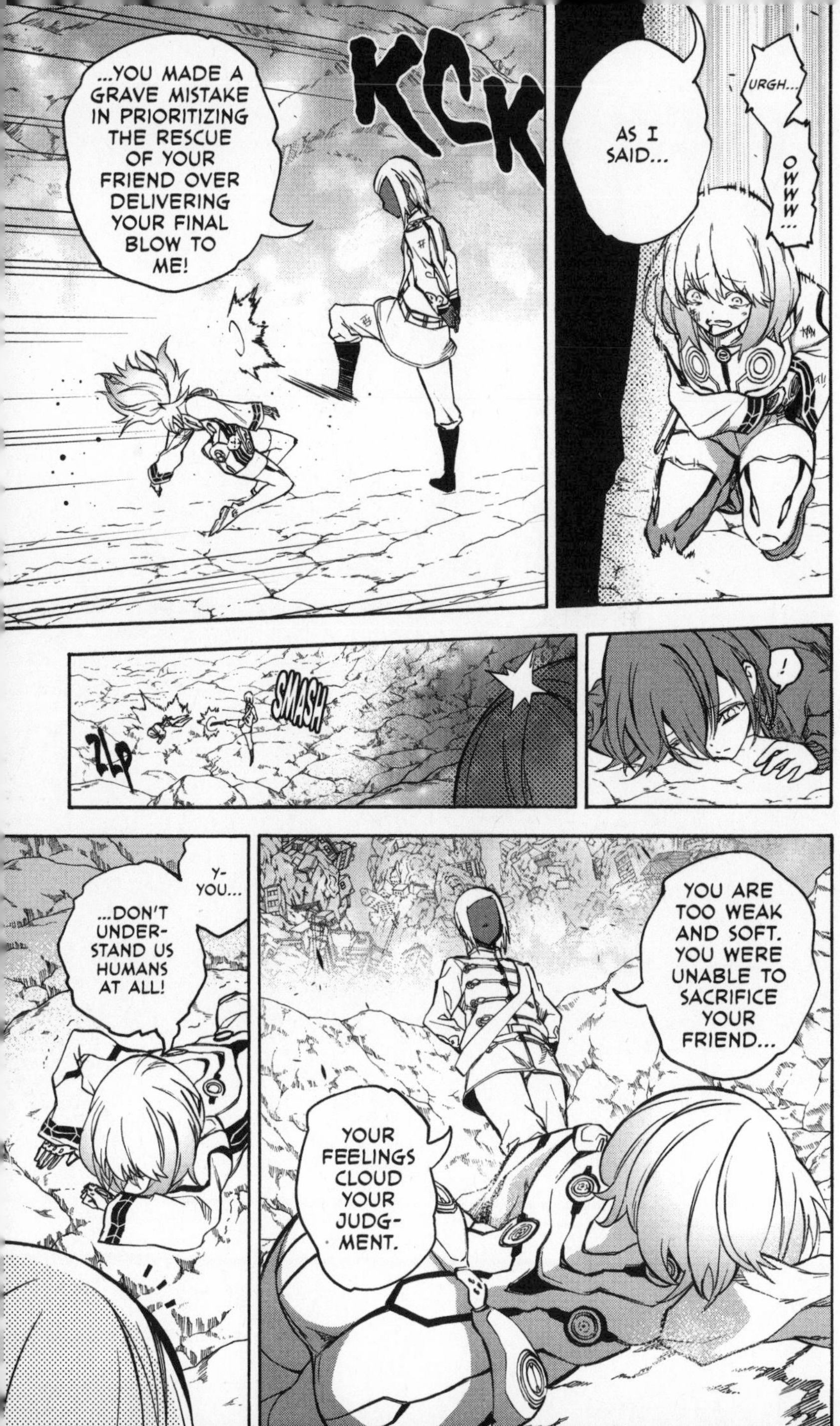
URGH...
OWWW...
AS I SAID...
KCK
...YOU MADE A GRAVE MISTAKE IN PRIORITIZING THE RESCUE OF YOUR FRIEND OVER DELIVERING YOUR FINAL BLOW TO ME!
!
SMASH
ZLP
YOU ARE TOO WEAK AND SOFT. YOU WERE UNABLE TO SACRIFICE YOUR FRIEND...
YOUR FEELINGS CLOUD YOUR JUDG-MENT.
Y-YOU...
...DON'T UNDER-STAND US HUMANS AT ALL!

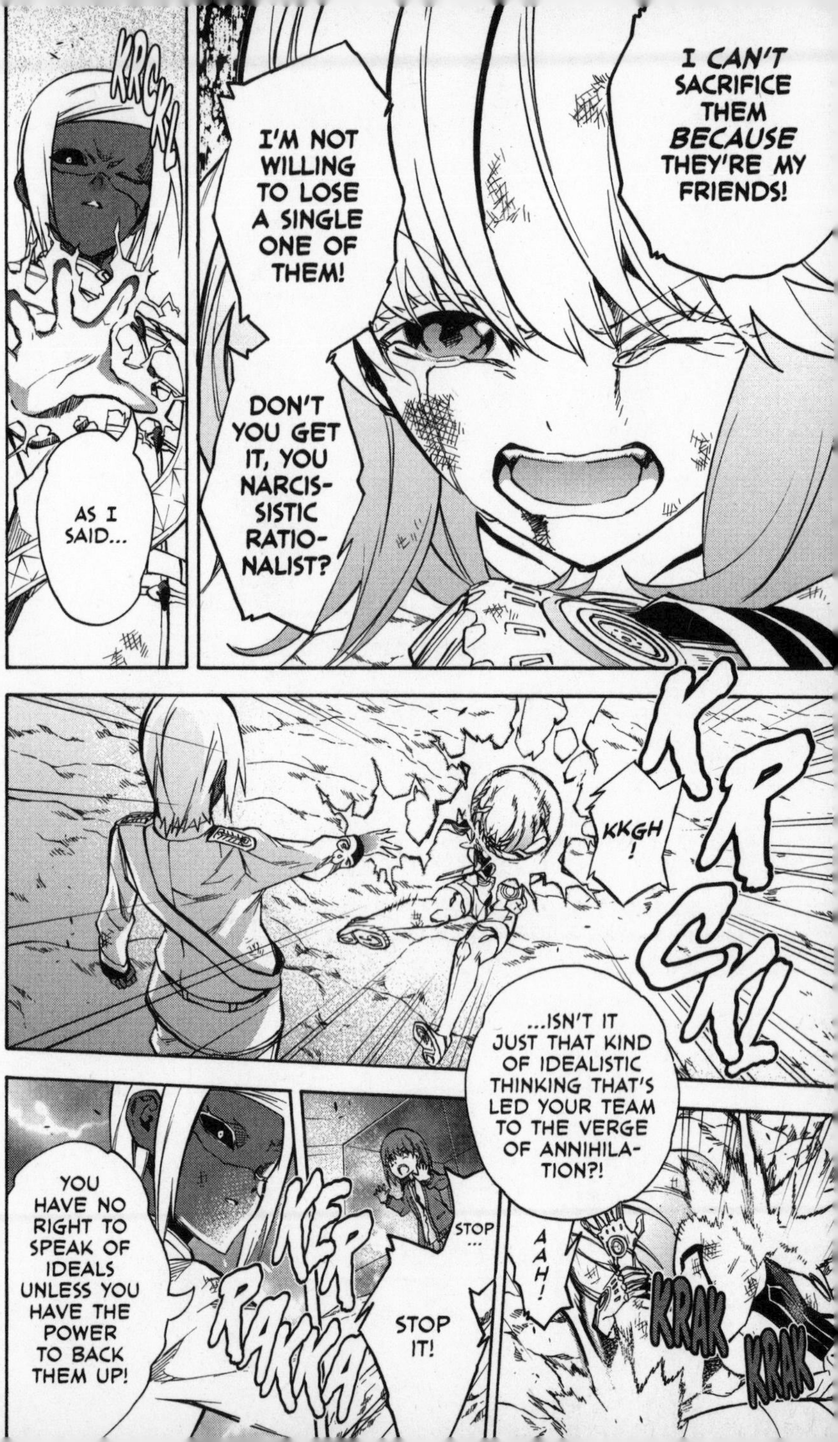
I CAN'T SACRIFICE THEM BECAUSE THEY'RE MY FRIENDS!
I'M NOT WILLING TO LOSE A SINGLE ONE OF THEM!
DON'T YOU GET IT, YOU NARCISSISTIC RATIONALIST?
KRCKL
AS I SAID...
KRCKL
KKGH!
...ISN'T IT JUST THAT KIND OF IDEALISTIC THINKING THAT'S LED YOUR TEAM TO THE VERGE OF ANNIHILATION?!
AAH!
KRAK
KRAK
STOP...
STOP IT!
KEP
RAKKA
YOU HAVE NO RIGHT TO SPEAK OF IDEALS UNLESS YOU HAVE THE POWER TO BACK THEM UP!

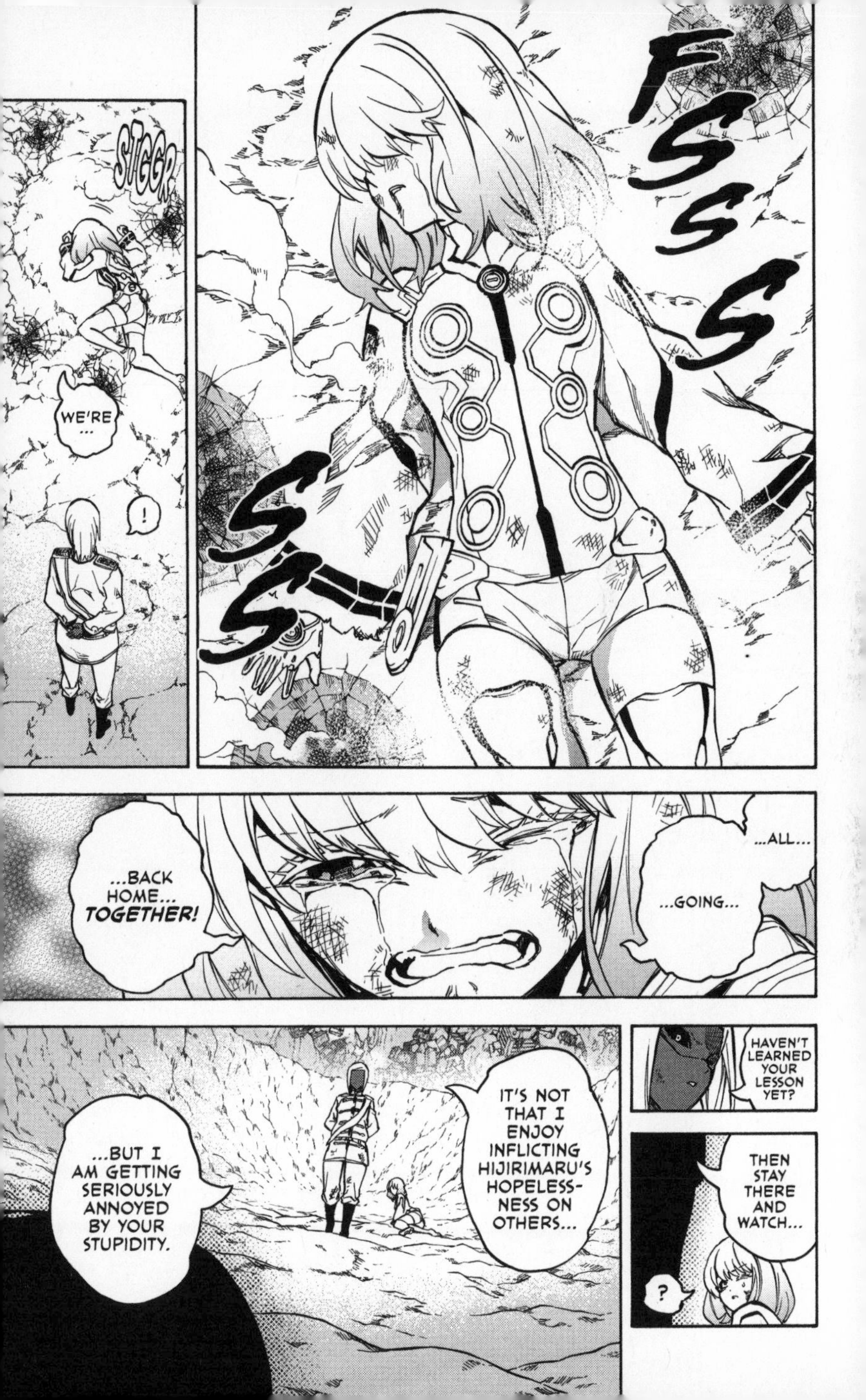
FSSSS
SSS
STGGR
WE'RE...
!
...ALL...
...GOING...
...BACK HOME... TOGETHER!
HAVEN'T LEARNED YOUR LESSON YET?
THEN STAY THERE AND WATCH...
?
IT'S NOT THAT I ENJOY INFLICTING HIJIRIMARU'S HOPELESS-NESS ON OTHERS...
...BUT I AM GETTING SERIOUSLY ANNOYED BY YOUR STUPIDITY.

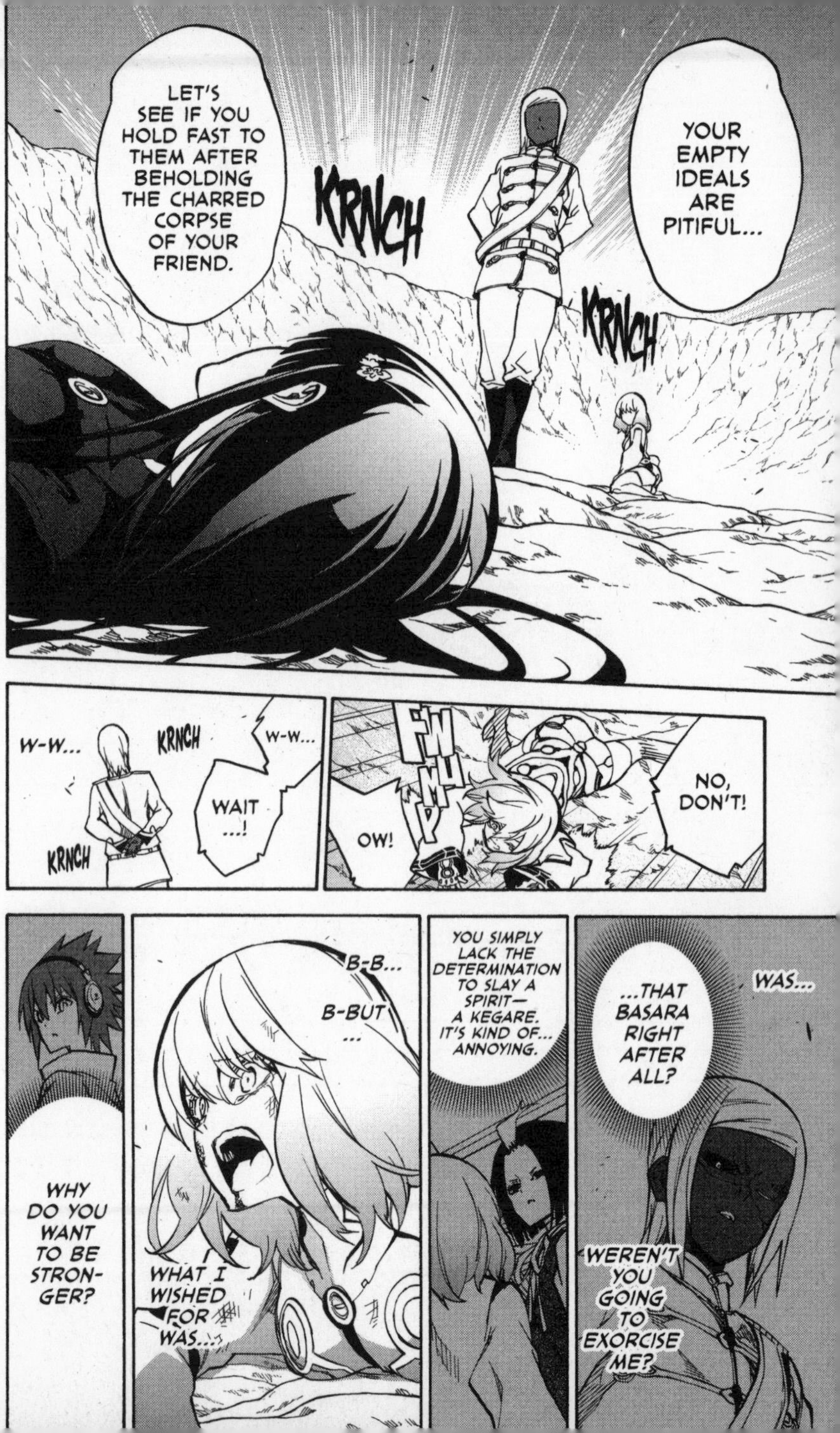
YOUR EMPTY IDEALS ARE PITIFUL...
KRNCH
KRNCH
LET'S SEE IF YOU HOLD FAST TO THEM AFTER BEHOLDING THE CHARRED CORPSE OF YOUR FRIEND.
NO, DON'T!
FWUMP
OW!
W-W...
WAIT ...!
KRNCH
W-W...
KRNCH
WAS...
...THAT BASARA RIGHT AFTER ALL?
WEREN'T YOU GOING TO EXORCISE ME?
YOU SIMPLY LACK THE DETERMINATION TO SLAY A SPIRIT— A KEGARE. IT'S KIND OF... ANNOYING.
B-B...
B-BUT ...
WHAT I WISHED FOR WAS...
WHY DO YOU WANT TO BE STRONGER?

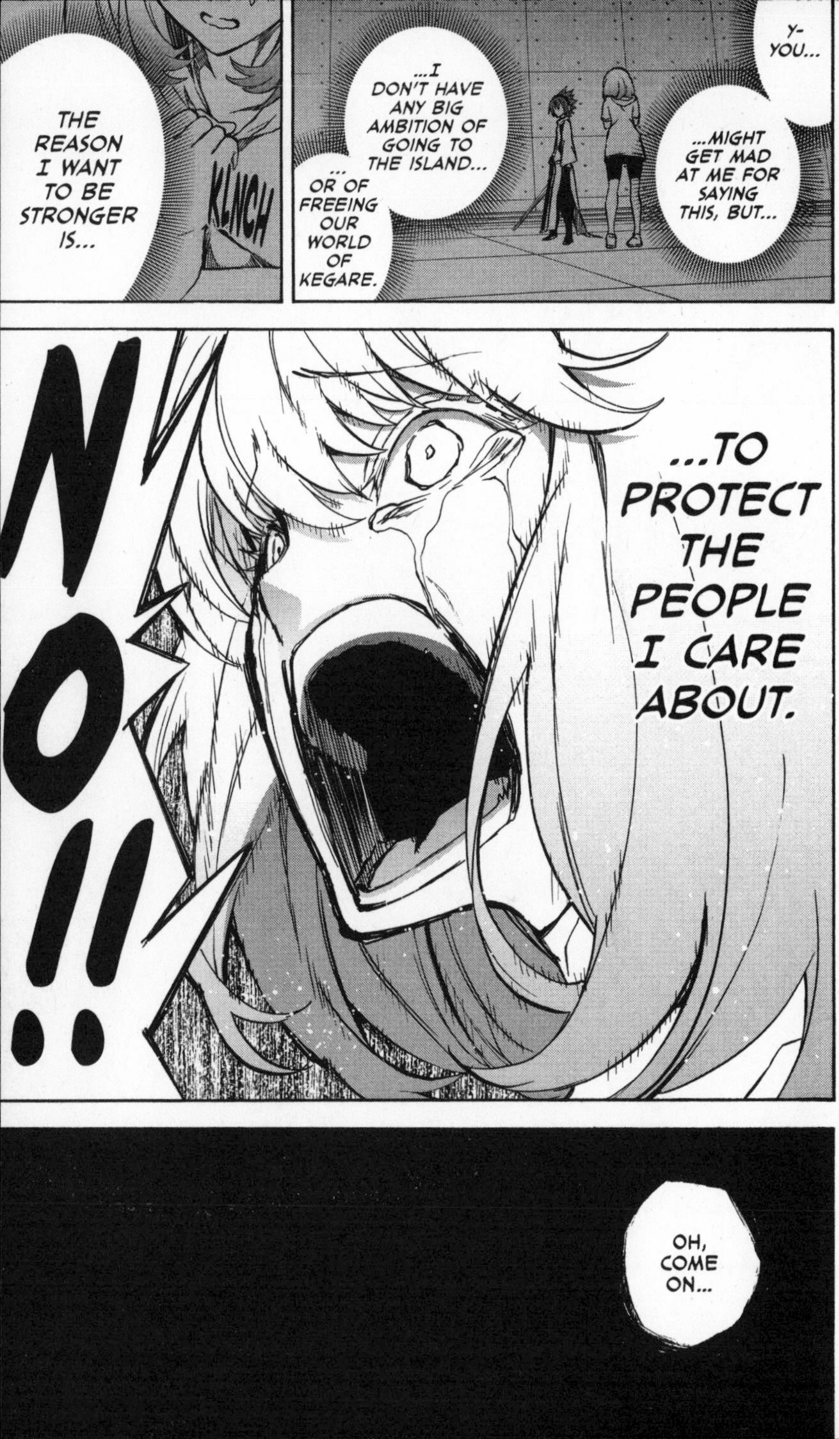
Y-YOU...
...MIGHT GET MAD AT ME FOR SAYING THIS, BUT...
...I DON'T HAVE ANY BIG AMBITION OF GOING TO THE ISLAND...
...OR OF FREEING OUR WORLD OF KEGARE.
KLNCH
THE REASON I WANT TO BE STRONGER IS...
...TO PROTECT THE PEOPLE I CARE ABOUT.
NO!!
OH, COME ON...

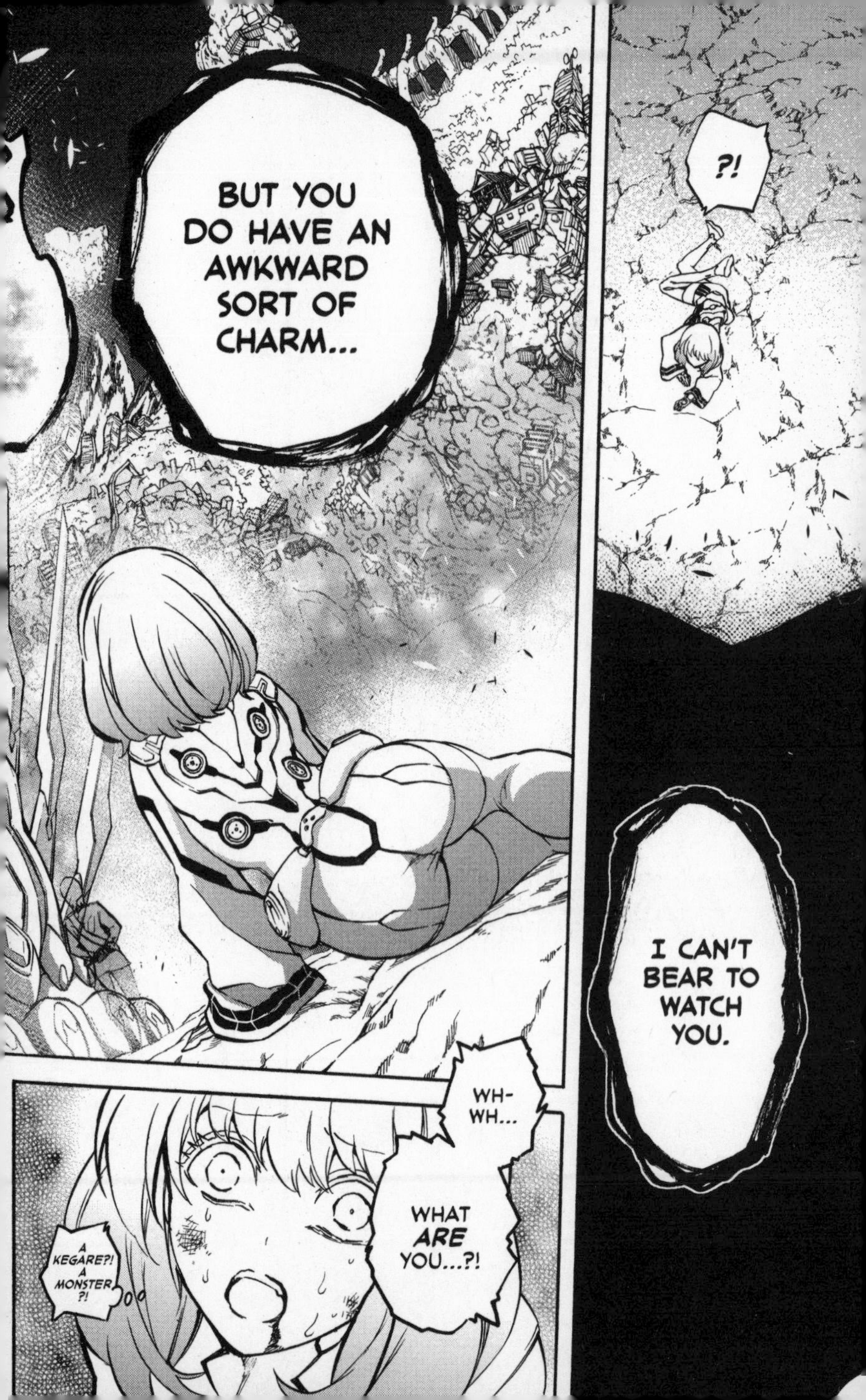
?!
BUT YOU DO HAVE AN AWKWARD SORT OF CHARM...
I CAN'T BEAR TO WATCH YOU.
WH- WH...
WHAT *ARE* YOU...?!
A KEGARE?! A MONSTER?!

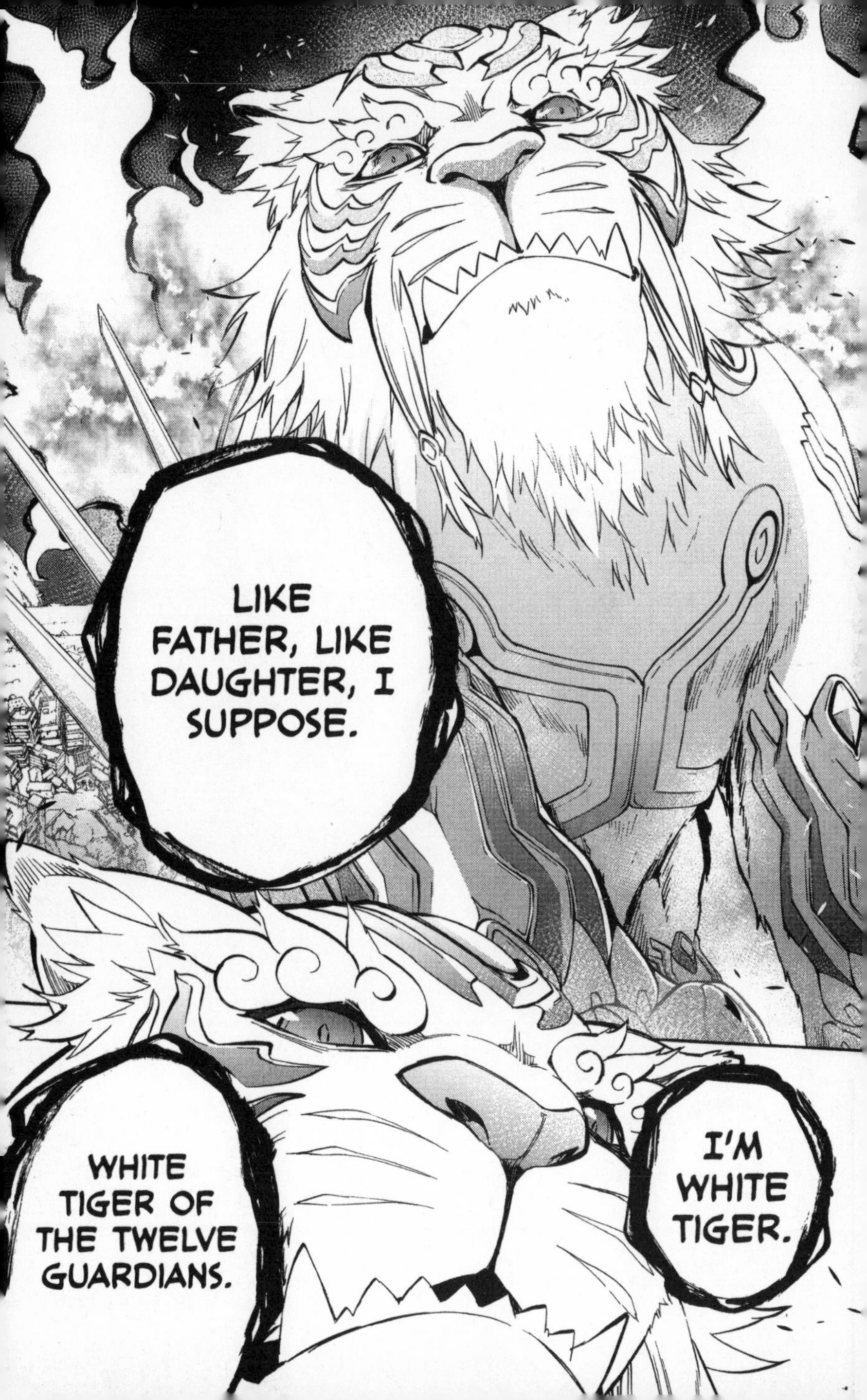
LIKE FATHER, LIKE DAUGHTER, I SUPPOSE.
I'M WHITE TIGER.
WHITE TIGER OF THE TWELVE GUARDIANS.

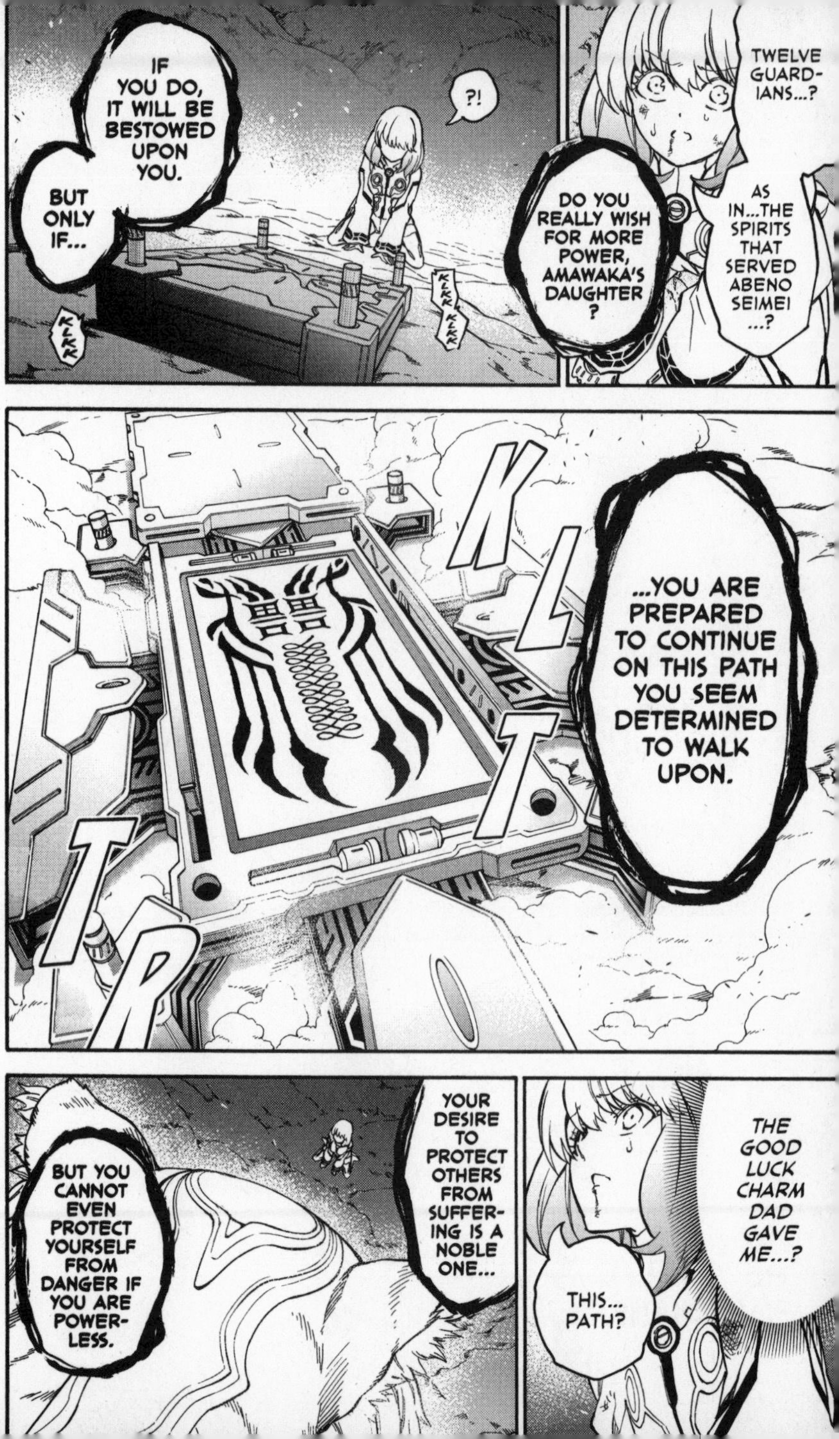
TWELVE GUARDIANS...?
AS IN...THE SPIRITS THAT SERVED ABENO SEIMEI...?
DO YOU REALLY WISH FOR MORE POWER, AMAWAKA'S DAUGHTER?
?!
IF YOU DO, IT WILL BE BESTOWED UPON YOU.
KLKK KLKK
BUT ONLY IF...
KLKK
...YOU ARE PREPARED TO CONTINUE ON THIS PATH YOU SEEM DETERMINED TO WALK UPON.
KLTTR
THE GOOD LUCK CHARM DAD GAVE ME...?
THIS... PATH?
YOUR DESIRE TO PROTECT OTHERS FROM SUFFERING IS A NOBLE ONE...
BUT YOU CANNOT EVEN PROTECT YOURSELF FROM DANGER IF YOU ARE POWERLESS.

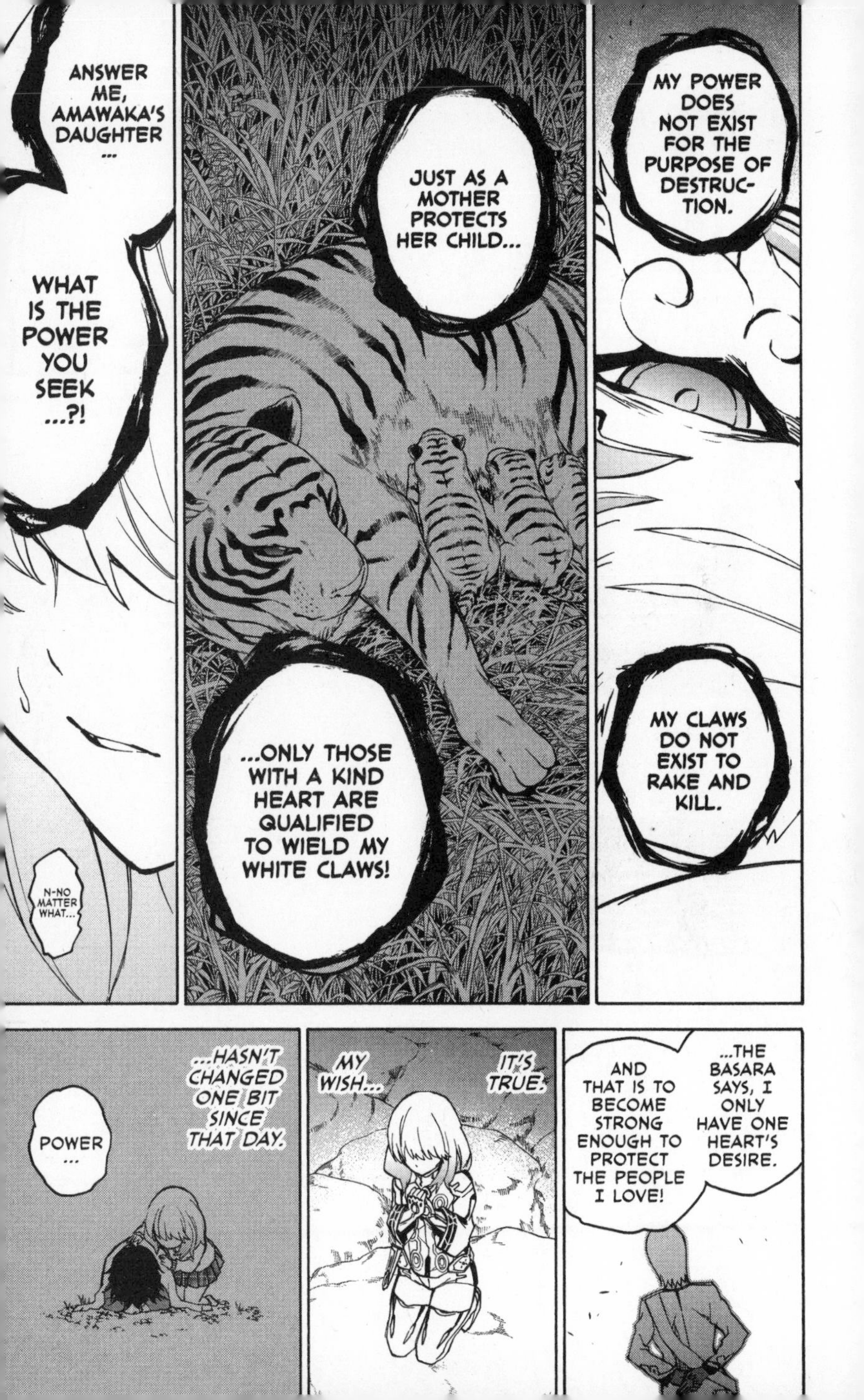
MY POWER DOES NOT EXIST FOR THE PURPOSE OF DESTRUCTION.
MY CLAWS DO NOT EXIST TO RAKE AND KILL.
JUST AS A MOTHER PROTECTS HER CHILD...
...ONLY THOSE WITH A KIND HEART ARE QUALIFIED TO WIELD MY WHITE CLAWS!
ANSWER ME, AMAWAKA'S DAUGHTER ...
WHAT IS THE POWER YOU SEEK ...?!
N-NO MATTER WHAT...
...THE BASARA SAYS, I ONLY HAVE ONE HEART'S DESIRE.
AND THAT IS TO BECOME STRONG ENOUGH TO PROTECT THE PEOPLE I LOVE!
IT'S TRUE.
MY WISH...
...HASN'T CHANGED ONE BIT SINCE THAT DAY.
POWER ...

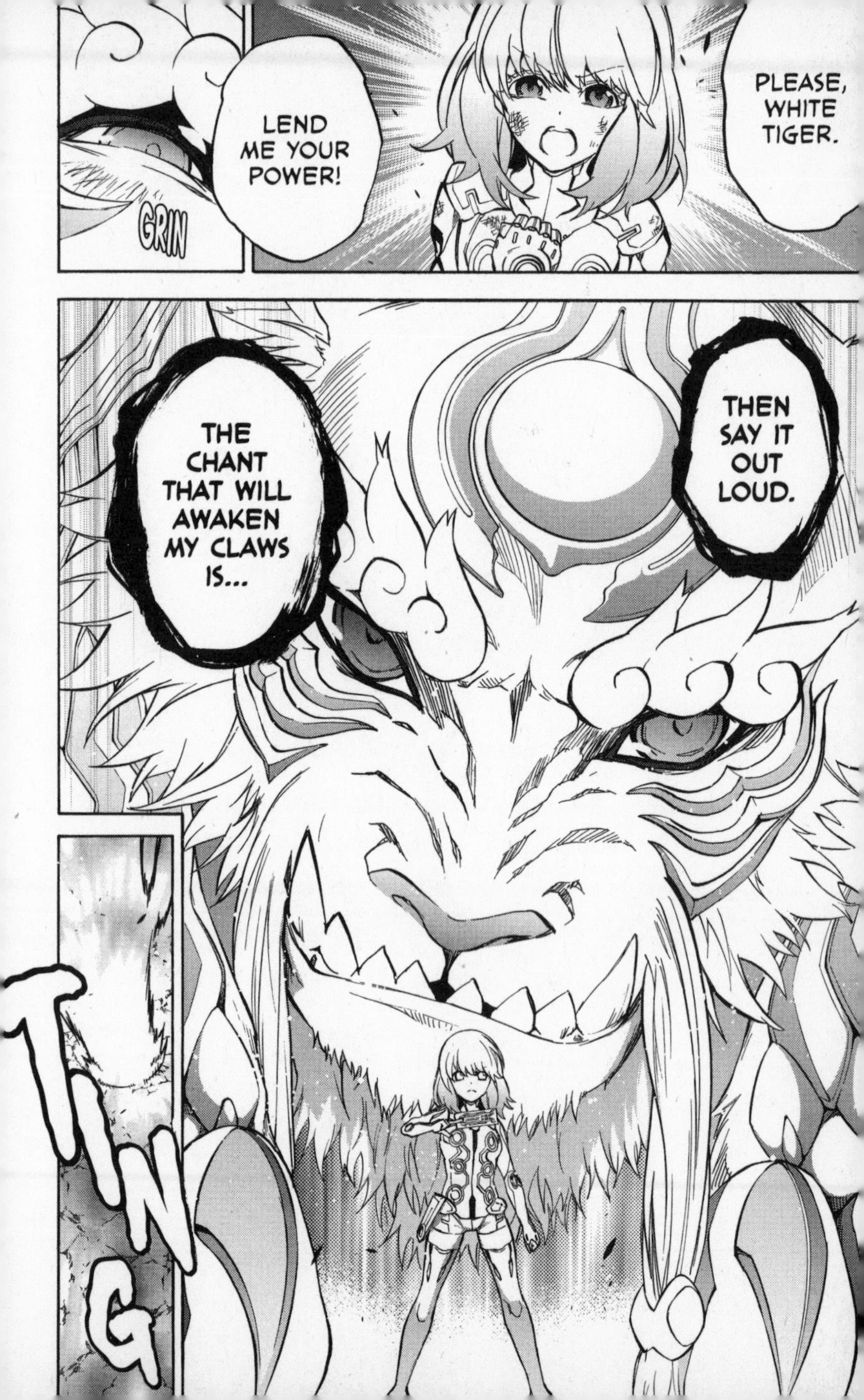
PLEASE, WHITE TIGER.
LEND ME YOUR POWER!
GRIN
THEN SAY IT OUT LOUD.
THE CHANT THAT WILL AWAKEN MY CLAWS IS...
TING

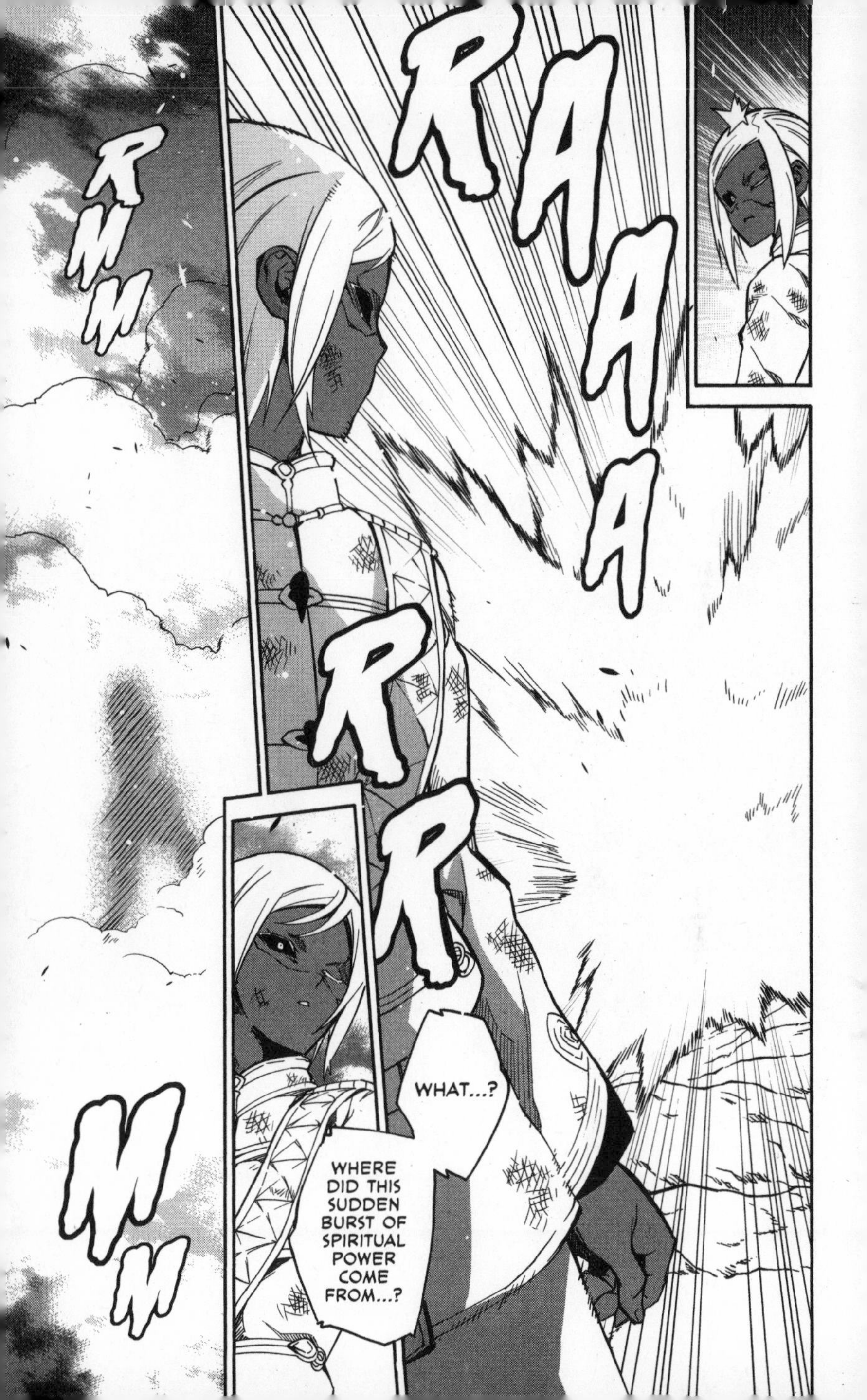
RAAAA
RRMM
WHAT...?
WHERE DID THIS SUDDEN BURST OF SPIRITUAL POWER COME FROM...?
RRMM

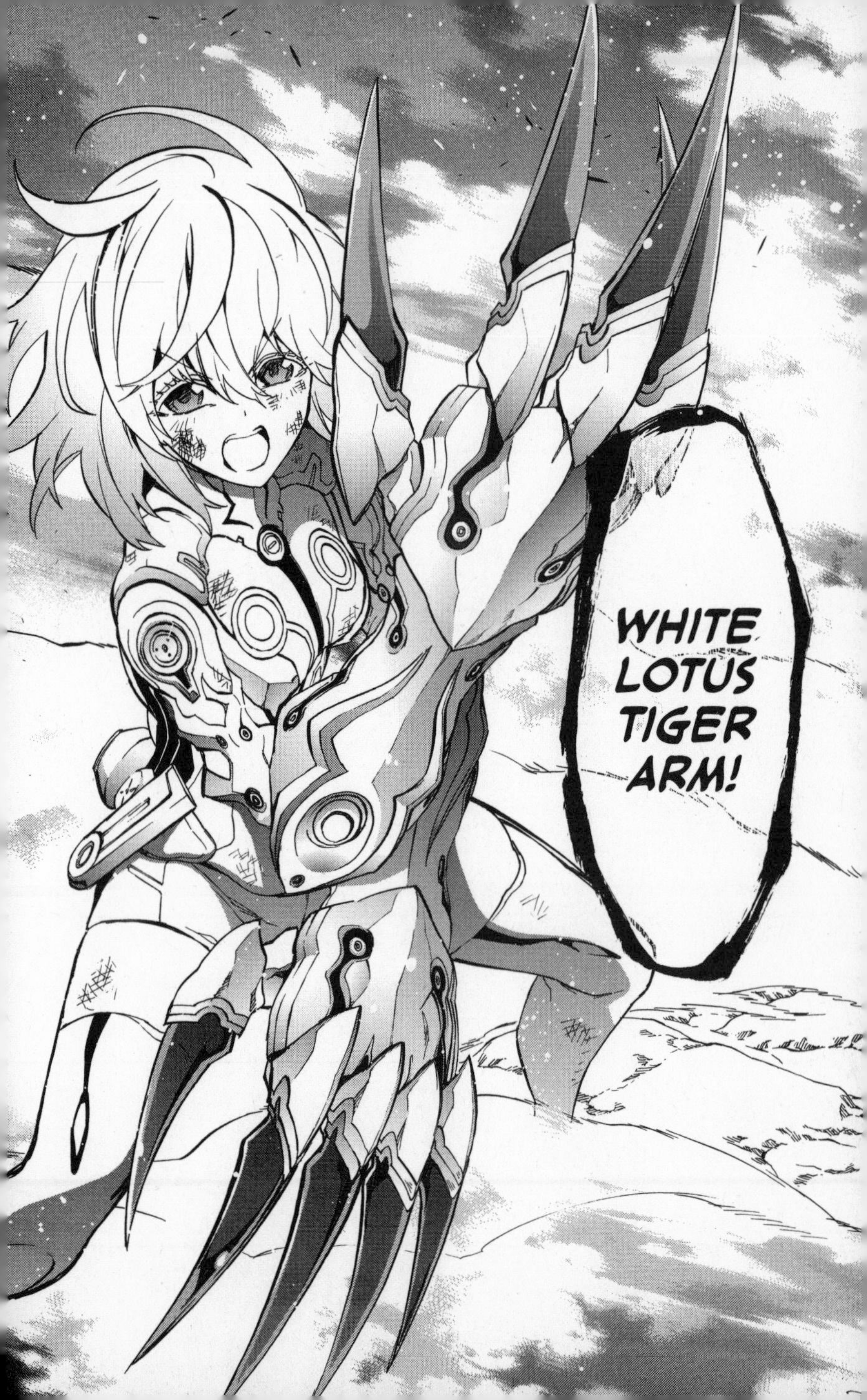
WHITE LOTUS TIGER ARM!

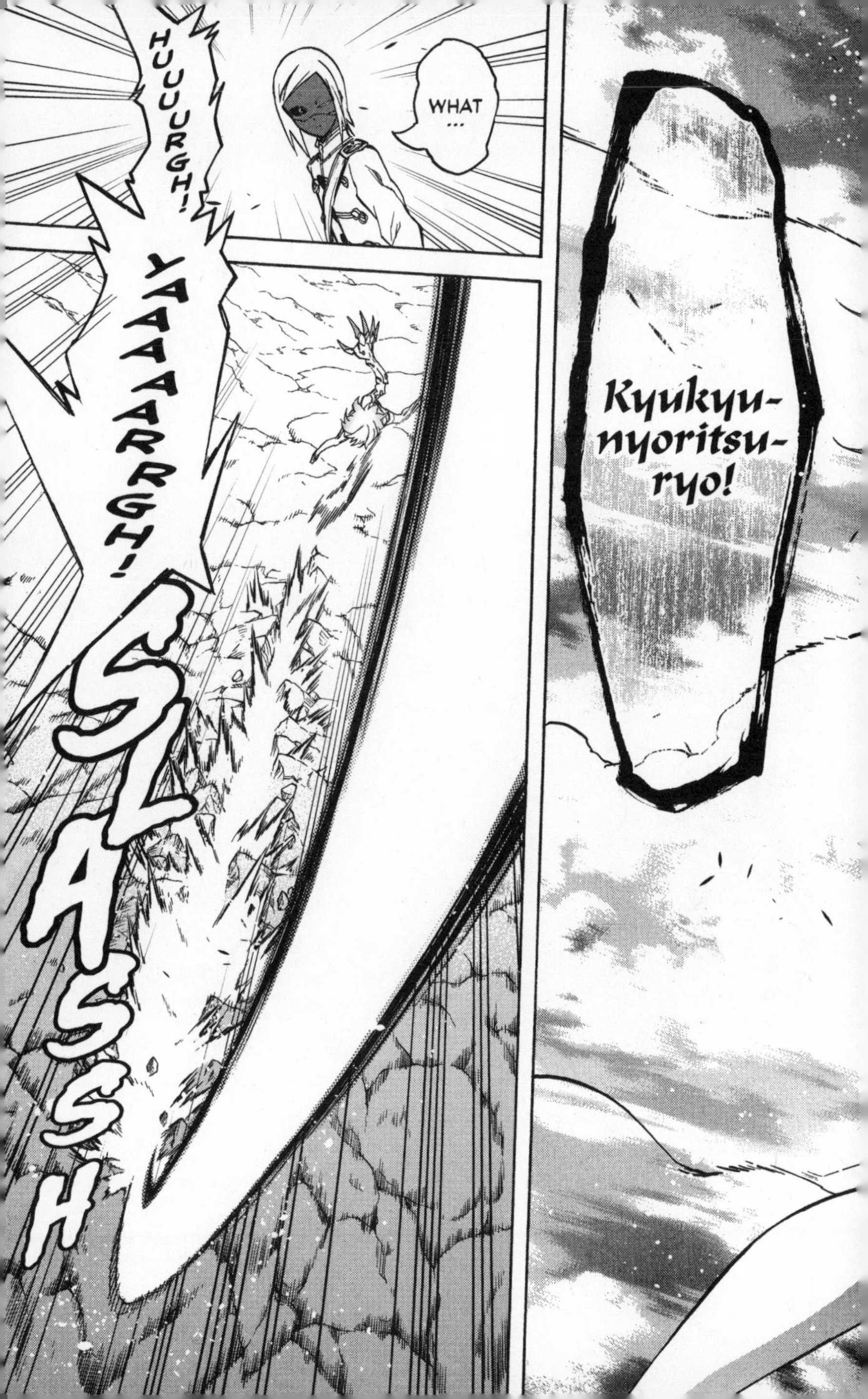
Kyukyu-nyoritsu-ryo!
WHAT ...
HUUUURGH!
YAAAAARRGH!
SLAASSH

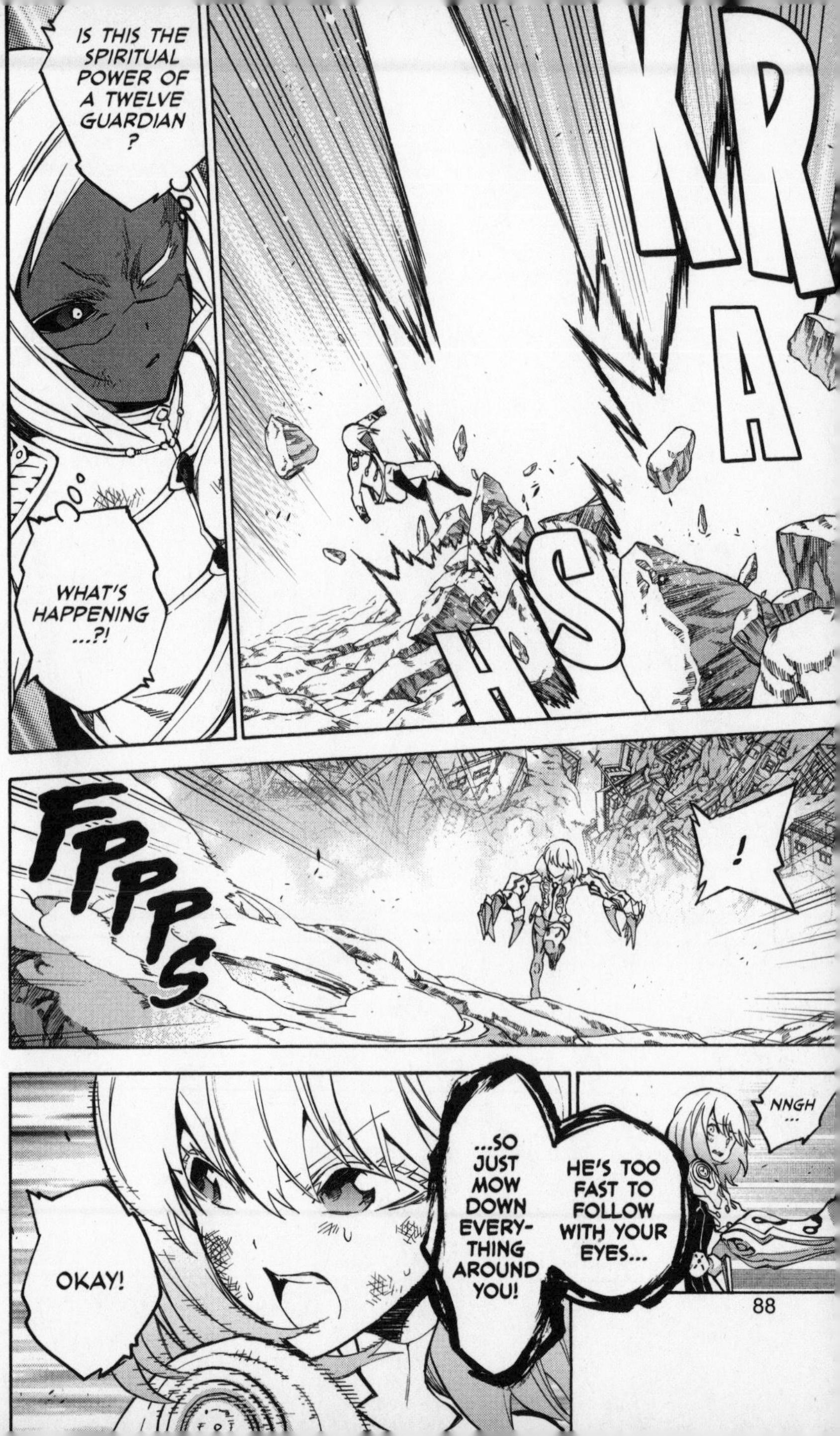
KRASH
IS THIS THE SPIRITUAL POWER OF A TWELVE GUARDIAN?
WHAT'S HAPPENING...?!
!
FPPPS
NNGH...
HE'S TOO FAST TO FOLLOW WITH YOUR EYES...
...SO JUST MOW DOWN EVERY-THING AROUND YOU!
OKAY!

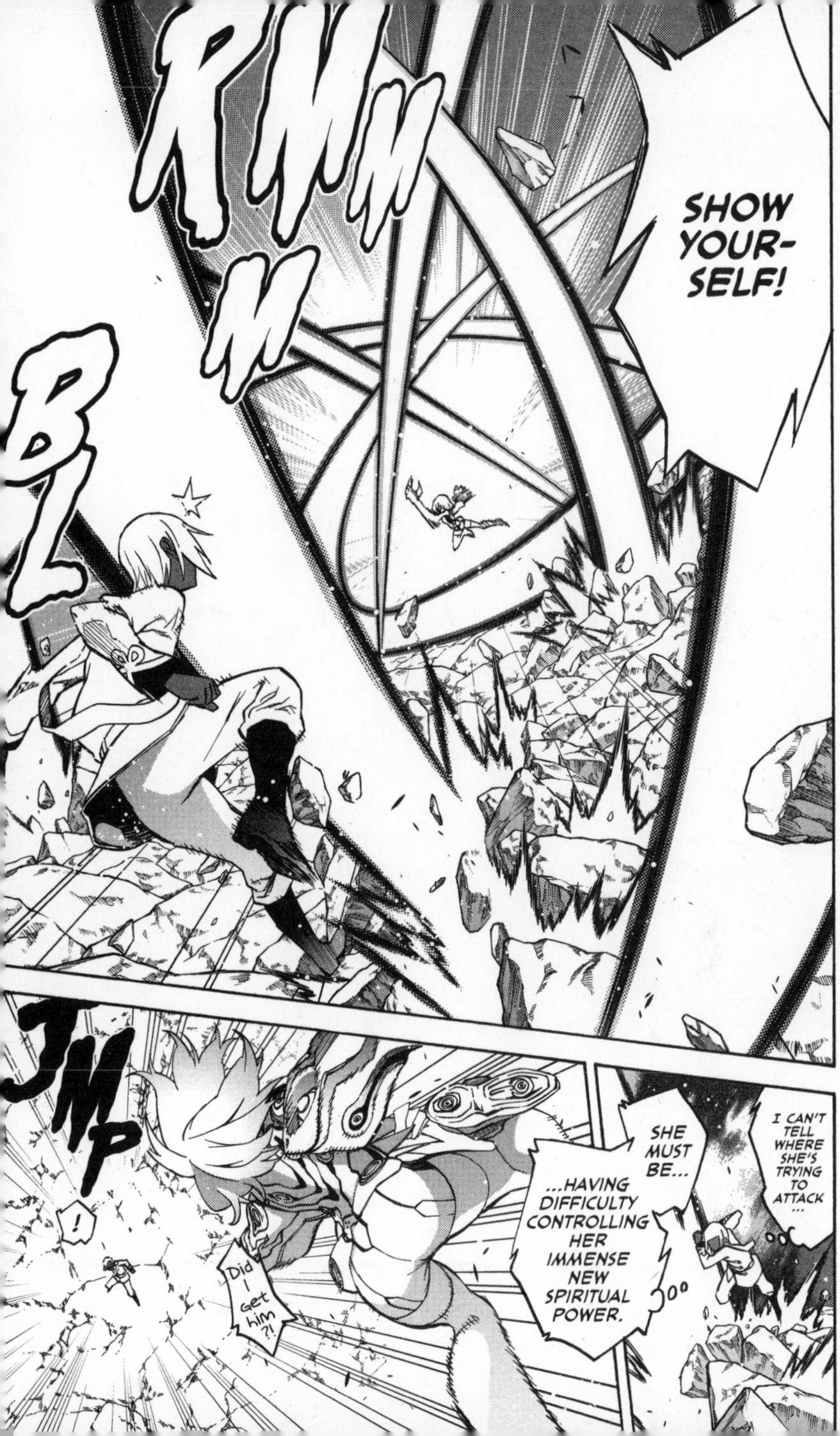
SHOW YOUR-SELF!
I CAN'T TELL WHERE SHE'S TRYING TO ATTACK...
SHE MUST BE...
...HAVING DIFFICULTY CONTROLLING HER IMMENSE NEW SPIRITUAL POWER.
Did I get him?!
!

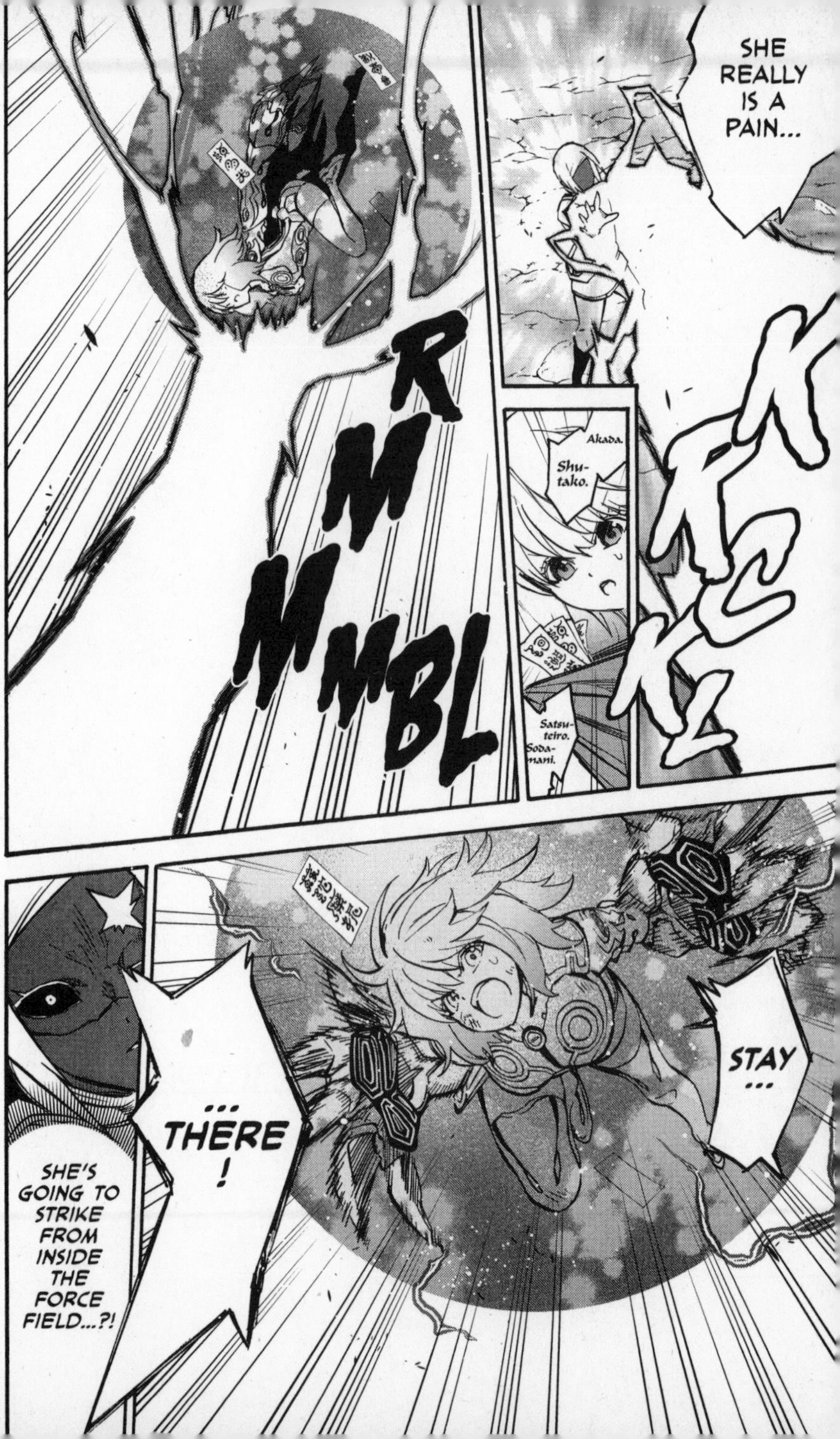
SHE REALLY IS A PAIN...
RMMMBL
KRKK
Akada.
Shu-tako.
Satsu-teiro.
Soda-mani.
STAY ...
... THERE!
SHE'S GOING TO STRIKE FROM INSIDE THE FORCE FIELD...?!

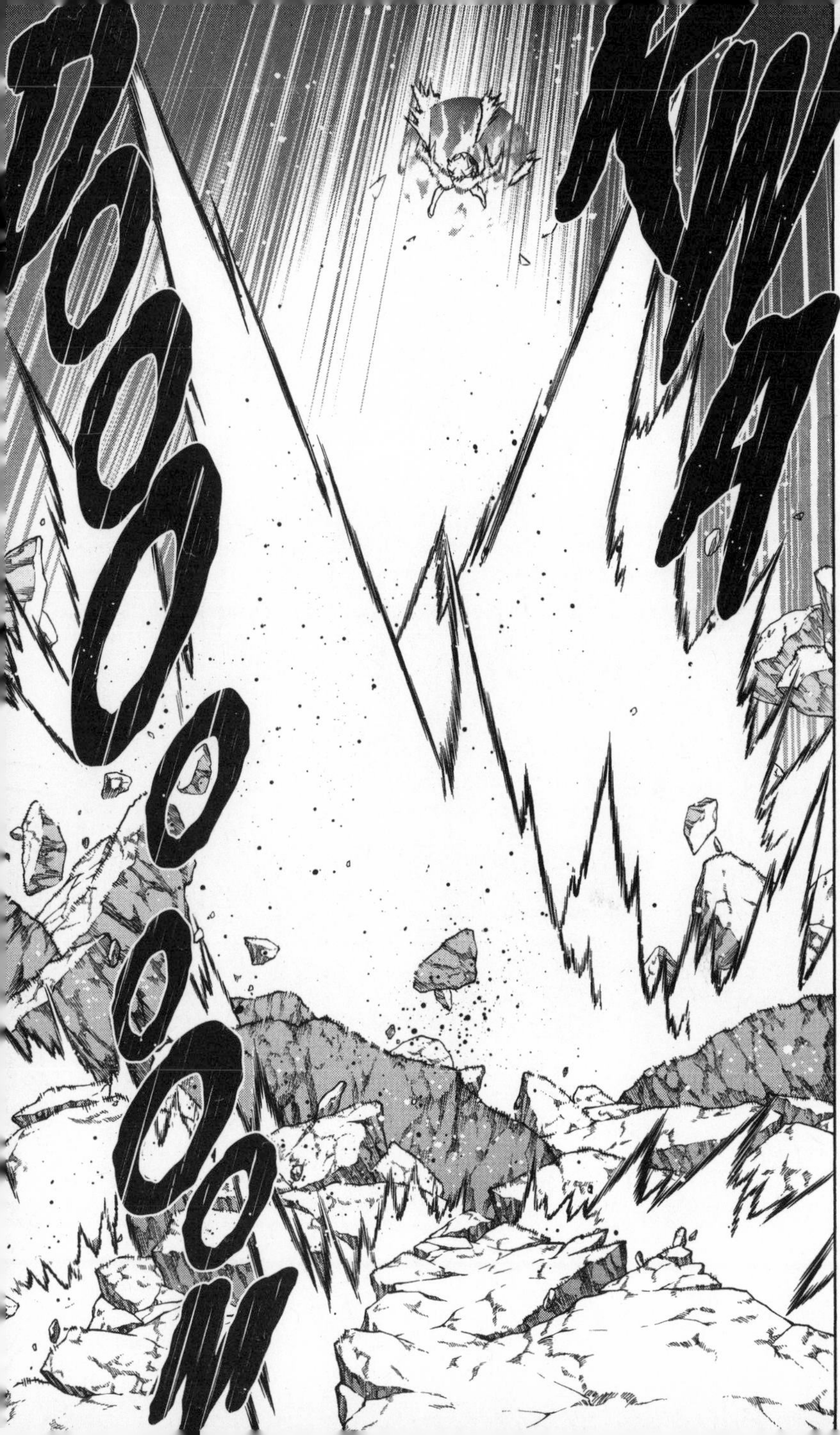
TOOOOOOOM!!

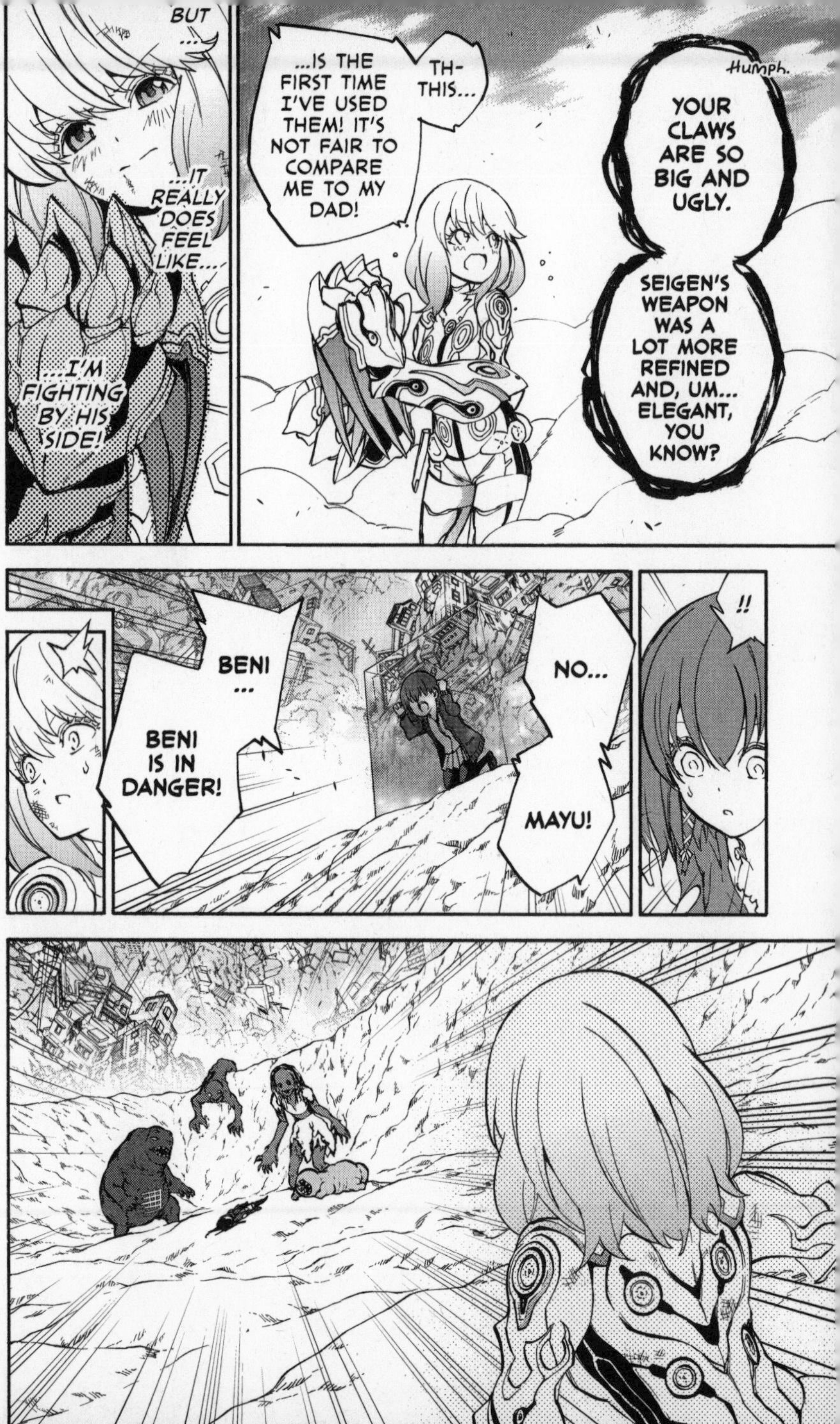
Humph.
YOUR CLAWS ARE SO BIG AND UGLY.
SEIGEN'S WEAPON WAS A LOT MORE REFINED AND, UM... ELEGANT, YOU KNOW?
TH- THIS...
...IS THE FIRST TIME I'VE USED THEM! IT'S NOT FAIR TO COMPARE ME TO MY DAD!
BUT ...
...IT REALLY DOES FEEL LIKE...
...I'M FIGHTING BY HIS SIDE!
!!
NO...
MAYU!
BENI ...
BENI IS IN DANGER!

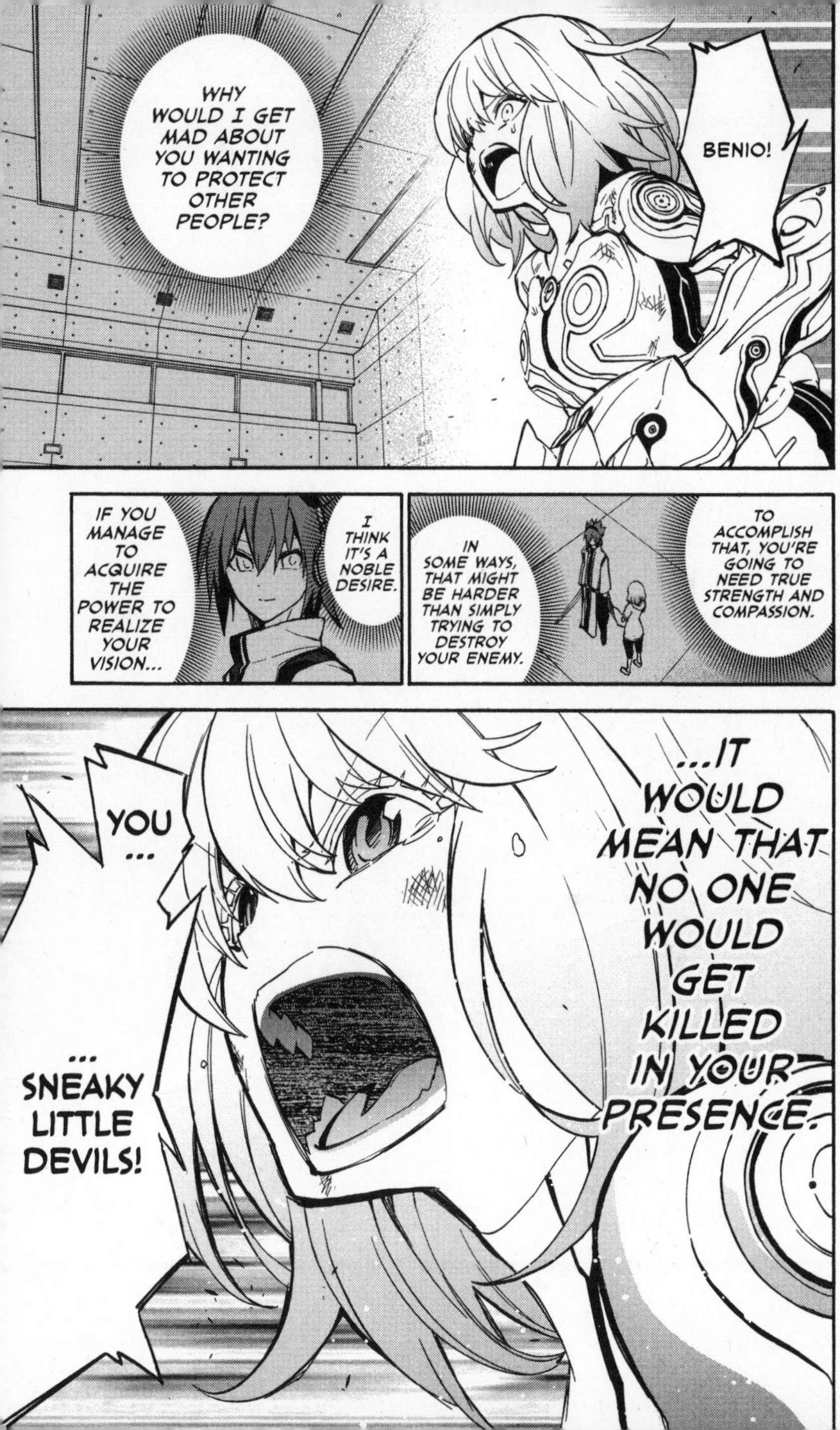
BENIO!
WHY WOULD I GET MAD ABOUT YOU WANTING TO PROTECT OTHER PEOPLE?
TO ACCOMPLISH THAT, YOU'RE GOING TO NEED TRUE STRENGTH AND COMPASSION.
IN SOME WAYS, THAT MIGHT BE HARDER THAN SIMPLY TRYING TO DESTROY YOUR ENEMY.
I THINK IT'S A NOBLE DESIRE.
IF YOU MANAGE TO ACQUIRE THE POWER TO REALIZE YOUR VISION...
...IT WOULD MEAN THAT NO ONE WOULD GET KILLED IN YOUR PRESENCE.
YOU...
...SNEAKY LITTLE DEVILS!

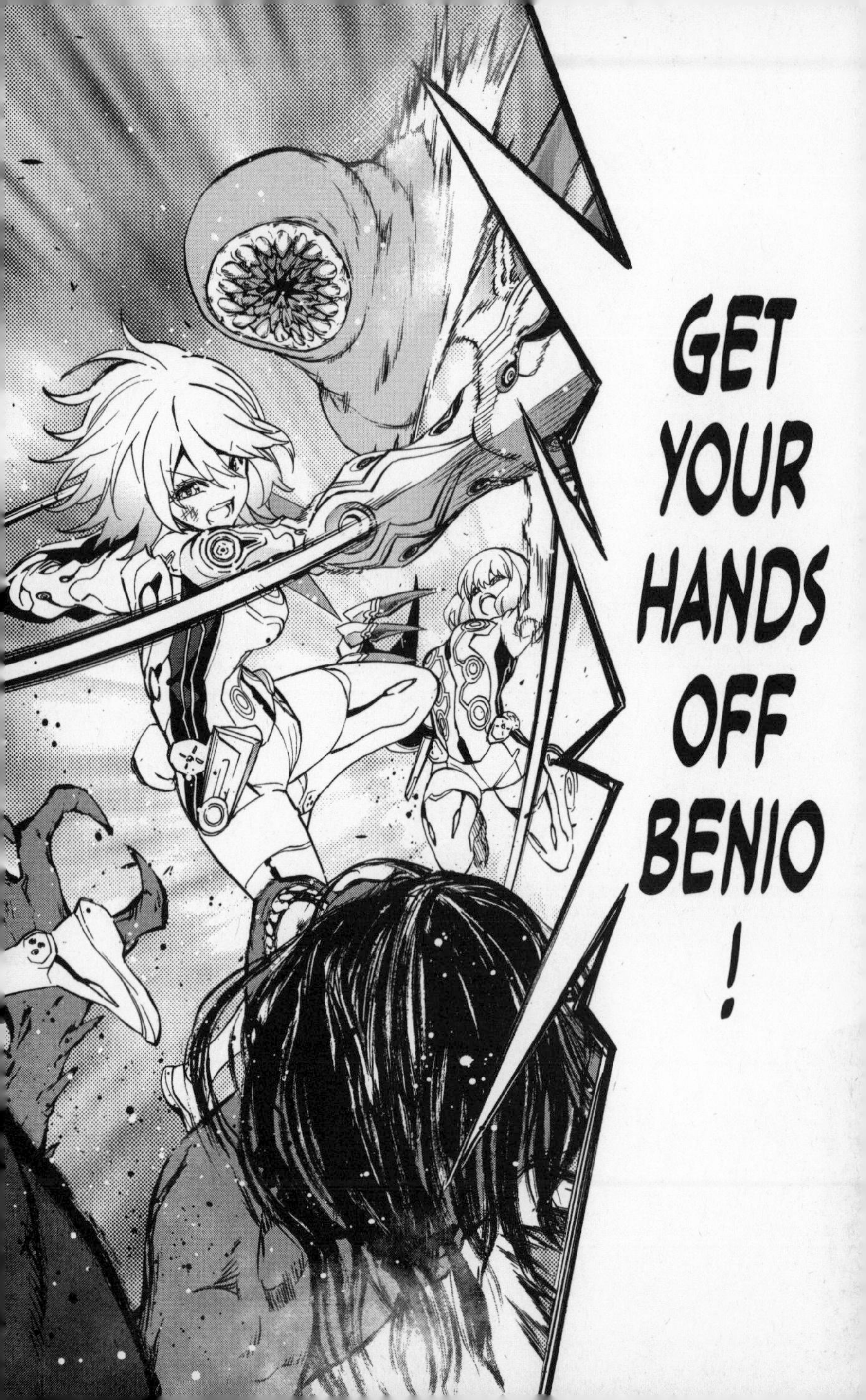
GET YOUR HANDS OFF BENIO!

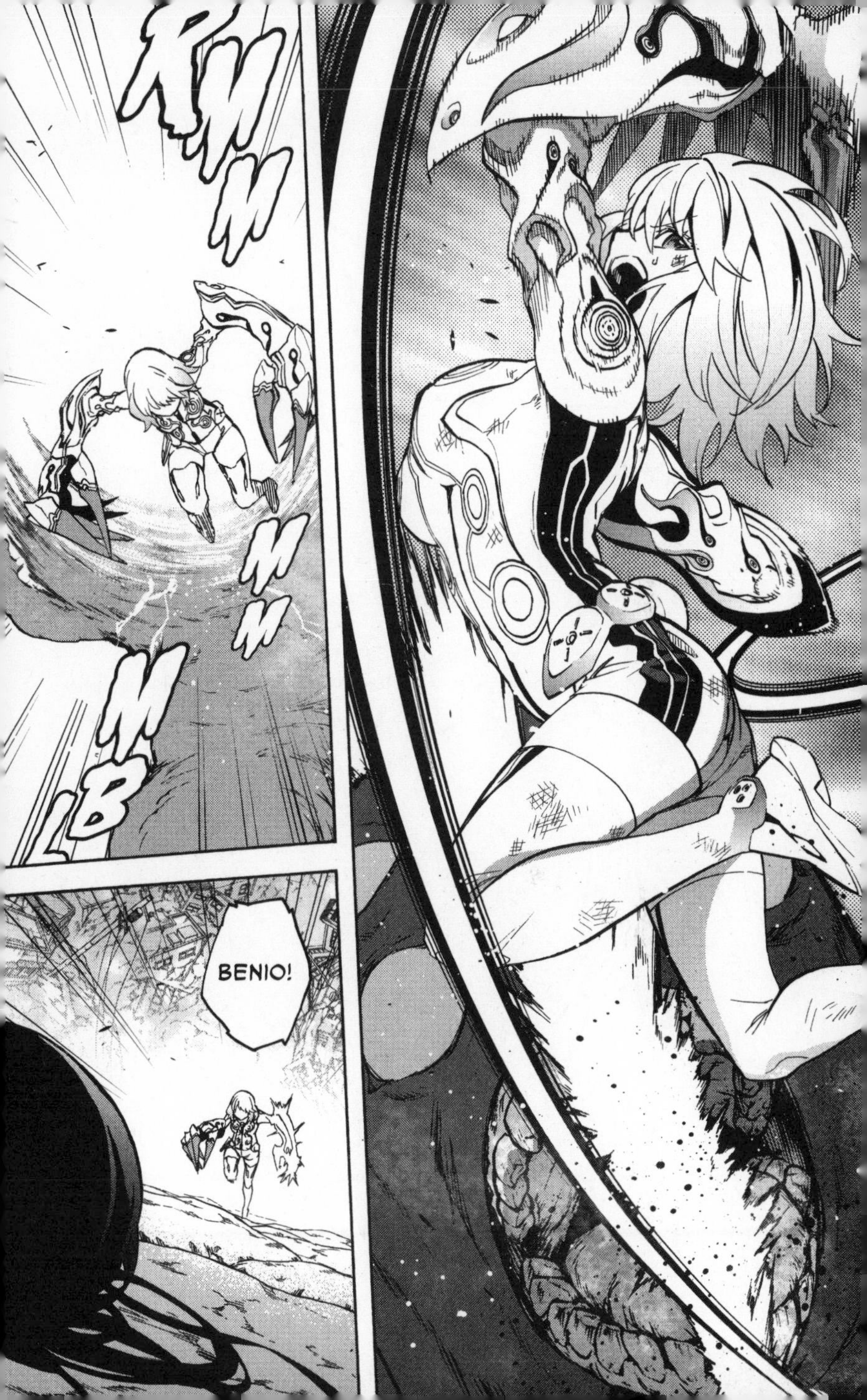
RMMMMMBL
BENIO!

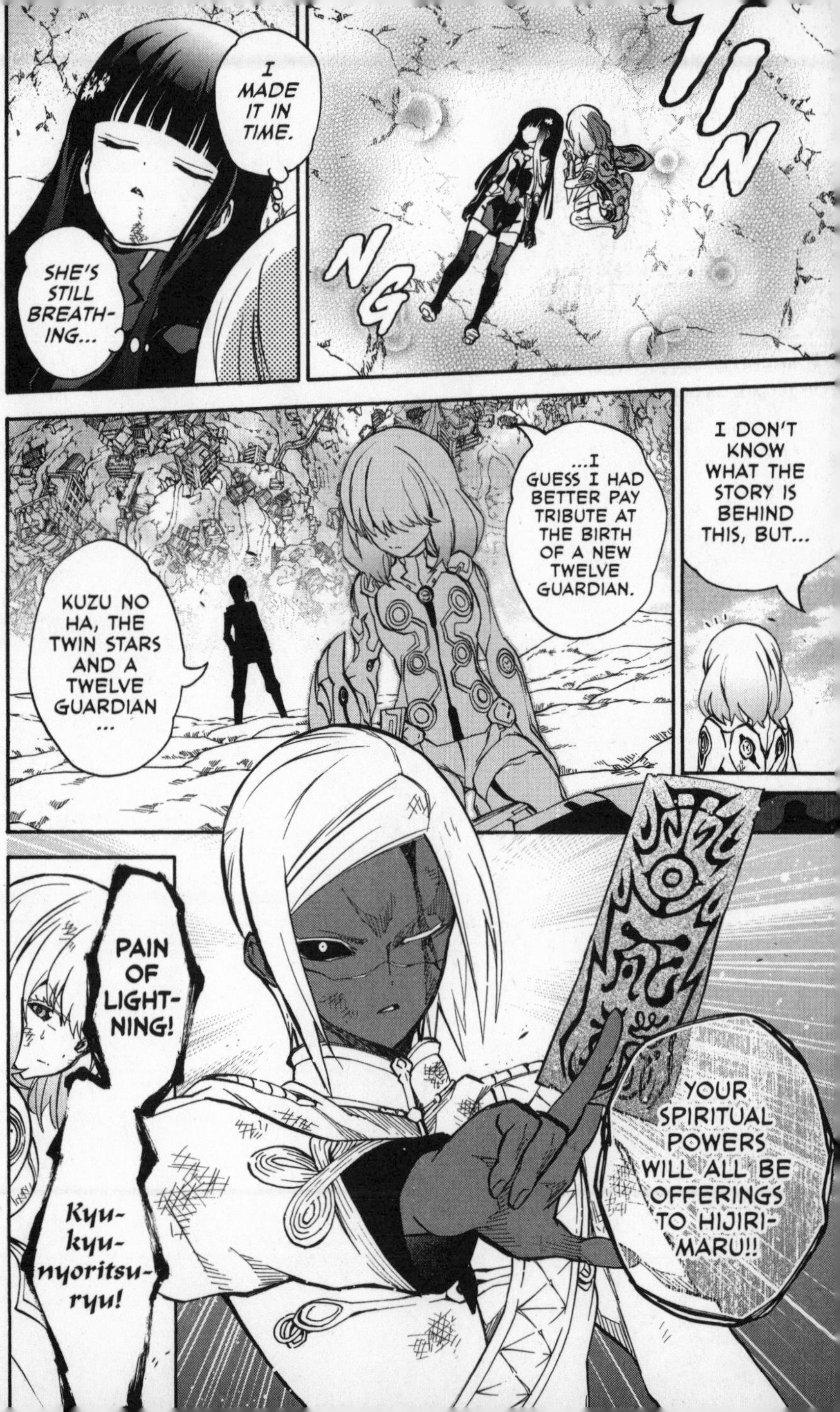
VIIN
NG
I MADE IT IN TIME.
SHE'S STILL BREATHING...
I DON'T KNOW WHAT THE STORY IS BEHIND THIS, BUT...
...I GUESS I HAD BETTER PAY TRIBUTE AT THE BIRTH OF A NEW TWELVE GUARDIAN.
KUZU NO HA, THE TWIN STARS AND A TWELVE GUARDIAN...
YOUR SPIRITUAL POWERS WILL ALL BE OFFERINGS TO HIJIRIMARU!!
PAIN OF LIGHTNING!
Kyukyunyoritsuryu!

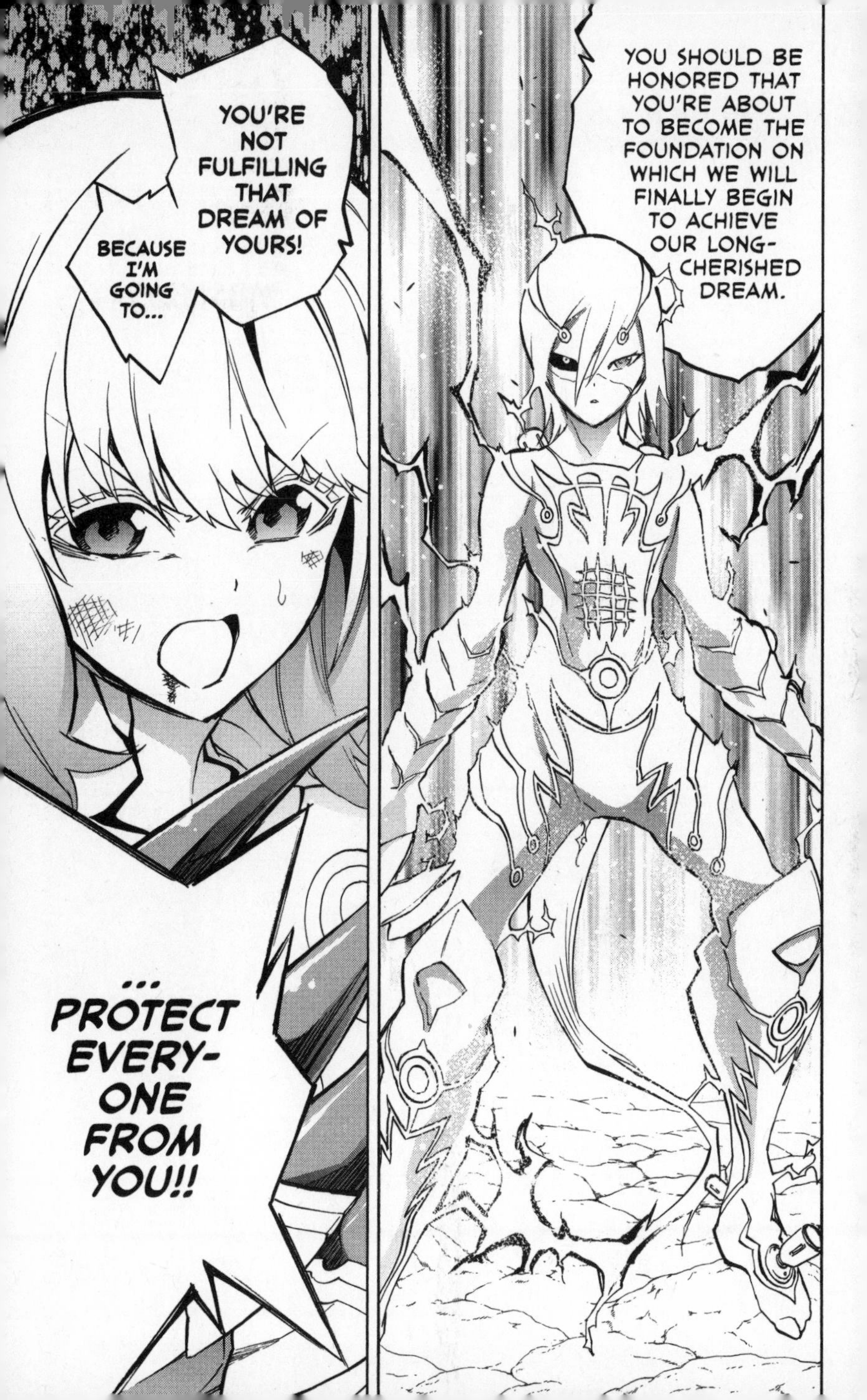
YOU SHOULD BE HONORED THAT YOU'RE ABOUT TO BECOME THE FOUNDATION ON WHICH WE WILL FINALLY BEGIN TO ACHIEVE OUR LONG-CHERISHED DREAM.
YOU'RE NOT FULFILLING THAT DREAM OF YOURS!
BECAUSE I'M GOING TO...
...PROTECT EVERY-ONE FROM YOU!!

KEGARE CLASSIFICATION

Part 1

The dwellers of Magano, the Kegare. The Association of Unified Exorcists classifies Kegare in six risk categories. Here is a guide to the power levels and distinctions among these six types.

DEIGAN, OR MUD EYE

Risk Level: D, D+

The weakest and slowest of the Kegare. Deigan are not very intelligent and simply mob the prey (humans) they encounter. Their ability to do harm is no different from that of ordinary humans, so unless they attack in groups, an average exorcist would have no trouble exorcising them. A Kegare can steal spiritual power by killing another Kegare. Deigan hardly ever manage to kill humans, so their main tactic for acquiring greater spiritual power is to prey on other Deigan, which means they can only reach the next level by surviving a battle with one of their own.

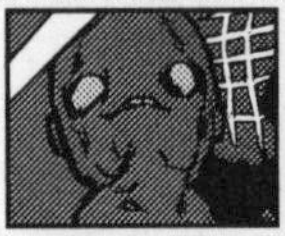
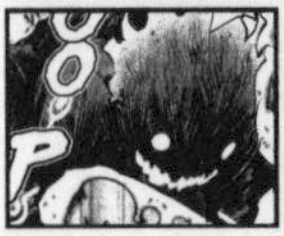

Ryogo Ratio 10:1

HANNYA, OR DEMON OF WISDOM

Risk Level: C, C+, CC

Hannya are larger and contain more spiritual power than Deigan. They can easily kill humans, but are not very intelligent or fast moving. The risk of fighting one is not that high, as long as you are well equipped. Note: Kegare can sense the spiritual power of a person, and it is their natural instinct to gather more of it to grow more powerful. However, Kegare do not hunger for food, so preying upon humans is merely for the purpose of absorbing their spiritual power, not eating their flesh.

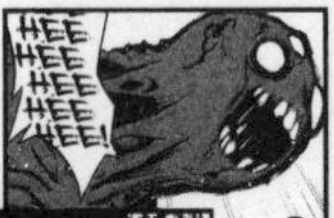
HEE HEE HEE HEE HEE!
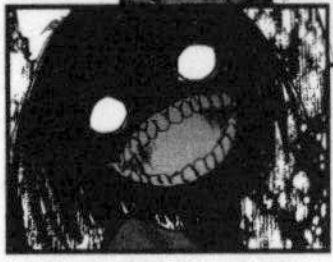

Ryogo Ratio 1:1

JA, OR SNAKE

Risk Level: B, B+, BB

Ja are far larger than Deigan or Hannya and cannot be exorcised without a platoon of exorcists working together. Ja gradually absorb the memories and external characteristics of the humans they kill, so unlike Deigan and Hannya, each has a unique appearance. Most of the Kegare on Tsuchimikado Island, the battle front line, are of the Ja variety. The weakest Kegare on the island is an upper-ranked Hannya.

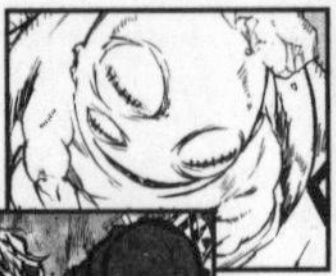
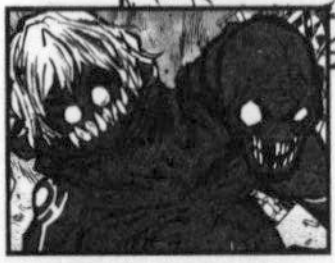

Ryogo Ratio 1:10

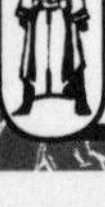

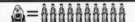

Explanation of the Unit

What is a "Ryogo Ratio"?

Let us assume that the unit of power to fight a Kegare is a "Ryogo." One Ryogo is equivalent to a grown man with the stamina and athletic skills of an average athlete, and contains enough spiritual power to exorcise a Kegare.

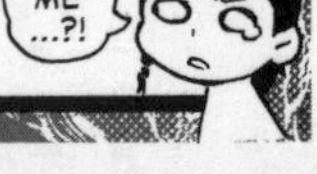
WHY ME ...?!

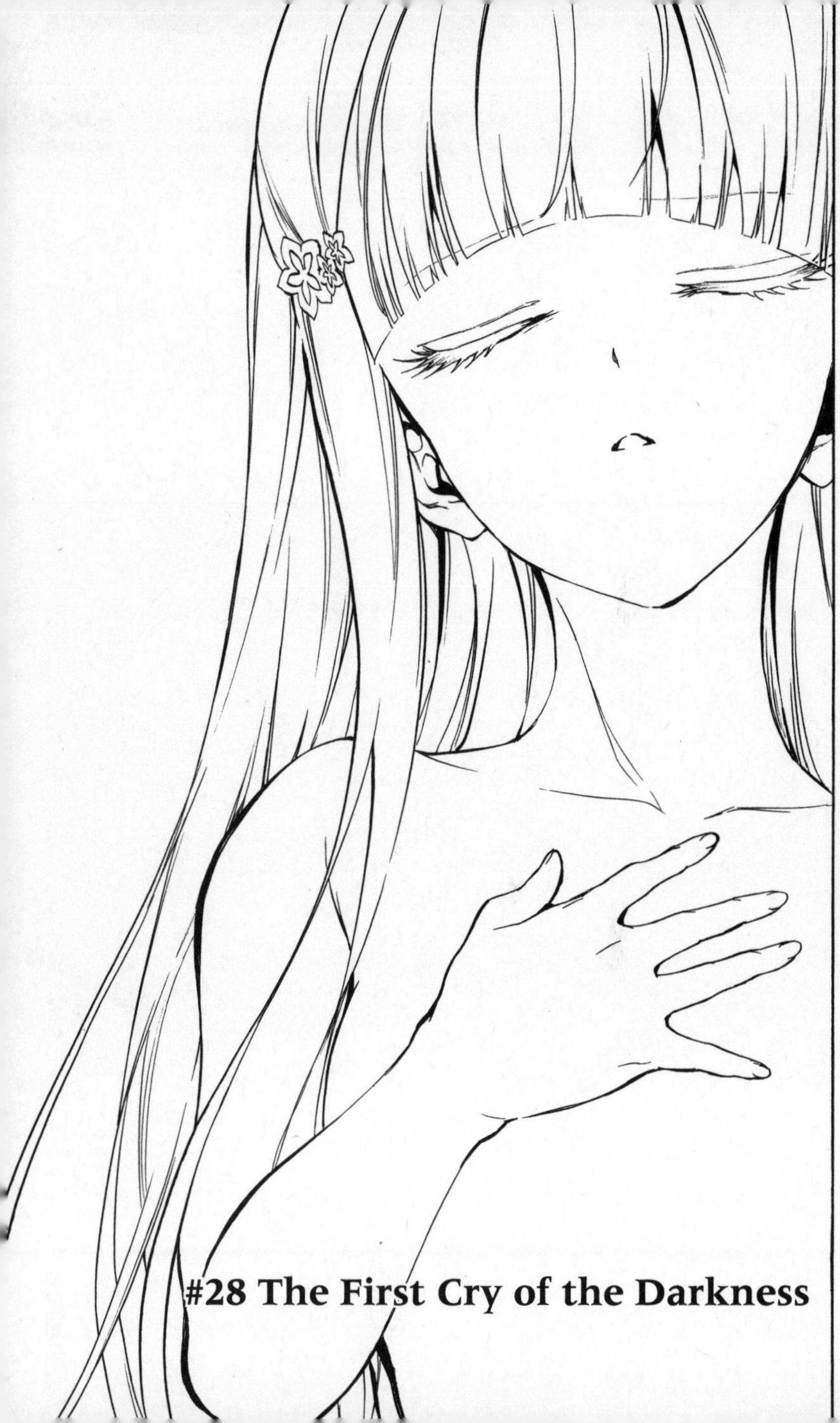

#28 The First Cry of the Darkness

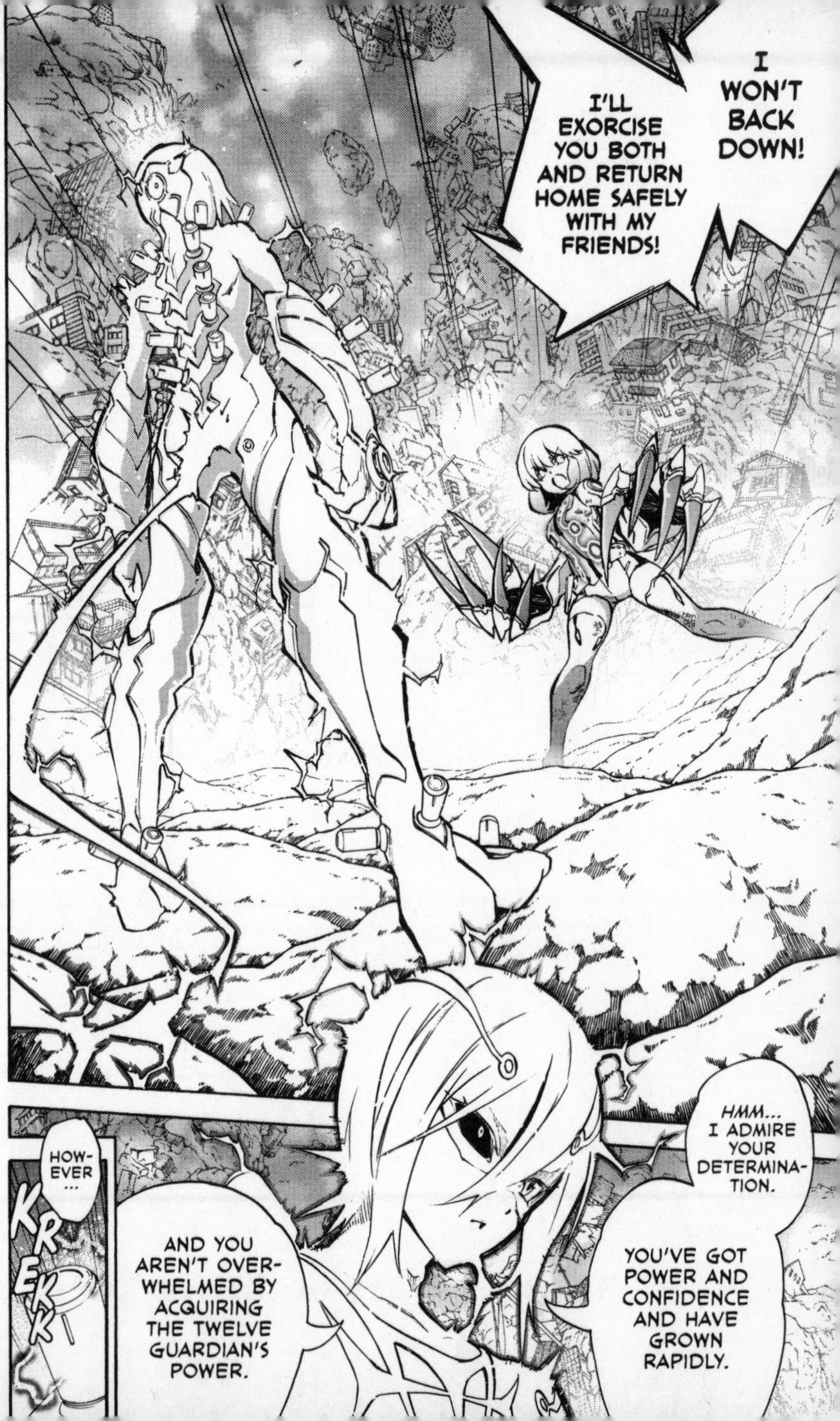
I WON'T BACK DOWN!
I'LL EXORCISE YOU BOTH AND RETURN HOME SAFELY WITH MY FRIENDS!
HMM... I ADMIRE YOUR DETERMINA-TION.
YOU'VE GOT POWER AND CONFIDENCE AND HAVE GROWN RAPIDLY.
AND YOU AREN'T OVER-WHELMED BY ACQUIRING THE TWELVE GUARDIAN'S POWER.
HOW-EVER...
KREKK

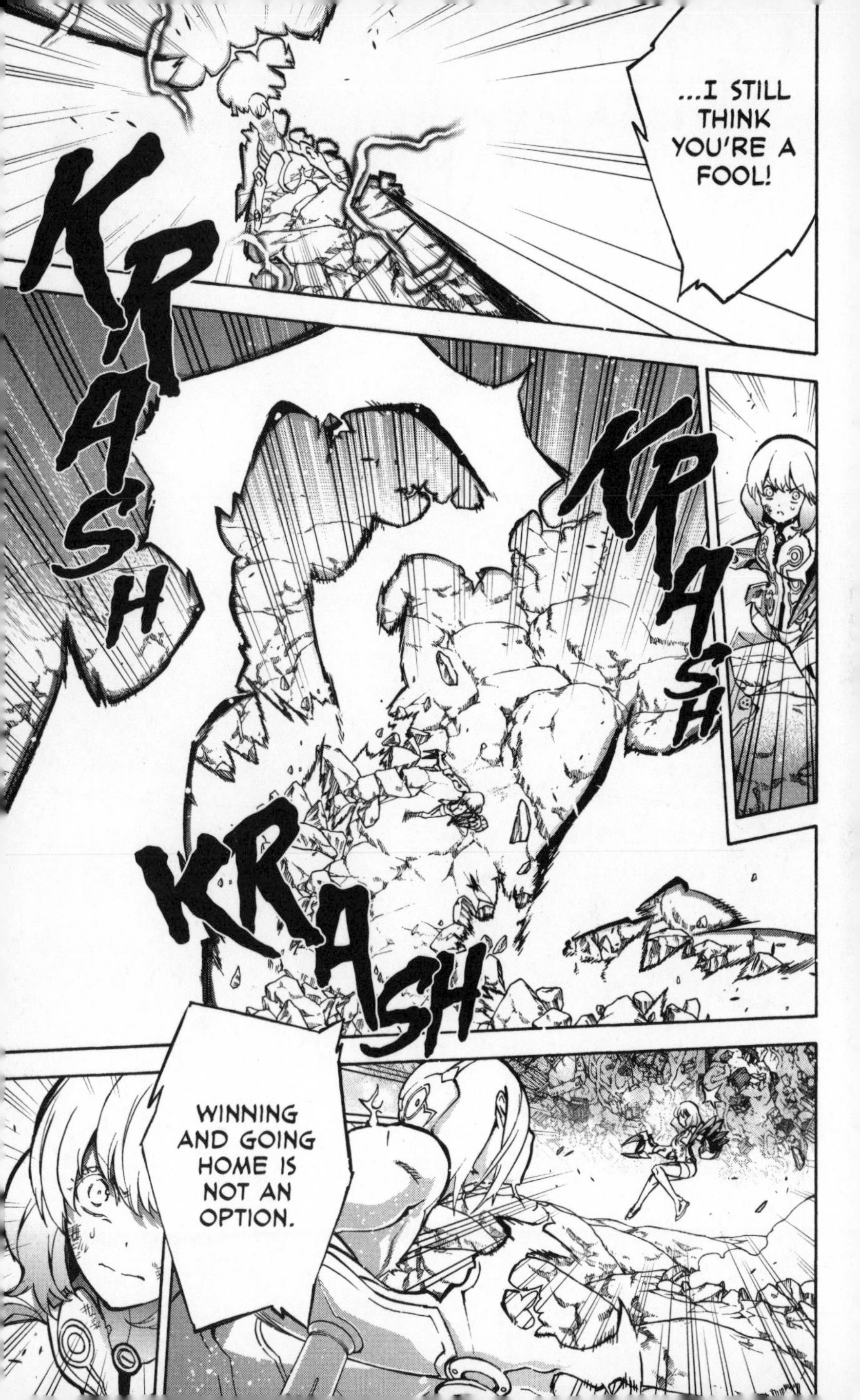
...I STILL THINK YOU'RE A FOOL!
KRASH
KRASH
KRASH
WINNING AND GOING HOME IS NOT AN OPTION.

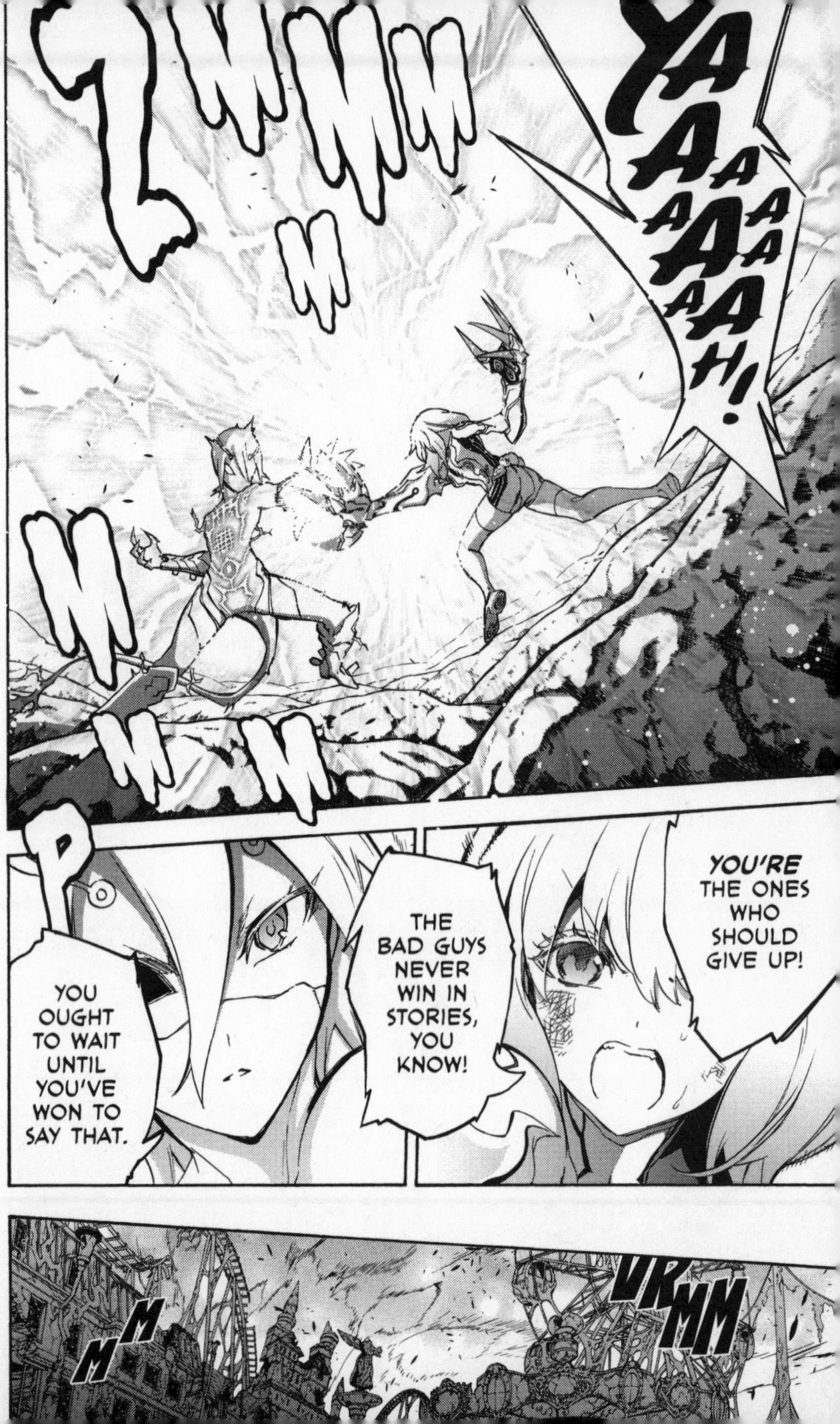
YAAAAAAAAAAAH!
ZMMMM
M
MMMM
YOU'RE THE ONES WHO SHOULD GIVE UP!
THE BAD GUYS NEVER WIN IN STORIES, YOU KNOW!
P
YOU OUGHT TO WAIT UNTIL YOU'VE WON TO SAY THAT.
VRMM
MMM

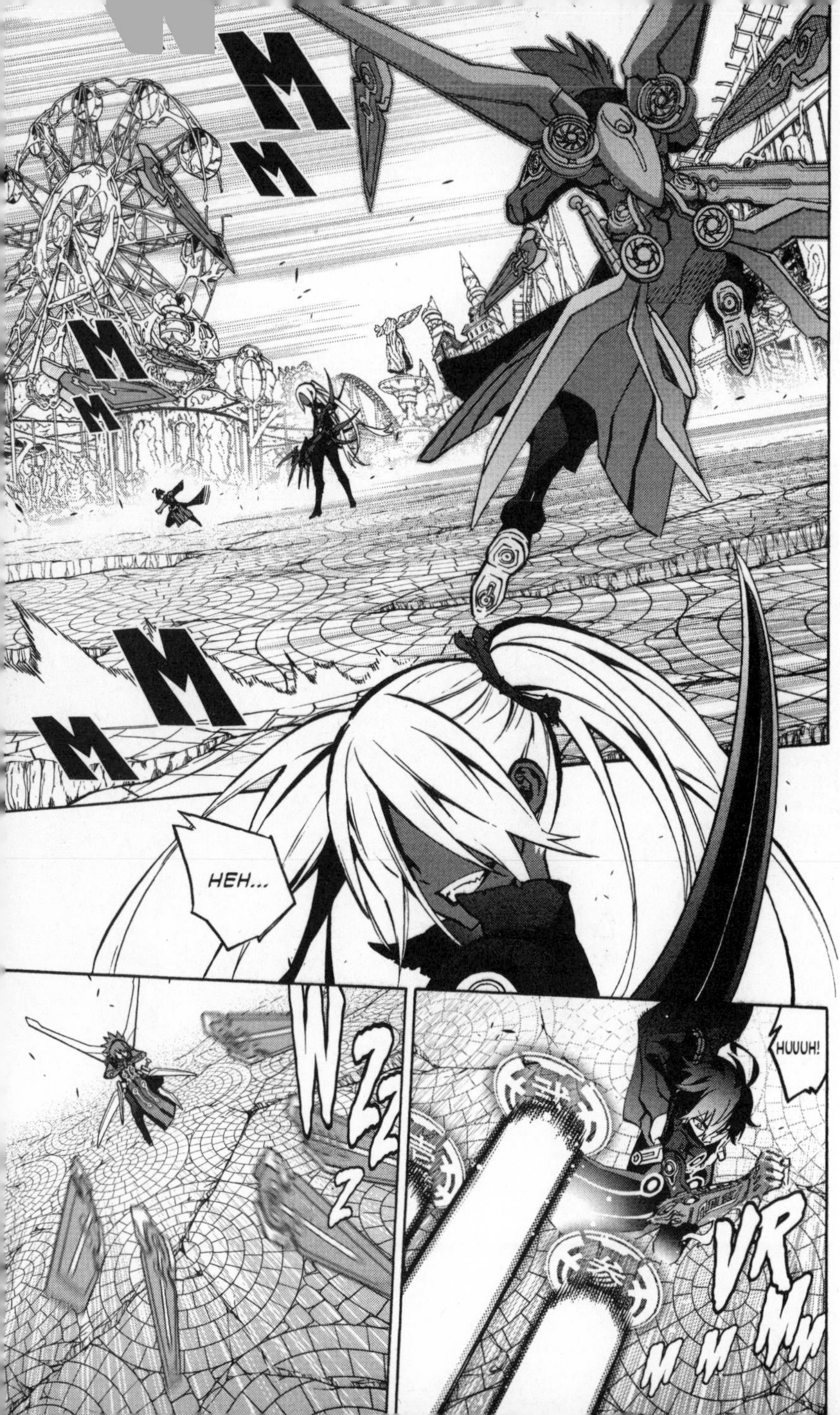
MM
MM
MM
HEH...
HUUUH!
VRMMMMM
WZZZ

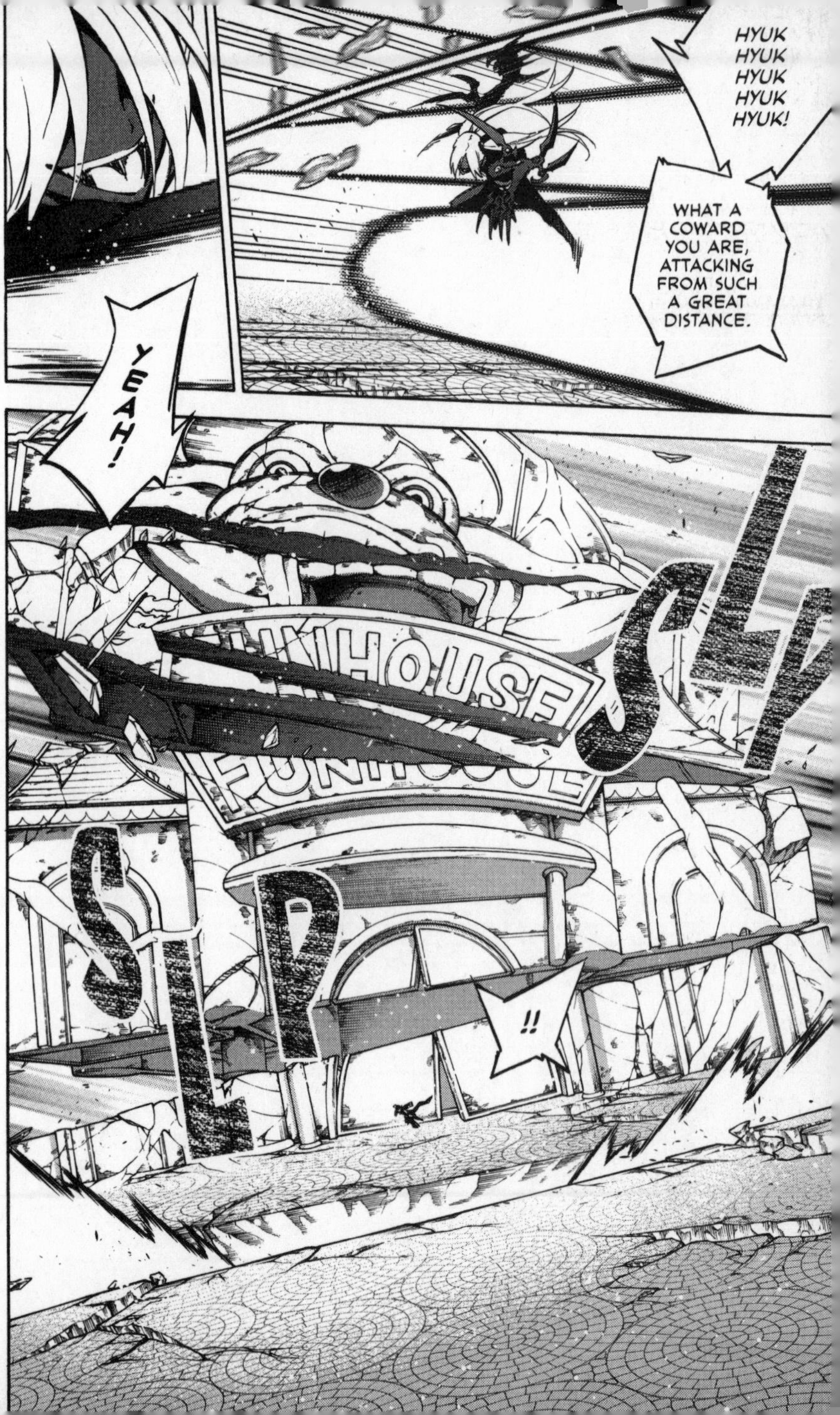
HYUK
HYUK
HYUK
HYUK
HYUK!
WHAT A COWARD YOU ARE, ATTACKING FROM SUCH A GREAT DISTANCE.
YEAH!
FUNHOUSE
!!

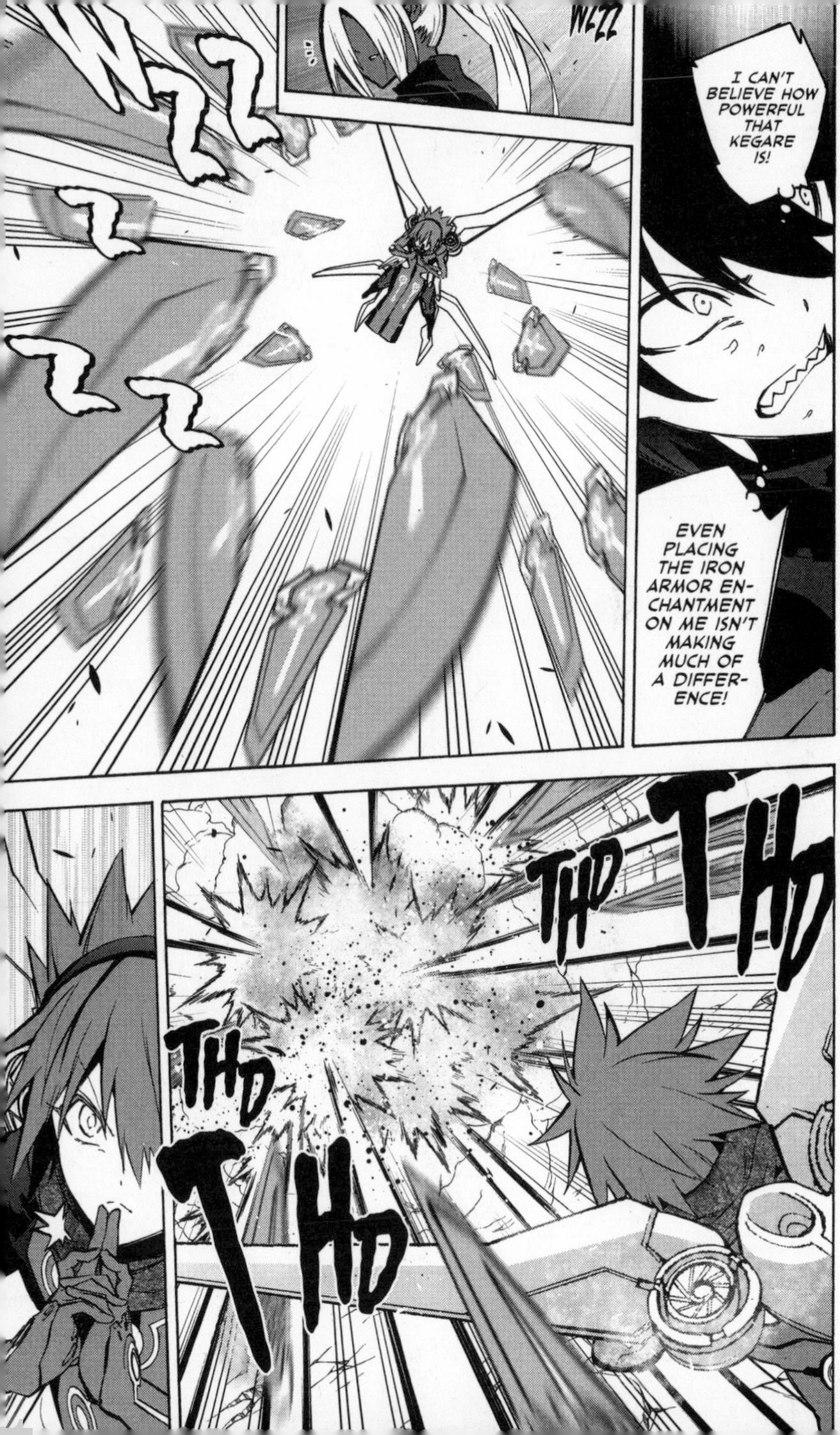
WZZZZZ
WZZZ
I CAN'T BELIEVE HOW POWERFUL THAT KEGARE IS!
EVEN PLACING THE IRON ARMOR EN-CHANTMENT ON ME ISN'T MAKING MUCH OF A DIFFER-ENCE!
THD THD
THD THD

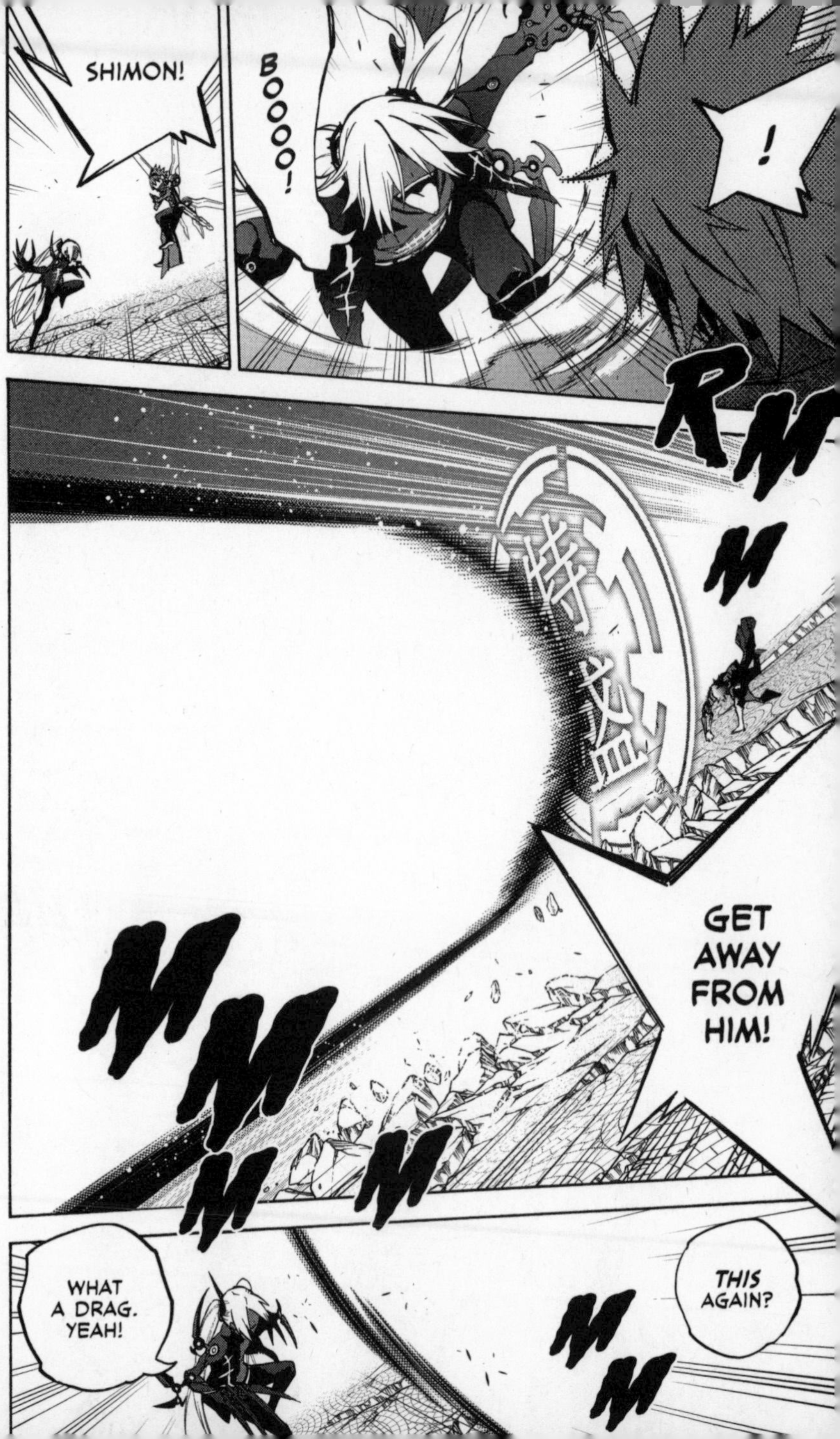
!
BOOOOO!
SHIMON!
RMMMMMMM
GET AWAY FROM HIM!
THIS AGAIN?
WHAT A DRAG. YEAH!

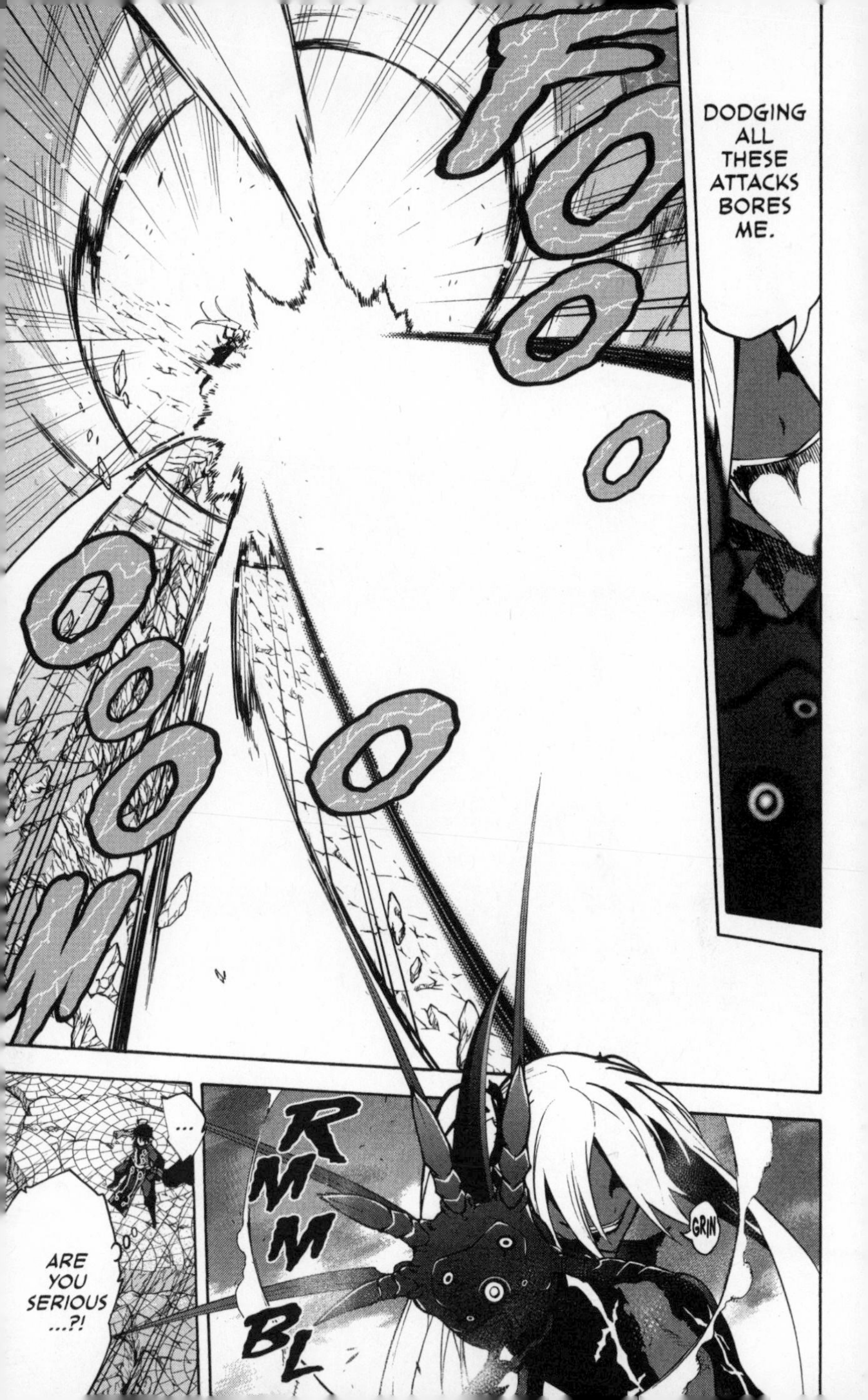
DODGING ALL THESE ATTACKS BORES ME.
FOOOOOOOM
RMMBL
GRIN
...
ARE YOU SERIOUS ...?!

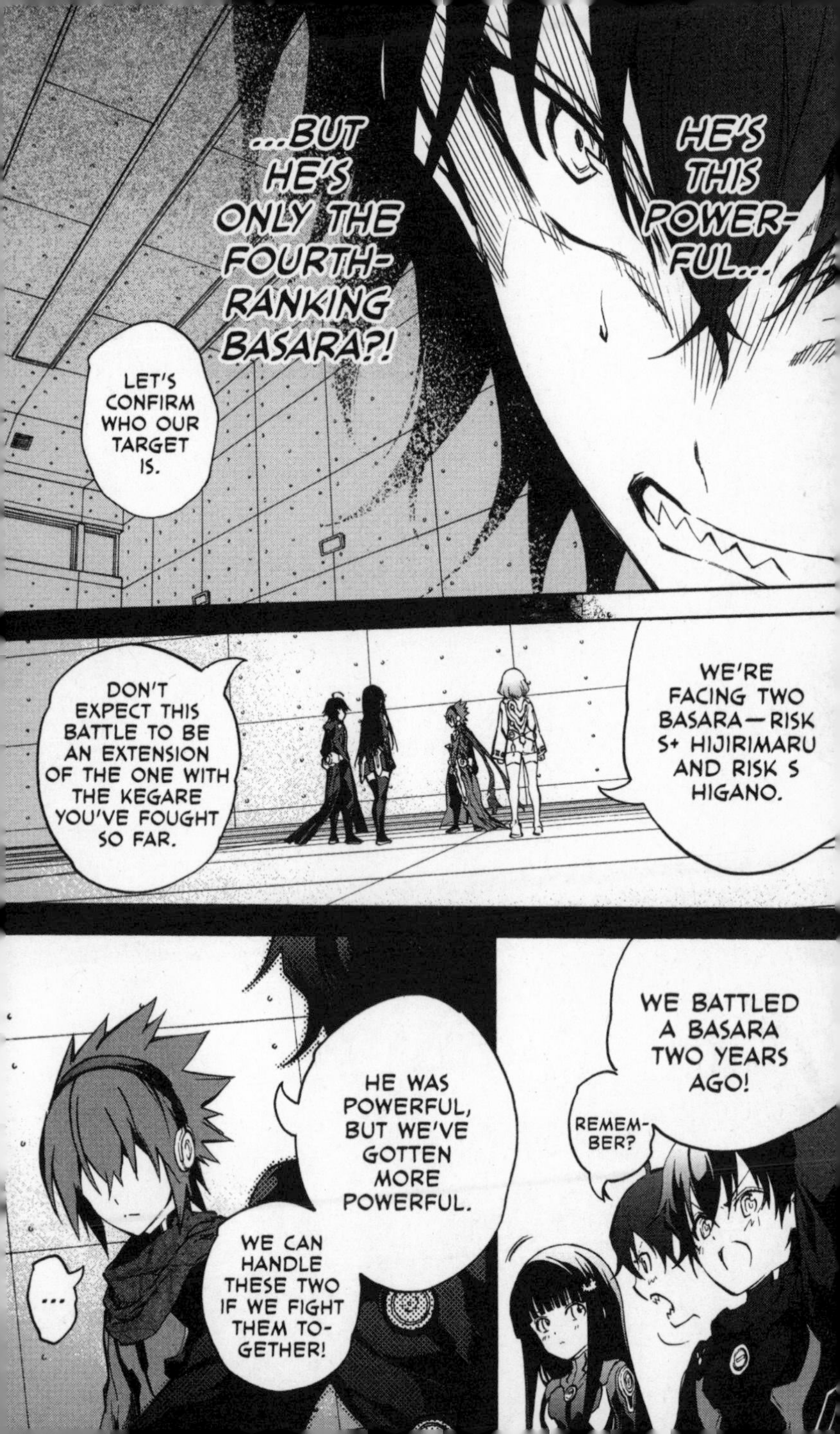
HE'S THIS POWERFUL...
...BUT HE'S ONLY THE FOURTH-RANKING BASARA?!
LET'S CONFIRM WHO OUR TARGET IS.
WE'RE FACING TWO BASARA—RISK S+ HIJIRIMARU AND RISK S HIGANO.
DON'T EXPECT THIS BATTLE TO BE AN EXTENSION OF THE ONE WITH THE KEGARE YOU'VE FOUGHT SO FAR.
WE BATTLED A BASARA TWO YEARS AGO!
REMEMBER?
HE WAS POWERFUL, BUT WE'VE GOTTEN MORE POWERFUL.
WE CAN HANDLE THESE TWO IF WE FIGHT THEM TOGETHER!
...

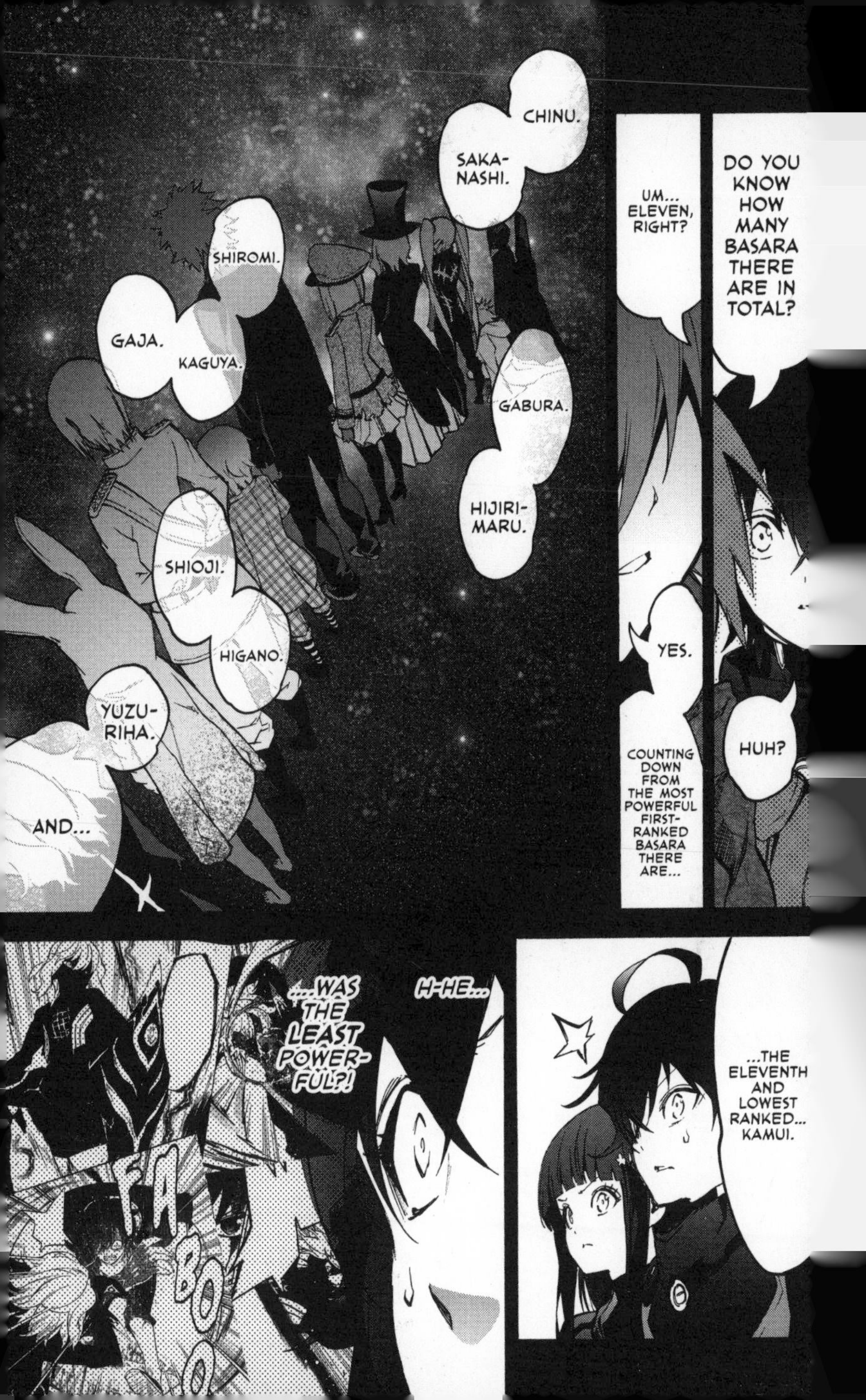
DO YOU KNOW HOW MANY BASARA THERE ARE IN TOTAL?
HUH?
UM... ELEVEN, RIGHT?
YES.
COUNTING DOWN FROM THE MOST POWERFUL FIRST-RANKED BASARA THERE ARE...
CHINU.
SAKA-NASHI.
SHIROMI.
GAJA.
KAGUYA.
GABURA.
HIJIRI-MARU.
SHIOJI.
HIGANO.
YUZU-RIHA.
AND...
...THE ELEVENTH AND LOWEST RANKED... KAMUI.
H-HE...
...WAS THE LEAST POWER-FUL?!

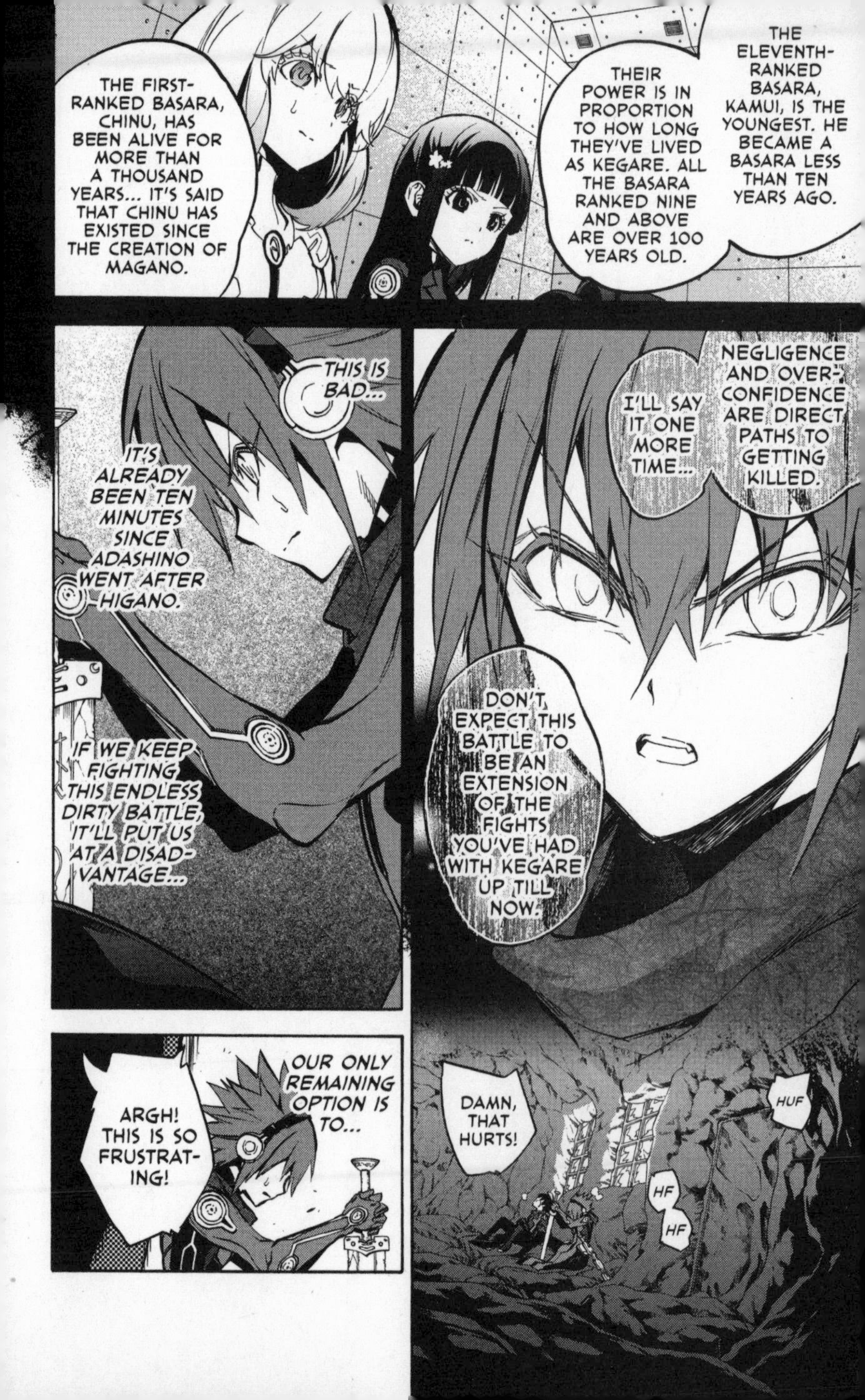
THE ELEVENTH-RANKED BASARA, KAMUI, IS THE YOUNGEST. HE BECAME A BASARA LESS THAN TEN YEARS AGO.
THEIR POWER IS IN PROPORTION TO HOW LONG THEY'VE LIVED AS KEGARE. ALL THE BASARA RANKED NINE AND ABOVE ARE OVER 100 YEARS OLD.
THE FIRST-RANKED BASARA, CHINU, HAS BEEN ALIVE FOR MORE THAN A THOUSAND YEARS... IT'S SAID THAT CHINU HAS EXISTED SINCE THE CREATION OF MAGANO.
NEGLIGENCE AND OVER-CONFIDENCE ARE DIRECT PATHS TO GETTING KILLED.
I'LL SAY IT ONE MORE TIME...
DON'T EXPECT THIS BATTLE TO BE AN EXTENSION OF THE FIGHTS YOU'VE HAD WITH KEGARE UP TILL NOW.
HUF
DAMN, THAT HURTS!
HF
HF
THIS IS BAD...
IT'S ALREADY BEEN TEN MINUTES SINCE ADASHINO WENT AFTER HIGANO.
IF WE KEEP FIGHTING THIS ENDLESS DIRTY BATTLE, IT'LL PUT US AT A DISAD-VANTAGE...
OUR ONLY REMAINING OPTION IS TO...
ARGH! THIS IS SO FRUSTRAT-ING!

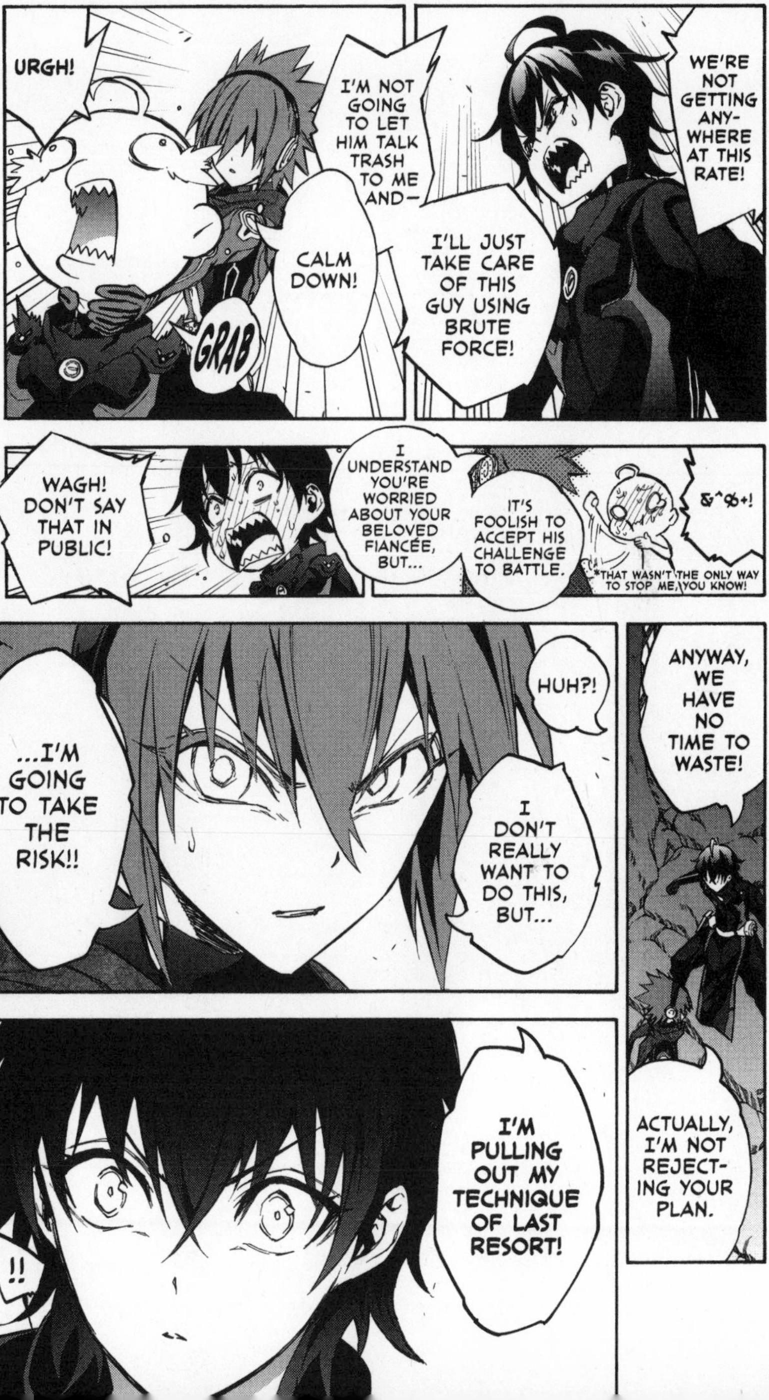
WE'RE NOT GETTING ANY-WHERE AT THIS RATE!
I'LL JUST TAKE CARE OF THIS GUY USING BRUTE FORCE!
I'M NOT GOING TO LET HIM TALK TRASH TO ME AND—
URGH!
CALM DOWN!
GRAB
&^%+!
I UNDERSTAND YOU'RE WORRIED ABOUT YOUR BELOVED FIANCÉE, BUT...
IT'S FOOLISH TO ACCEPT HIS CHALLENGE TO BATTLE.
*THAT WASN'T THE ONLY WAY TO STOP ME, YOU KNOW!
WAGH! DON'T SAY THAT IN PUBLIC!
ANYWAY, WE HAVE NO TIME TO WASTE!
ACTUALLY, I'M NOT REJECT-ING YOUR PLAN.
HUH?!
I DON'T REALLY WANT TO DO THIS, BUT...
...I'M GOING TO TAKE THE RISK!!
I'M PULLING OUT MY TECHNIQUE OF LAST RESORT!
!!

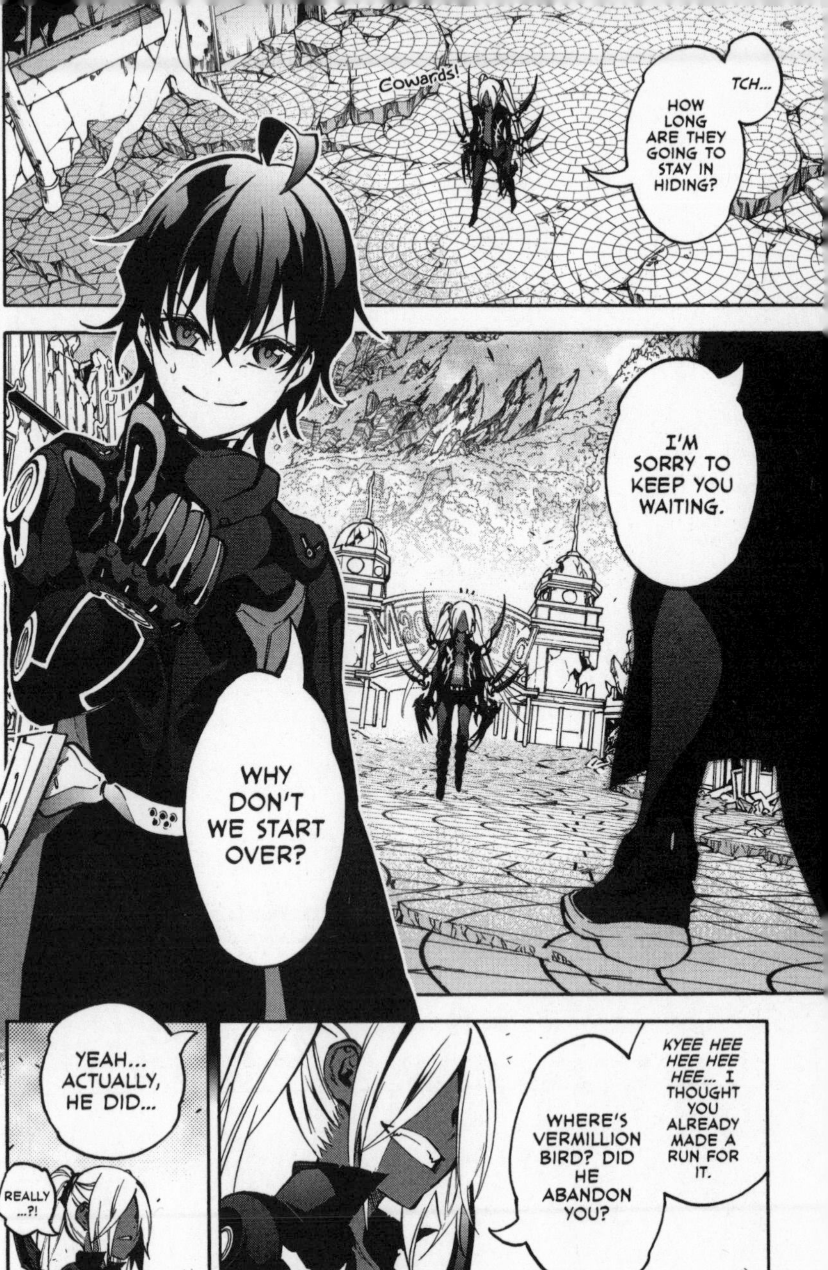
TCH... HOW LONG ARE THEY GOING TO STAY IN HIDING?
Cowards!
I'M SORRY TO KEEP YOU WAITING.
WHY DON'T WE START OVER?
KYEE HEE HEE HEE HEE... I THOUGHT YOU ALREADY MADE A RUN FOR IT.
WHERE'S VERMILLION BIRD? DID HE ABANDON YOU?
YEAH... ACTUALLY, HE DID...
REALLY ...?!

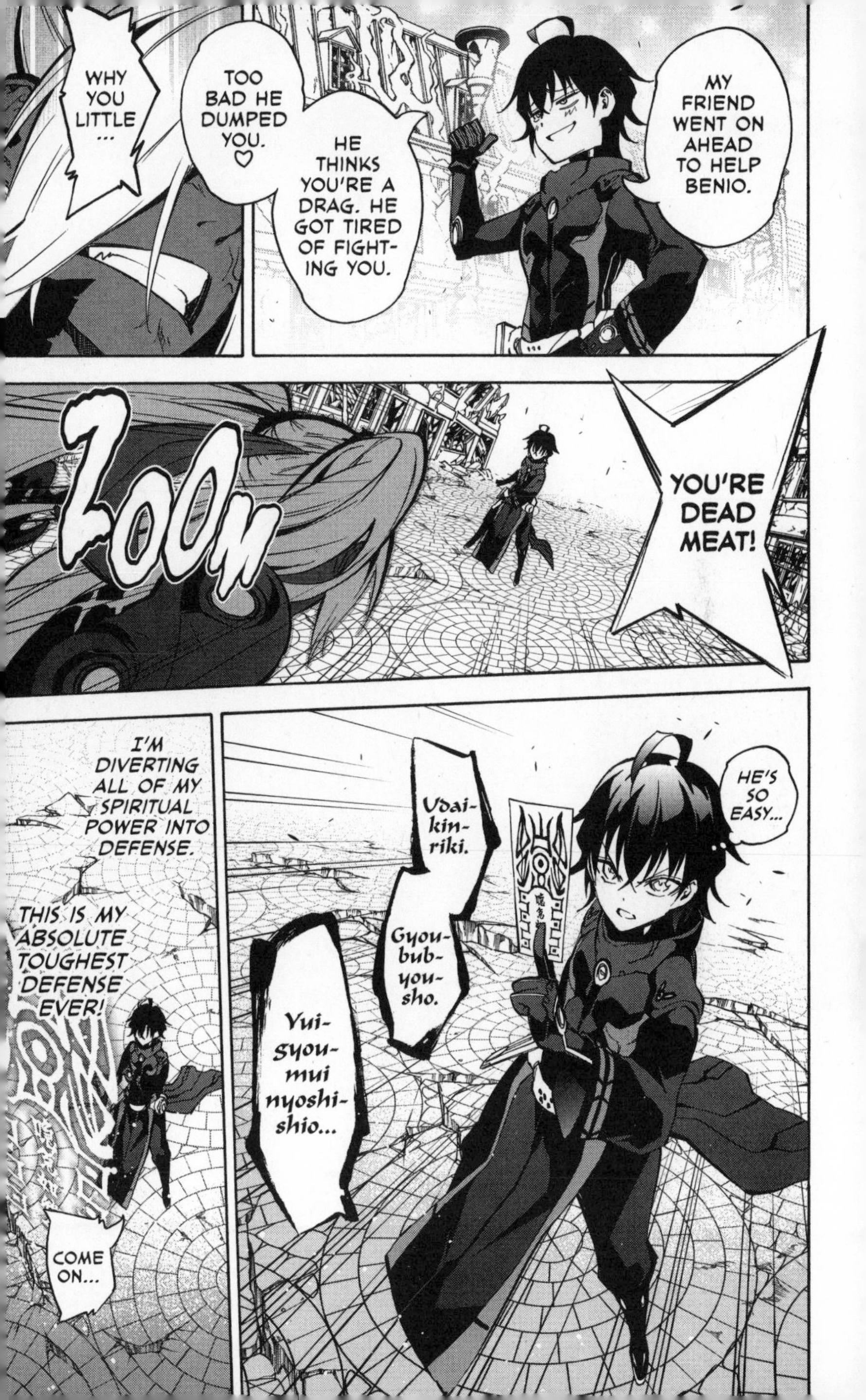
MY FRIEND WENT ON AHEAD TO HELP BENIO.
HE THINKS YOU'RE A DRAG. HE GOT TIRED OF FIGHT-ING YOU.
TOO BAD HE DUMPED YOU. ♡
WHY YOU LITTLE ...
YOU'RE DEAD MEAT!
ZOOM
HE'S SO EASY...
Udai-kin-riki.
Gyou-bub-you-sho.
Yui-syou-mui nyoshi-shio...
I'M DIVERTING ALL OF MY SPIRITUAL POWER INTO DEFENSE.
THIS IS MY ABSOLUTE TOUGHEST DEFENSE EVER!
COME ON...

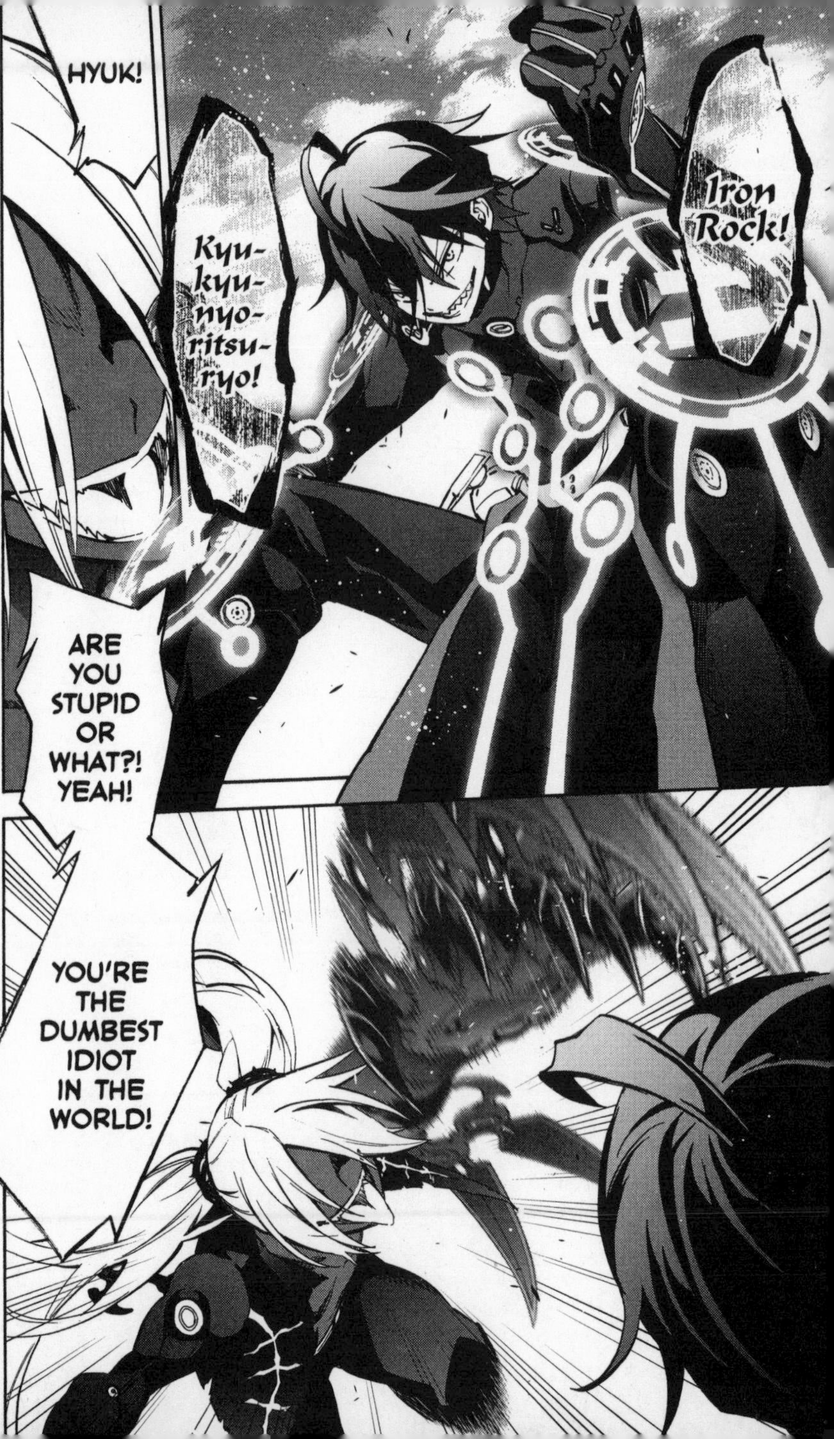
Iron Rock!
Kyu-kyu-nyo-ritsu-ryo!
HYUK!
ARE YOU STUPID OR WHAT?! YEAH!
YOU'RE THE DUMBEST IDIOT IN THE WORLD!

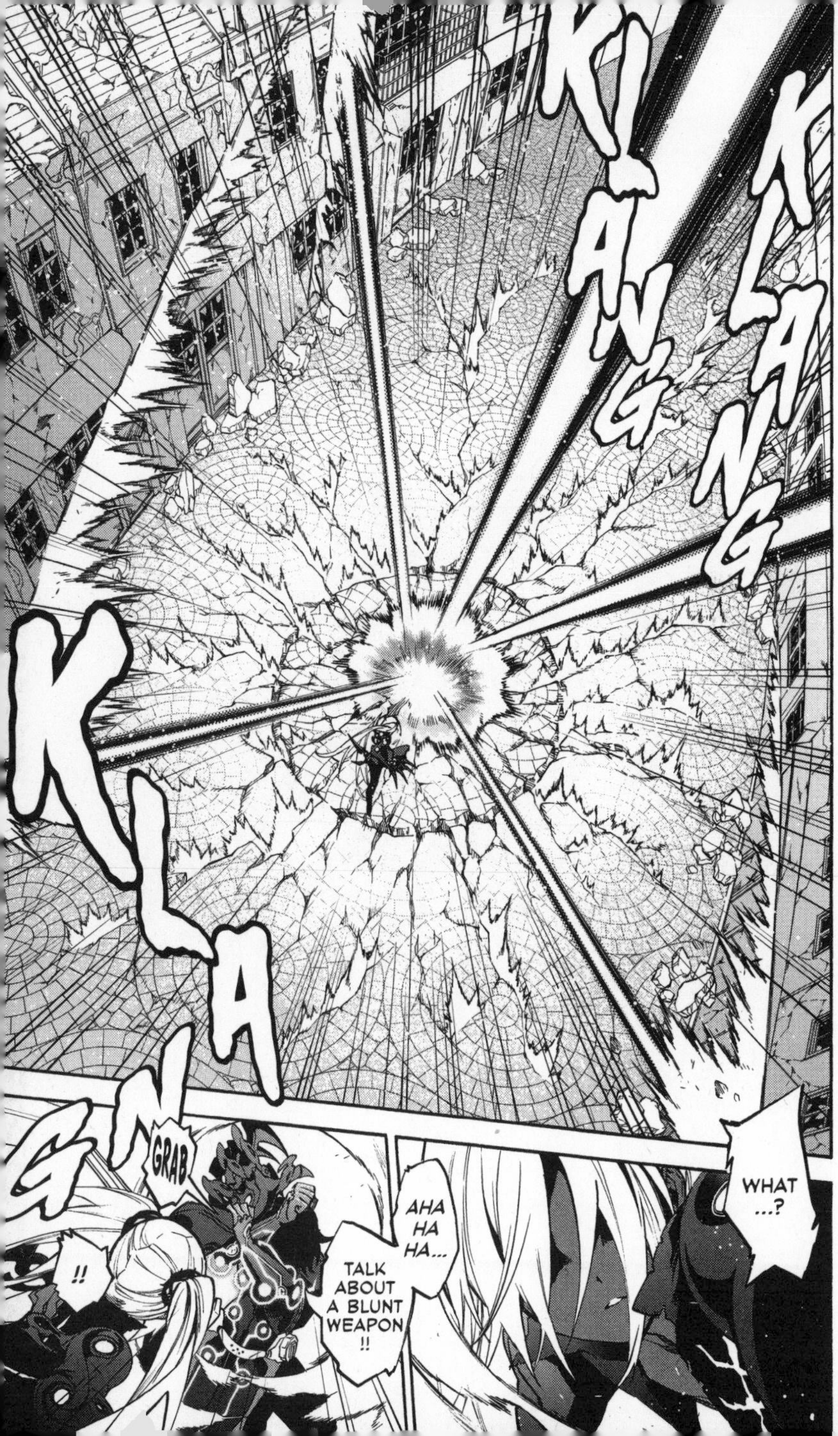
KLANG
KLANG
WHAT ...?
AHA HA HA...
TALK ABOUT A BLUNT WEAPON !!
GRAB
!!

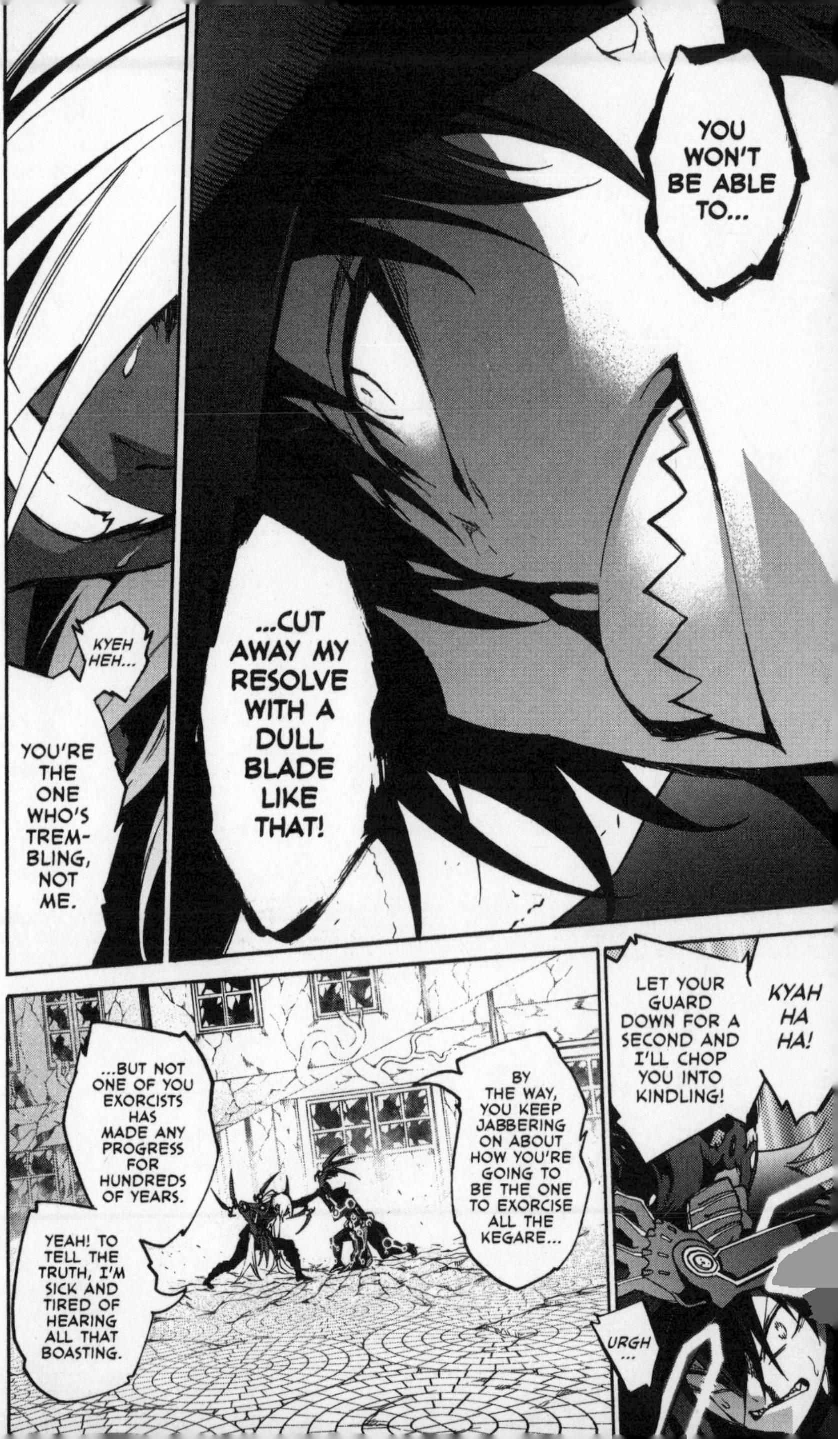
YOU WON'T BE ABLE TO...
...CUT AWAY MY RESOLVE WITH A DULL BLADE LIKE THAT!
KYEH HEH...
YOU'RE THE ONE WHO'S TREMBLING, NOT ME.
KYAH HA HA!
LET YOUR GUARD DOWN FOR A SECOND AND I'LL CHOP YOU INTO KINDLING!
URGH...
BY THE WAY, YOU KEEP JABBERING ON ABOUT HOW YOU'RE GOING TO BE THE ONE TO EXORCISE ALL THE KEGARE...
...BUT NOT ONE OF YOU EXORCISTS HAS MADE ANY PROGRESS FOR HUNDREDS OF YEARS.
YEAH! TO TELL THE TRUTH, I'M SICK AND TIRED OF HEARING ALL THAT BOASTING.

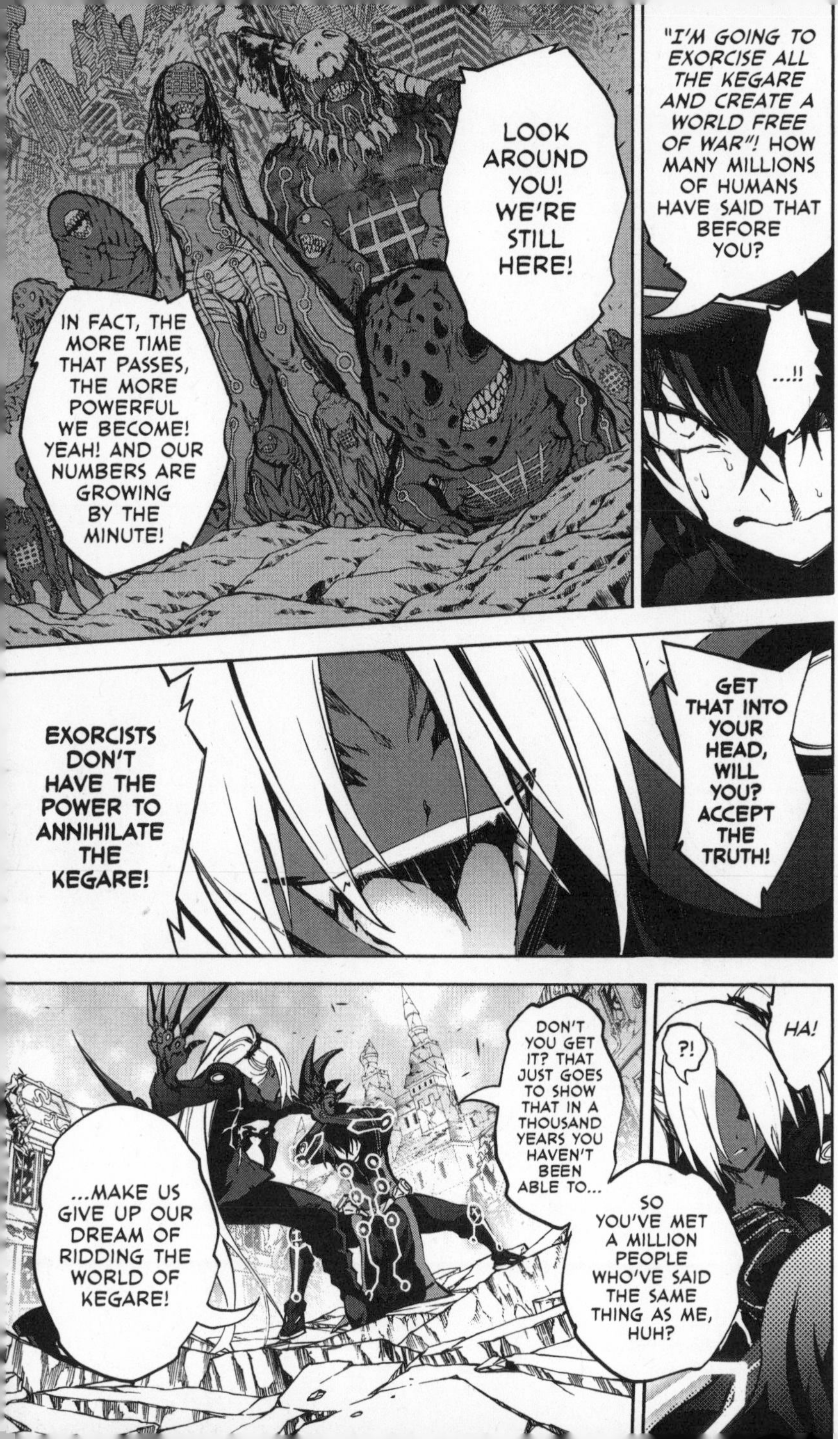
"I'M GOING TO EXORCISE ALL THE KEGARE AND CREATE A WORLD FREE OF WAR"! HOW MANY MILLIONS OF HUMANS HAVE SAID THAT BEFORE YOU?
...!!
LOOK AROUND YOU! WE'RE STILL HERE!
IN FACT, THE MORE TIME THAT PASSES, THE MORE POWERFUL WE BECOME! YEAH! AND OUR NUMBERS ARE GROWING BY THE MINUTE!
GET THAT INTO YOUR HEAD, WILL YOU? ACCEPT THE TRUTH!
EXORCISTS DON'T HAVE THE POWER TO ANNIHILATE THE KEGARE!
HA!
?!
SO YOU'VE MET A MILLION PEOPLE WHO'VE SAID THE SAME THING AS ME, HUH?
DON'T YOU GET IT? THAT JUST GOES TO SHOW THAT IN A THOUSAND YEARS YOU HAVEN'T BEEN ABLE TO...
...MAKE US GIVE UP OUR DREAM OF RIDDING THE WORLD OF KEGARE!

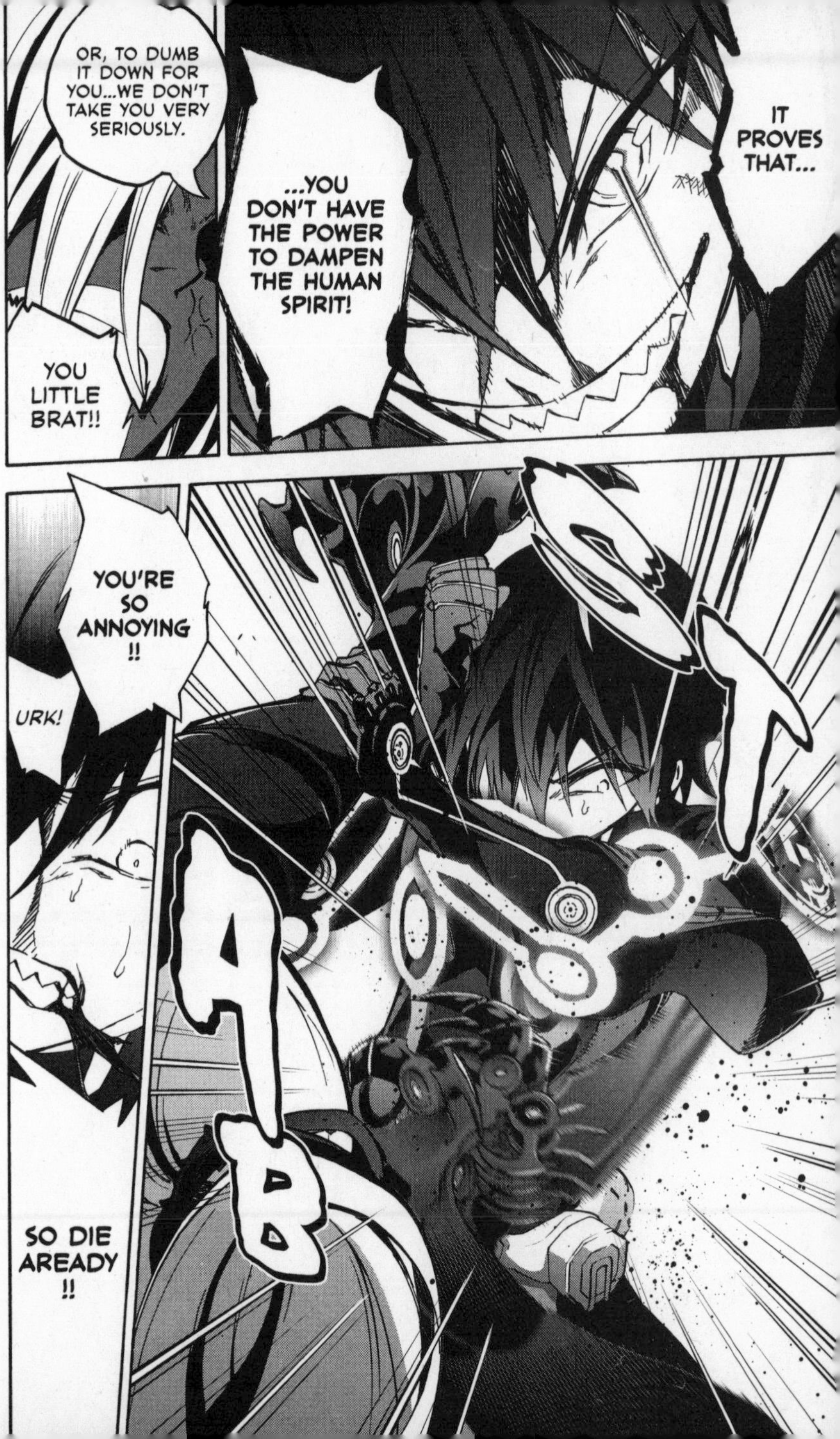
IT PROVES THAT...
...YOU DON'T HAVE THE POWER TO DAMPEN THE HUMAN SPIRIT!
OR, TO DUMB IT DOWN FOR YOU...WE DON'T TAKE YOU VERY SERIOUSLY.
YOU LITTLE BRAT!!
YOU'RE SO ANNOYING !!
URK!
SO DIE AREADY !!

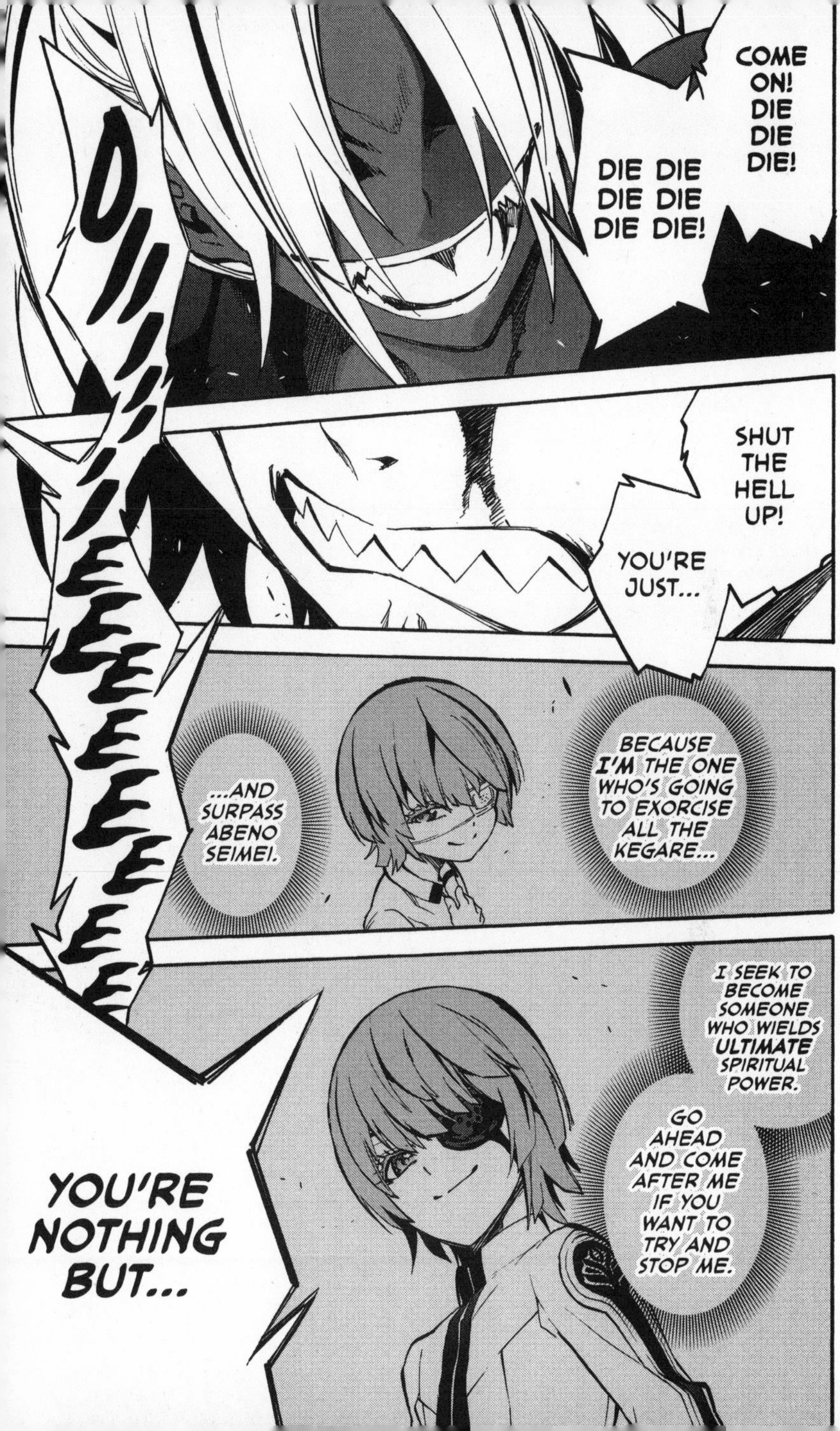
COME ON! DIE DIE DIE!
DIE DIE DIE DIE DIE DIE!
DIIIIEEEEEEEEEE
SHUT THE HELL UP!
YOU'RE JUST...
BECAUSE I'M THE ONE WHO'S GOING TO EXORCISE ALL THE KEGARE...
...AND SURPASS ABENO SEIMEI.
I SEEK TO BECOME SOMEONE WHO WIELDS ULTIMATE SPIRITUAL POWER.
GO AHEAD AND COME AFTER ME IF YOU WANT TO TRY AND STOP ME.
YOU'RE NOTHING BUT...

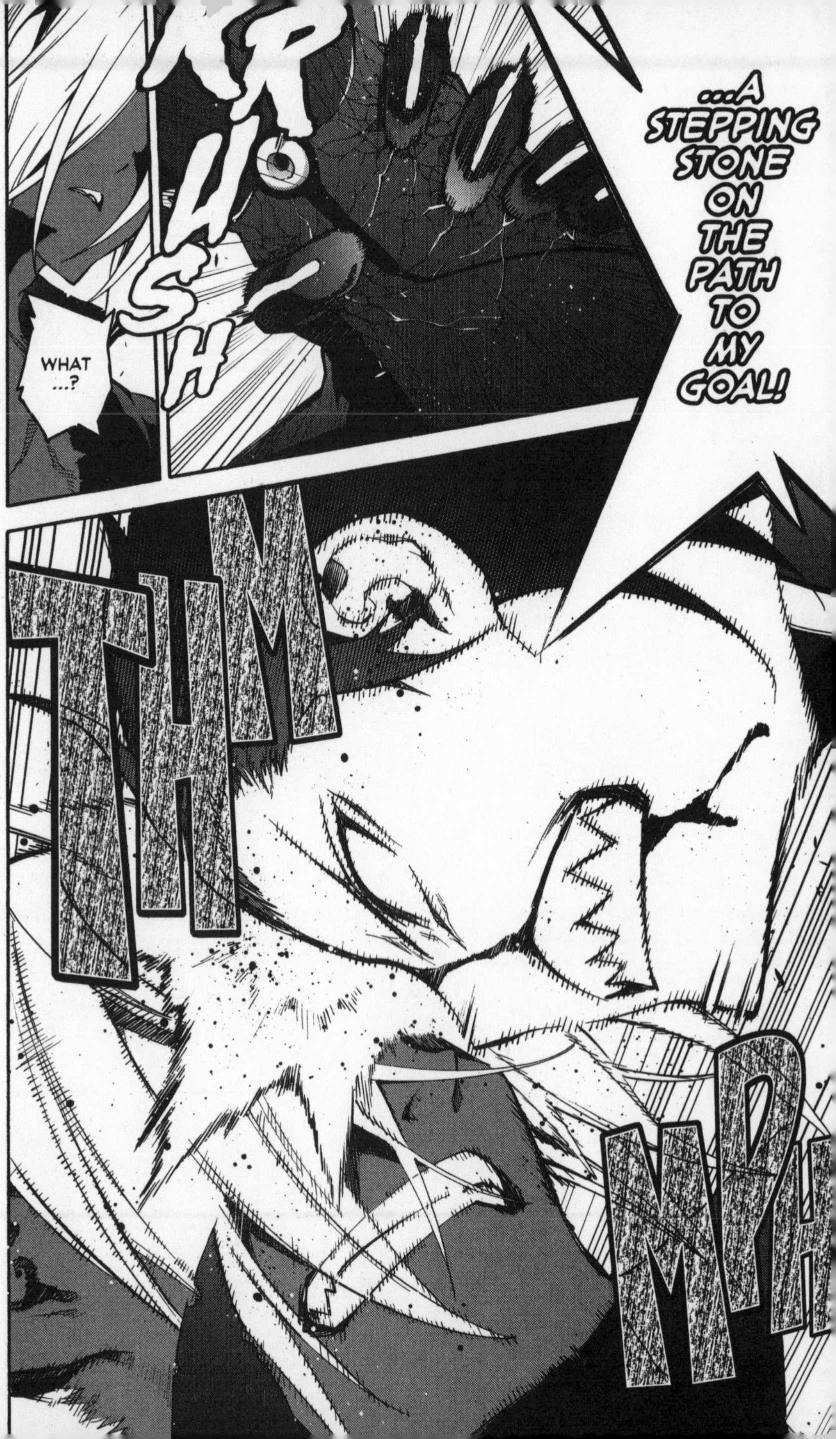
...A STEPPING STONE ON THE PATH TO MY GOAL!
KRUSH
WHAT ...?
THM
MP

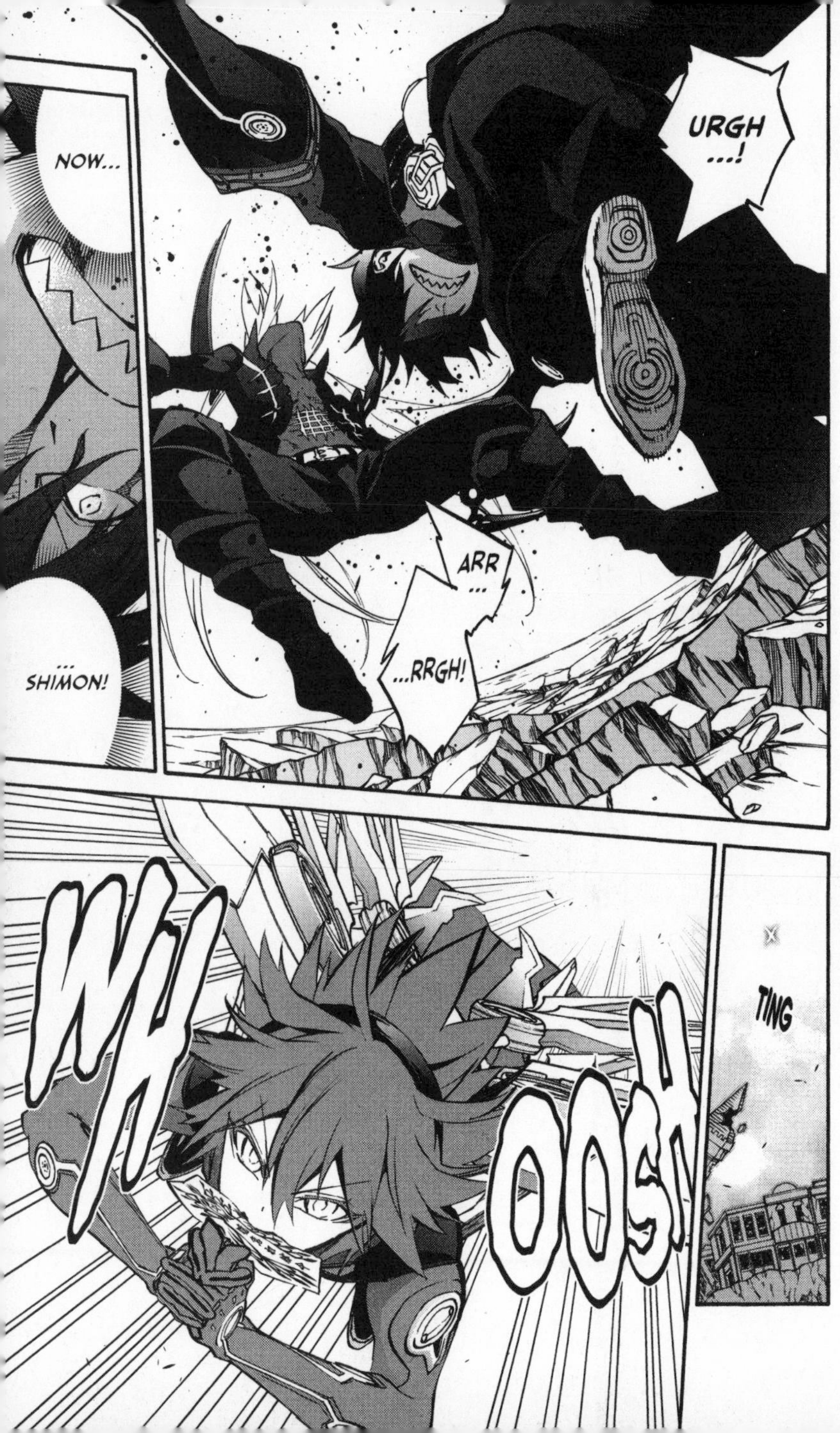
URGH...!
ARR...
...RRGH!
NOW...
...SHIMON!
TING
WHOOSH

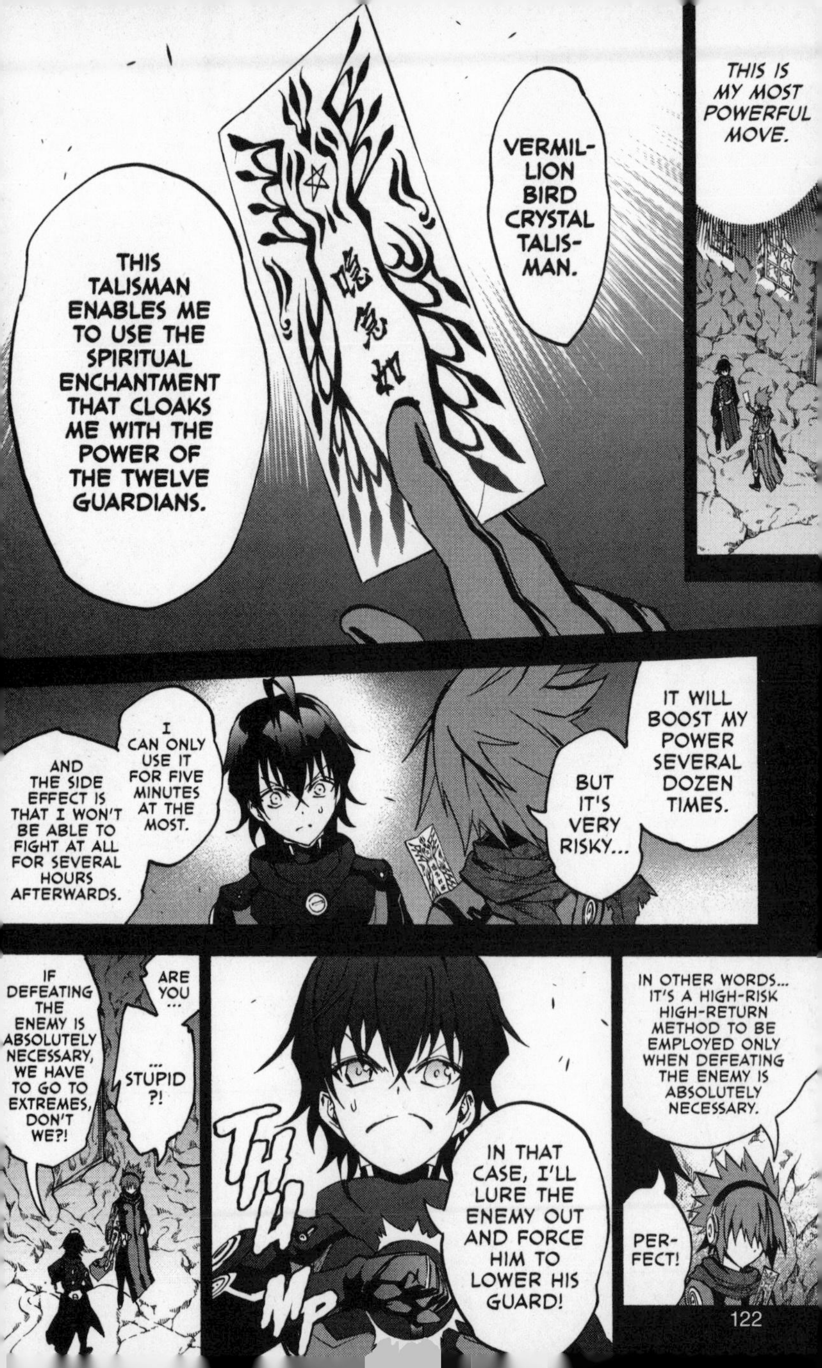
THIS IS MY MOST POWERFUL MOVE.
VERMIL-LION BIRD CRYSTAL TALIS-MAN.
THIS TALISMAN ENABLES ME TO USE THE SPIRITUAL ENCHANTMENT THAT CLOAKS ME WITH THE POWER OF THE TWELVE GUARDIANS.
IT WILL BOOST MY POWER SEVERAL DOZEN TIMES.
BUT IT'S VERY RISKY...
I CAN ONLY USE IT FOR FIVE MINUTES AT THE MOST.
AND THE SIDE EFFECT IS THAT I WON'T BE ABLE TO FIGHT AT ALL FOR SEVERAL HOURS AFTERWARDS.
IN OTHER WORDS... IT'S A HIGH-RISK HIGH-RETURN METHOD TO BE EMPLOYED ONLY WHEN DEFEATING THE ENEMY IS ABSOLUTELY NECESSARY.
PER-FECT!
IN THAT CASE, I'LL LURE THE ENEMY OUT AND FORCE HIM TO LOWER HIS GUARD!
THUMP
ARE YOU...
...STUPID?!
IF DEFEATING THE ENEMY IS ABSOLUTELY NECESSARY, WE HAVE TO GO TO EXTREMES, DON'T WE?!

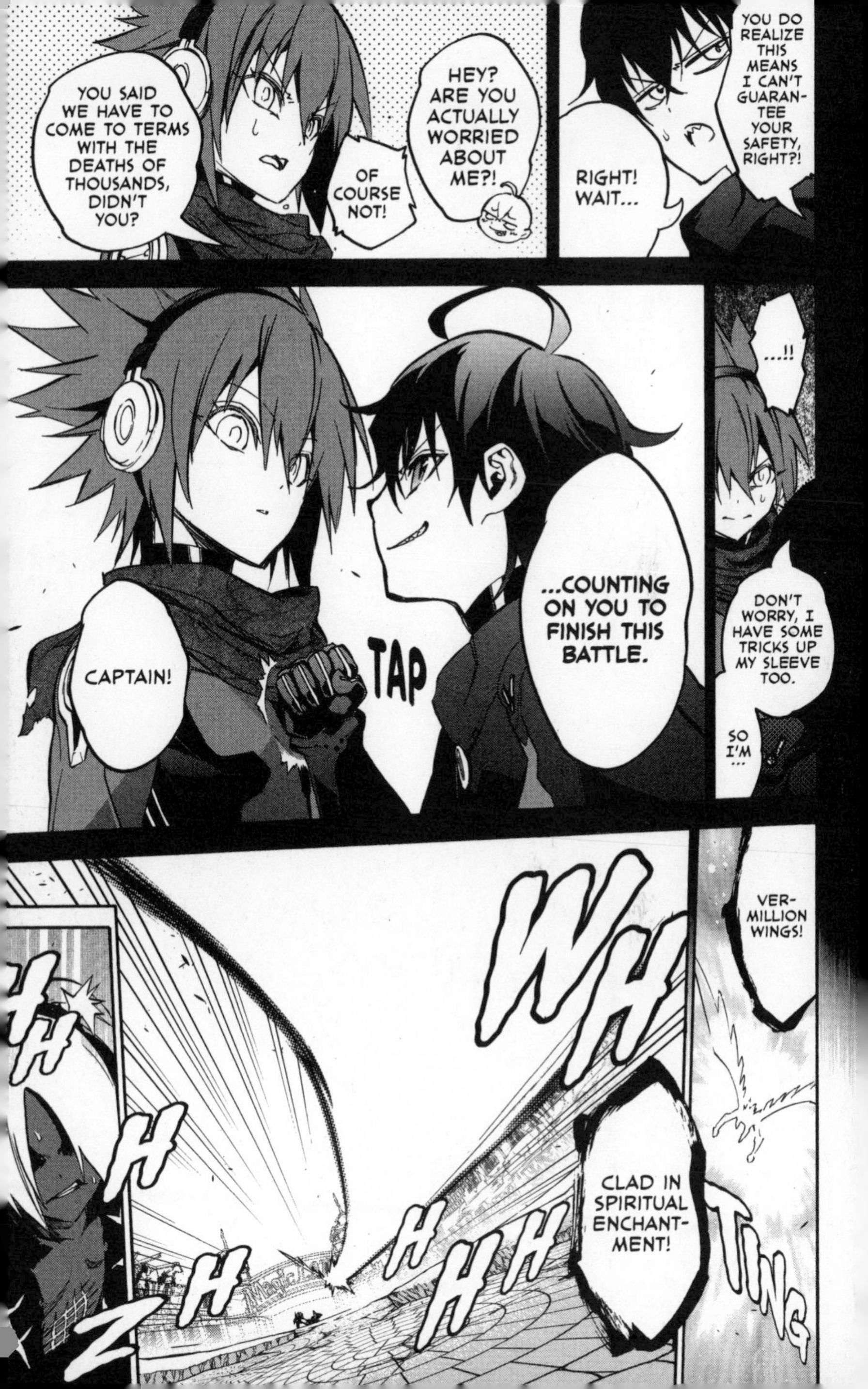
YOU DO REALIZE THIS MEANS I CAN'T GUARAN-TEE YOUR SAFETY, RIGHT?!
RIGHT! WAIT...
HEY? ARE YOU ACTUALLY WORRIED ABOUT ME?!
OF COURSE NOT!
YOU SAID WE HAVE TO COME TO TERMS WITH THE DEATHS OF THOUSANDS, DIDN'T YOU?
...!!
DON'T WORRY, I HAVE SOME TRICKS UP MY SLEEVE TOO.
SO I'M...
...COUNTING ON YOU TO FINISH THIS BATTLE.
TAP
CAPTAIN!
VER-MILLION WINGS!
WH
CLAD IN SPIRITUAL ENCHANT-MENT!
TING

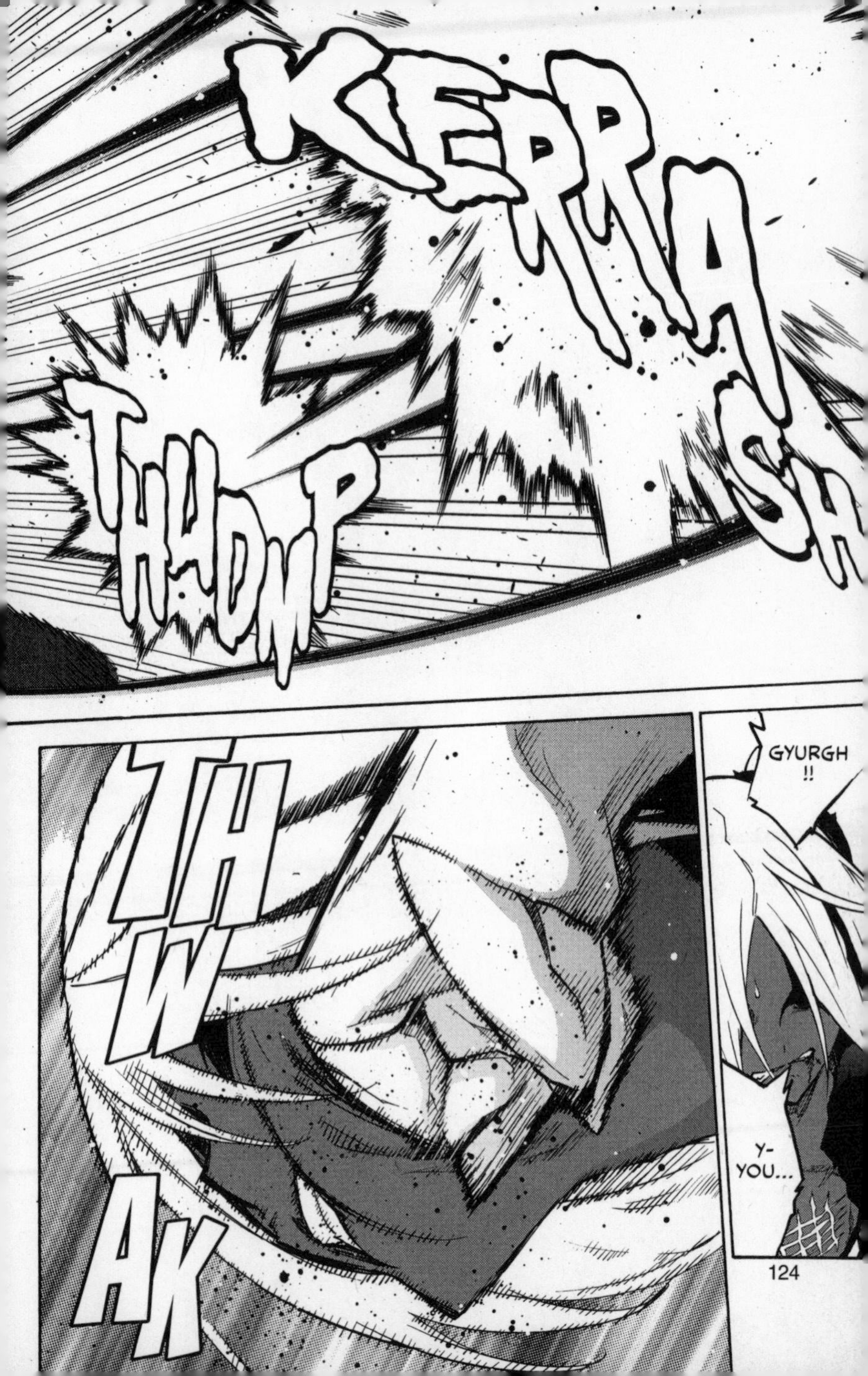
KERRASH
THUDMP
GYURGH !!
Y- YOU...
THWAK

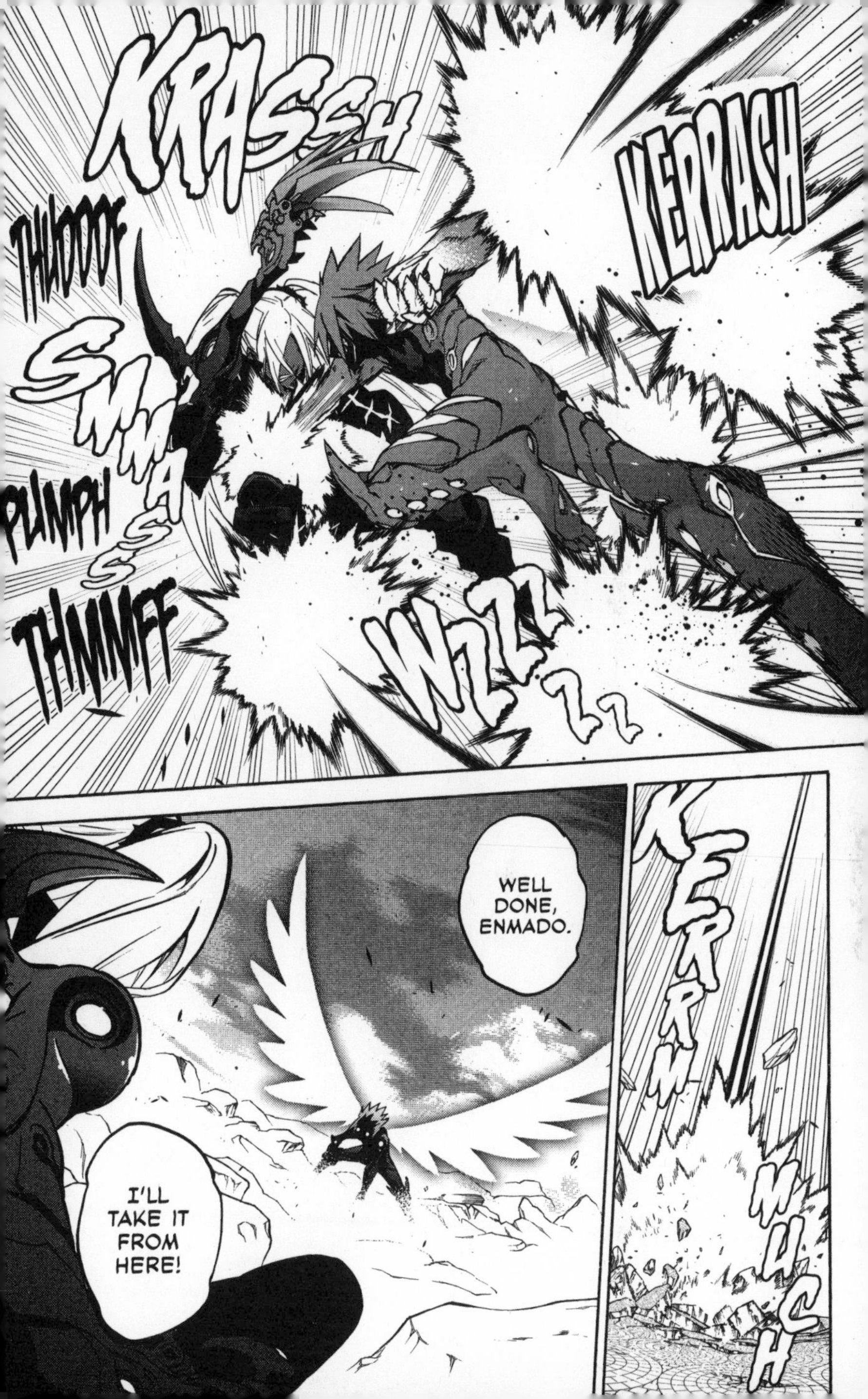
KERRASH
KRASSH
THUDOOF
SMMASSS
THMMFF
WZZZZZ
WELL DONE, ENMADO.
I'LL TAKE IT FROM HERE!

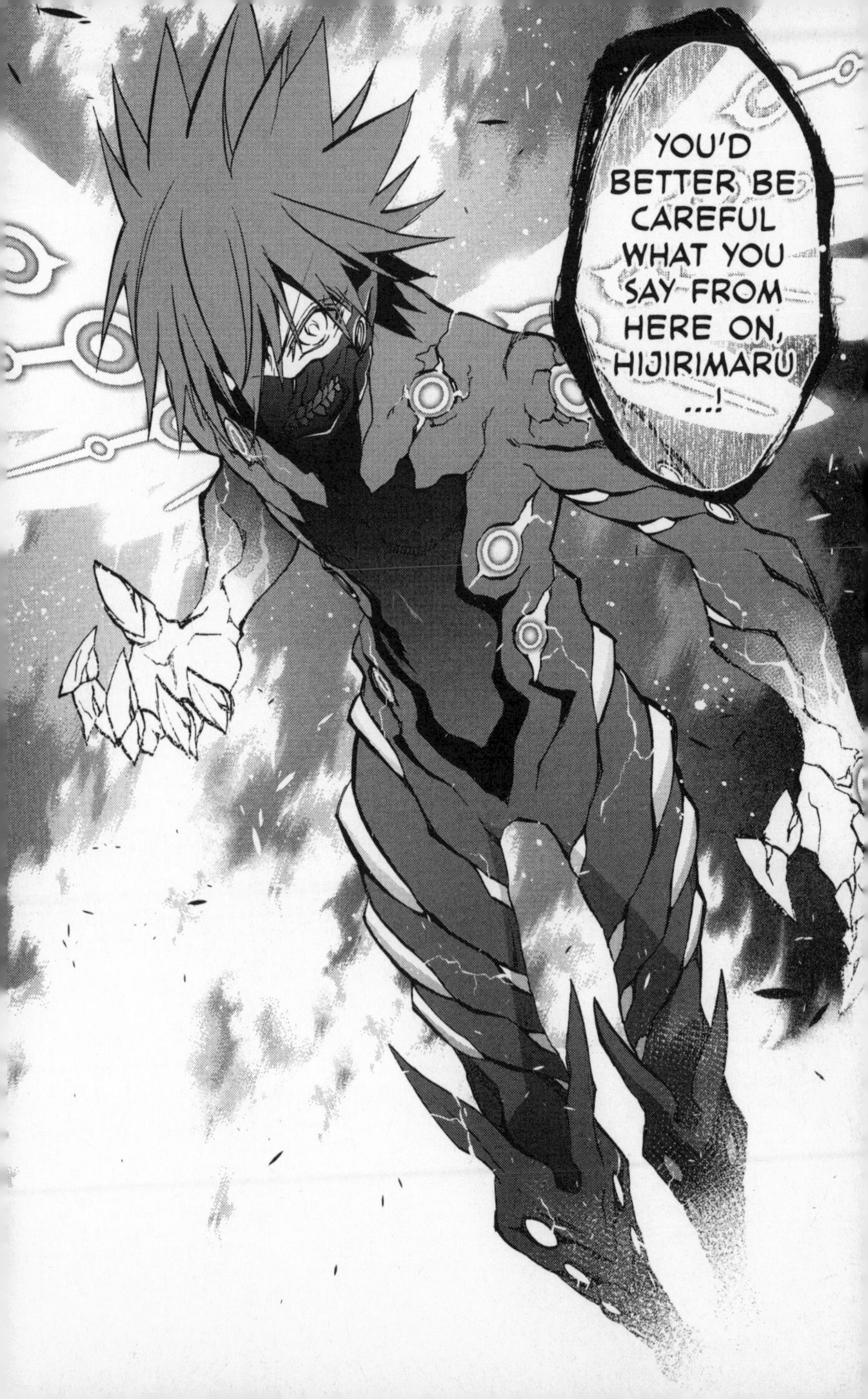
YOU'D BETTER BE CAREFUL WHAT YOU SAY FROM HERE ON, HIJIRIMARU ...!

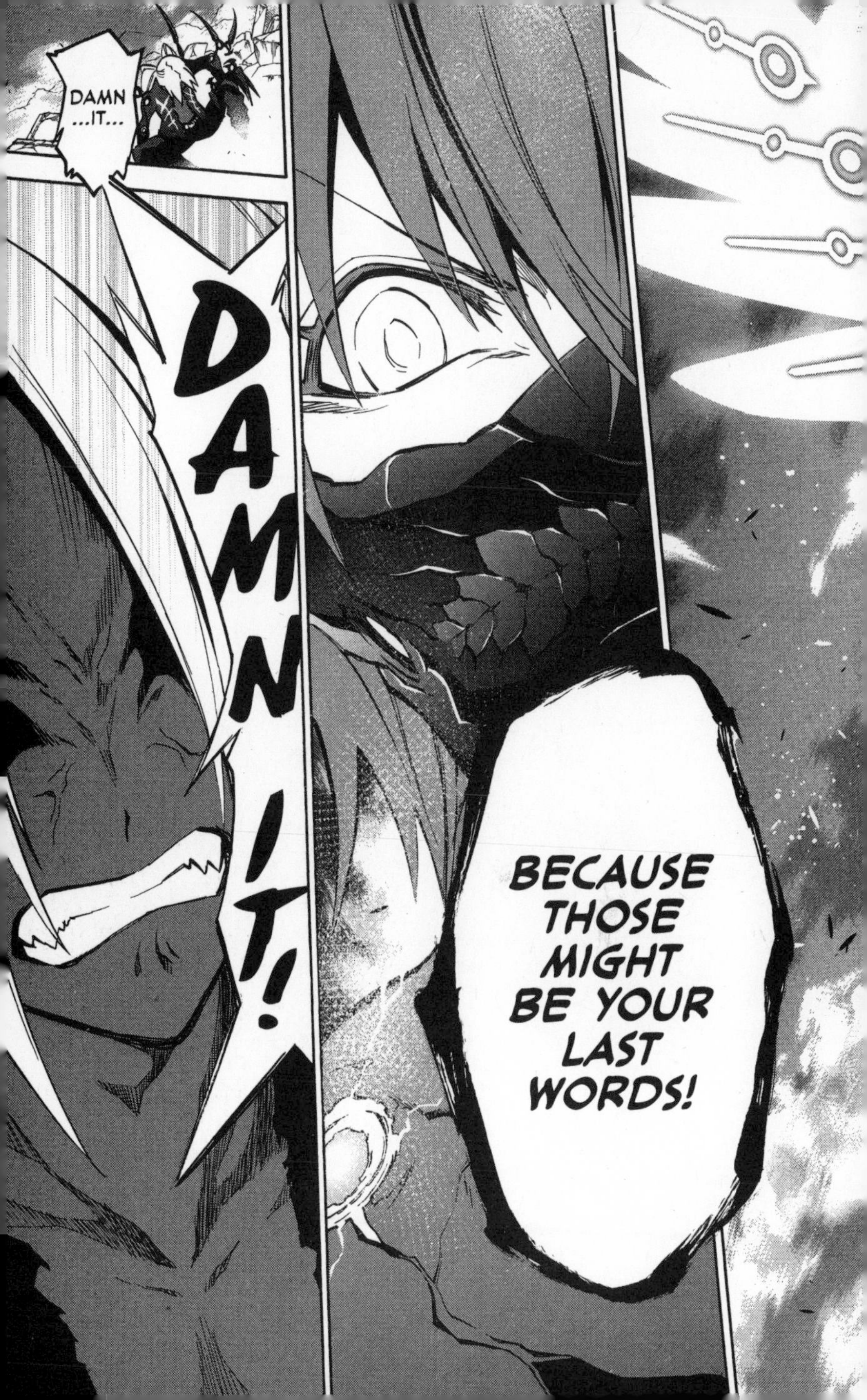
BECAUSE THOSE MIGHT BE YOUR LAST WORDS!
DAMN ...IT...
DAMNIT!

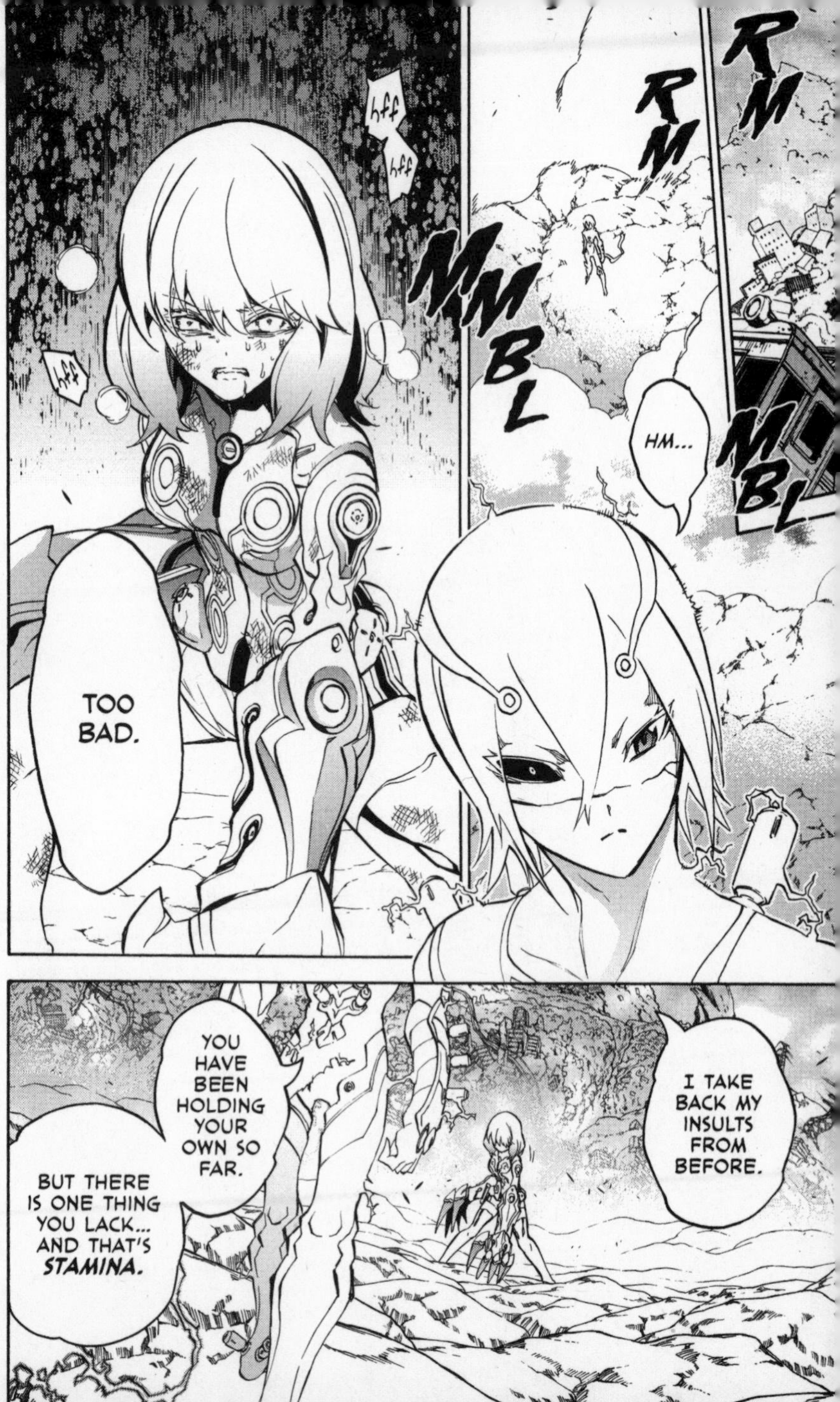
RM
MMBL
RM
HM...
MMMBL
hff
hff
hff
TOO BAD.
I TAKE BACK MY INSULTS FROM BEFORE.
YOU HAVE BEEN HOLDING YOUR OWN SO FAR.
BUT THERE IS ONE THING YOU LACK... AND THAT'S *STAMINA*.

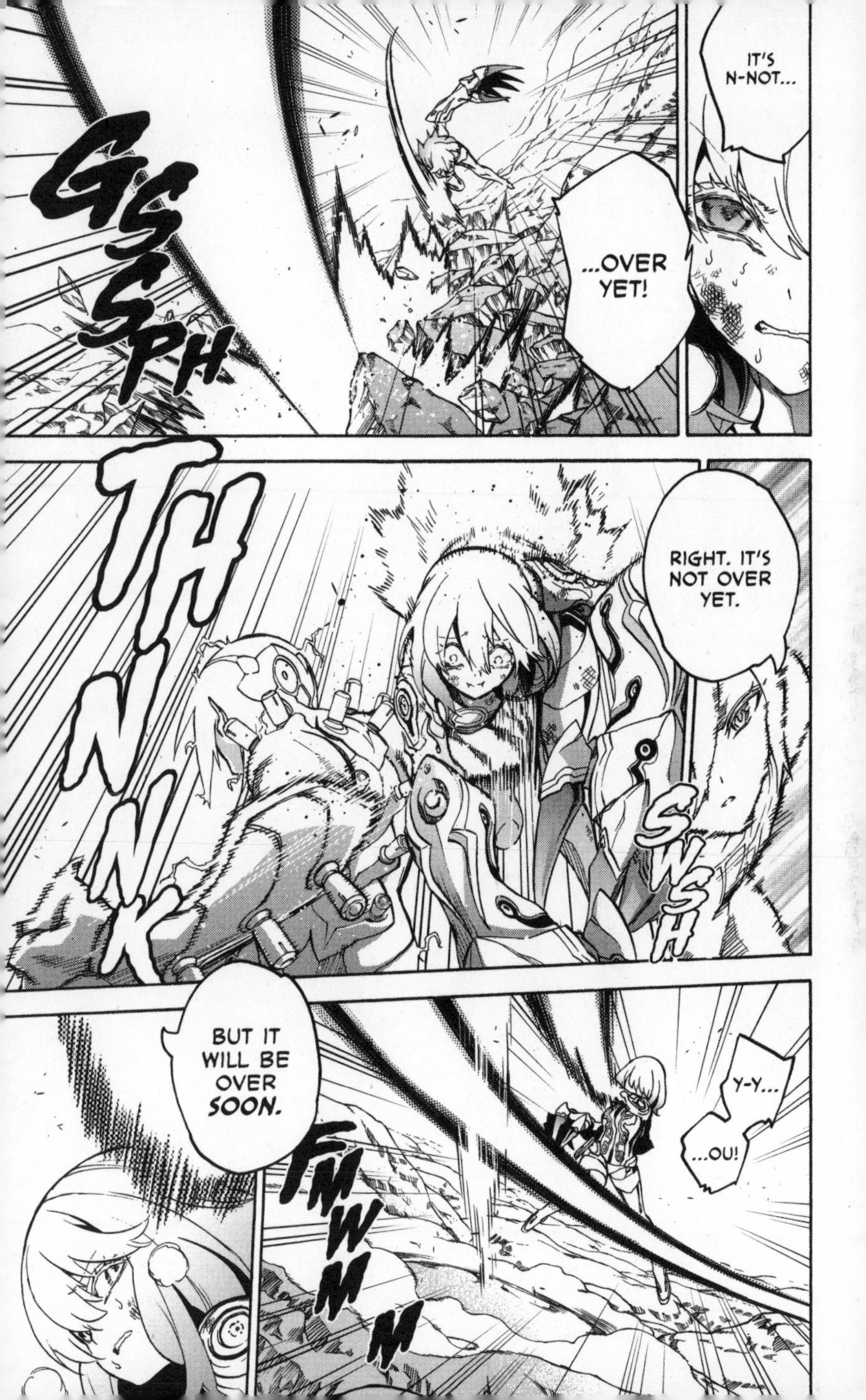
IT'S N-NOT...
...OVER YET!
GSSPH
RIGHT. IT'S NOT OVER YET.
SWSH
THNNK
Y-Y...
...OU!
BUT IT WILL BE OVER SOON.
FMWMM

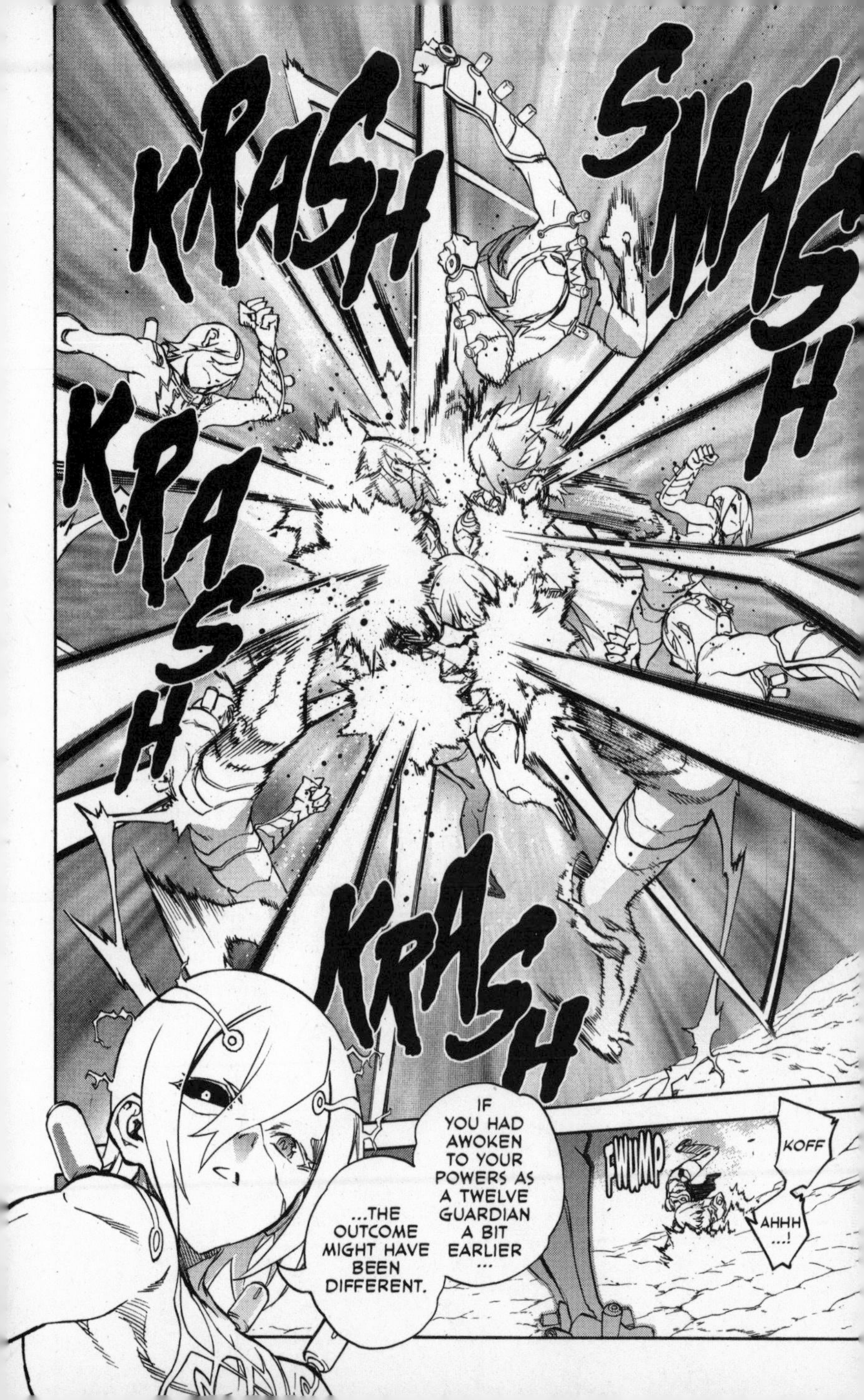
SMASH
KRASH
KRASH
KRASH
KOFF
FWUMP
AHHH ...!
IF YOU HAD AWOKEN TO YOUR POWERS AS A TWELVE GUARDIAN A BIT EARLIER ...
...THE OUTCOME MIGHT HAVE BEEN DIFFERENT.

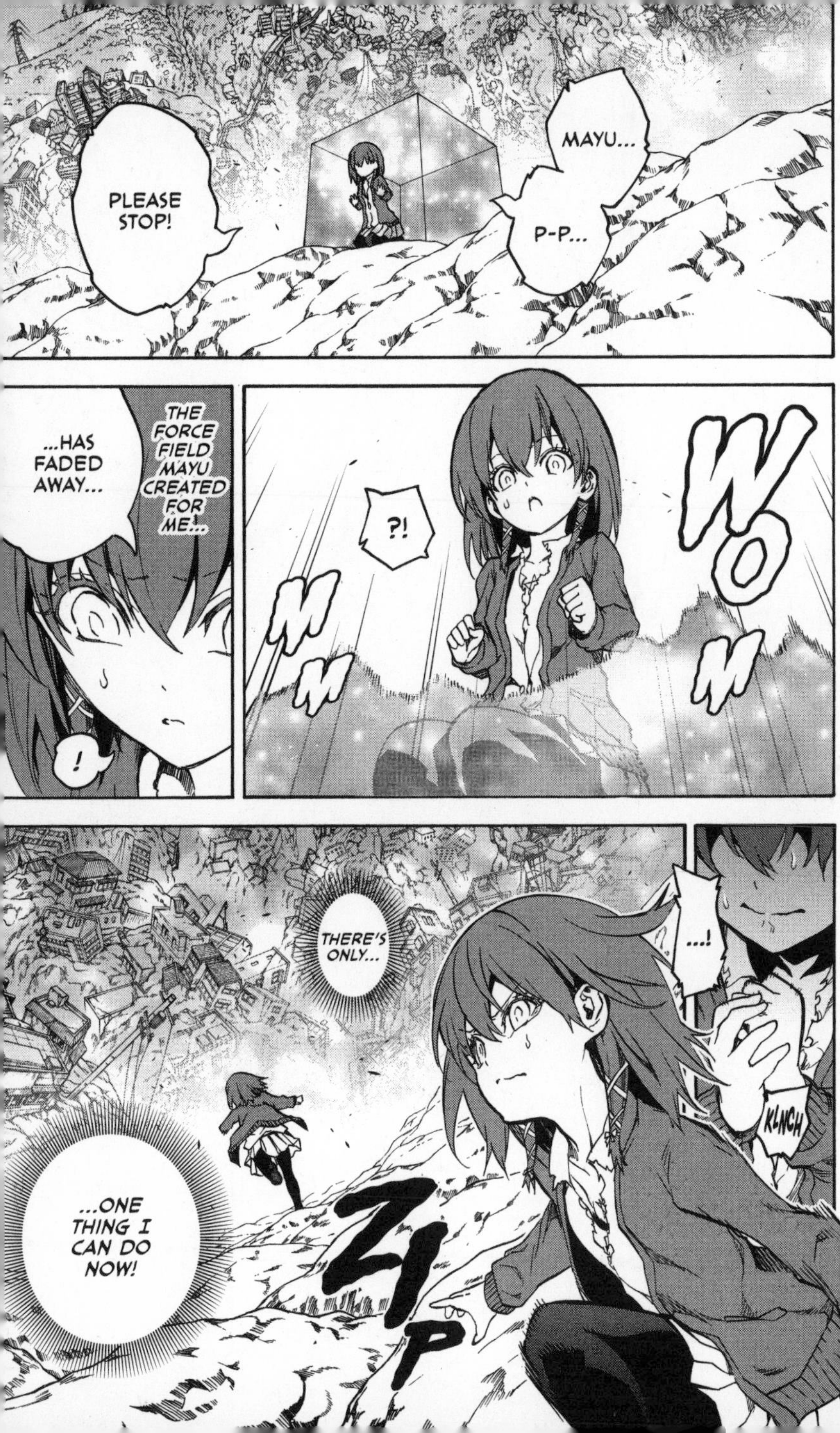
MAYU...
P-P...
PLEASE STOP!
WOMM
?!
THE FORCE FIELD MAYU CREATED FOR ME...
...HAS FADED AWAY...
!
...!
KLNCH
THERE'S ONLY...
...ONE THING I CAN DO NOW!
ZIP

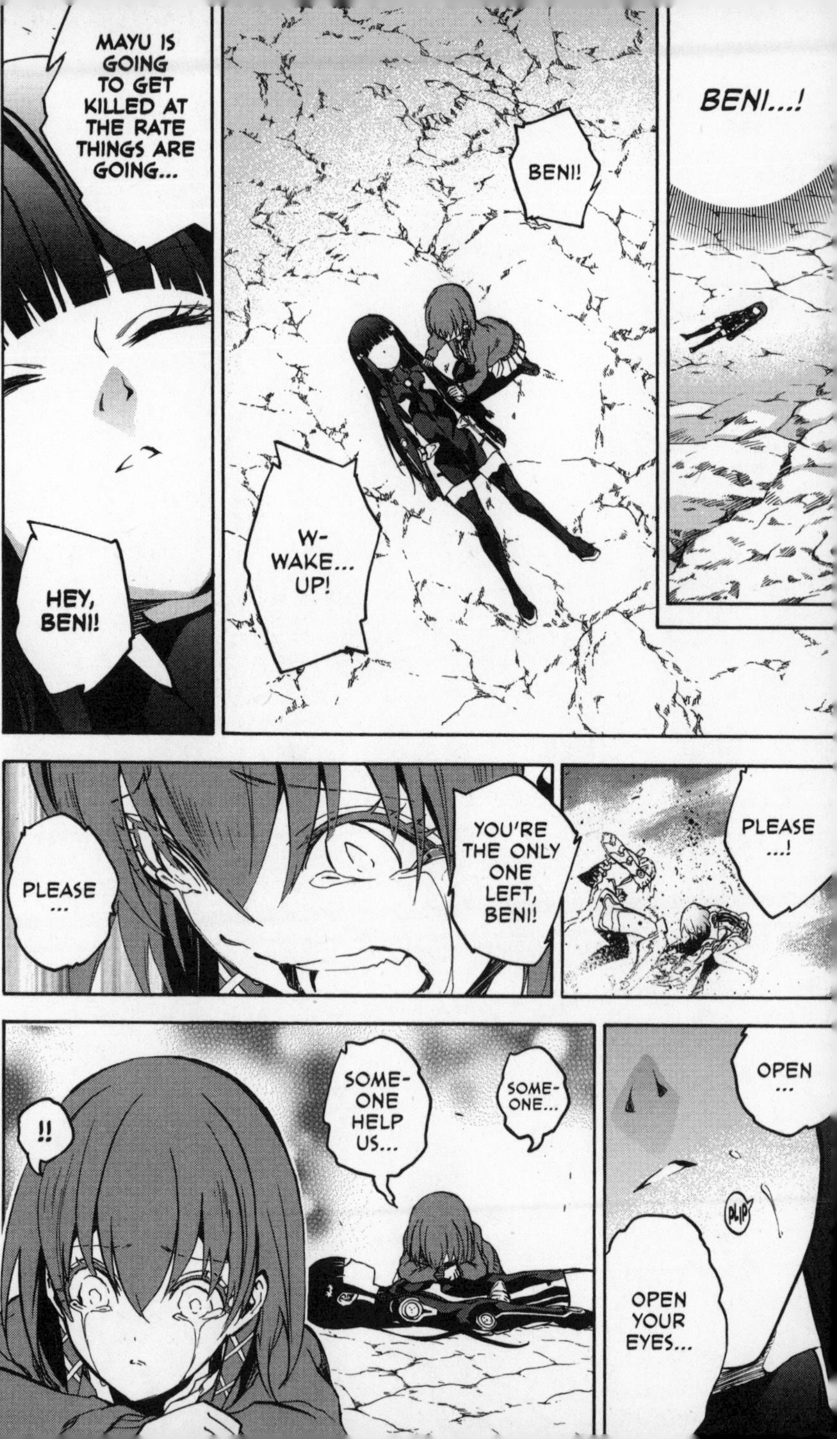
BENI...!
BENI!
W-WAKE... UP!
MAYU IS GOING TO GET KILLED AT THE RATE THINGS ARE GOING...
HEY, BENI!
PLEASE...!
YOU'RE THE ONLY ONE LEFT, BENI!
PLEASE...
OPEN...
PLIP
OPEN YOUR EYES...
SOME-ONE...
SOME-ONE HELP US...
!!

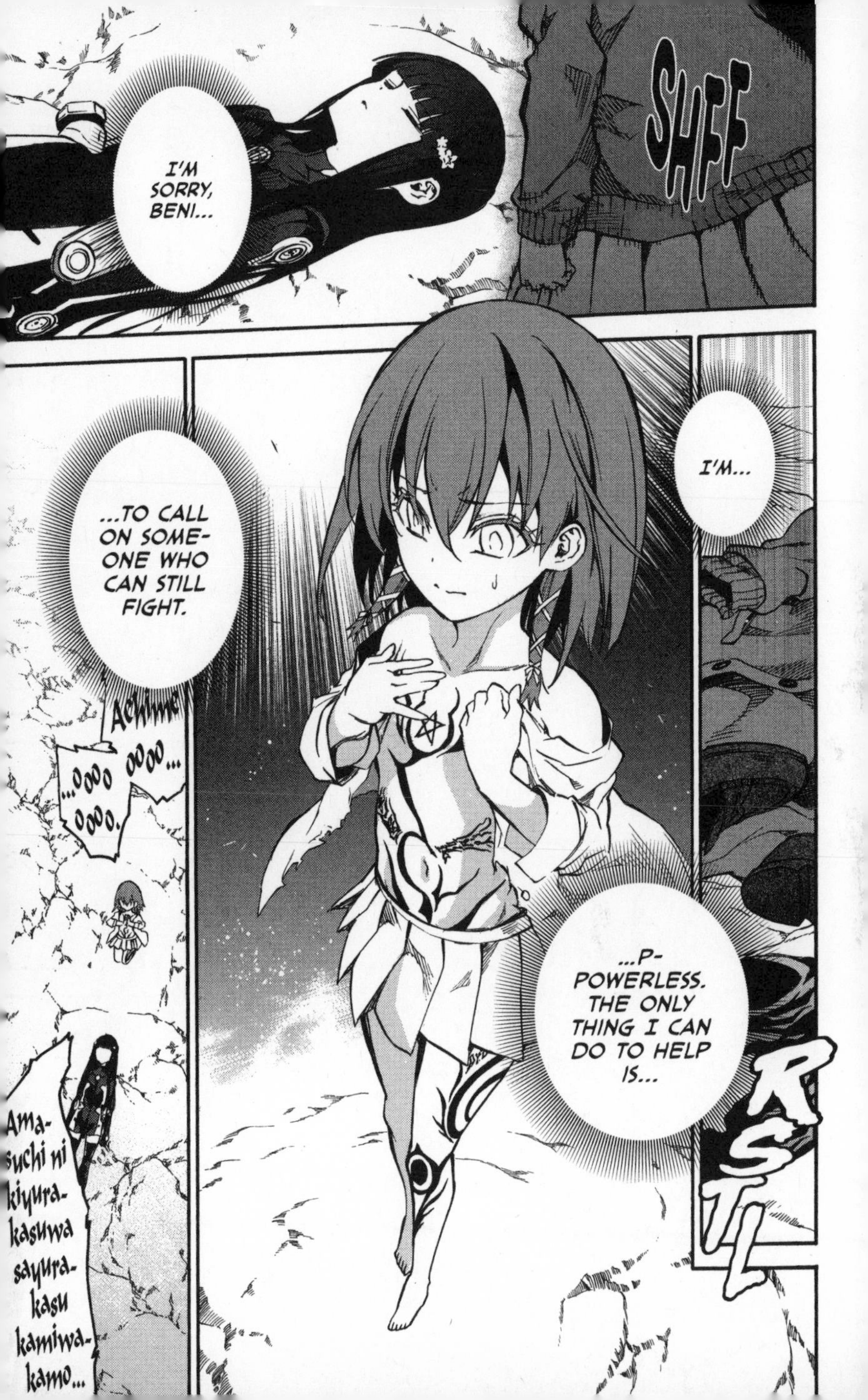
SHFF
I'M SORRY, BENI...
I'M...
...P-POWERLESS. THE ONLY THING I CAN DO TO HELP IS...
RSTL
...TO CALL ON SOME-ONE WHO CAN STILL FIGHT.
Achime
...oooo oooo... oooo.
Ama-suchi ni kiyura-kasuwa sayura-kasu kamiwa-kamo...

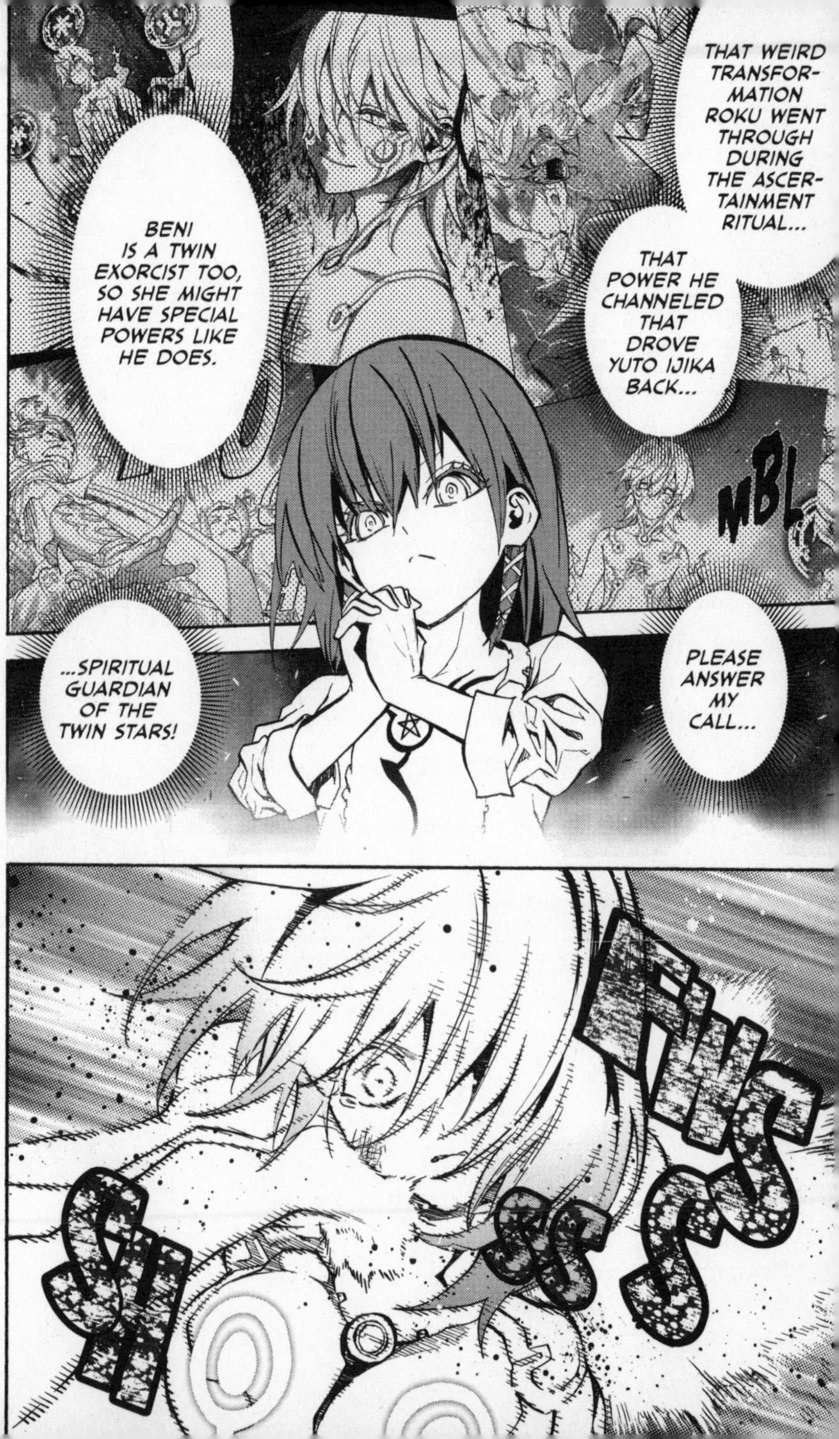
THAT WEIRD TRANSFORMATION ROKU WENT THROUGH DURING THE ASCERTAINMENT RITUAL...
THAT POWER HE CHANNELED THAT DROVE YUTO IJIKA BACK...
BENI IS A TWIN EXORCIST TOO, SO SHE MIGHT HAVE SPECIAL POWERS LIKE HE DOES.
MBL
PLEASE ANSWER MY CALL...
...SPIRITUAL GUARDIAN OF THE TWIN STARS!

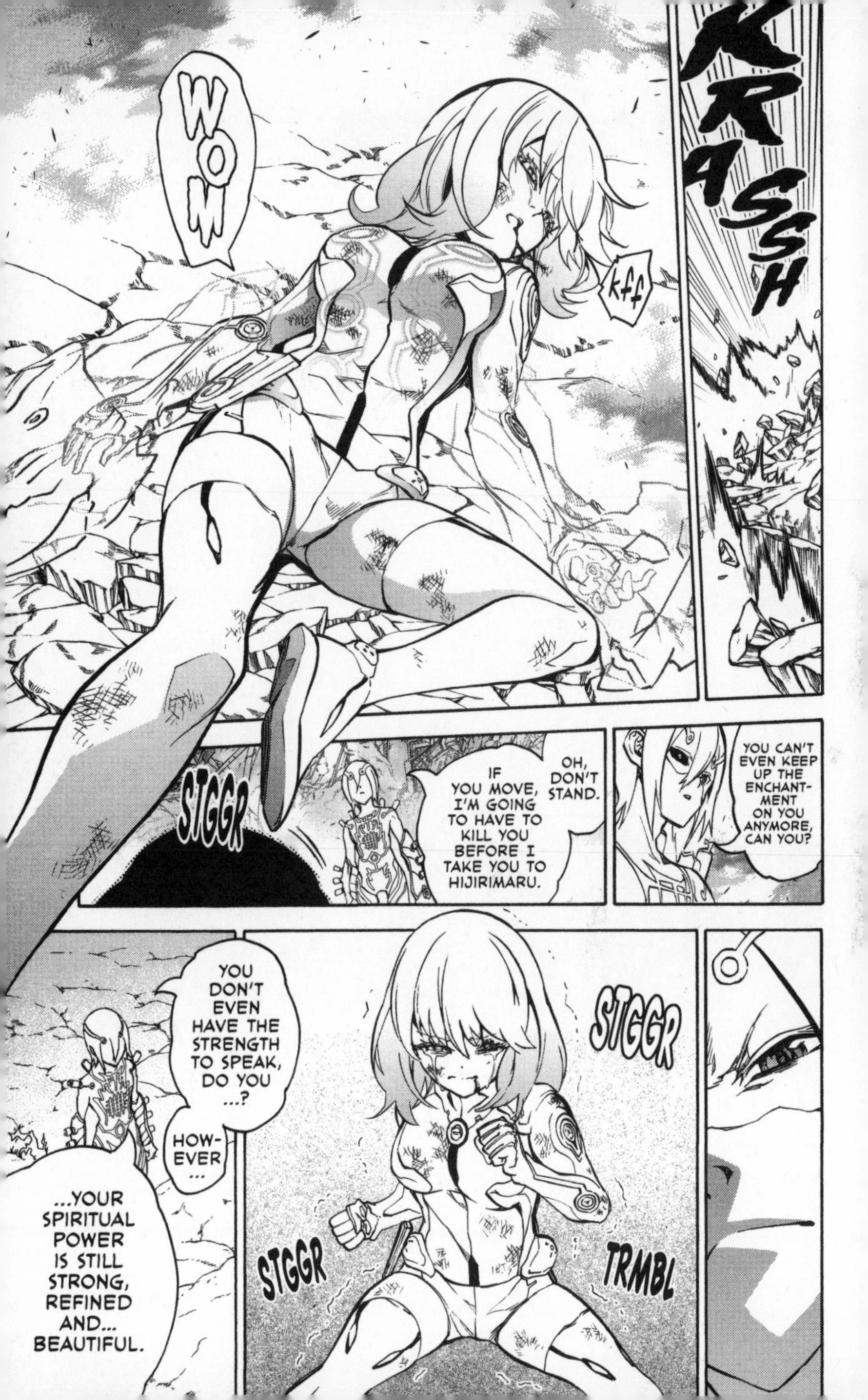

KRASSH
WOW
kff
YOU CAN'T EVEN KEEP UP THE ENCHANTMENT ON YOU ANYMORE, CAN YOU?
OH, DON'T STAND.
IF YOU MOVE, I'M GOING TO HAVE TO KILL YOU BEFORE I TAKE YOU TO HIJIRIMARU.
STGGR
STGGR
YOU DON'T EVEN HAVE THE STRENGTH TO SPEAK, DO YOU ...?
HOWEVER ...
TRMBL
STGGR
...YOUR SPIRITUAL POWER IS STILL STRONG, REFINED AND... BEAUTIFUL.

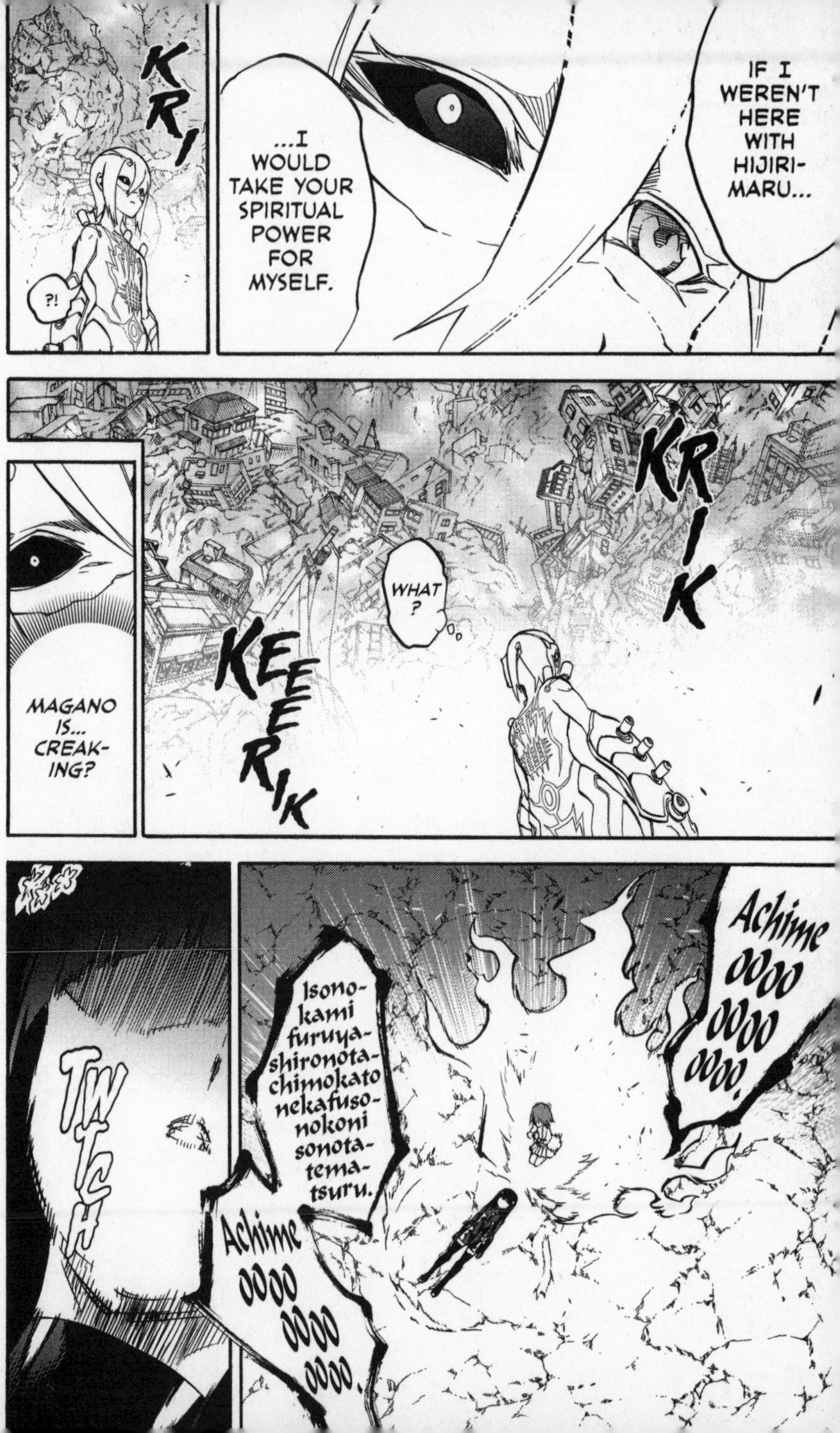
IF I WEREN'T HERE WITH HIJIRI-MARU...
...I WOULD TAKE YOUR SPIRITUAL POWER FOR MYSELF.
KRI
?!
KRRIK
WHAT?
KEEEERIK
MAGANO IS... CREAKING?
Achime oooooooooooo.
Isonokami furuyashironotachimokatonekafusonokoni sonotatematsuru.
Achime oooooooooooo.
TWITCH

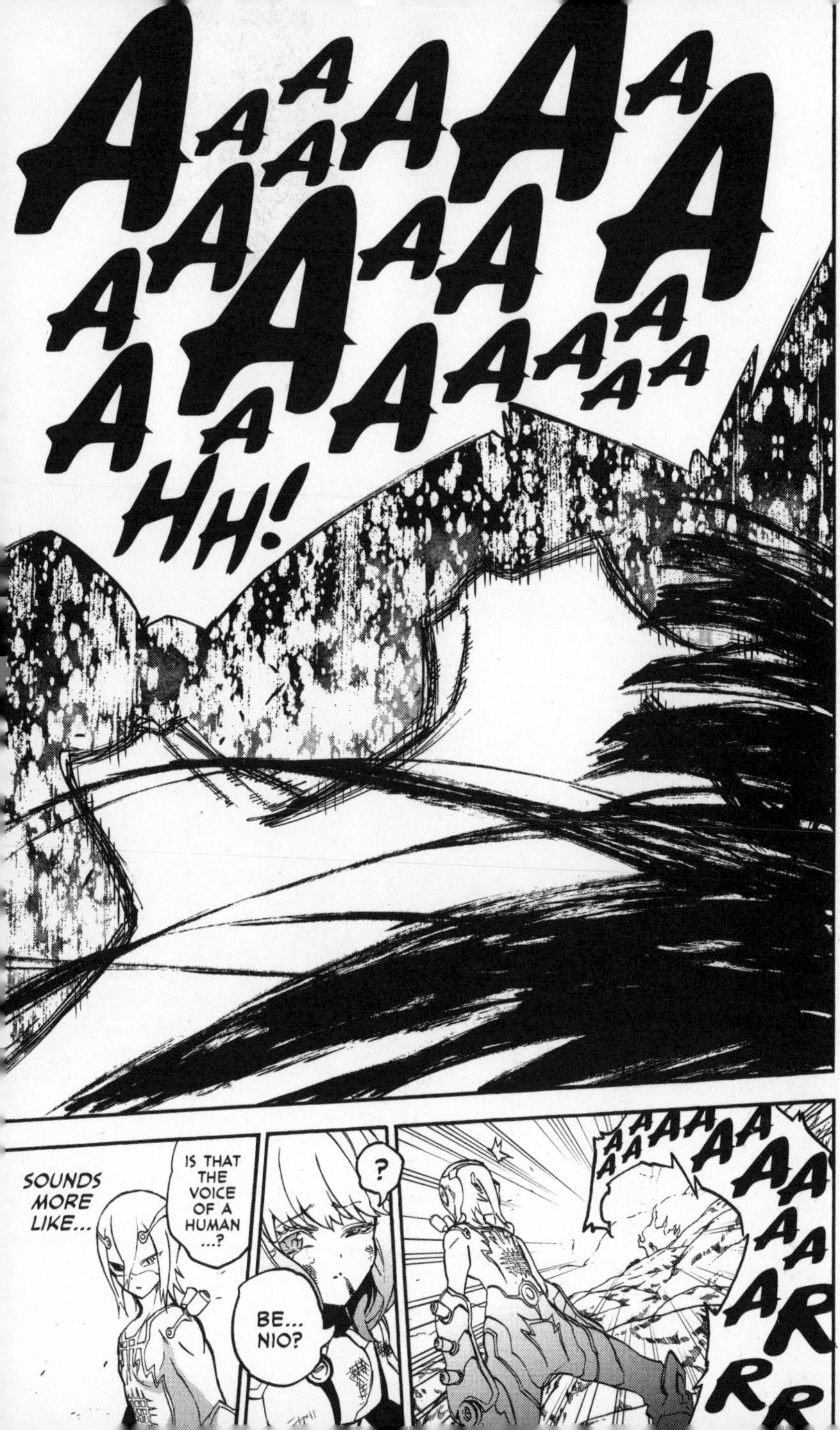

AAAAAAAAAAAAAAAAAAAAAAAAHH!
AAAAAAAAAAARRR
?
IS THAT THE VOICE OF A HUMAN ...?
SOUNDS MORE LIKE...
BE... NIO?

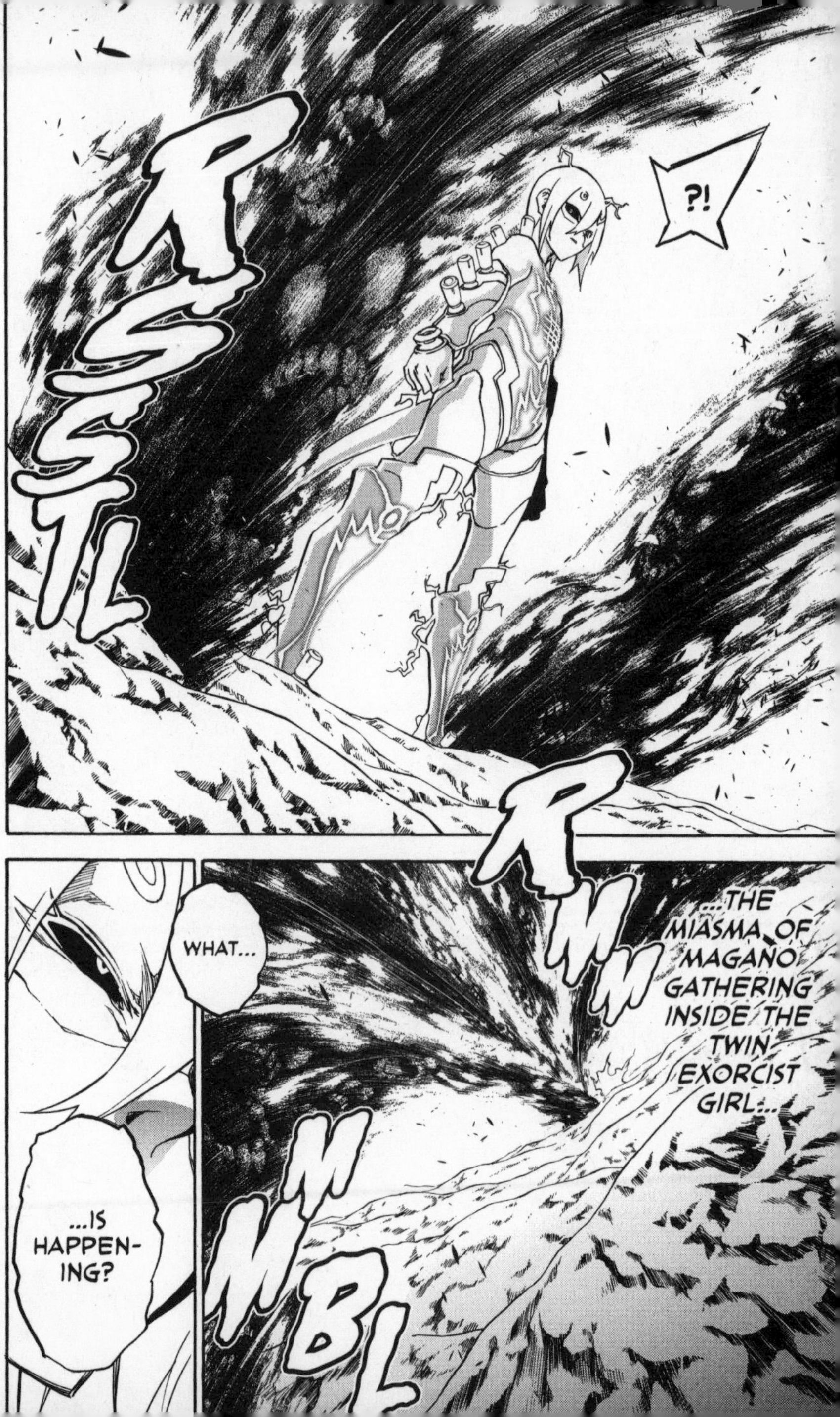
?!
...THE MIASMA OF MAGANO GATHERING INSIDE THE TWIN EXORCIST GIRL...
WHAT...
...IS HAPPENING?

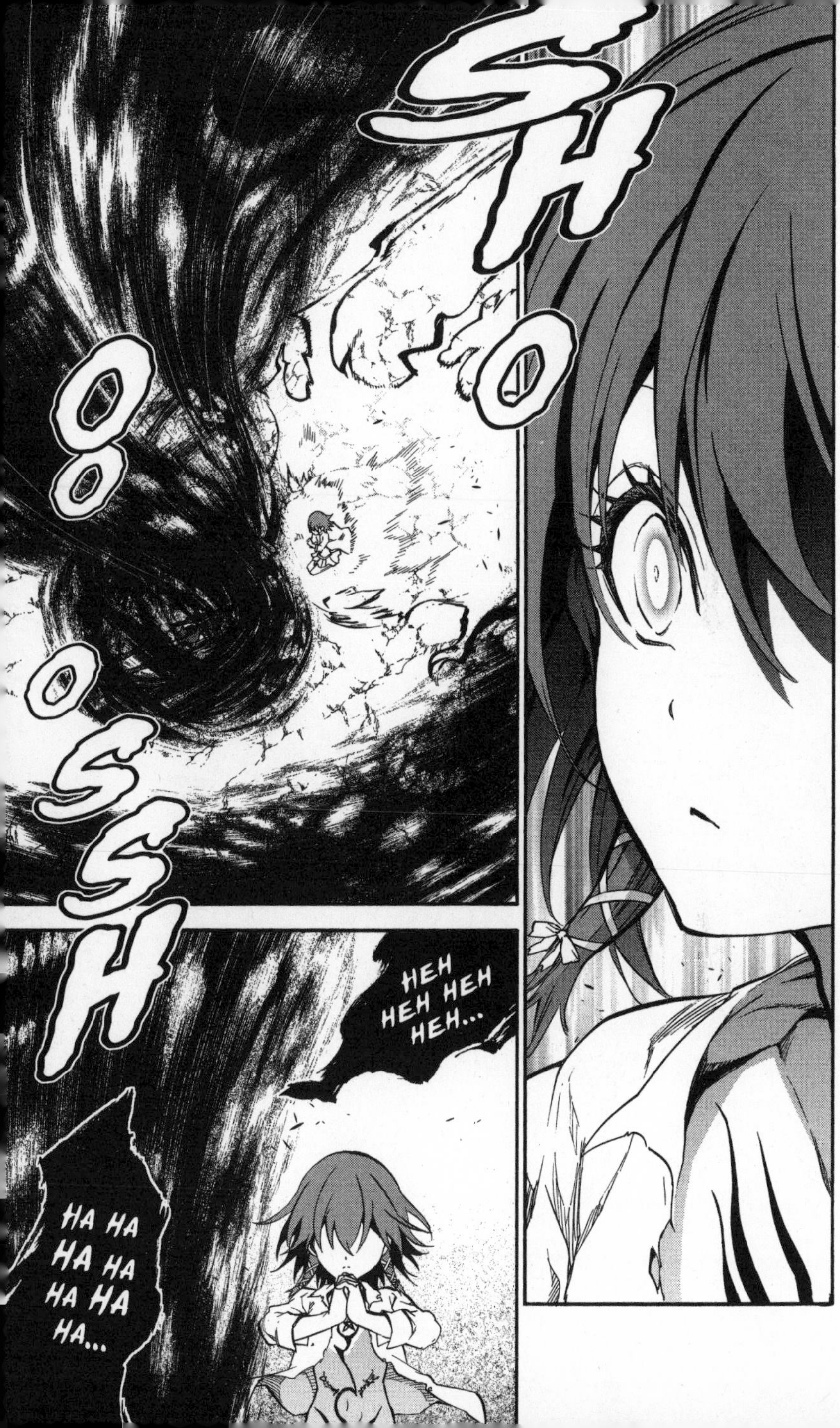
SHOOOOOOSSH
HEH HEH HEH HEH...
HA HA HA HA HA HA HA...

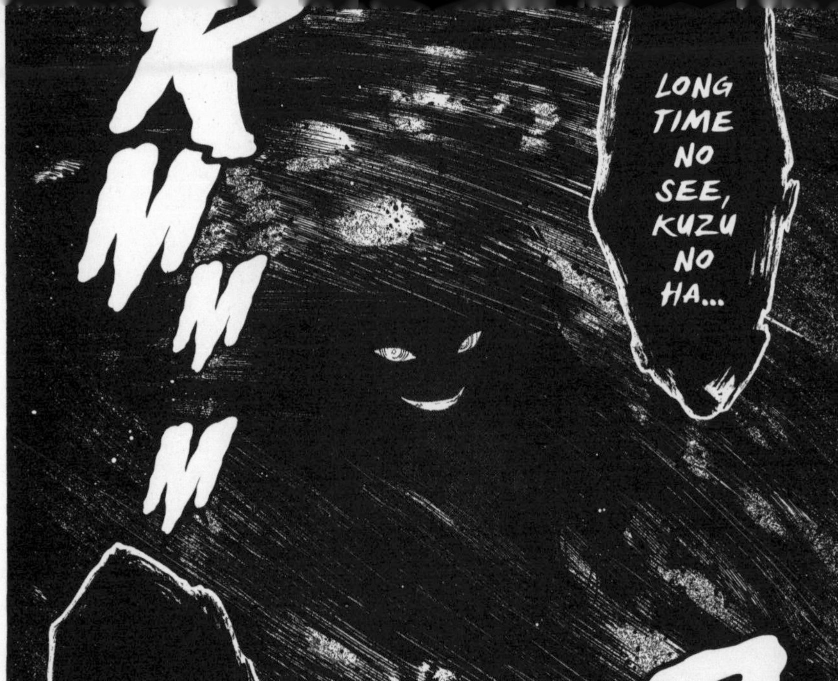
LONG TIME NO SEE, KUZU NO HA...
KMMM
BL
I NEVER EXPECTED YOU TO SUMMON ME LIKE THIS.
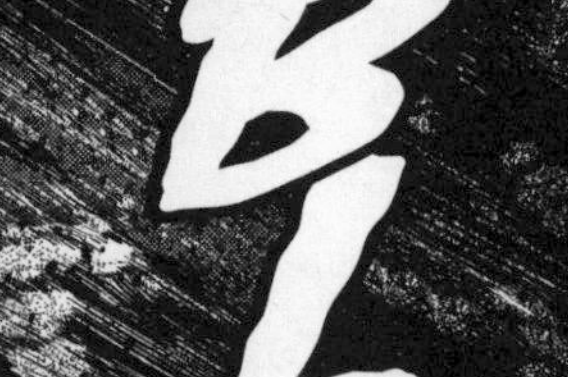
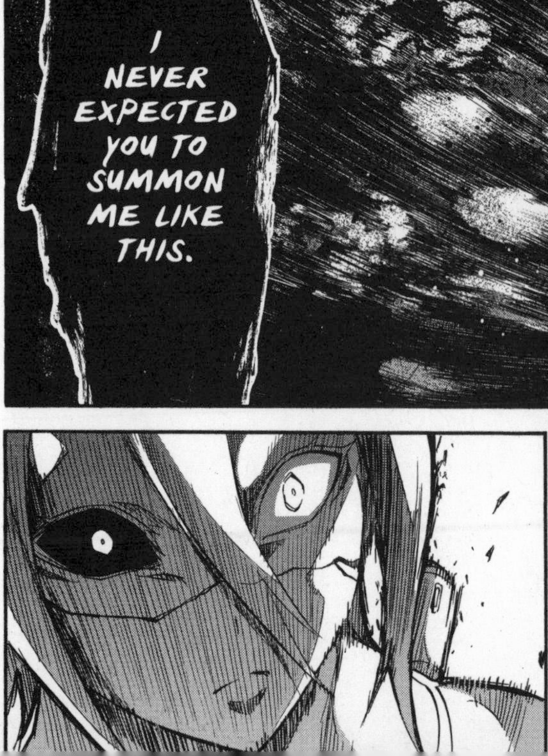

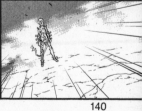

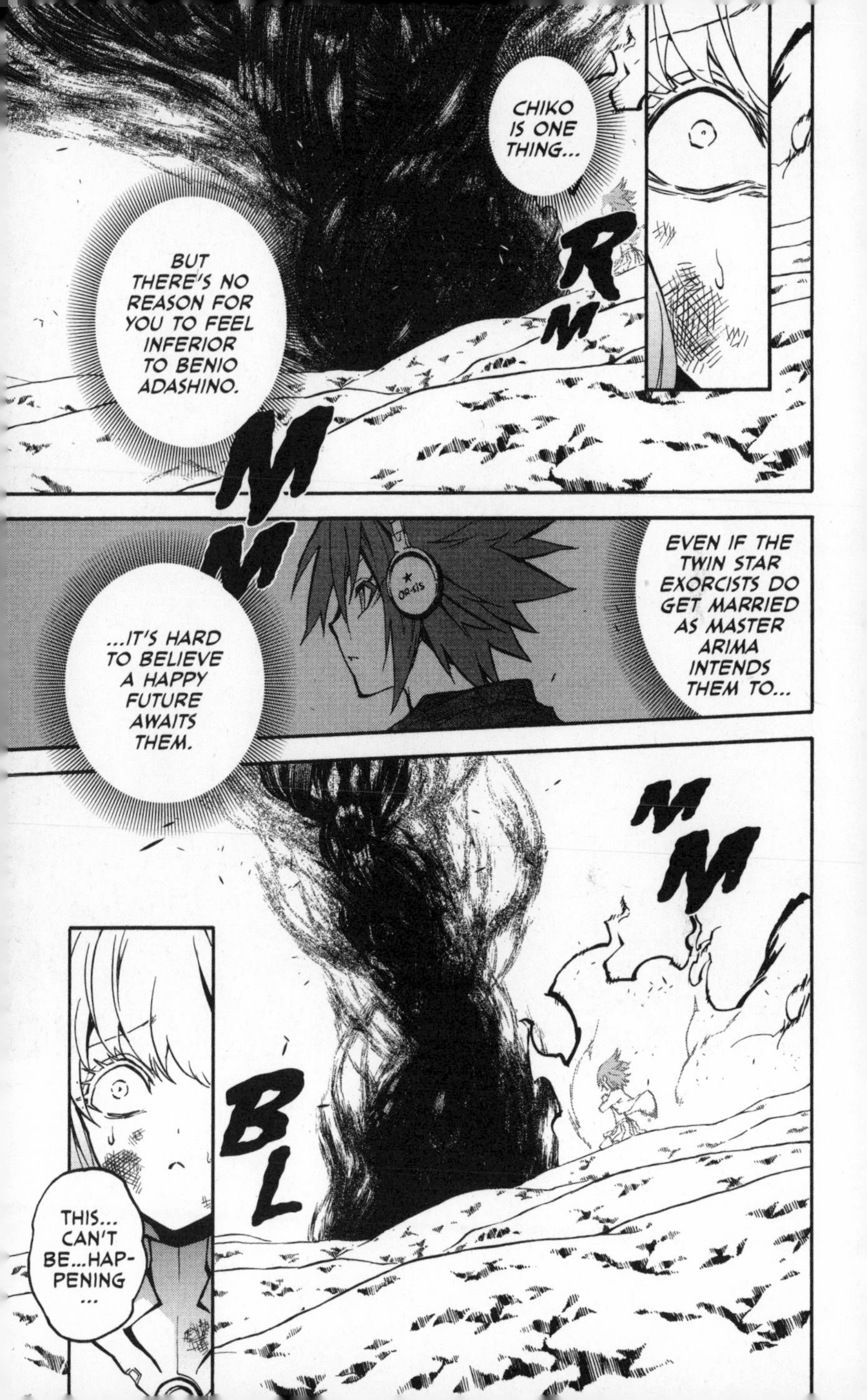
CHIKO IS ONE THING...
RM
BUT THERE'S NO REASON FOR YOU TO FEEL INFERIOR TO BENIO ADASHINO.
MM
EVEN IF THE TWIN STAR EXORCISTS DO GET MARRIED AS MASTER ARIMA INTENDS THEM TO...
...IT'S HARD TO BELIEVE A HAPPY FUTURE AWAITS THEM.
MM
BL
THIS... CAN'T BE...HAP-PENING...

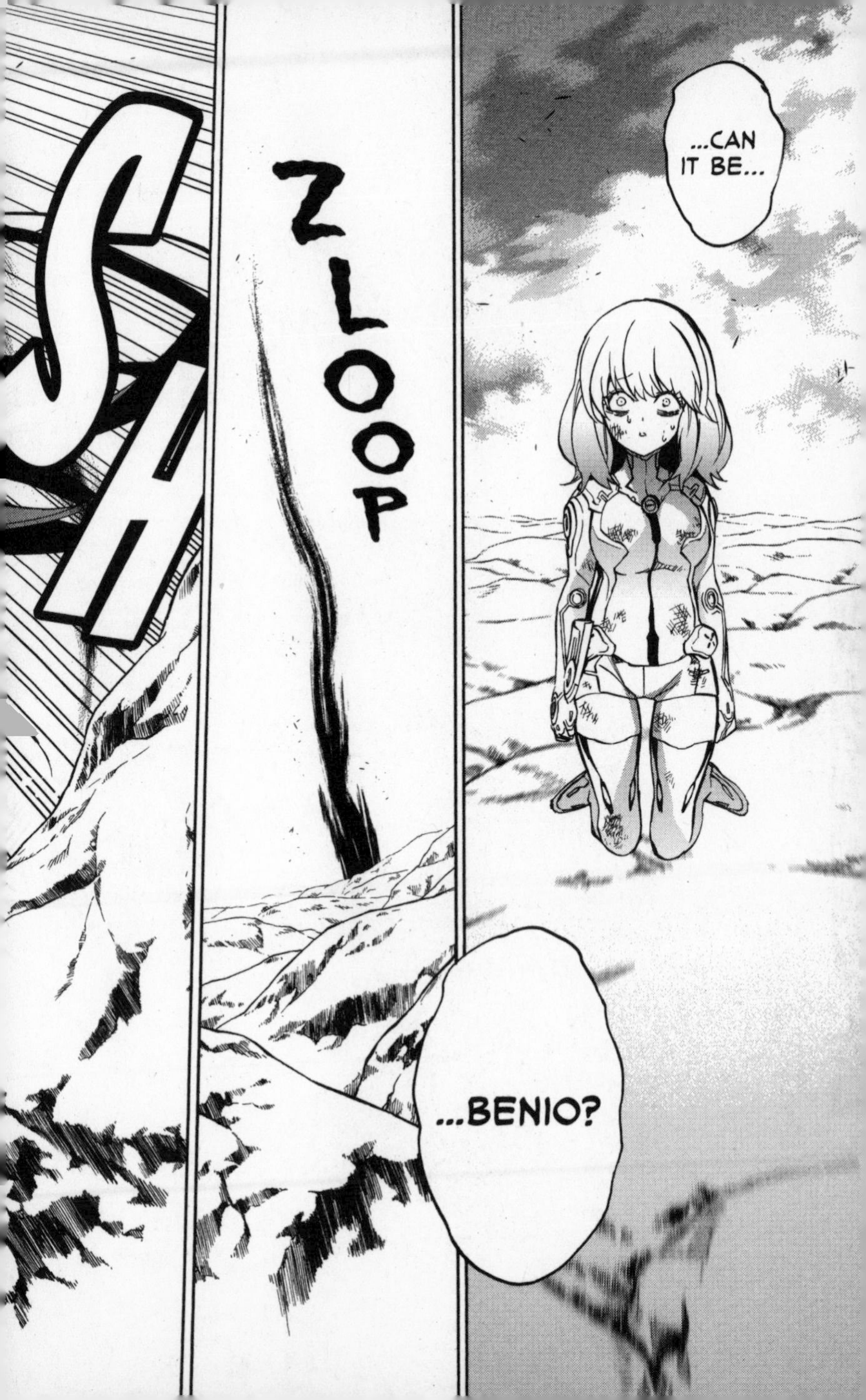
...CAN IT BE...
...BENIO?
ZLOOP
SH

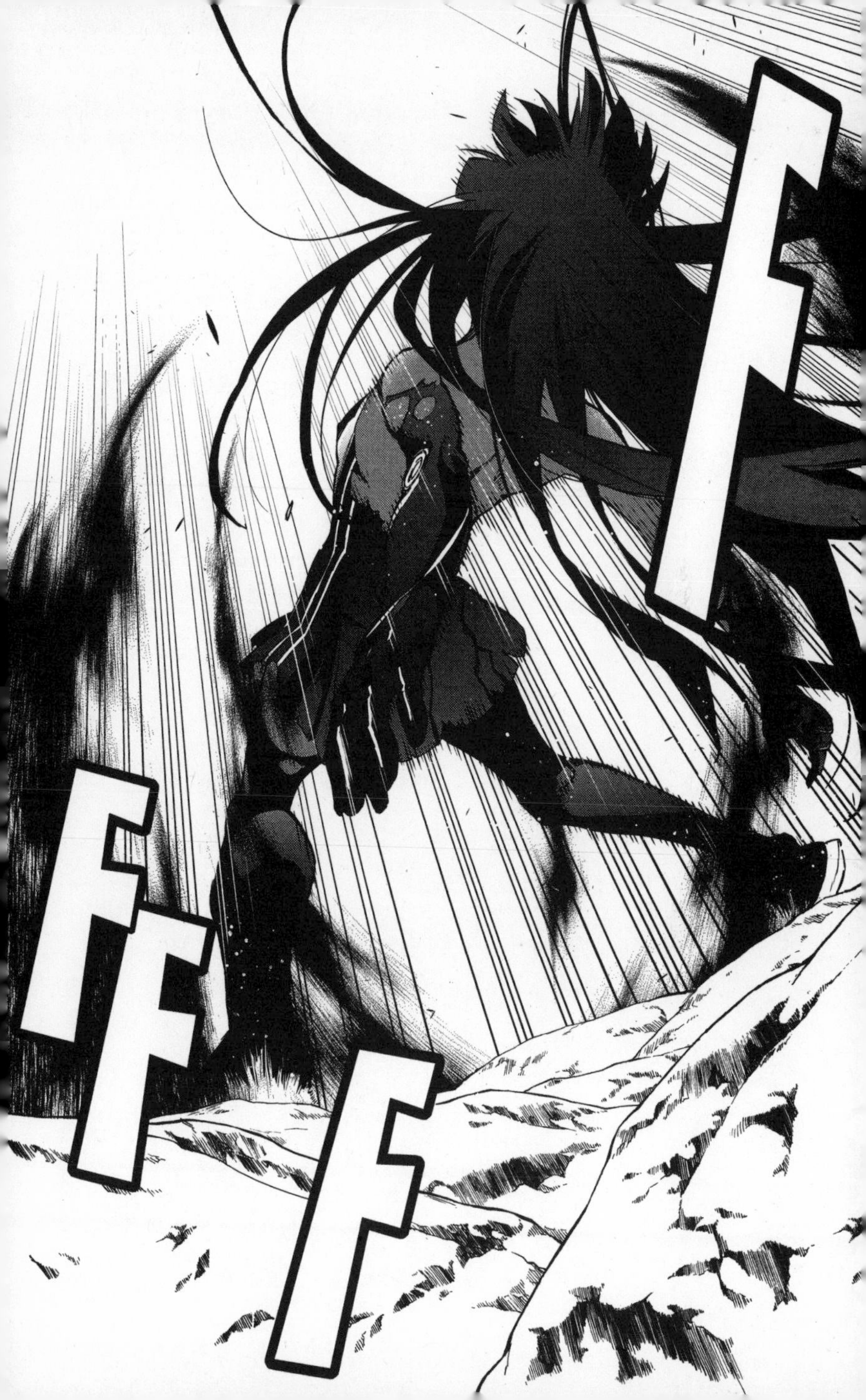
F
FFF

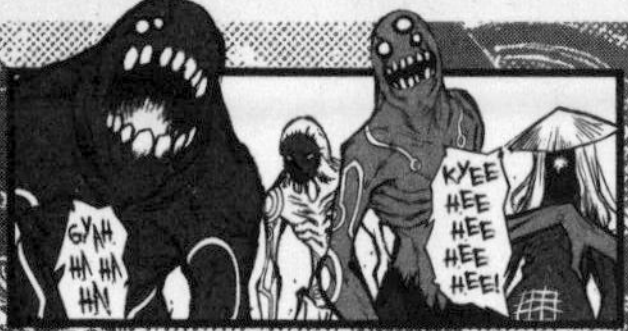
KYEE HEE HEE HEE HEE!
GYAH HA HA HA!

KEGARE CLASSIFICATION

Part 2

SHINJA (TRUE SNAKE)

Risk Level: A, A+, AA

A powerful Kegare that you could think of as a "candidate" for the level of Basara. These Kegare have developed great intelligence and can speak. They also use techniques and spells acquired from exorcists. Even a platoon of moderately skilled exorcists would be no match for them. Exorcising Shinja requires at least a Twelve Guardian or a company consisting of several high-ranking exorcists. Only a handful of Kegare are ranked above Risk A, but that's probably because the battle for spiritual power between the Kegare is fiercer than ever.

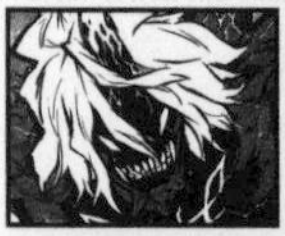

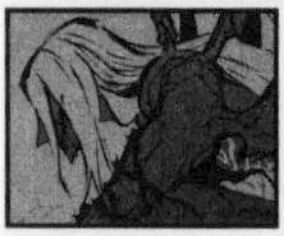

Ryogo Ratio 1:50

BASARA

Risk Level: S, S+, SSC

A Basara is the ultimate form of a Kegare, one who has acquired as much spiritual power as possible over the course of its evolution. The incredible amount of energy stored inside a Basara's human-sized body is said to be equivalent to that of a company of exorcists that includes several Twelve Guardians. A Kegare's intelligence at this level is equal to that of humans, and they can employ exorcist spells as well as wield an enchantment spell known as "Drape Them in the Shroud of Death." There are currently eleven known Basara. Each of them has different goals and motives, so they only work in small groups. If all the Basara ever decided to form an alliance, exorcists would be unable to defeat them.

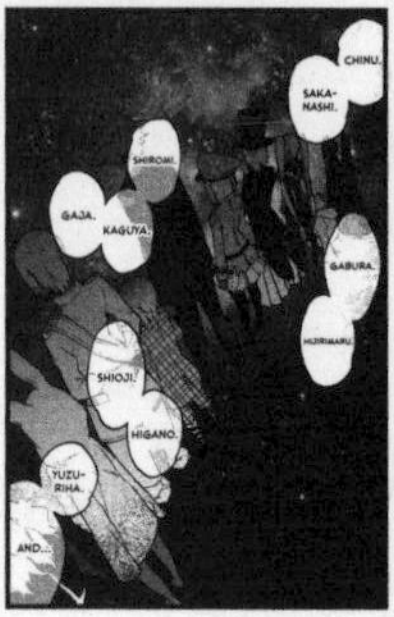
CHINU.
SAKA-NASHI.
SHIROMI.
KAGUYA.
GAJA.
GABURA.
HIJIRIMARU.
SHIOJI.
HIGANO.
YUZU-RIHA.
AND...

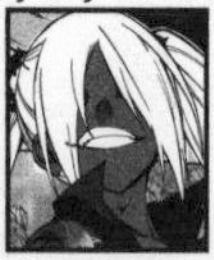

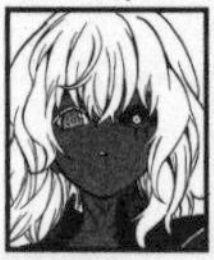

Ryogo Ratio 1:More than 100

NAMA-NARI

Risk Level: ex-A, ex-S

An exorcist who has acquired the body of a Kegare through the Kegare Curse, in which the yang spiritual power of an exorcist is inverted to that of the yin spiritual power of a Kegare. This was originally a black magic spell created as a means to defend against Kegare, but there are no records of it ever being used. It's also unclear how Yuto Ijika learned this forbidden spell.

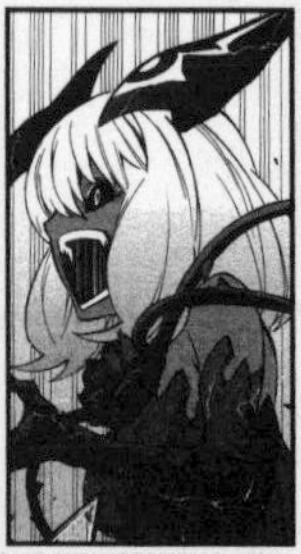

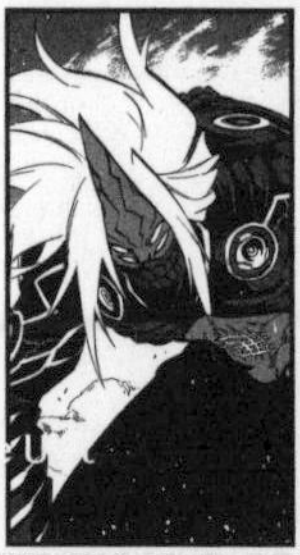

*By the way, Rokuro uses the term "C-Class" in Volume 6, but that was a mistake. It should have been "Risk B"! Sorry! —Sukeno

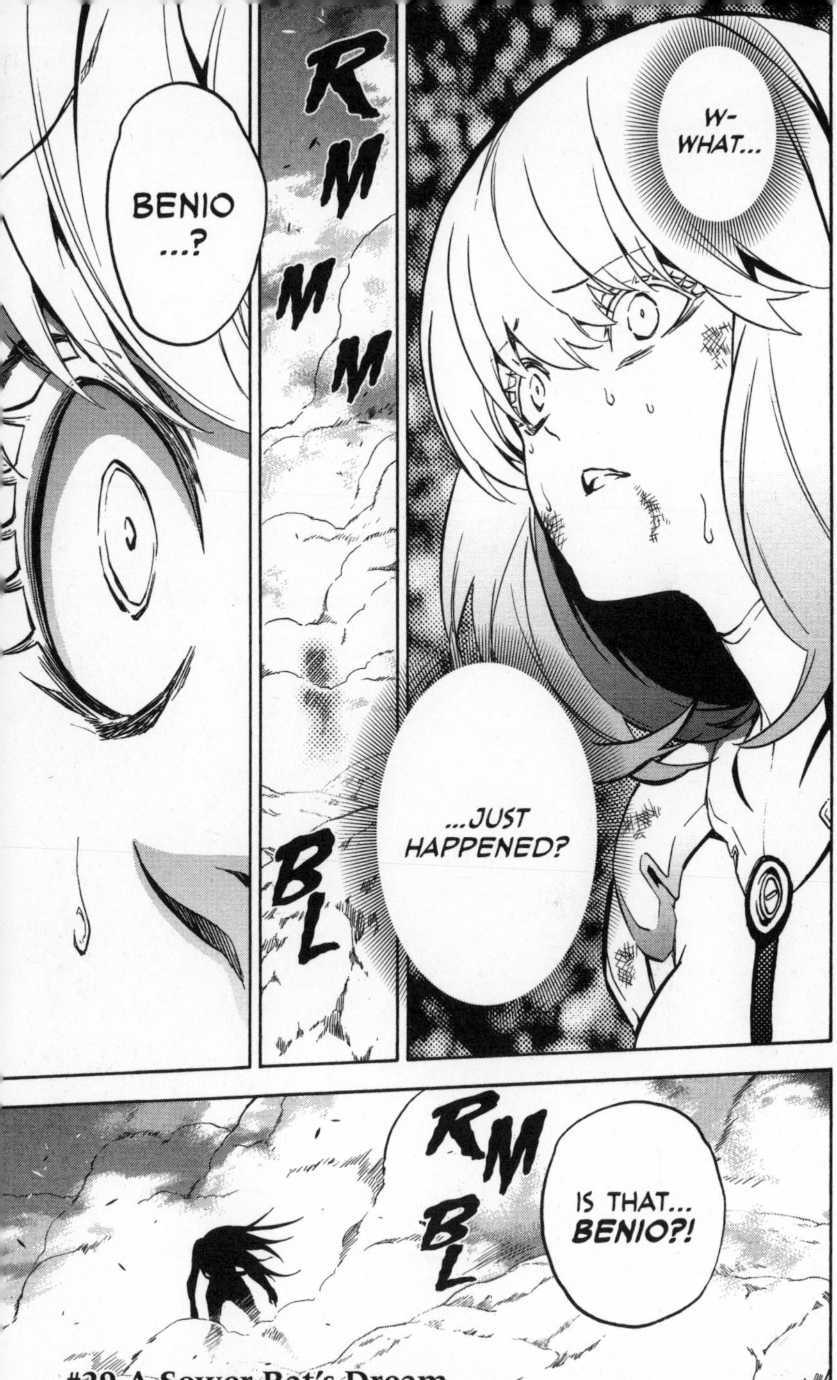
W-WHAT...
...JUST HAPPENED?
RMMMM
BL
BENIO ...?
RMBL
IS THAT... BENIO?!

#29 A Sewer Rat's Dream

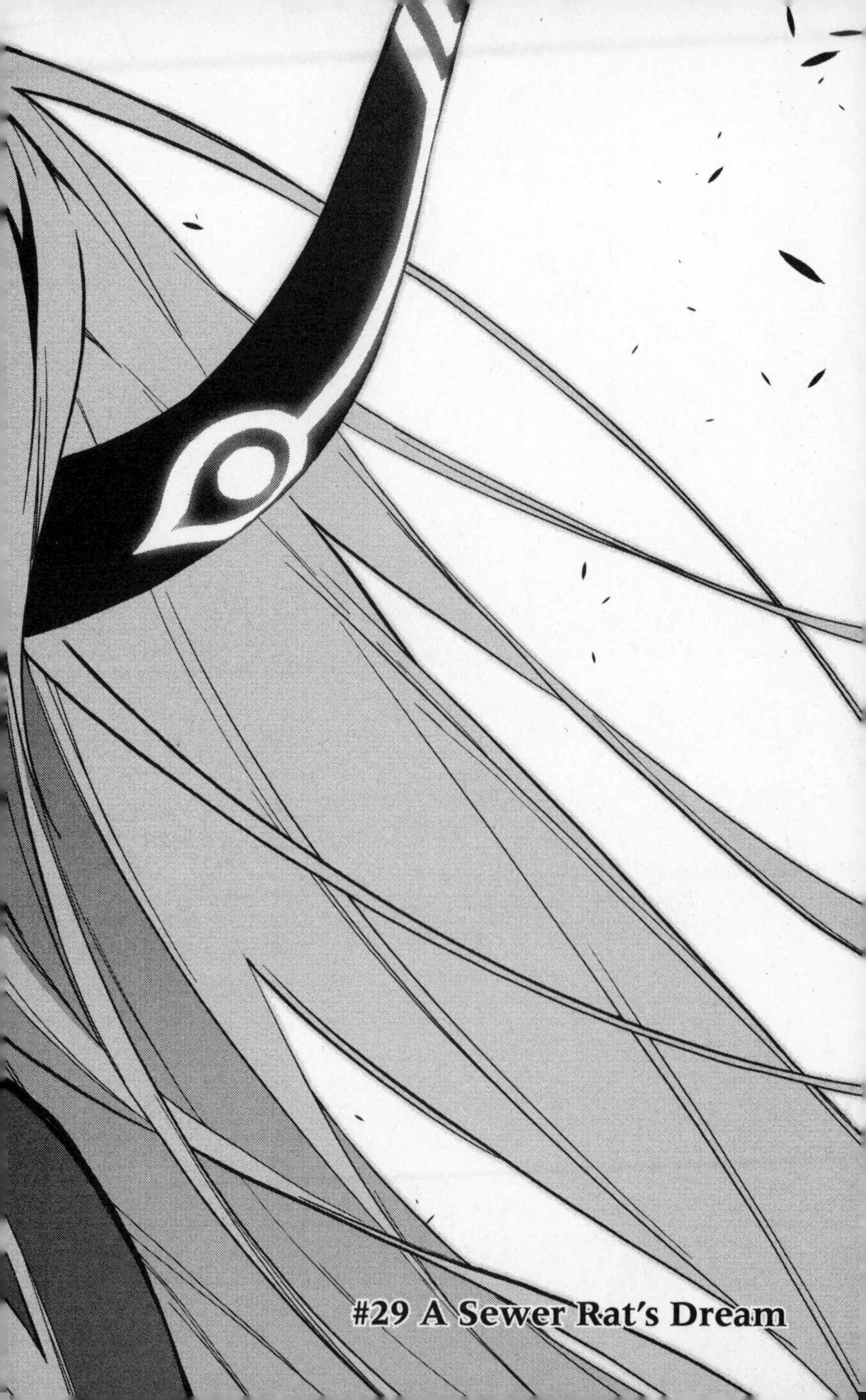

#29 A Sewer Rat's Dream

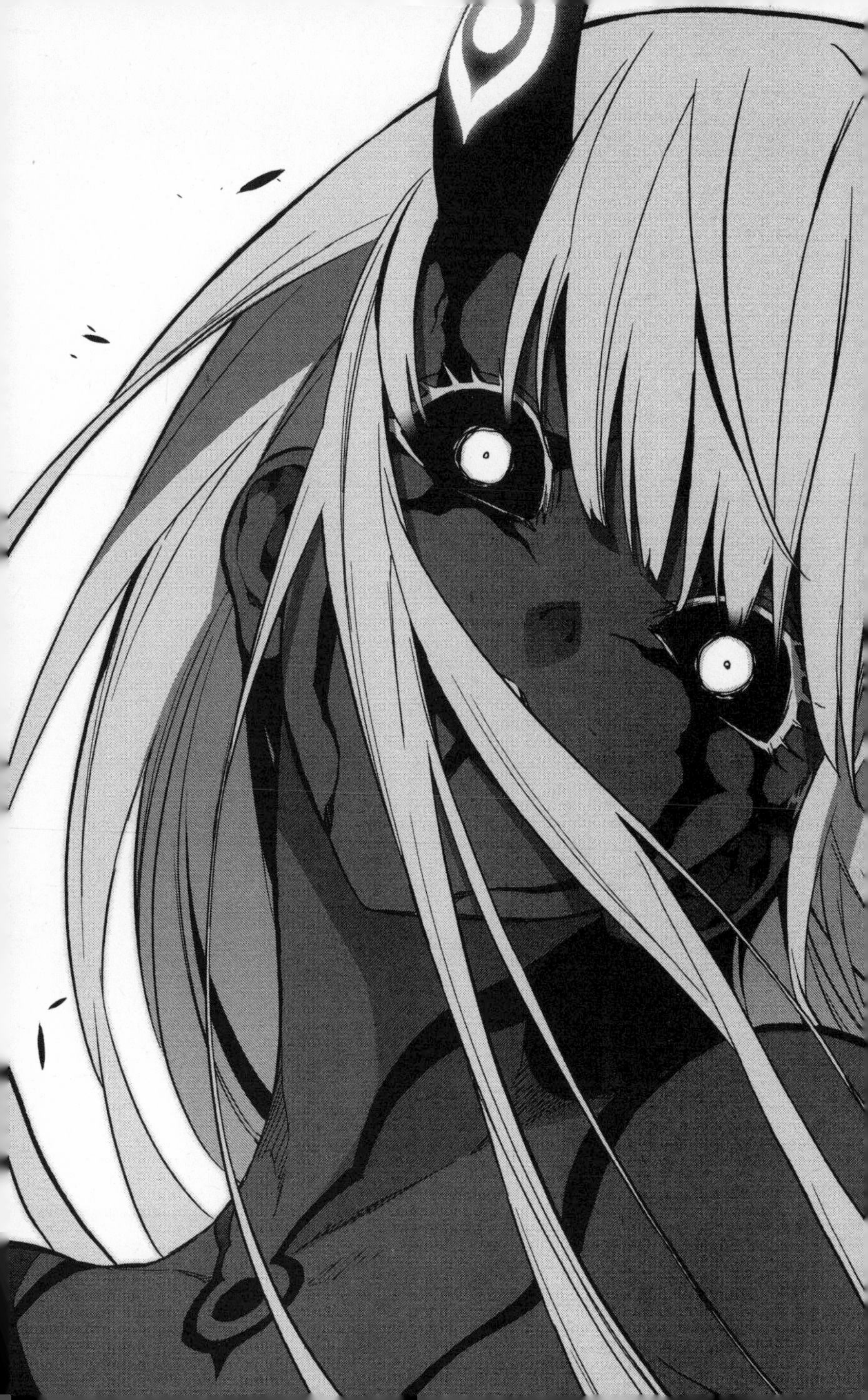

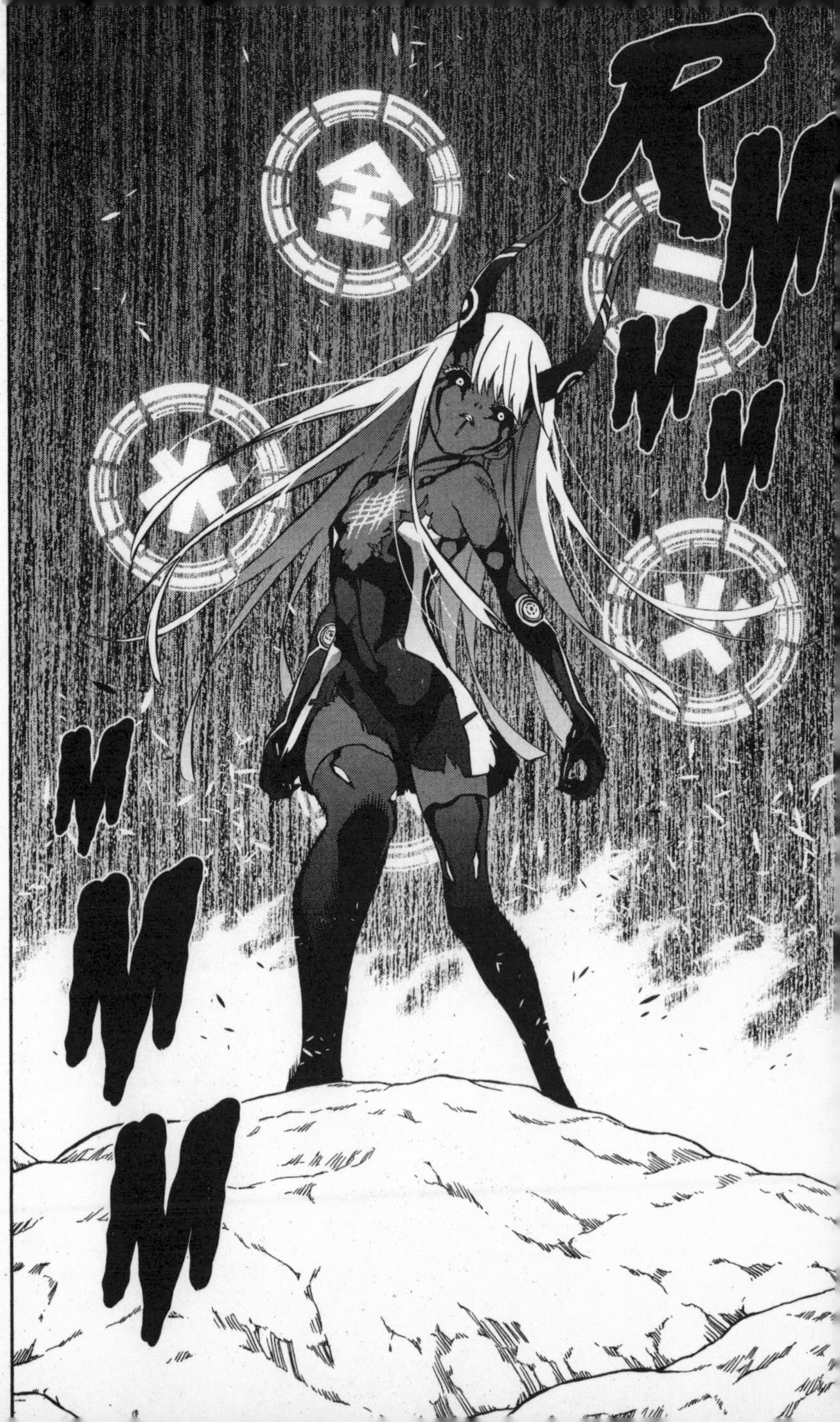
RMMMM
MMM

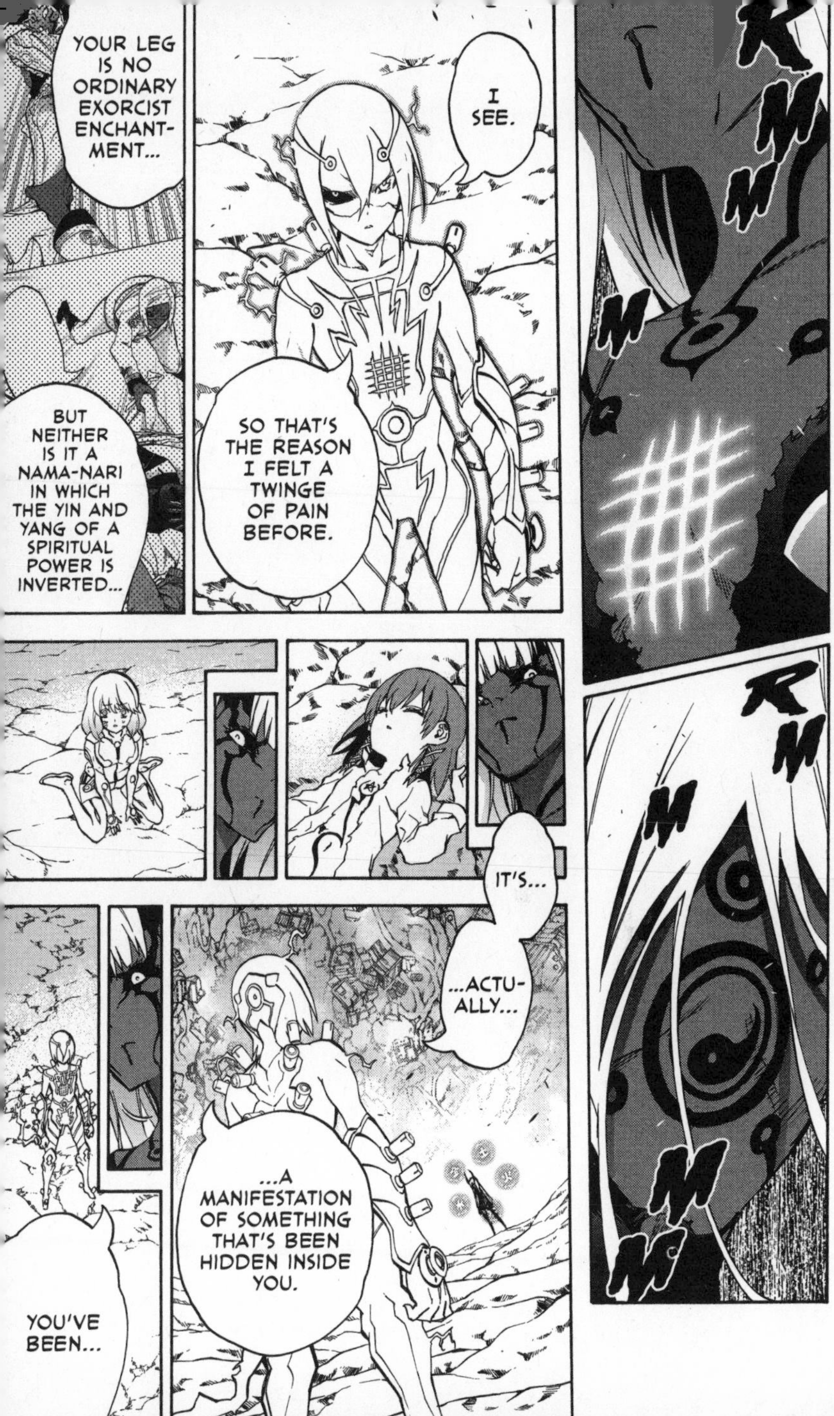

KMMMMM
I SEE.
SO THAT'S THE REASON I FELT A TWINGE OF PAIN BEFORE.
YOUR LEG IS NO ORDINARY EXORCIST ENCHANT-MENT...
BUT NEITHER IS IT A NAMA-NARI IN WHICH THE YIN AND YANG OF A SPIRITUAL POWER IS INVERTED...
RMMMMMM
IT'S...
...ACTU-ALLY...
...A MANIFESTATION OF SOMETHING THAT'S BEEN HIDDEN INSIDE YOU.
YOU'VE BEEN...

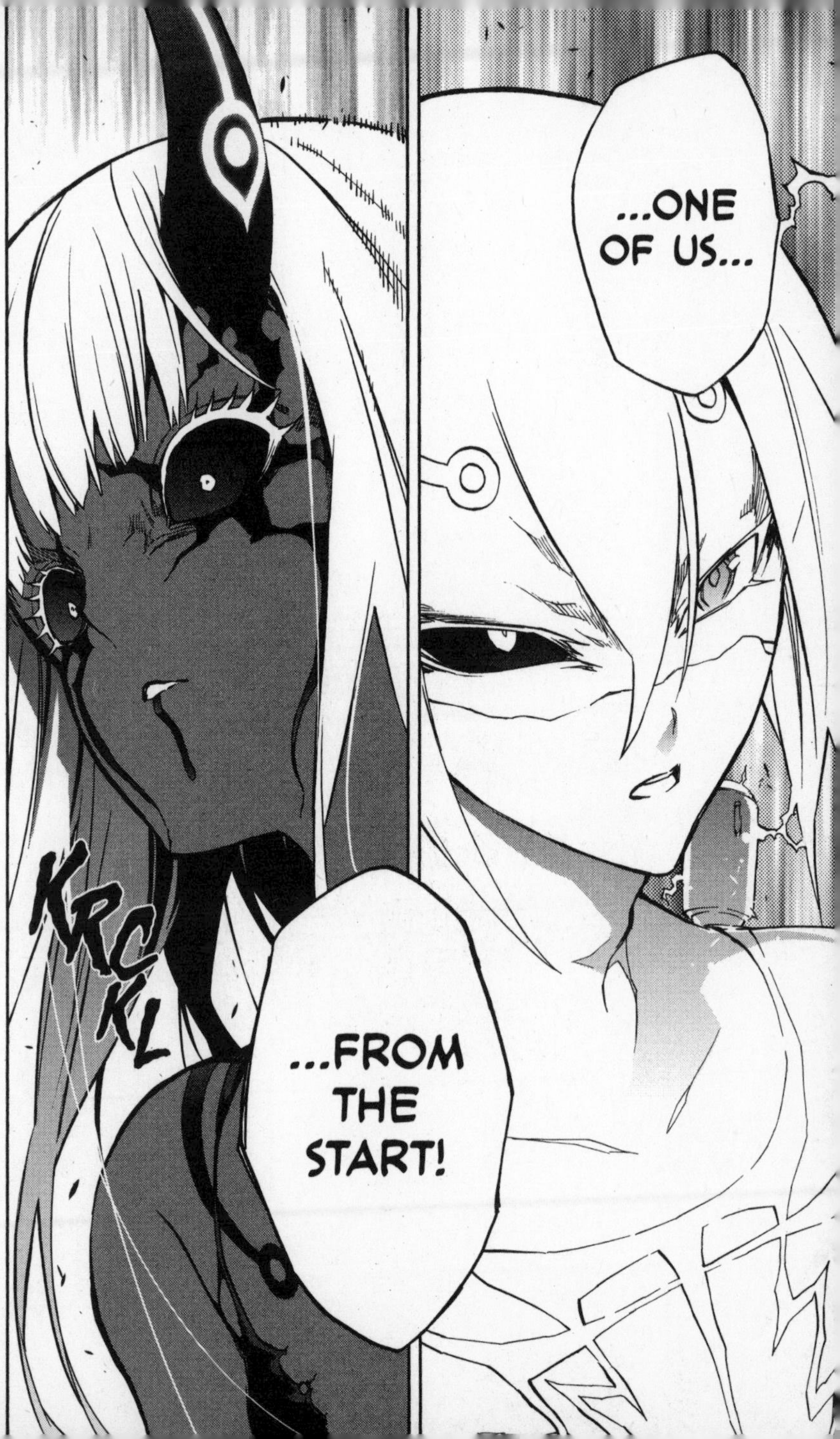
...ONE OF US...
...FROM THE START!
KRCKL

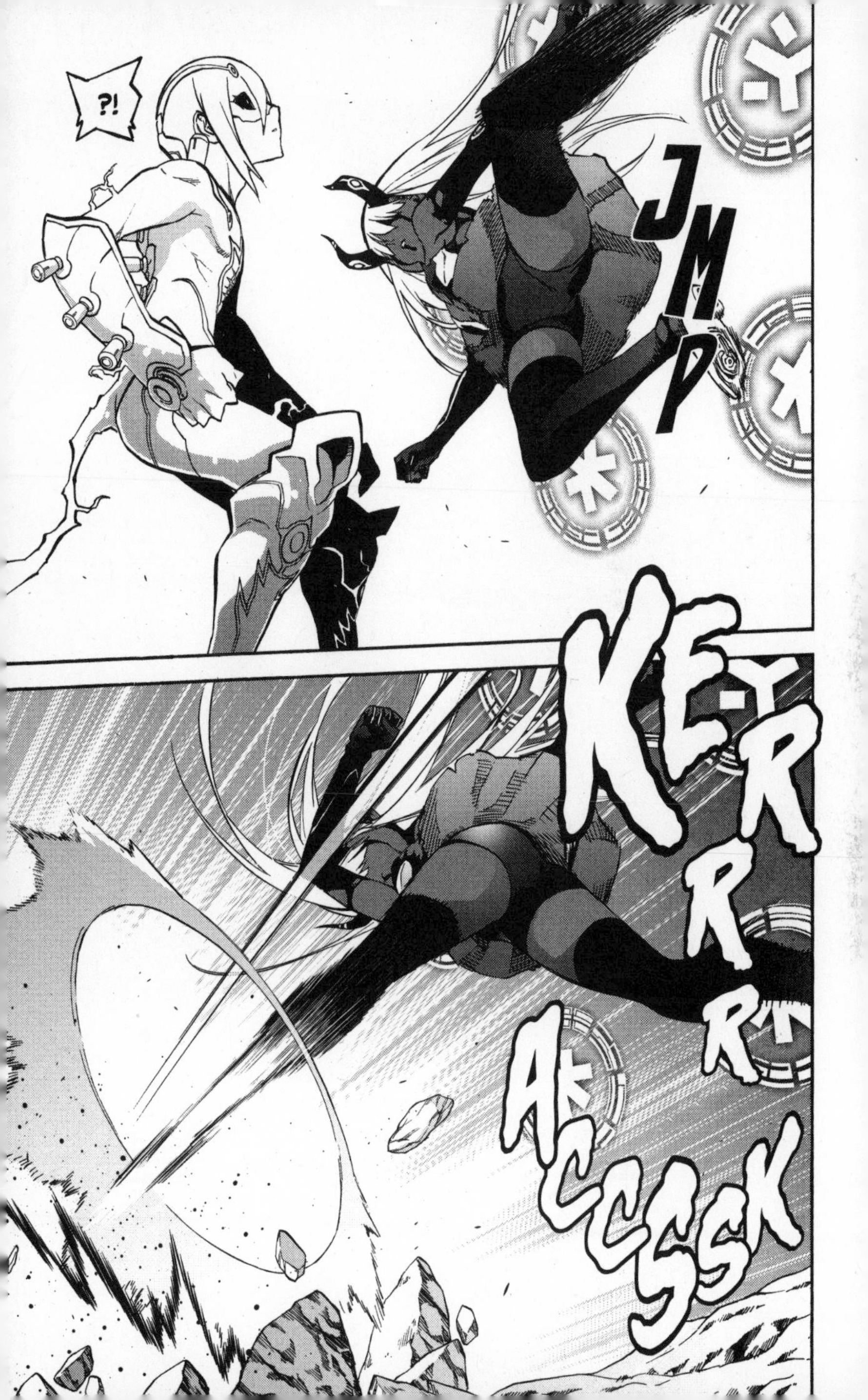
?!
JMP
KERRR
ACCSSK

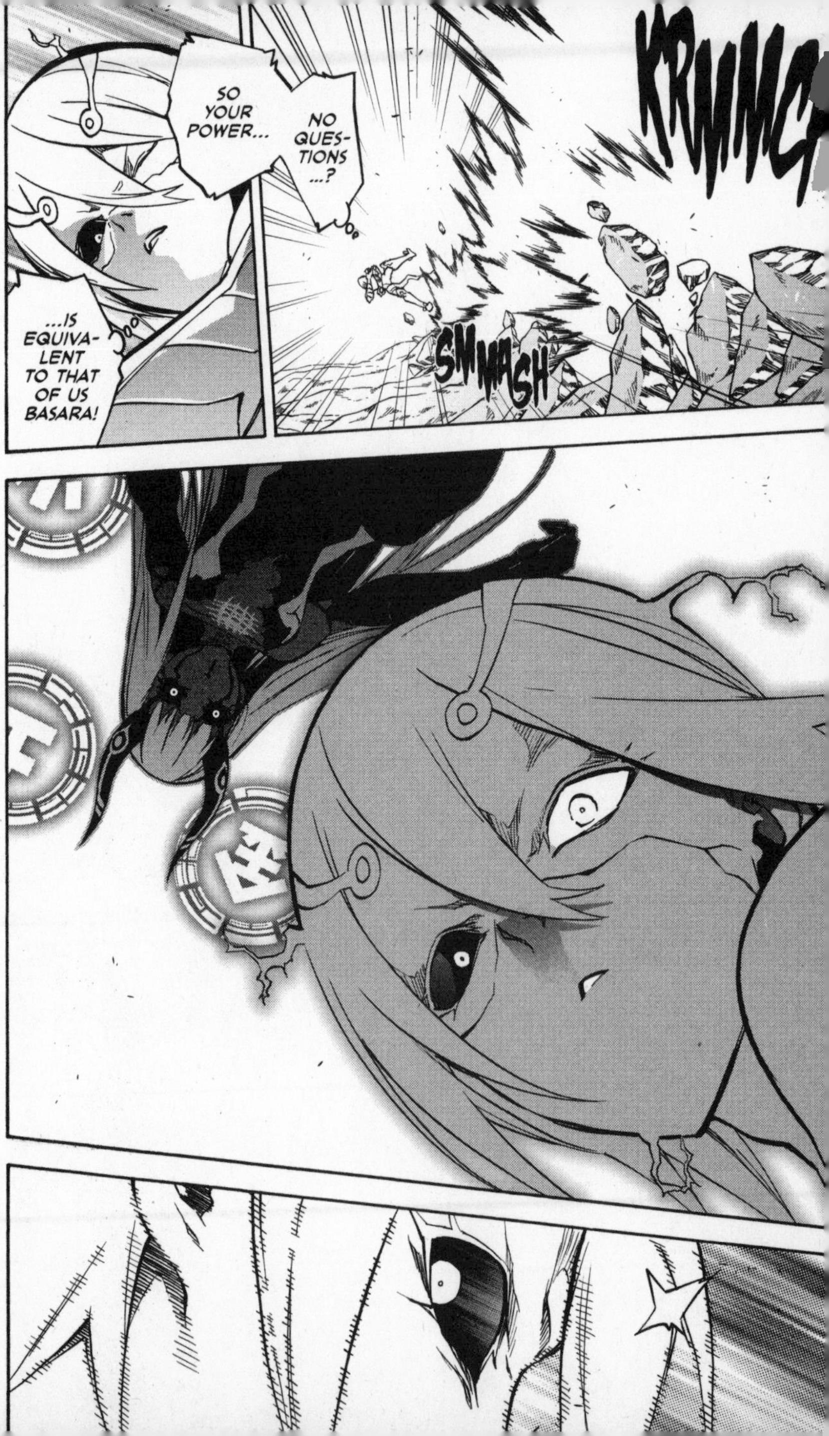

KRMMC
SMMASH
NO QUESTIONS...?
SO YOUR POWER...
...IS EQUIVALENT TO THAT OF US BASARA!

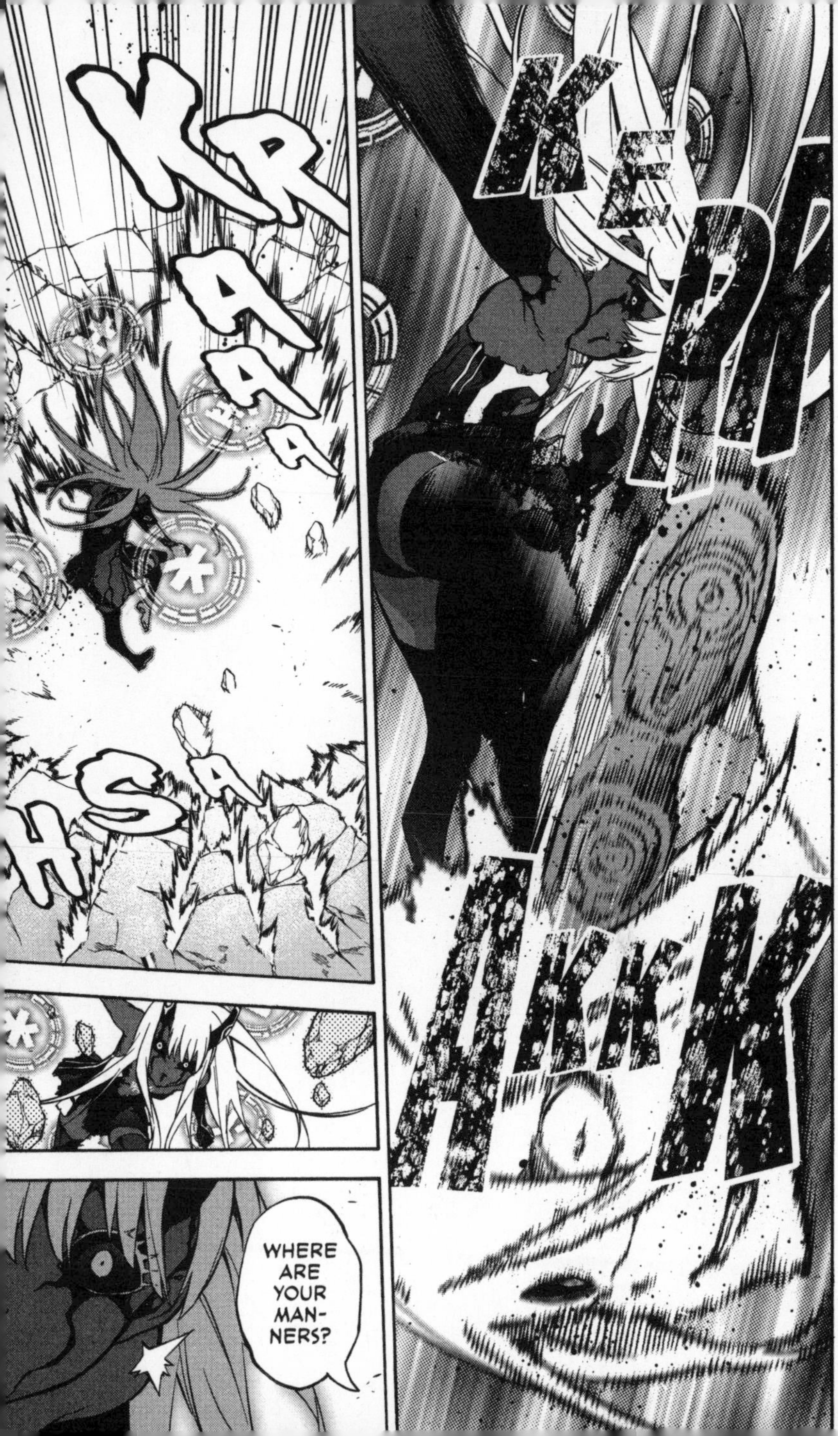
KRAAAA
WHERE ARE YOUR MAN-NERS?

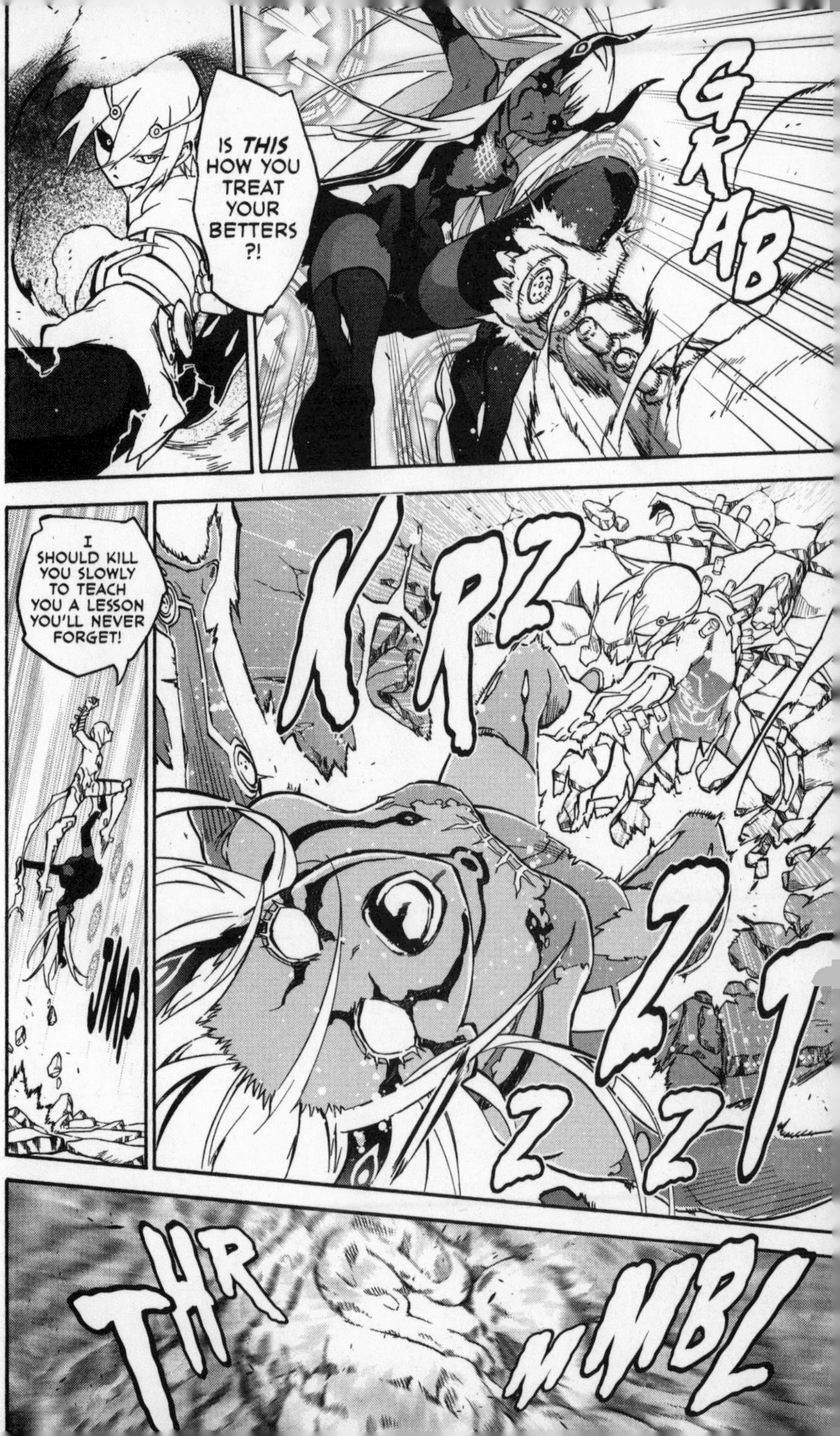
GRAB
IS THIS HOW YOU TREAT YOUR BETTERS?!
KRZ
ZZZT
I SHOULD KILL YOU SLOWLY TO TEACH YOU A LESSON YOU'LL NEVER FORGET!
THRMMBL

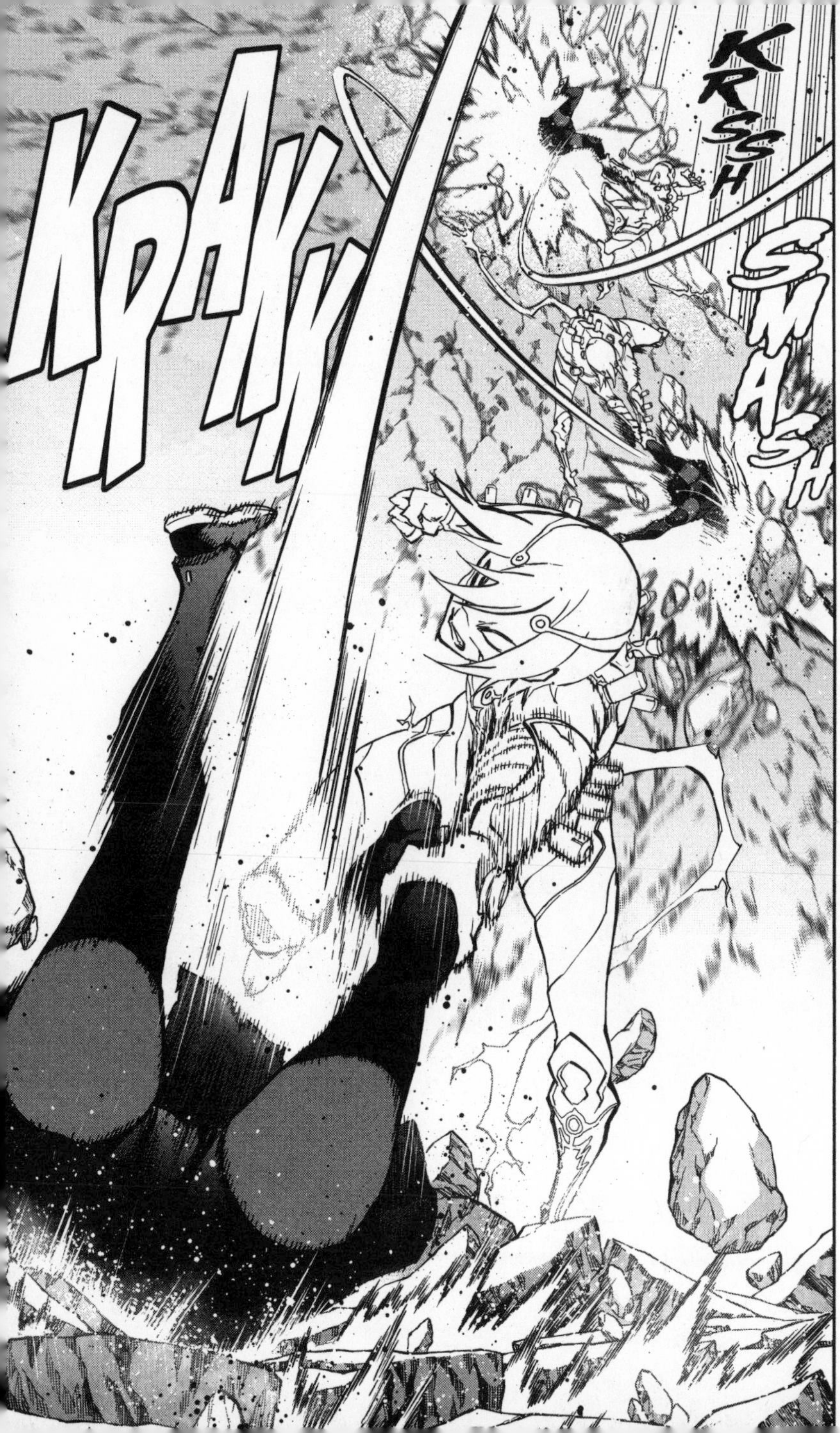
KRSSH
SMASH
KRAKK

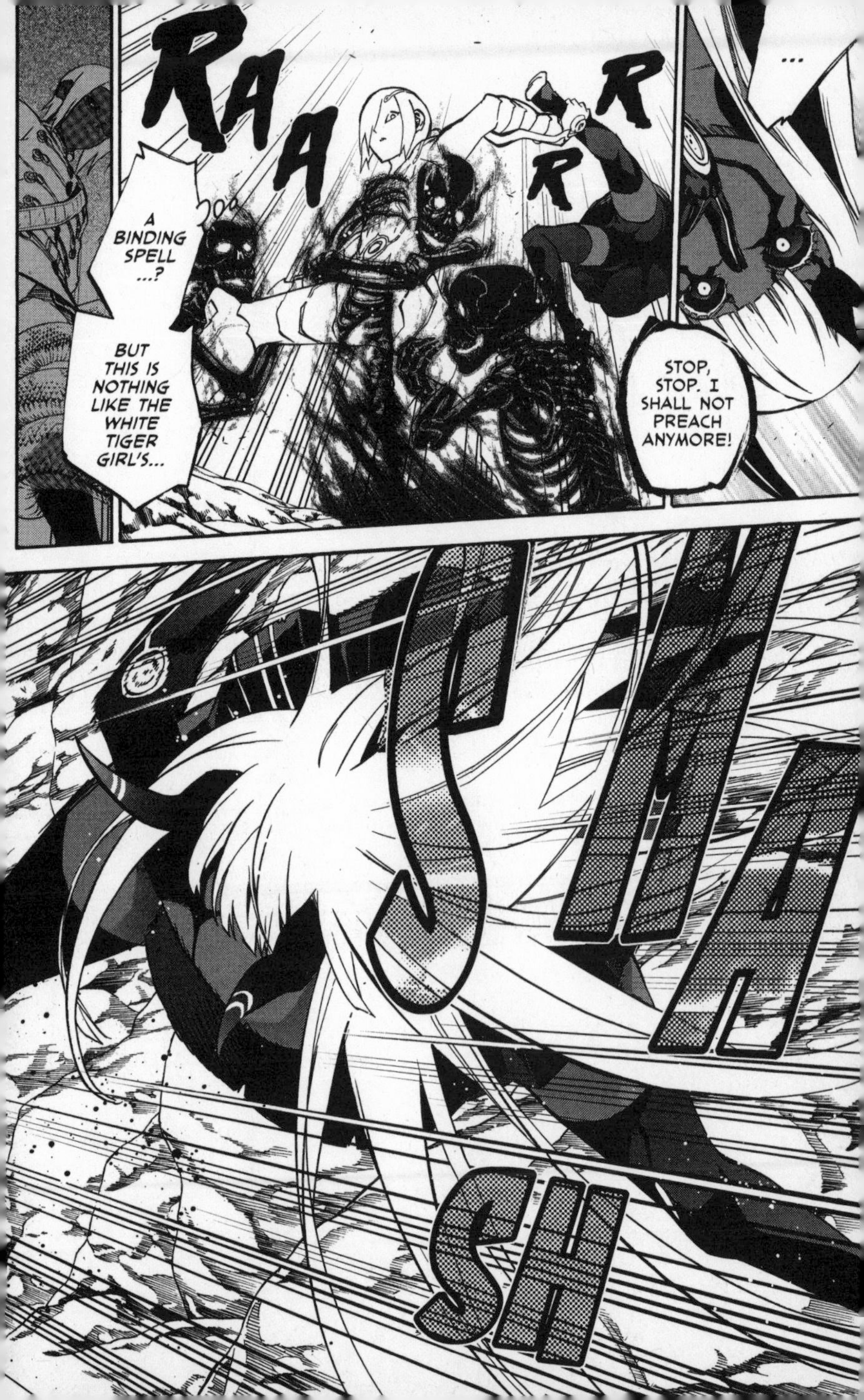
...
STOP, STOP. I SHALL NOT PREACH ANYMORE!
RAAARR
A BINDING SPELL ...?
BUT THIS IS NOTHING LIKE THE WHITE TIGER GIRL'S...
SH

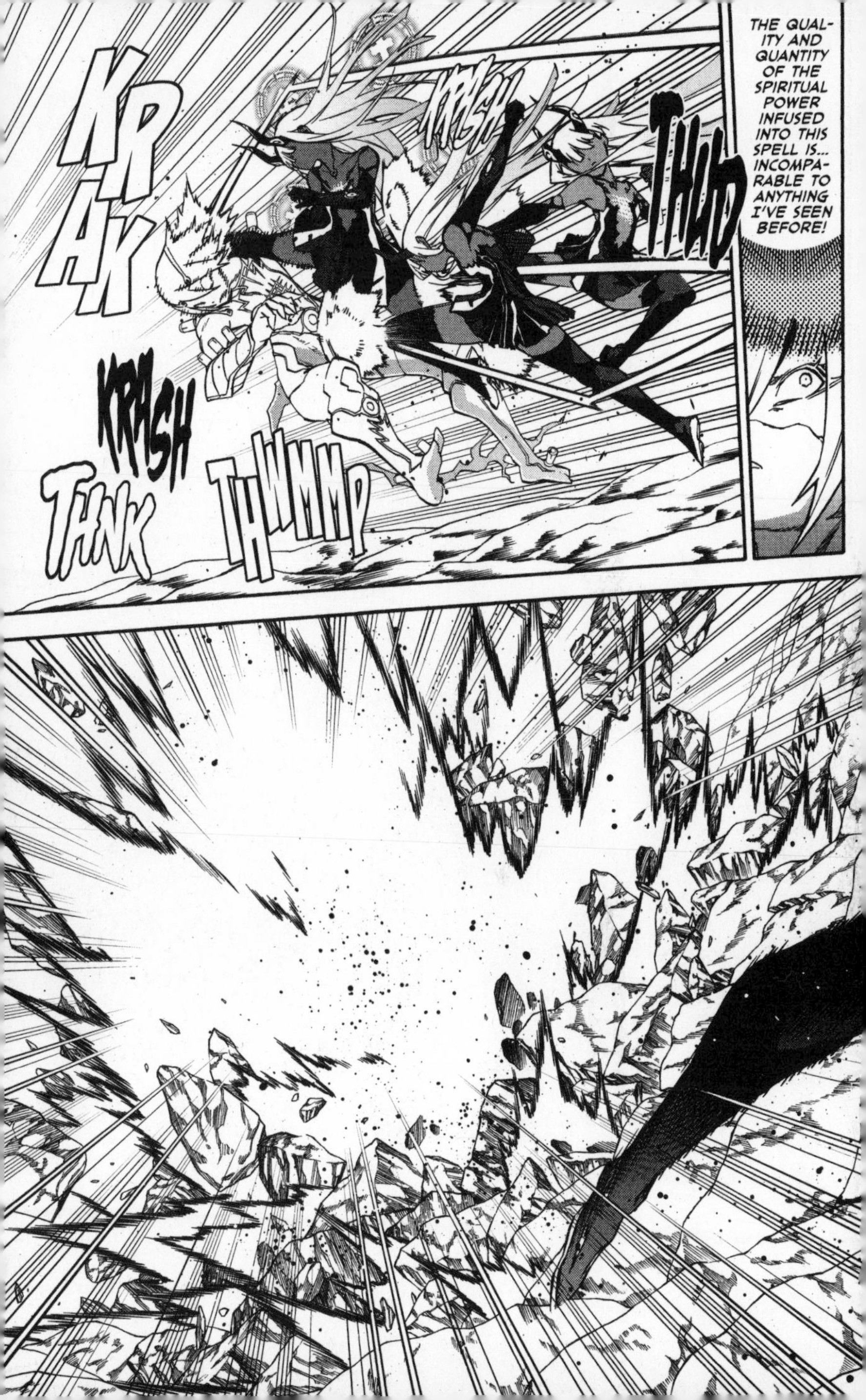
THE QUALITY AND QUANTITY OF THE SPIRITUAL POWER INFUSED INTO THIS SPELL IS... INCOMPARABLE TO ANYTHING I'VE SEEN BEFORE!
THUD
KRASH
KRAK
KRASH
THWMMP
THNK

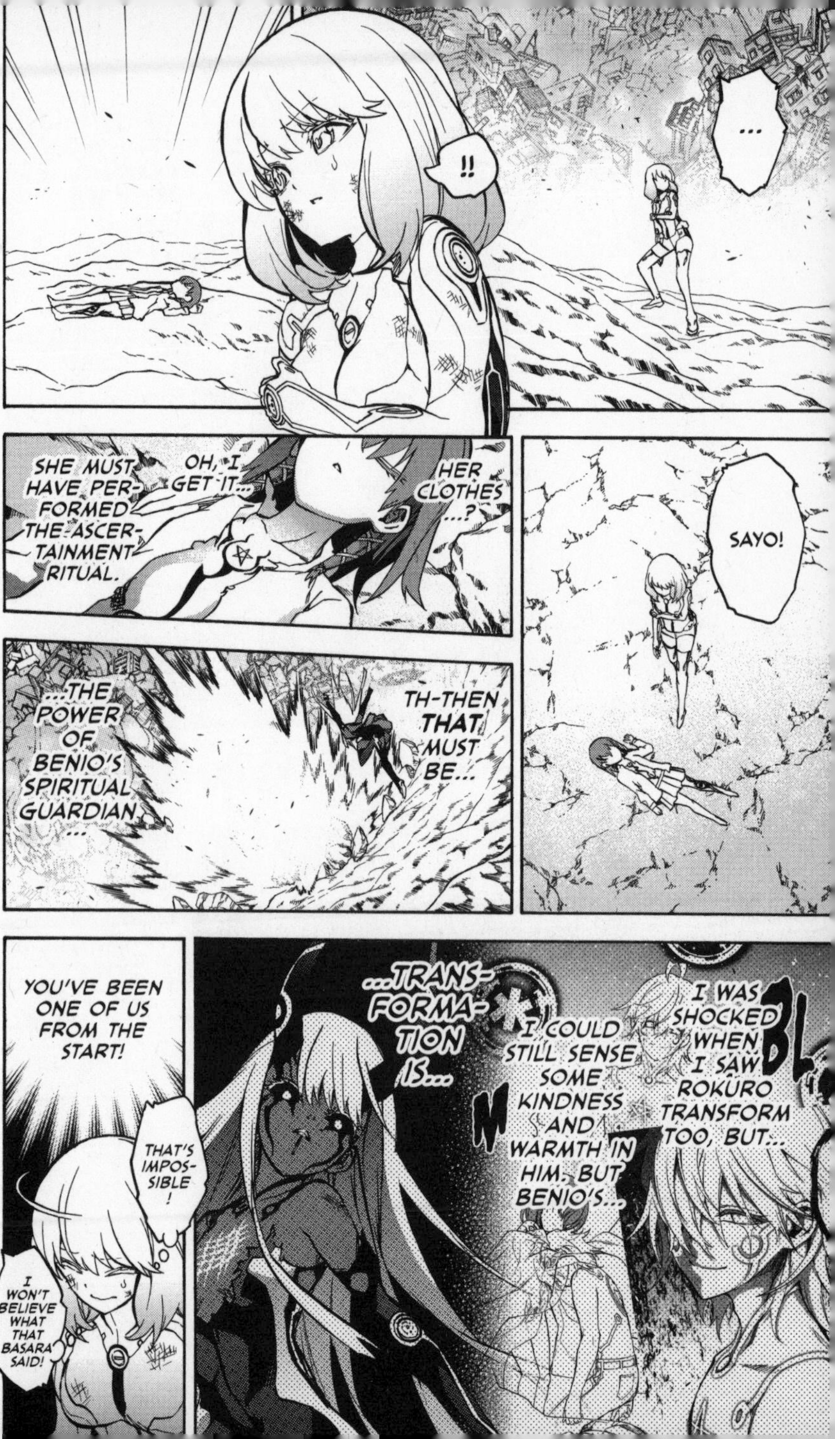
...
!!
SAYO!
HER CLOTHES ...?
OH, I GET IT...
SHE MUST HAVE PERFORMED THE ASCERTAINMENT RITUAL.
TH-THEN THAT MUST BE...
...THE POWER OF BENIO'S SPIRITUAL GUARDIAN...
I WAS SHOCKED WHEN I SAW ROKURO TRANSFORM TOO, BUT...
I COULD STILL SENSE SOME KINDNESS AND WARMTH IN HIM. BUT BENIO'S...
...TRANSFORMATION IS...
YOU'VE BEEN ONE OF US FROM THE START!
THAT'S IMPOSSIBLE!
I WON'T BELIEVE WHAT THAT BASARA SAID!

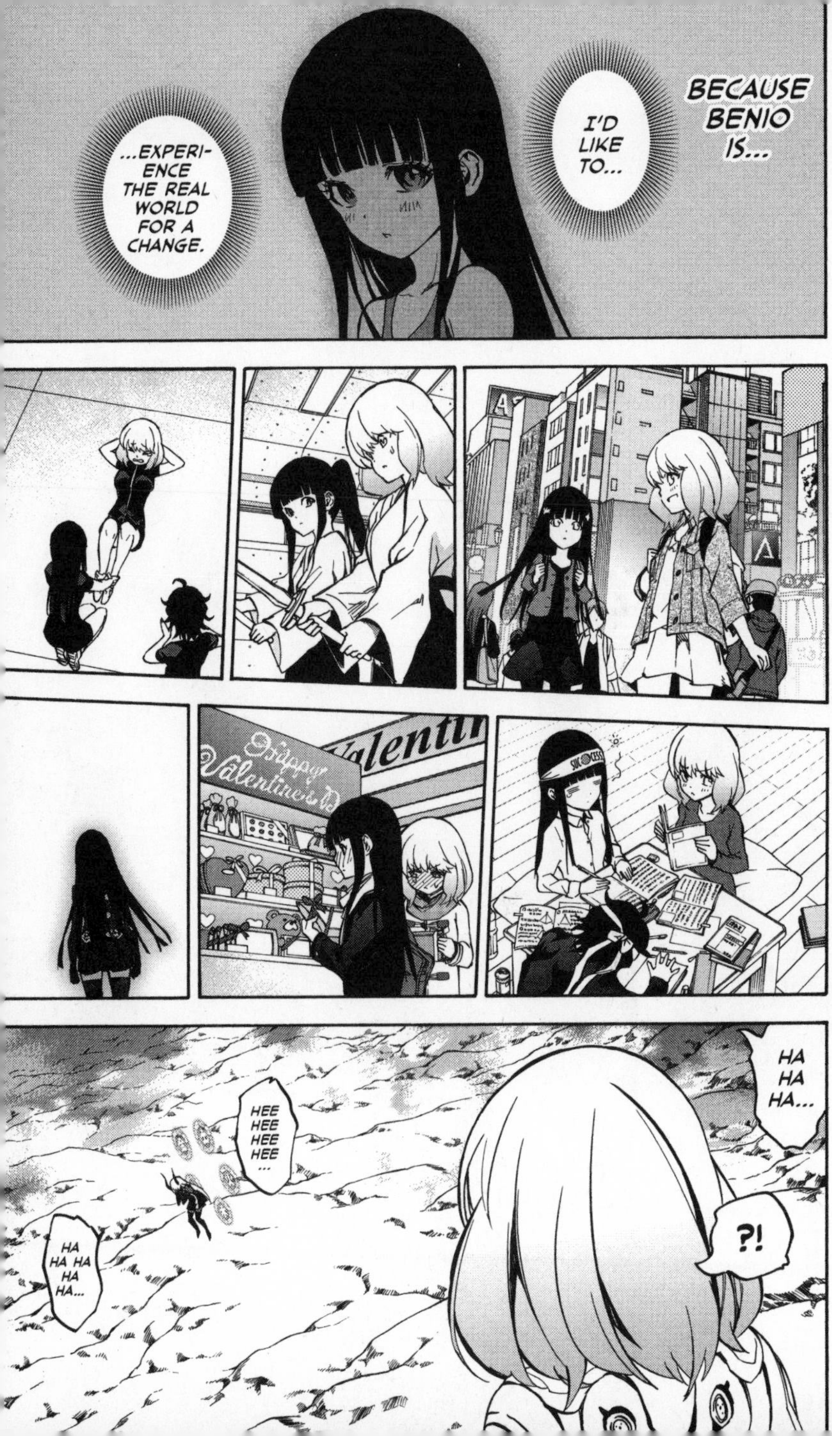
BECAUSE BENIO IS...
I'D LIKE TO...
...EXPERIENCE THE REAL WORLD FOR A CHANGE.
HA HA HA...
?!
HEE HEE HEE HEE ...
HA HA HA HA HA...

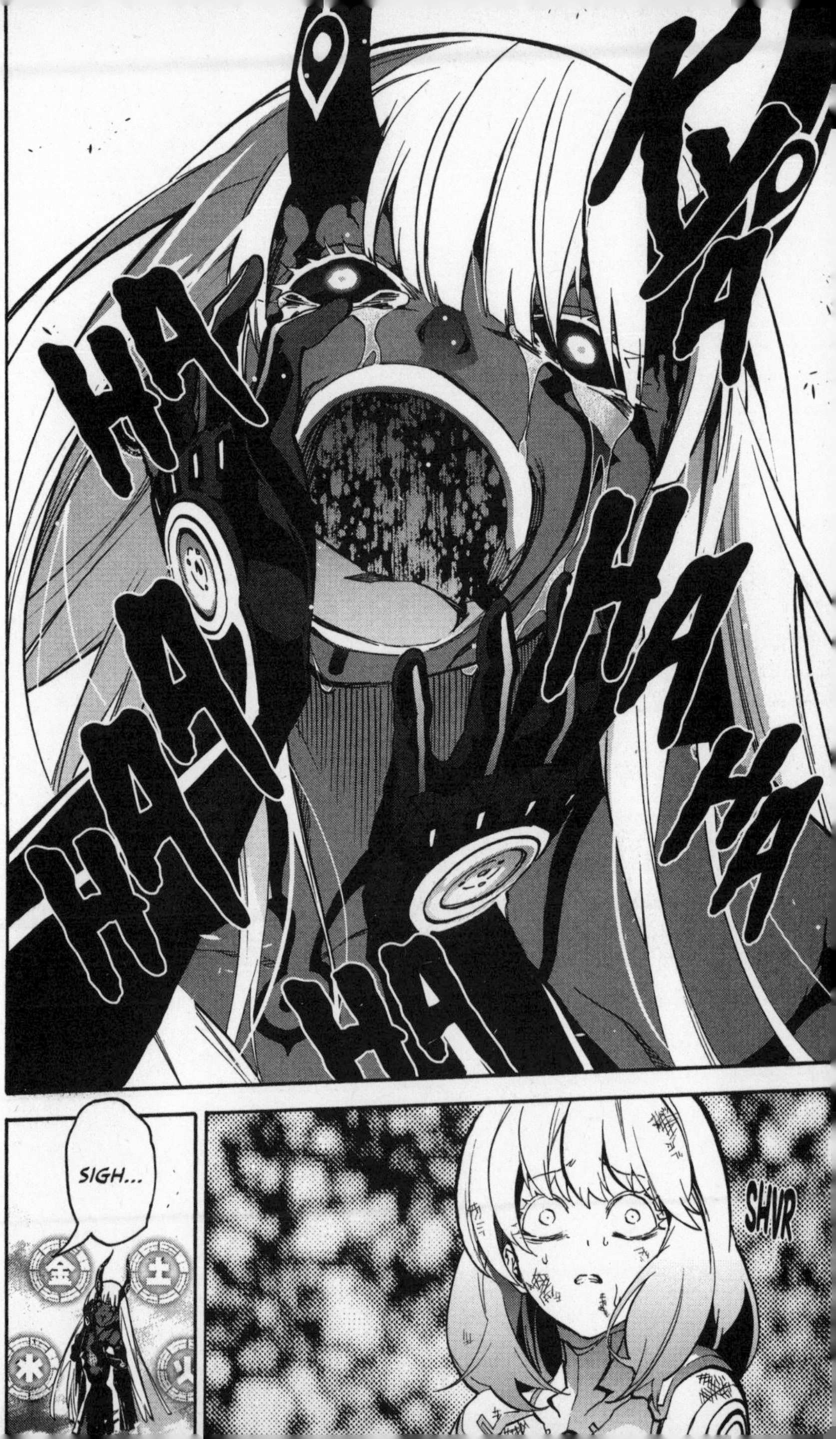
KYA
HA HA HA HA HA HA HA HA
SHVR
SIGH...

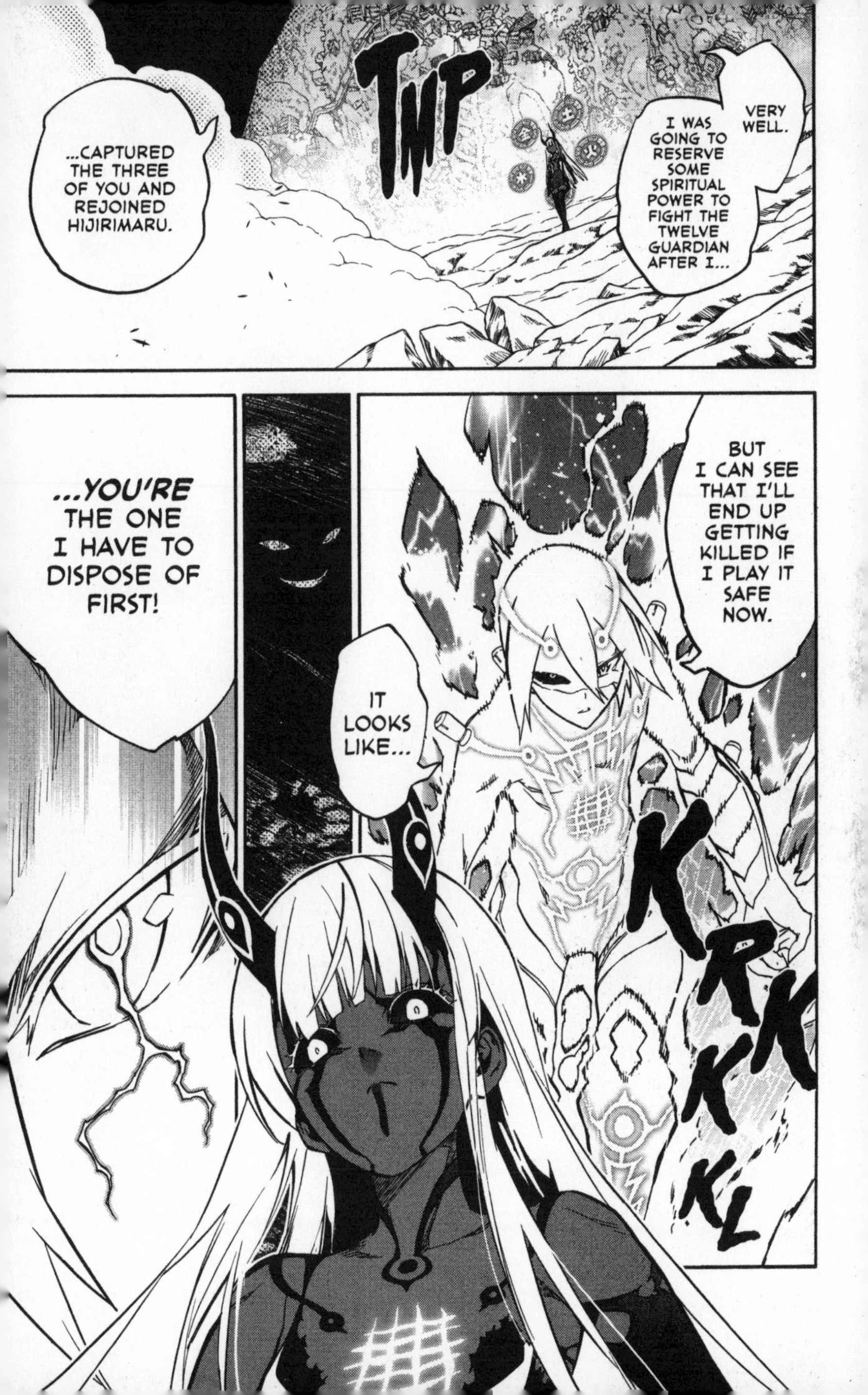
VERY WELL.
I WAS GOING TO RESERVE SOME SPIRITUAL POWER TO FIGHT THE TWELVE GUARDIAN AFTER I...
TMP
...CAPTURED THE THREE OF YOU AND REJOINED HIJIRIMARU.
BUT I CAN SEE THAT I'LL END UP GETTING KILLED IF I PLAY IT SAFE NOW.
IT LOOKS LIKE...
KRKKKL
...YOU'RE THE ONE I HAVE TO DISPOSE OF FIRST!

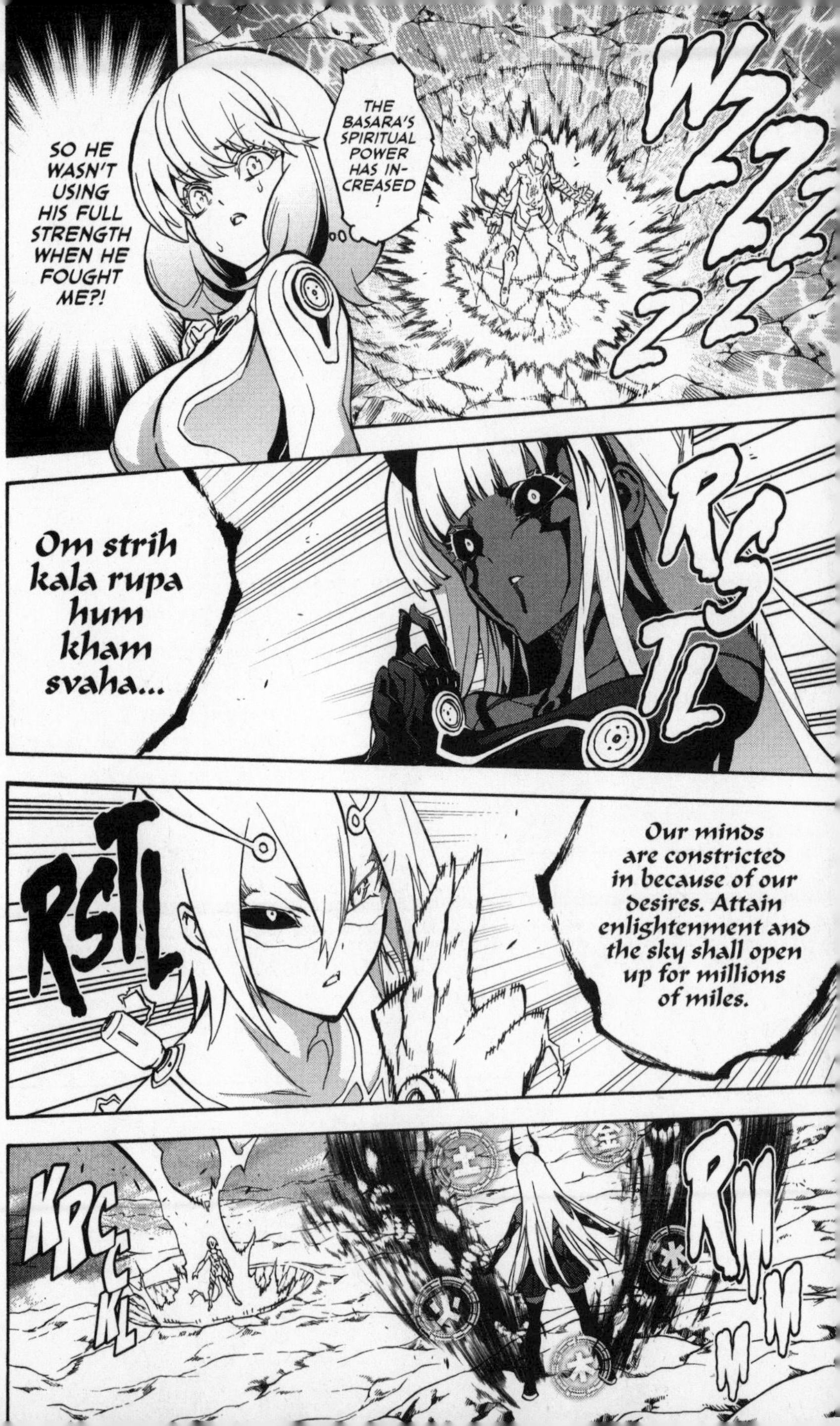
WZZZZZ
THE BASARA'S SPIRITUAL POWER HAS INCREASED!
SO HE WASN'T USING HIS FULL STRENGTH WHEN HE FOUGHT ME?!
RSTL
Om strih kala rupa hum kham svaha...
Our minds are constricted in because of our desires. Attain enlightenment and the sky shall open up for millions of miles.
RSTL
RMMMM
KRCKL

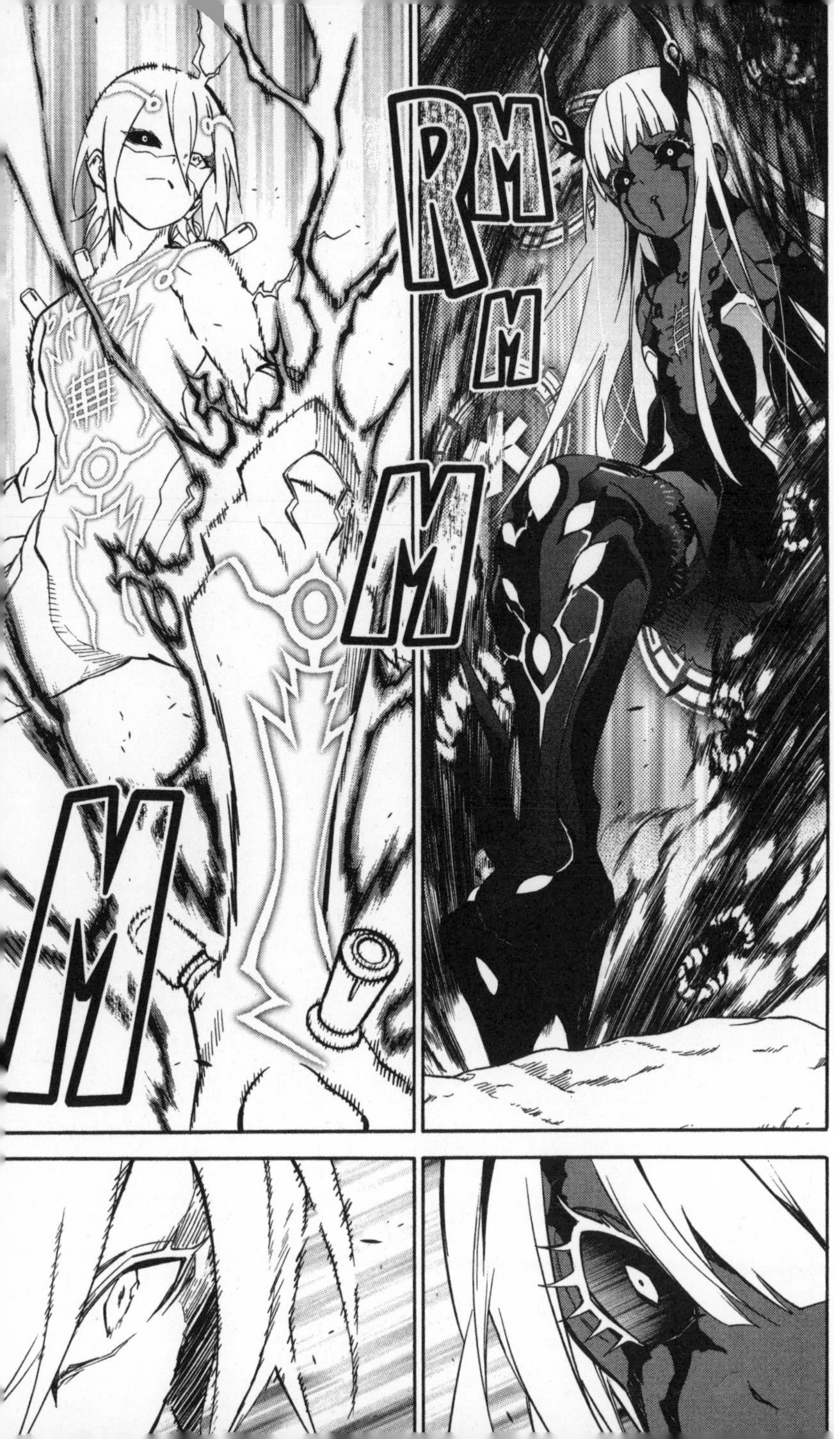
RMMMM

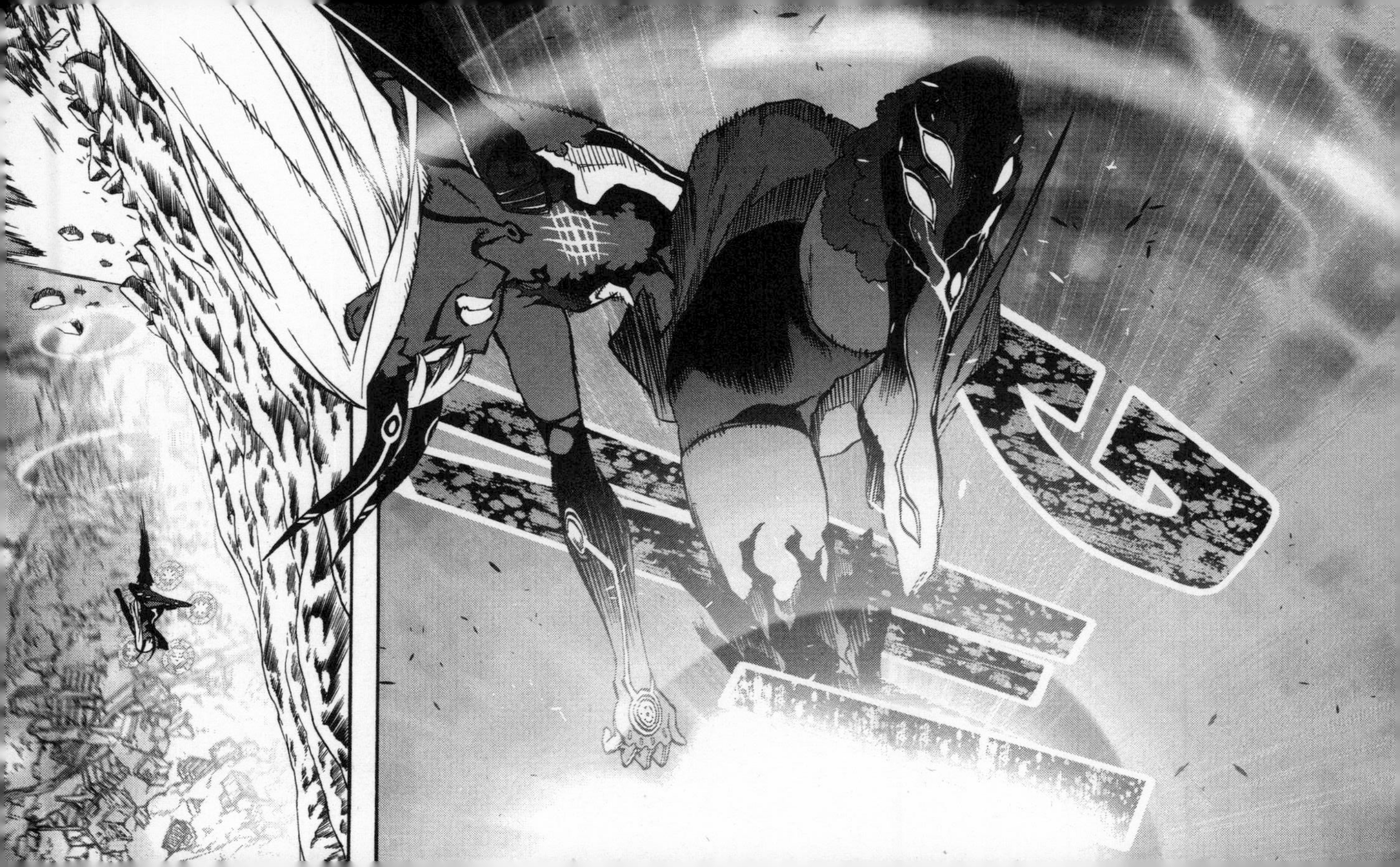

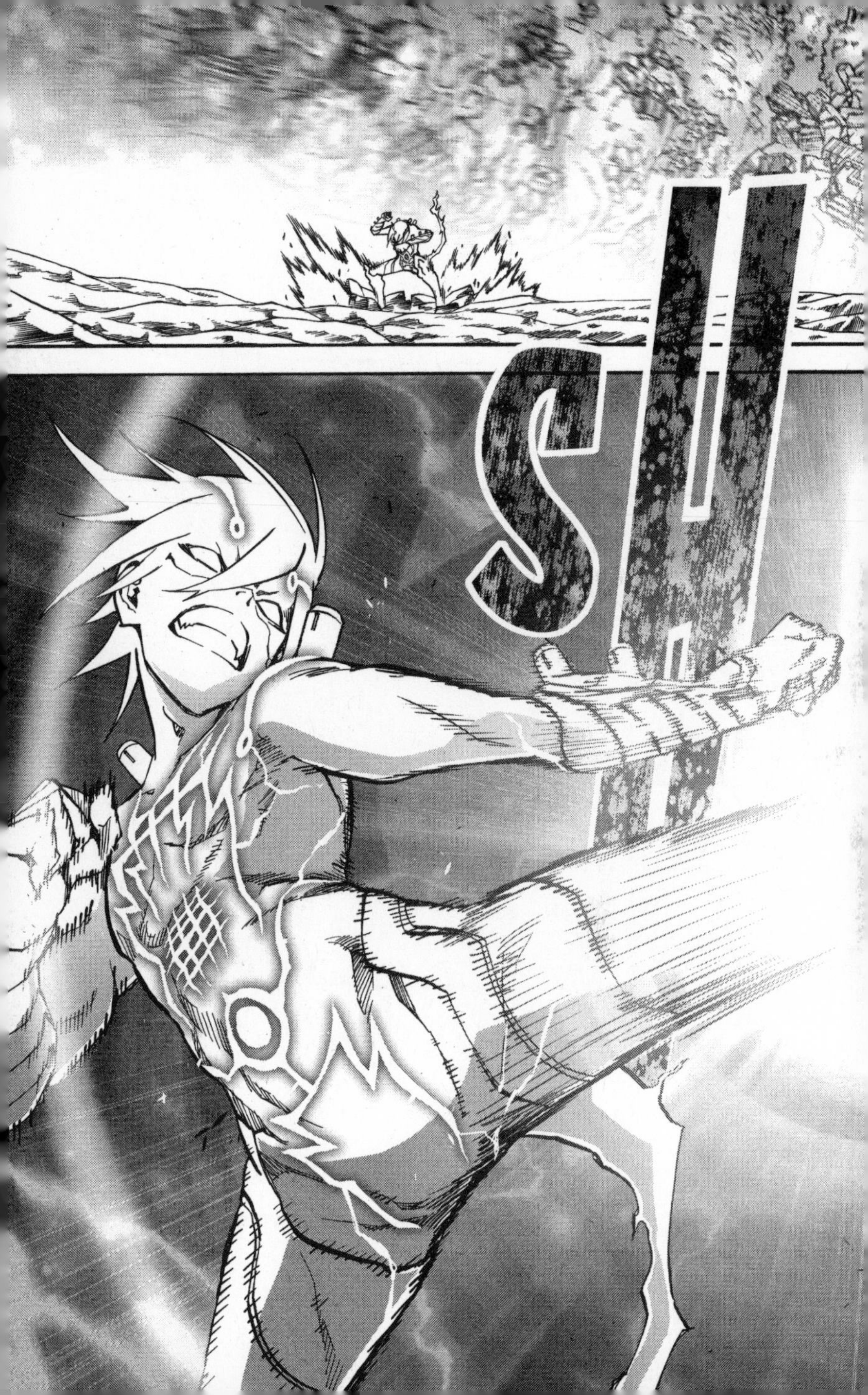
SH

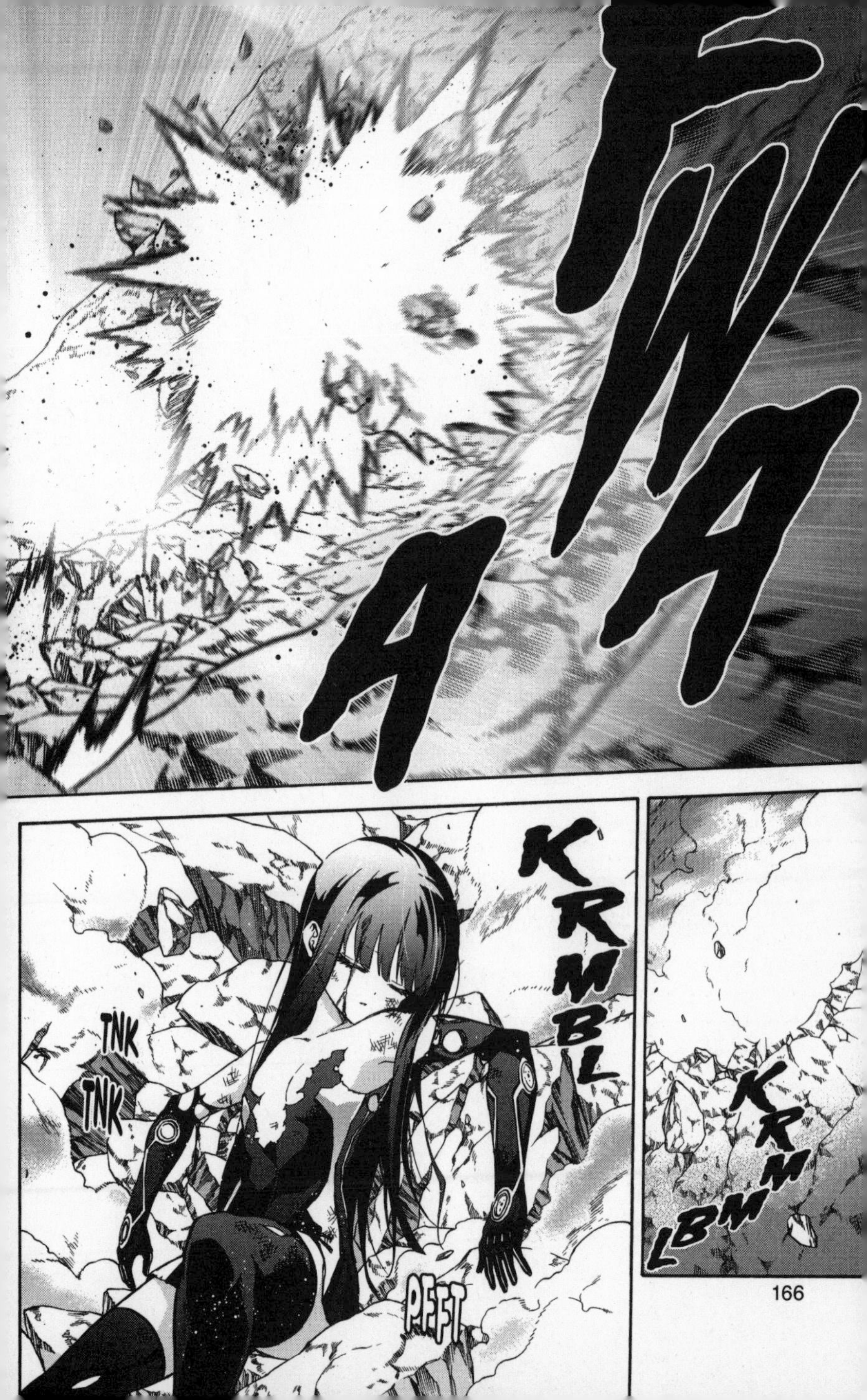
KRMMBL
KRMBL
TNK
TNK
PFFT

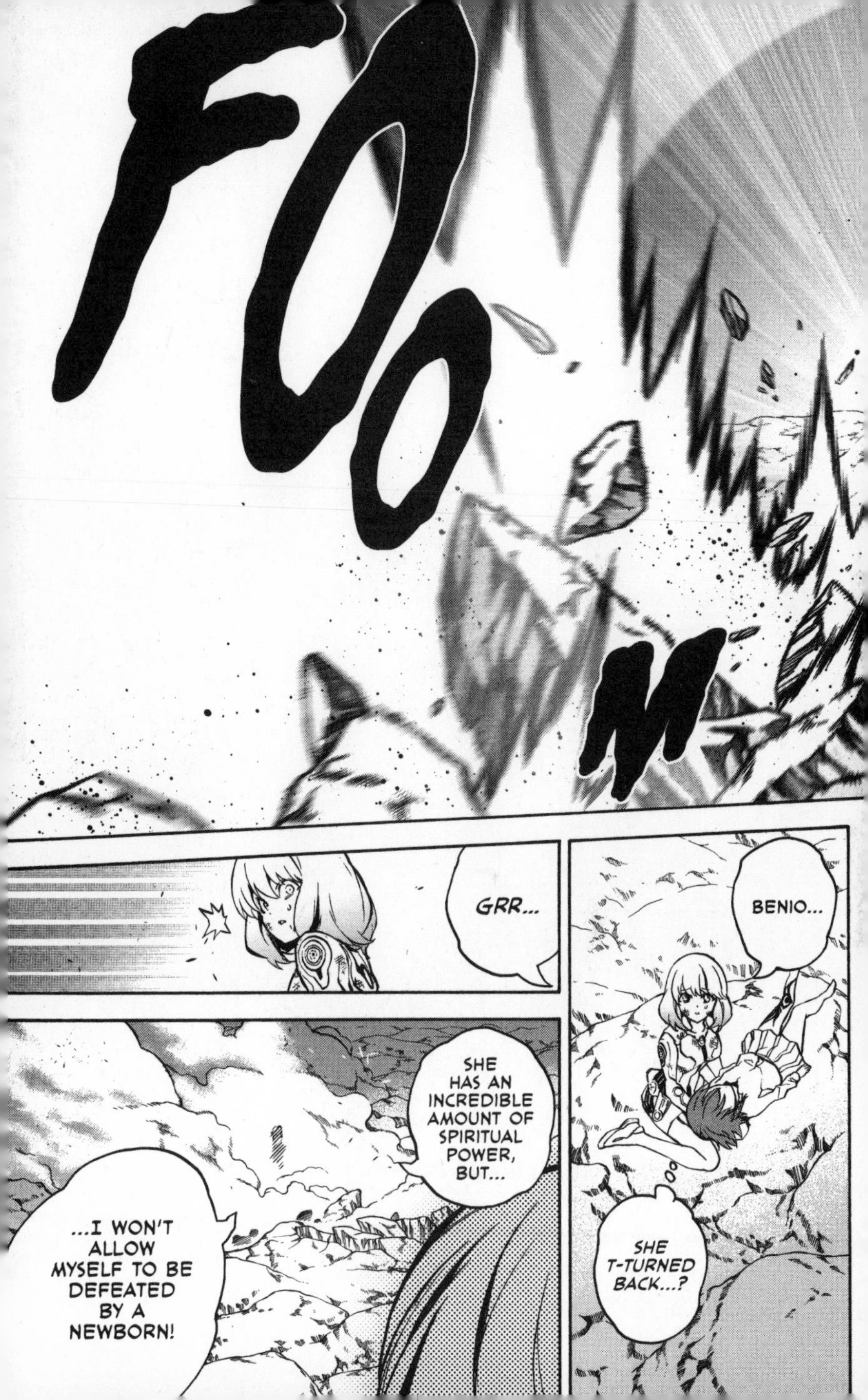
FOOM
BENIO...
SHE T-TURNED BACK...?
GRR...
SHE HAS AN INCREDIBLE AMOUNT OF SPIRITUAL POWER, BUT...
...I WON'T ALLOW MYSELF TO BE DEFEATED BY A NEWBORN!

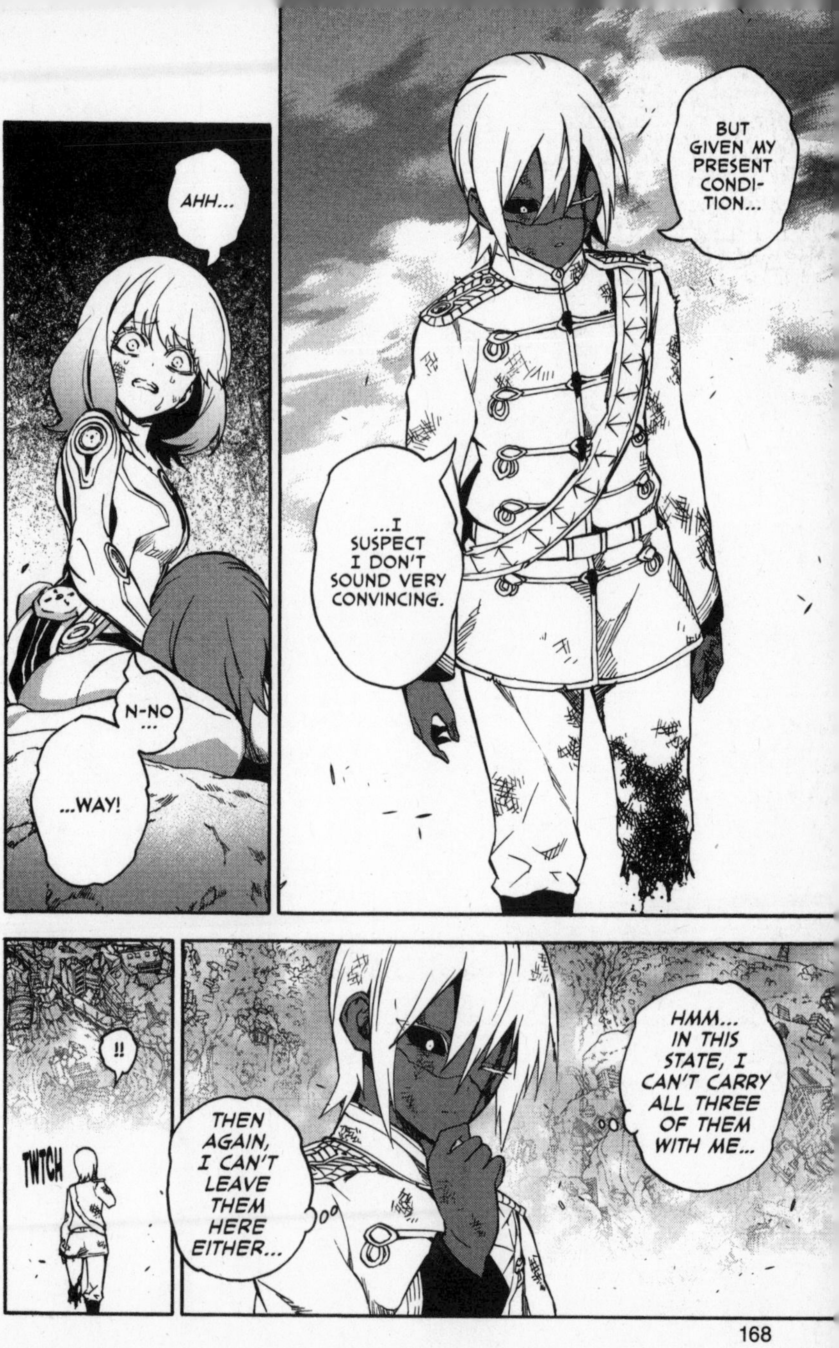
BUT GIVEN MY PRESENT CONDITION...
...I SUSPECT I DON'T SOUND VERY CONVINCING.
AHH...
N-NO...
...WAY!
HMM... IN THIS STATE, I CAN'T CARRY ALL THREE OF THEM WITH ME...
THEN AGAIN, I CAN'T LEAVE THEM HERE EITHER...
!!
TWTCH

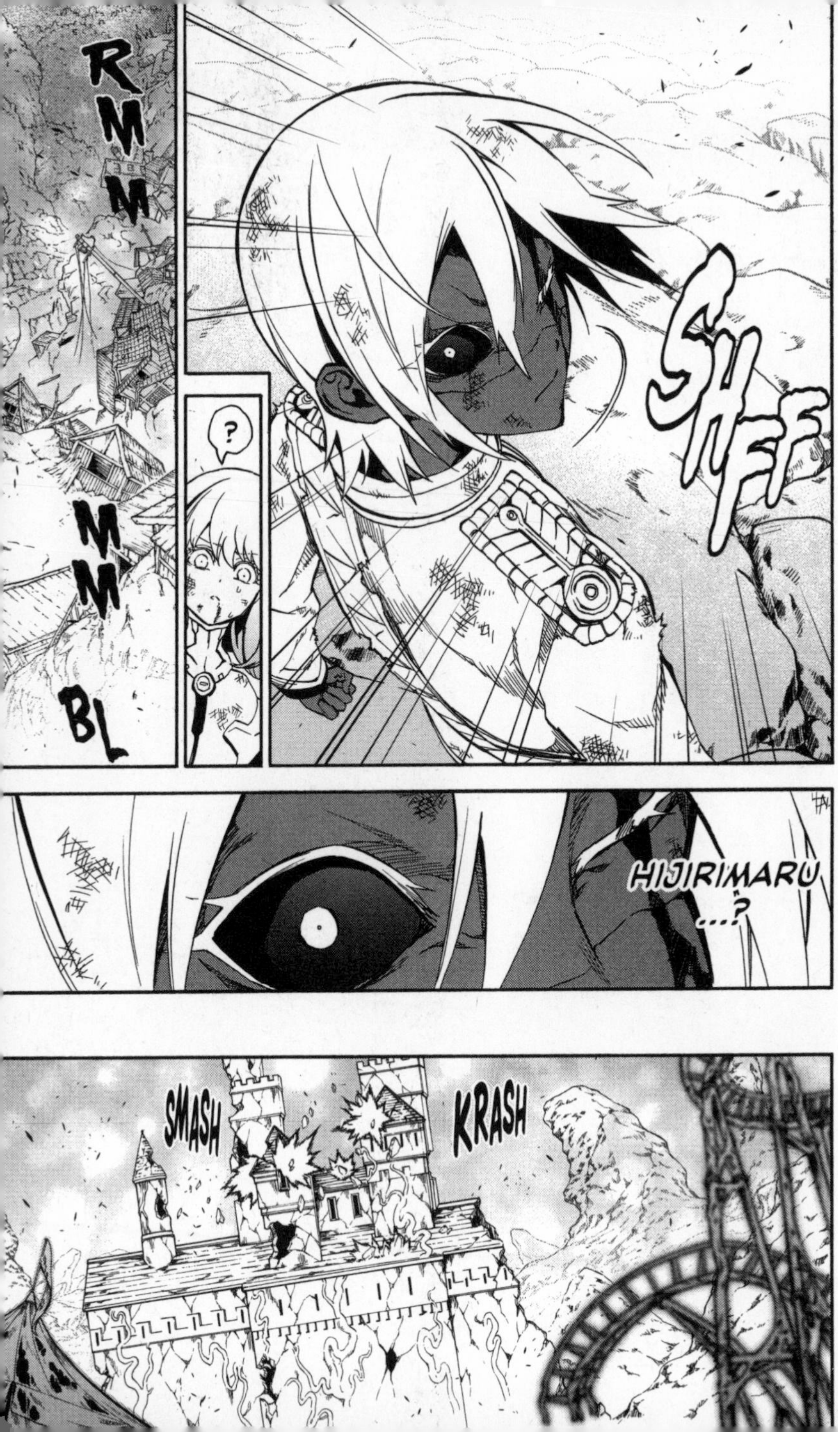
SHFF
?
RMM
MMM
BL
HIJIRIMARU ...?
KRASH
SMASH

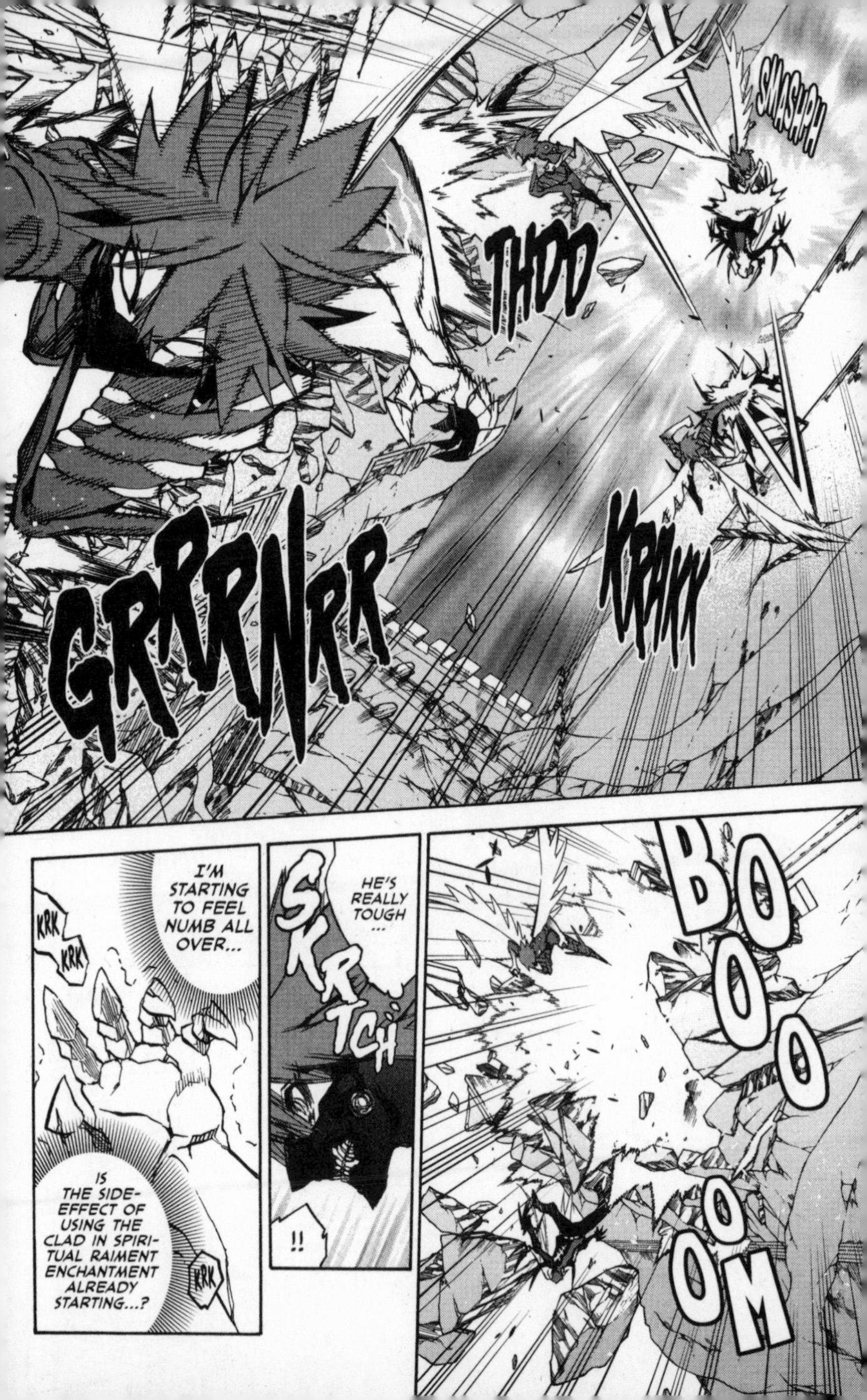
SHASHPH
THDD
KRAKK
GRRRNRR
BOOOOOOM
SKRRTCH
HE'S REALLY TOUGH ...
!!
I'M STARTING TO FEEL NUMB ALL OVER...
KRK
KRK
IS THE SIDE-EFFECT OF USING THE CLAD IN SPIRITUAL RAIMENT ENCHANTMENT ALREADY STARTING...?
KRK

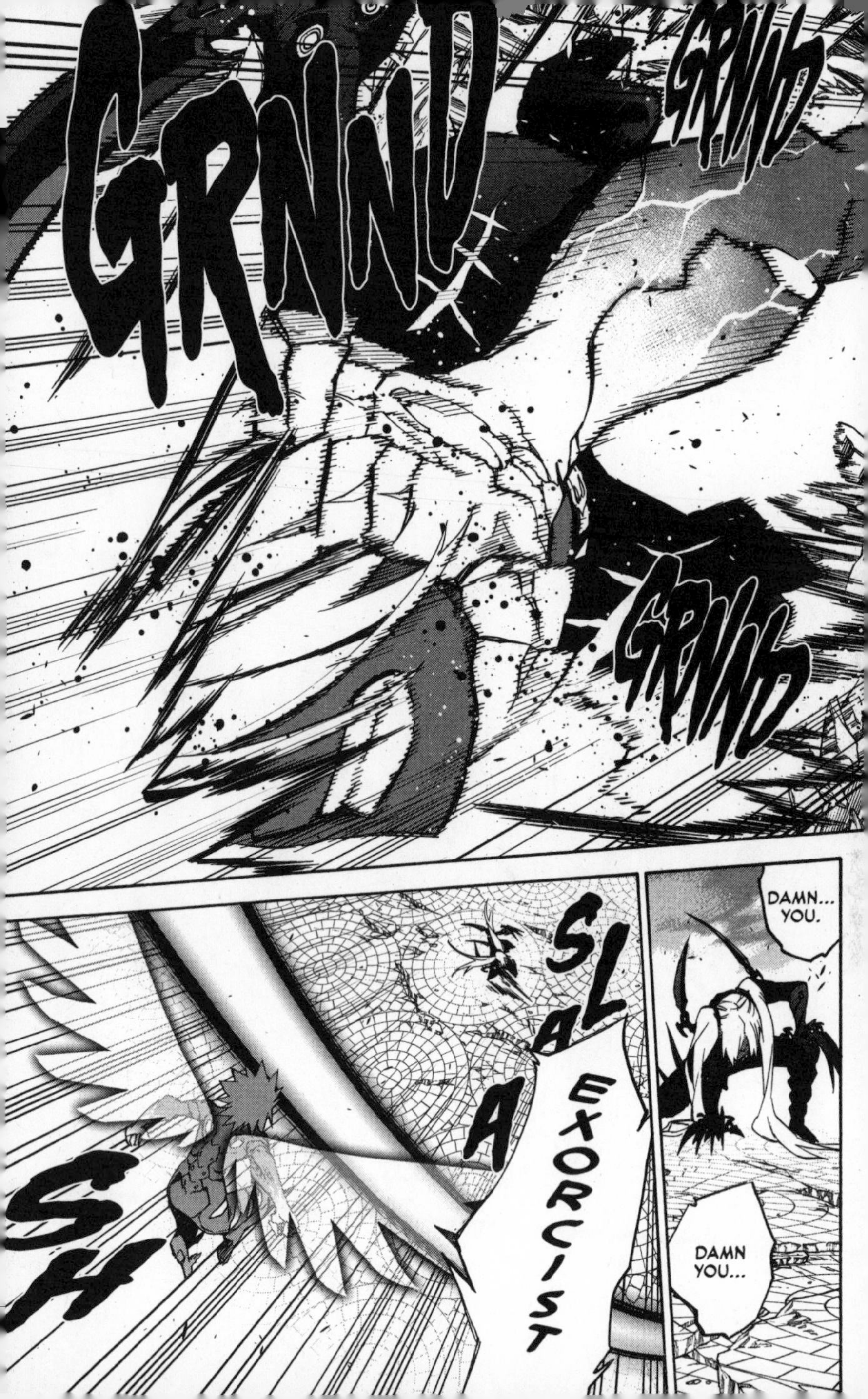
GRNND
GRNND
GRNND
DAMN... YOU.
DAMN YOU...
SLAA
EXORCIST
SH

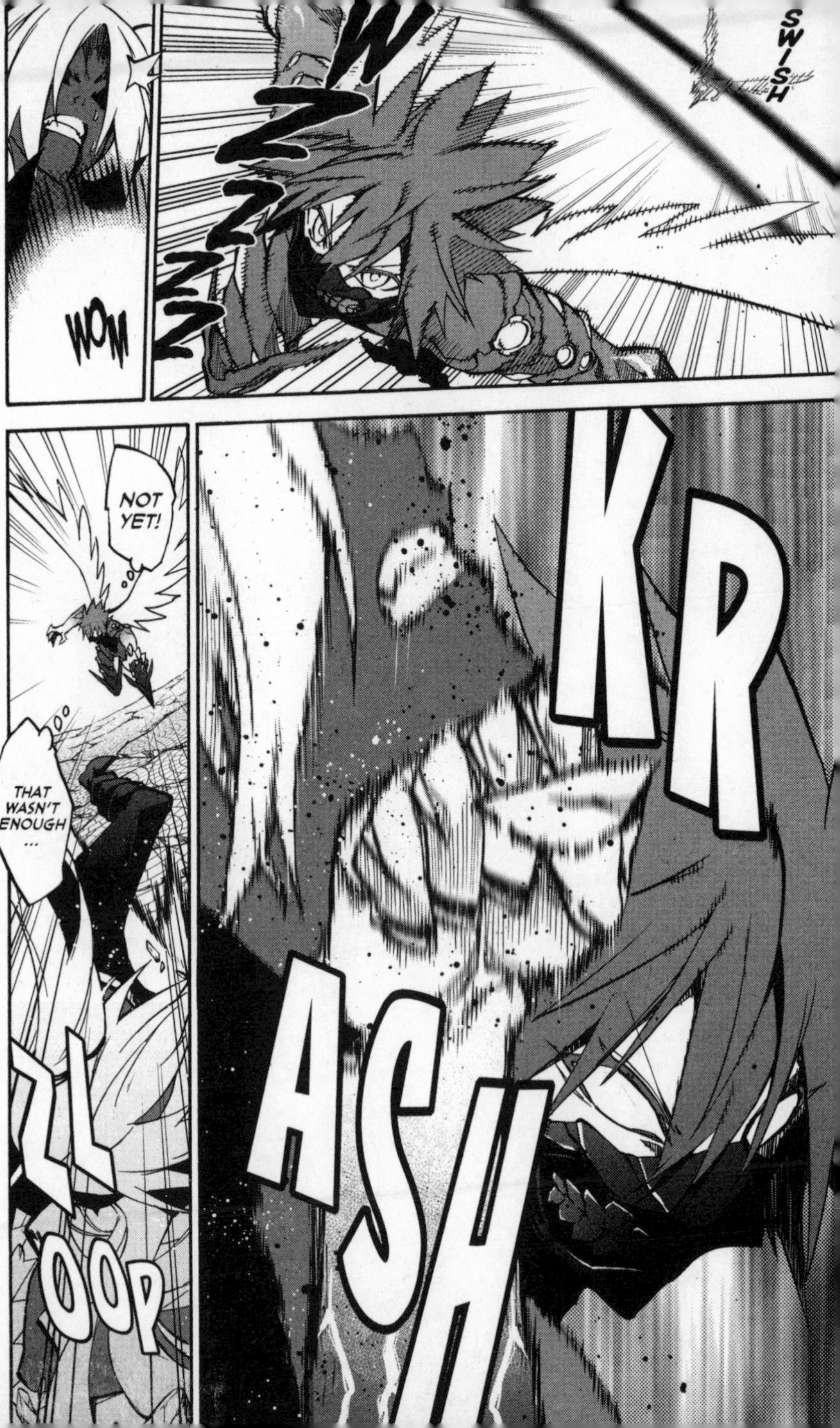
SWISH
WOM
KRASH
NOT YET!
THAT WASN'T ENOUGH ...

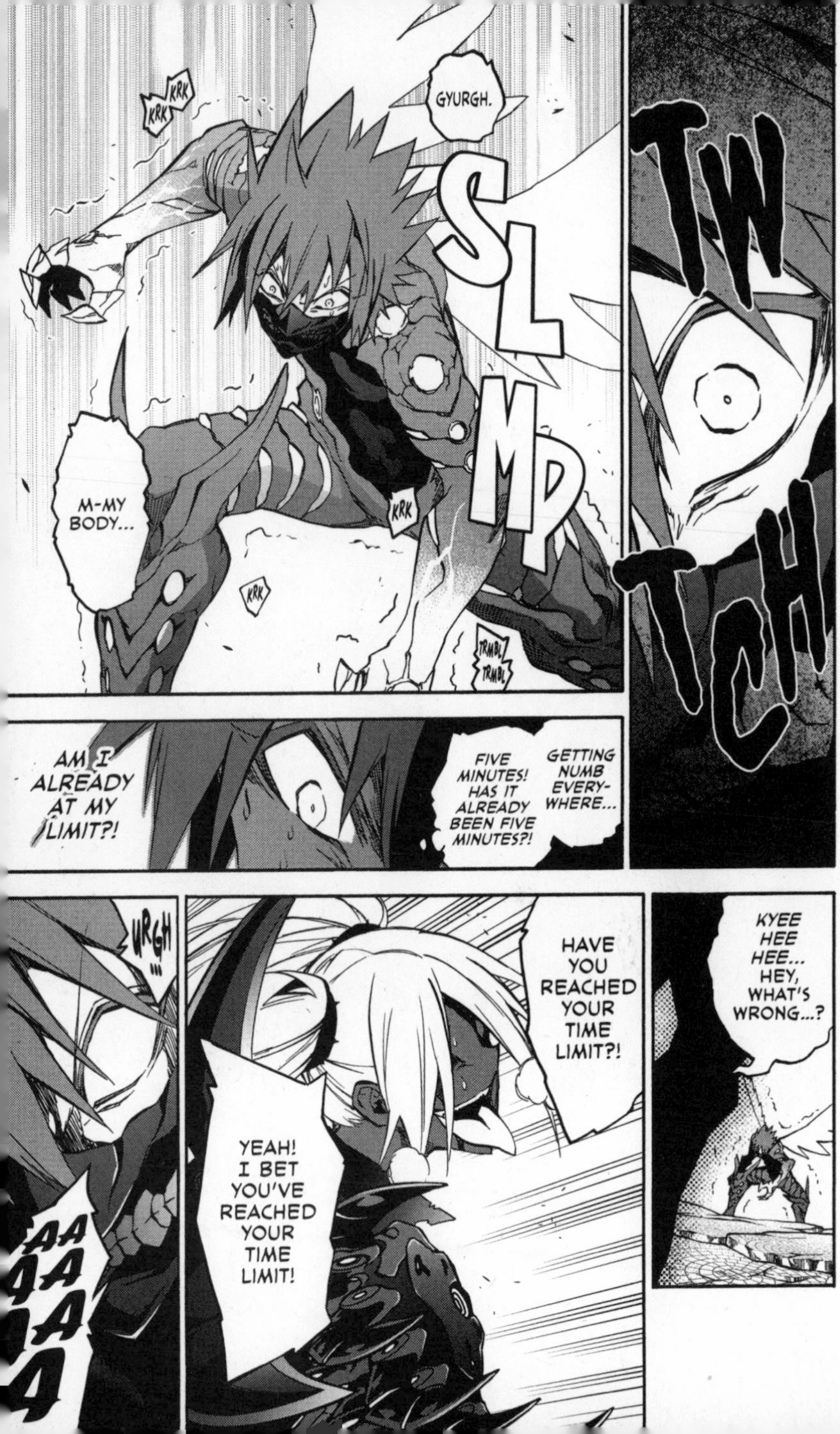
TWITCH
GYURGH.
SLMP
KRK KRK KRK
M-MY BODY...
KRK
KRK
TRMBL TRMBL
GETTING NUMB EVERY-WHERE...
FIVE MINUTES! HAS IT ALREADY BEEN FIVE MINUTES?!
AM I ALREADY AT MY LIMIT?!
KYEE HEE HEE... HEY, WHAT'S WRONG...?
HAVE YOU REACHED YOUR TIME LIMIT?!
YEAH! I BET YOU'VE REACHED YOUR TIME LIMIT!
URGH
AAAAAAA

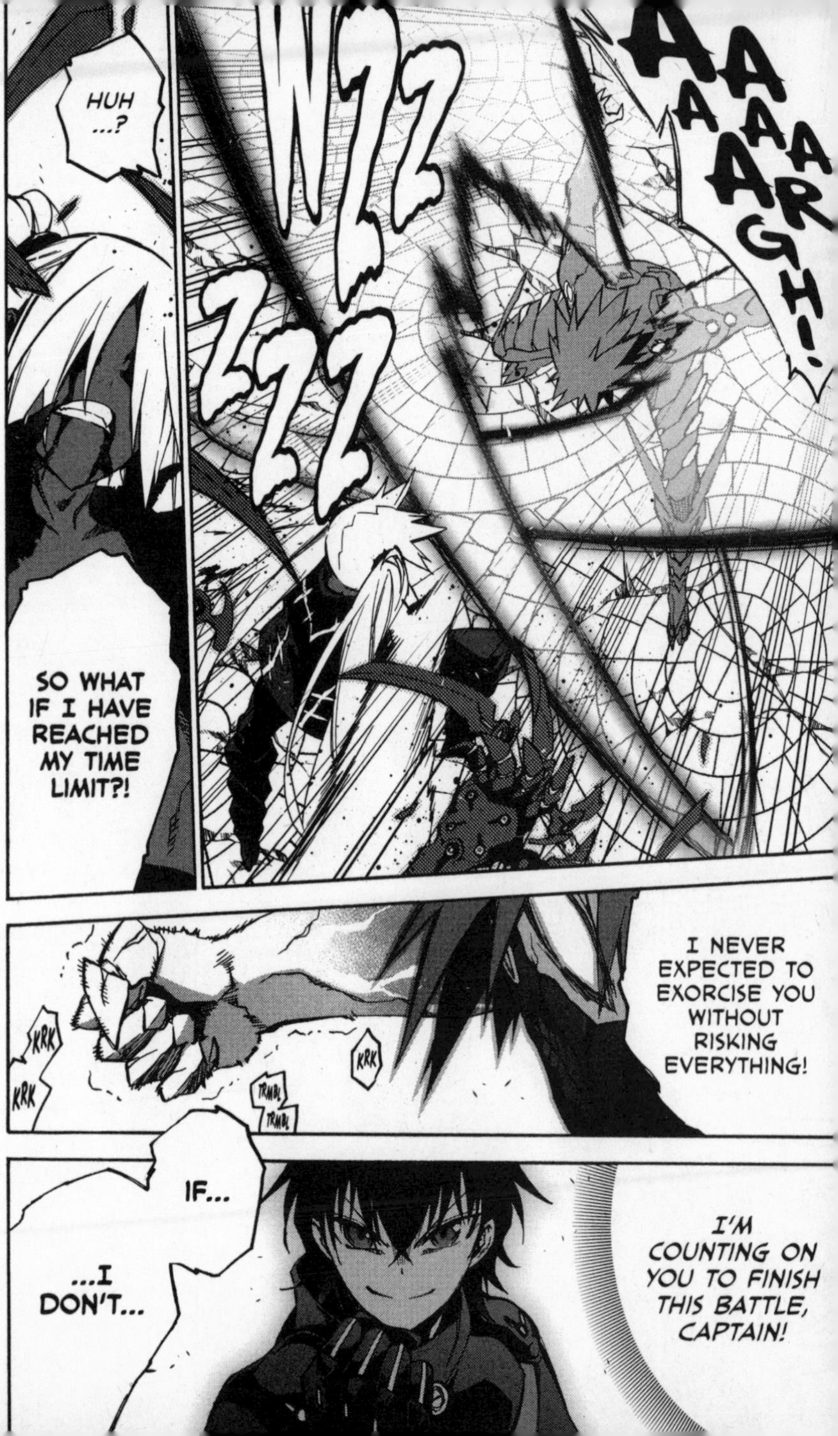

WZZ
ZZZ
AAAAAARGH!
HUH ...?
SO WHAT IF I HAVE REACHED MY TIME LIMIT?!
I NEVER EXPECTED TO EXORCISE YOU WITHOUT RISKING EVERYTHING!
KRK
TRMBL TRMBL
KRK
KRK
I'M COUNTING ON YOU TO FINISH THIS BATTLE, CAPTAIN!
IF...
...I DON'T...

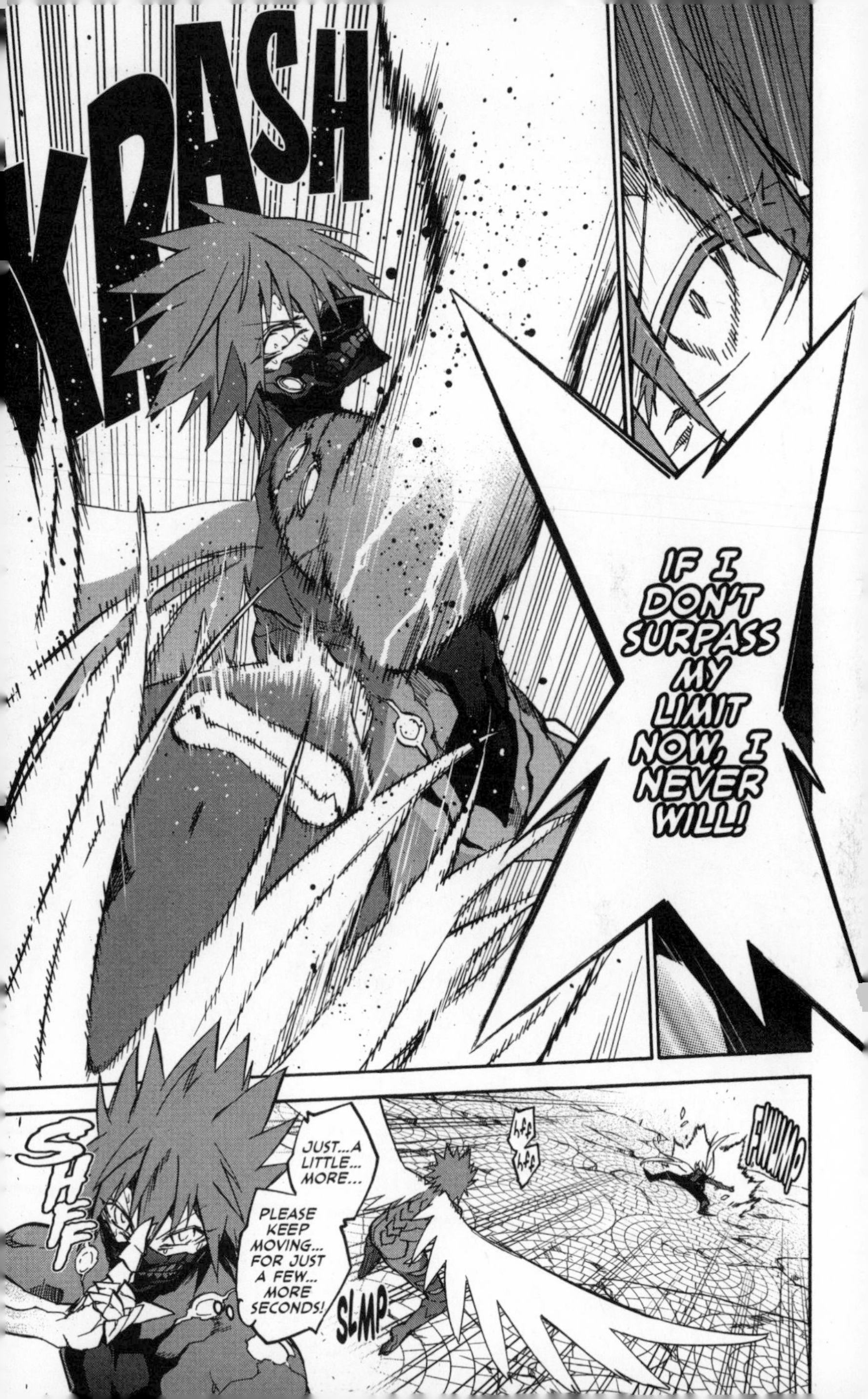
IF I DON'T SURPASS MY LIMIT NOW, I NEVER WILL!
KRASH
FWUMP
JUST...A LITTLE... MORE...
PLEASE KEEP MOVING... FOR JUST A FEW... MORE SECONDS!
SLMP
SHF

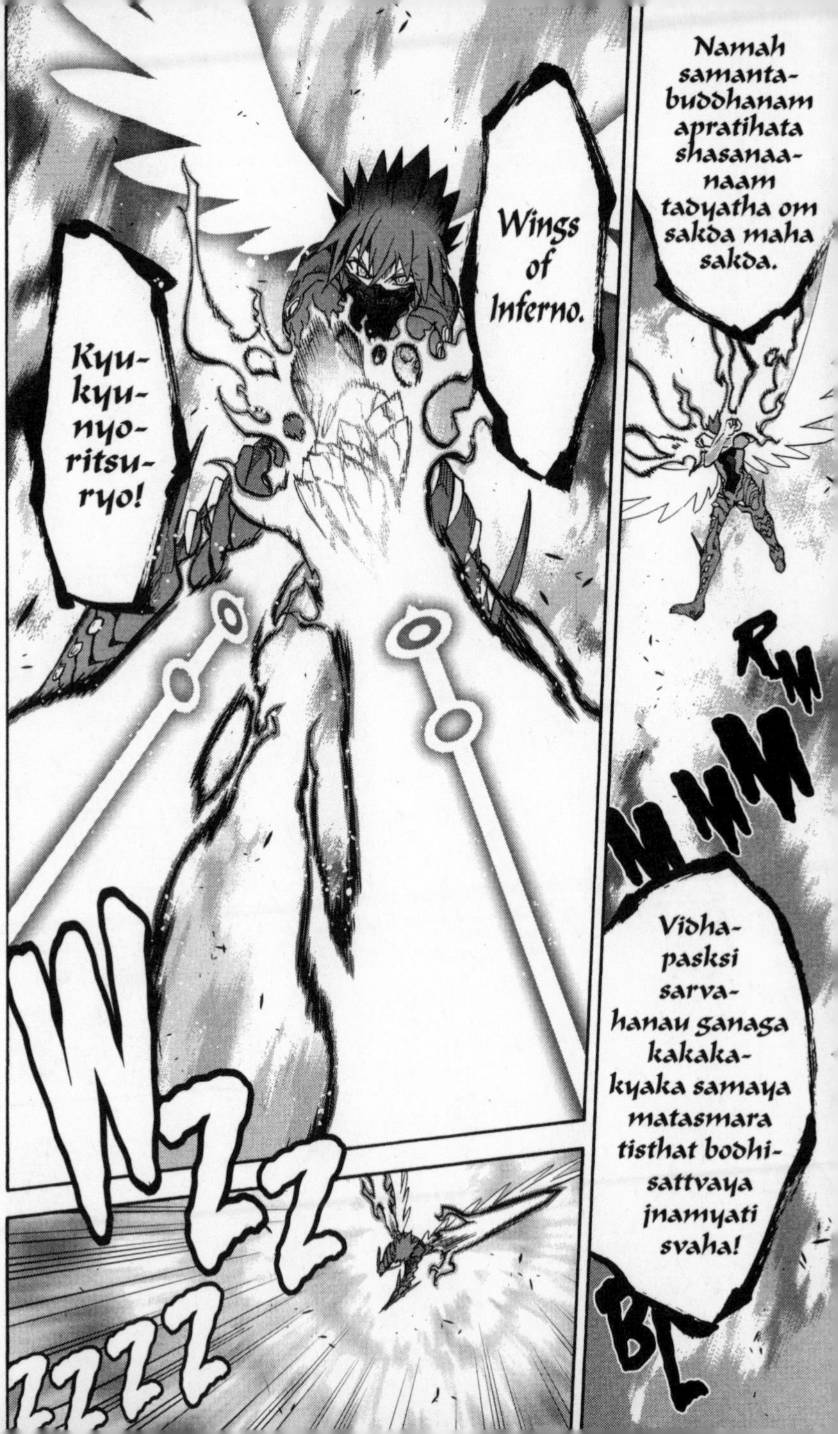
Namah samanta-buddhanam apratihata shasanaa-naam tadyatha om sakda maha sakda.
RMMMMM
Vidha-pasksi sarva-hanau ganaga kakaka-kyaka samaya matasmara tisthat bodhi-sattvaya jnamyati svaha!
BL
Wings of Inferno.
Kyu-kyu-nyo-ritsu-ryo!
WZZZ
ZZZZ

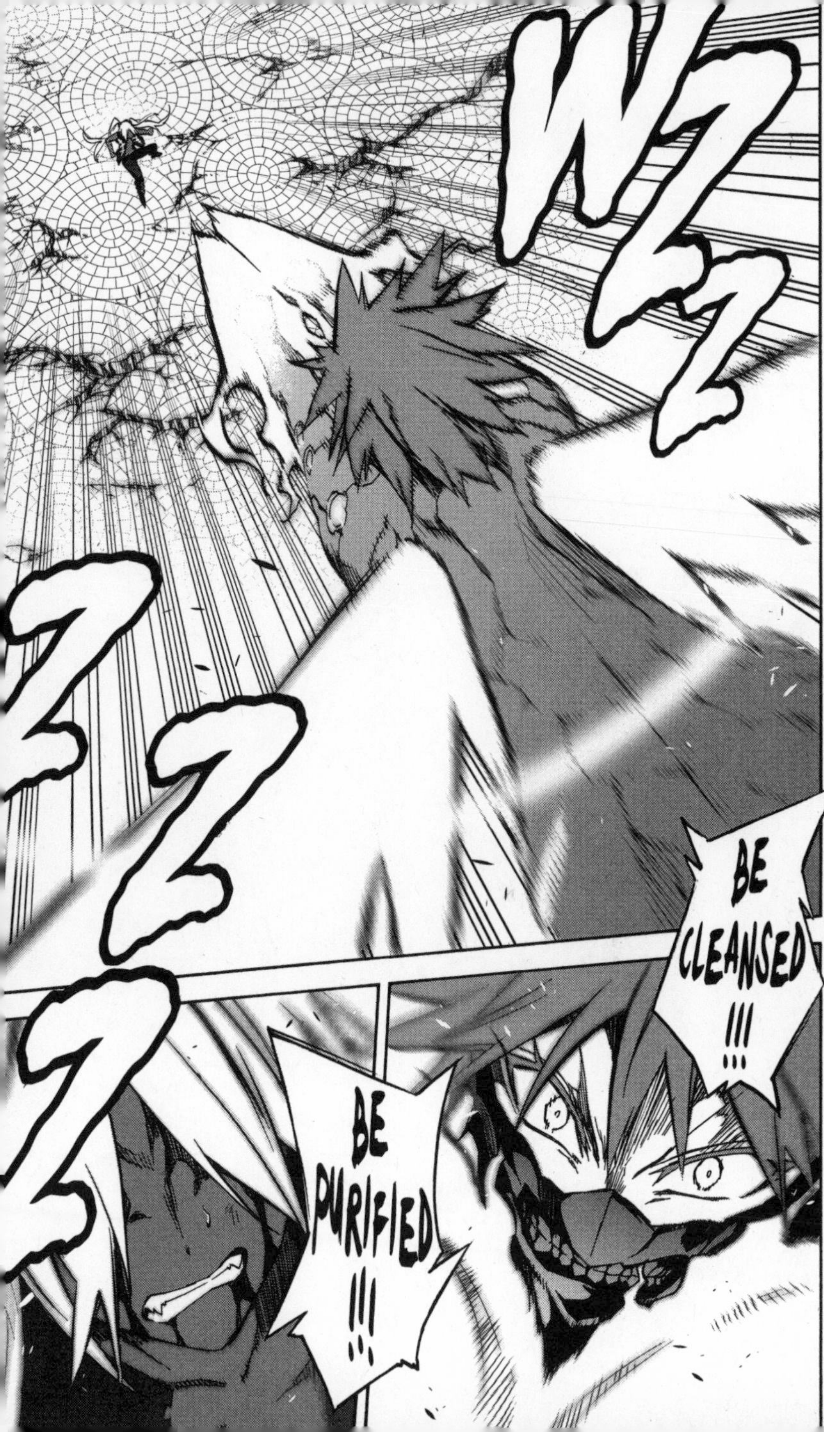
WZZ
ZZZ
BE CLEANSED!!!
BE PURIFIED!!!

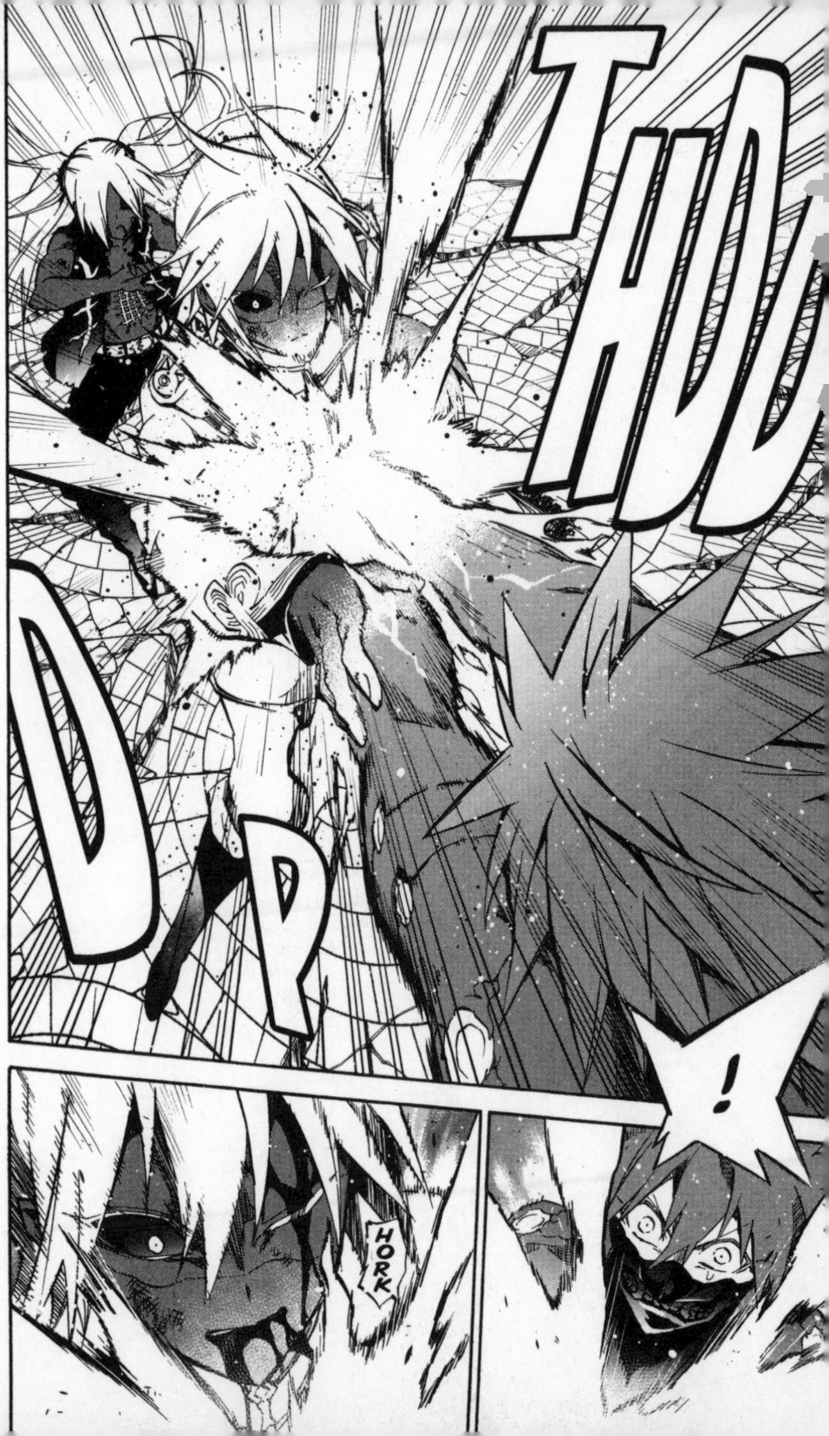
THUD
DUD
!
HORK

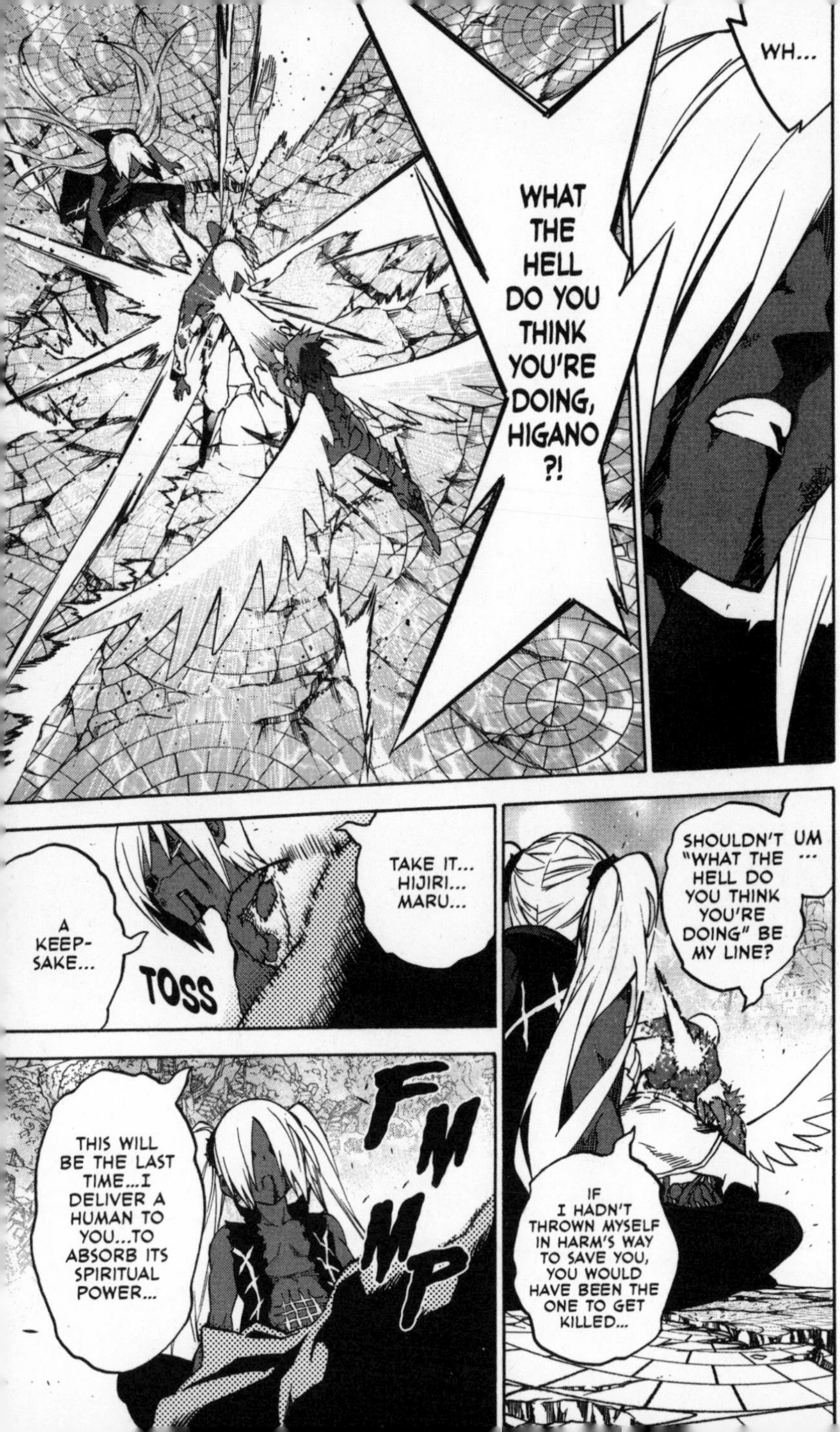
WH...
WHAT THE HELL DO YOU THINK YOU'RE DOING, HIGANO ?!
UM ...
SHOULDN'T "WHAT THE HELL DO YOU THINK YOU'RE DOING" BE MY LINE?
IF I HADN'T THROWN MYSELF IN HARM'S WAY TO SAVE YOU, YOU WOULD HAVE BEEN THE ONE TO GET KILLED...
TAKE IT... HIJIRI... MARU...
TOSS
A KEEP-SAKE...
FMMP
THIS WILL BE THE LAST TIME...I DELIVER A HUMAN TO YOU...TO ABSORB ITS SPIRITUAL POWER...

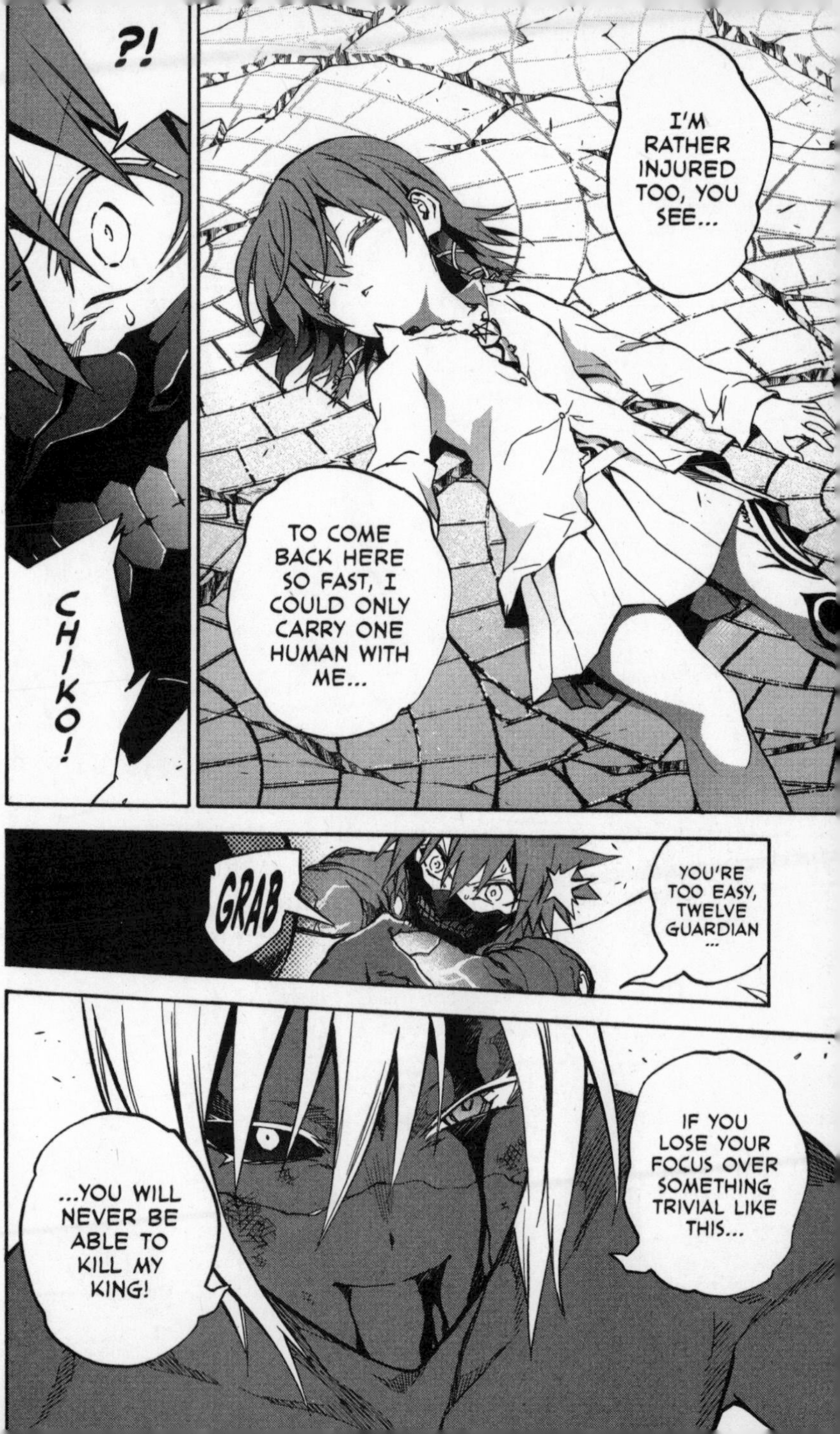
I'M RATHER INJURED TOO, YOU SEE...
TO COME BACK HERE SO FAST, I COULD ONLY CARRY ONE HUMAN WITH ME...
?!
CHIKO!
YOU'RE TOO EASY, TWELVE GUARDIAN...
GRAB
IF YOU LOSE YOUR FOCUS OVER SOMETHING TRIVIAL LIKE THIS...
...YOU WILL NEVER BE ABLE TO KILL MY KING!

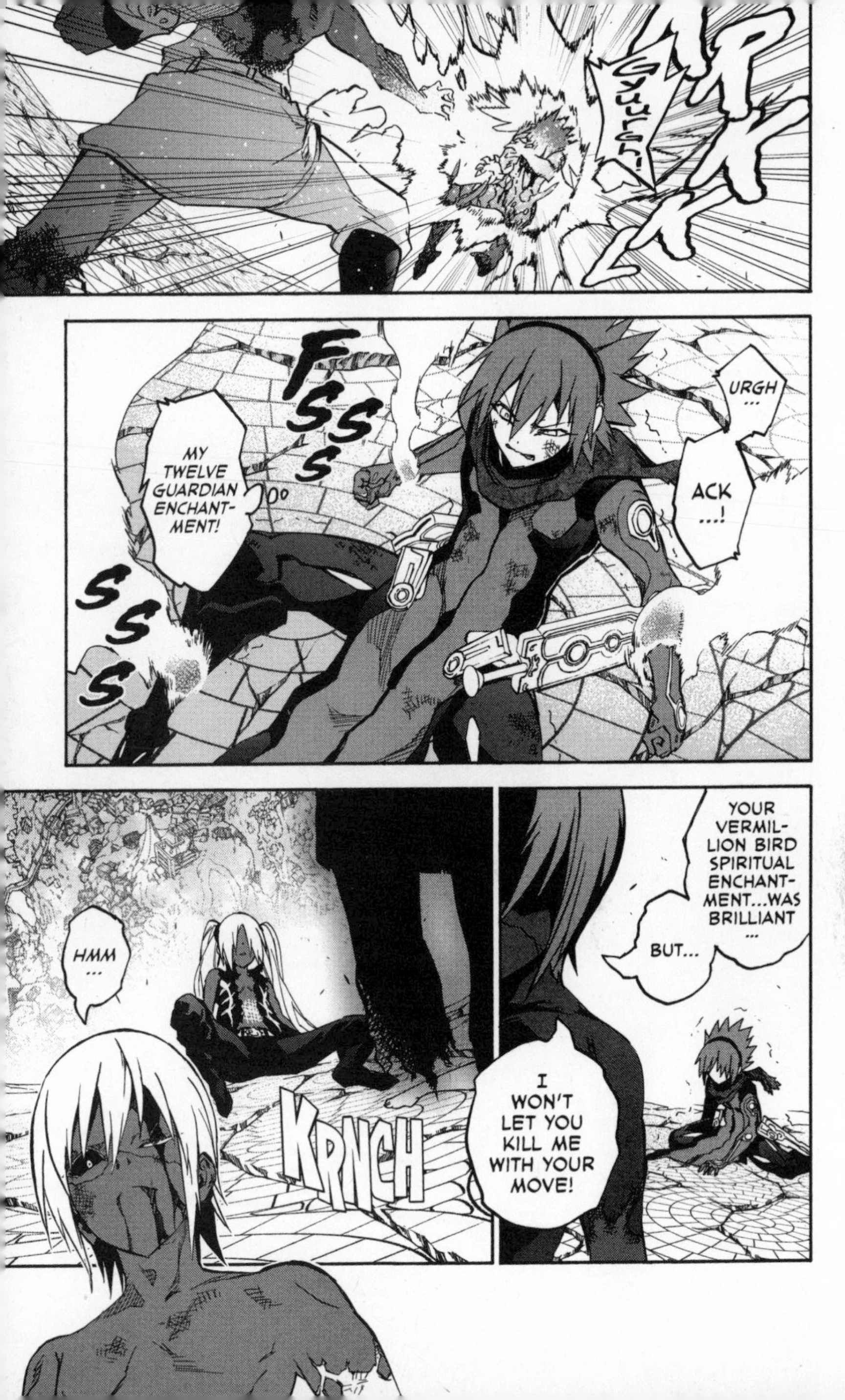
GYUUUGH!
URGH...
ACK...!
MY TWELVE GUARDIAN ENCHANTMENT!
FSSS
SSS
YOUR VERMILLION BIRD SPIRITUAL ENCHANTMENT...WAS BRILLIANT...
BUT...
I WON'T LET YOU KILL ME WITH YOUR MOVE!
HMM...
KRNCH

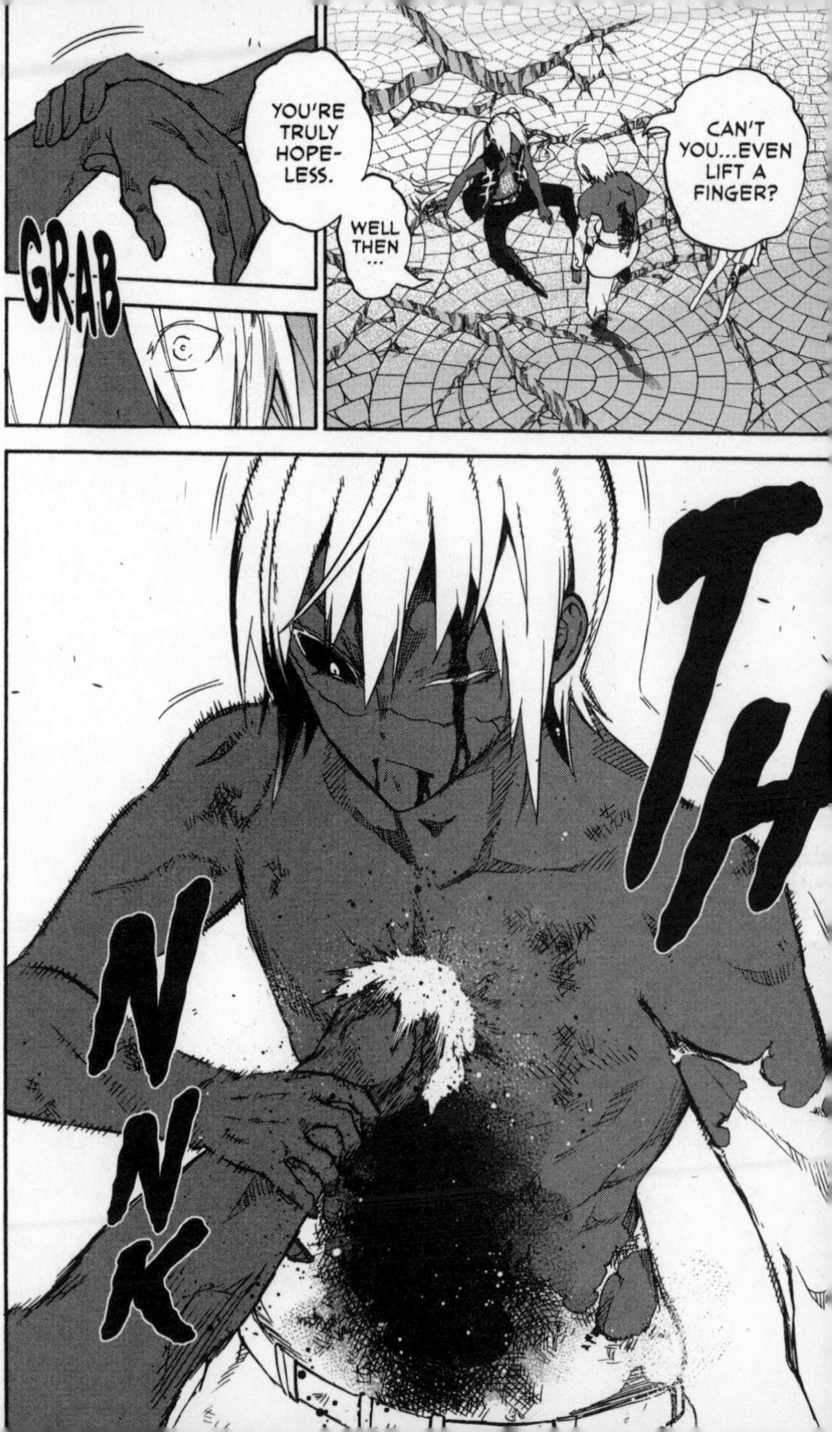
CAN'T YOU...EVEN LIFT A FINGER?
YOU'RE TRULY HOPE-LESS.
WELL THEN...
GRAB
TH
NNK

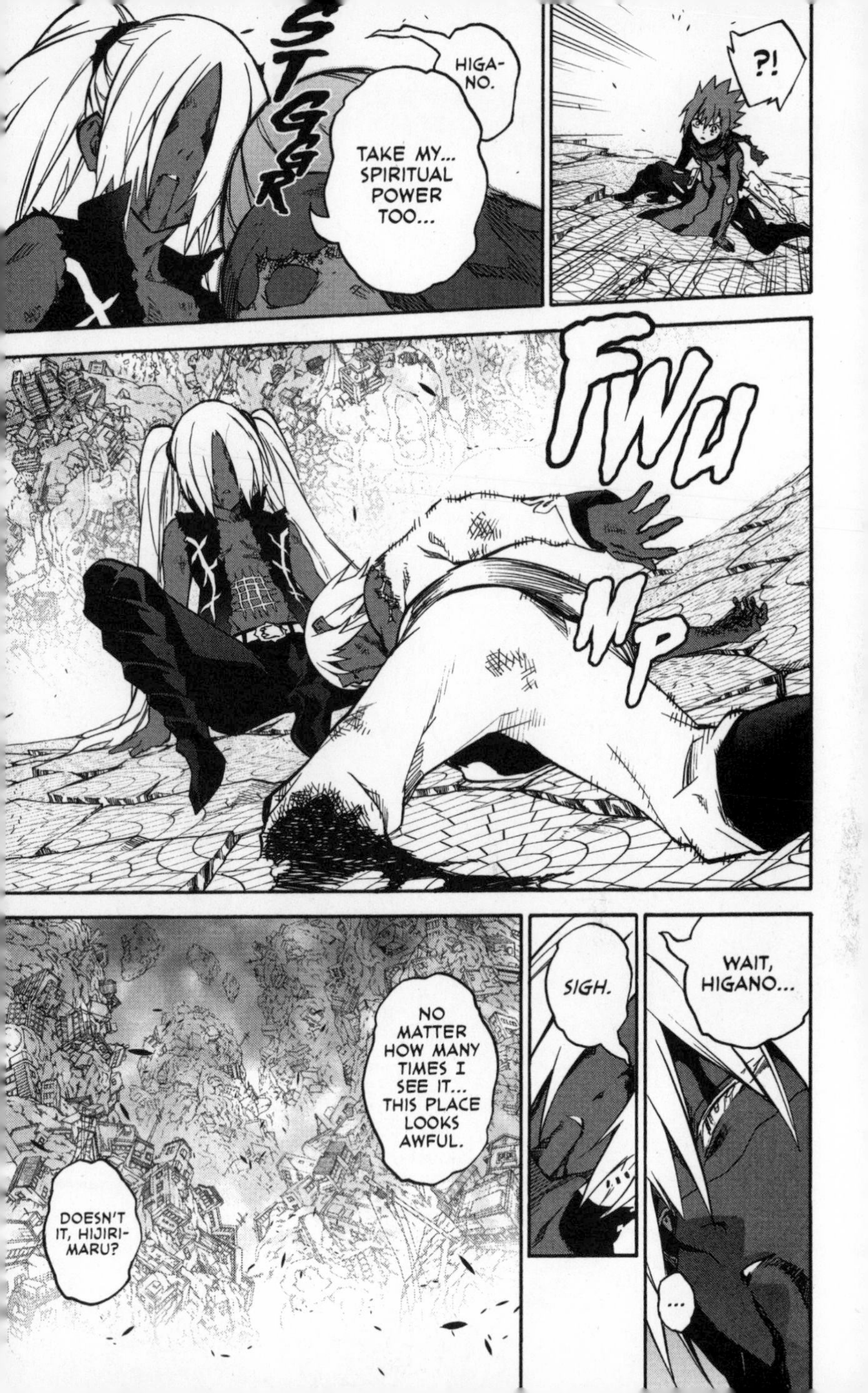
?!
HIGA-NO.
STGGR
TAKE MY... SPIRITUAL POWER TOO...
FWUMP
WAIT, HIGANO...
...
SIGH.
NO MATTER HOW MANY TIMES I SEE IT... THIS PLACE LOOKS AWFUL.
DOESN'T IT, HIJIRI-MARU?

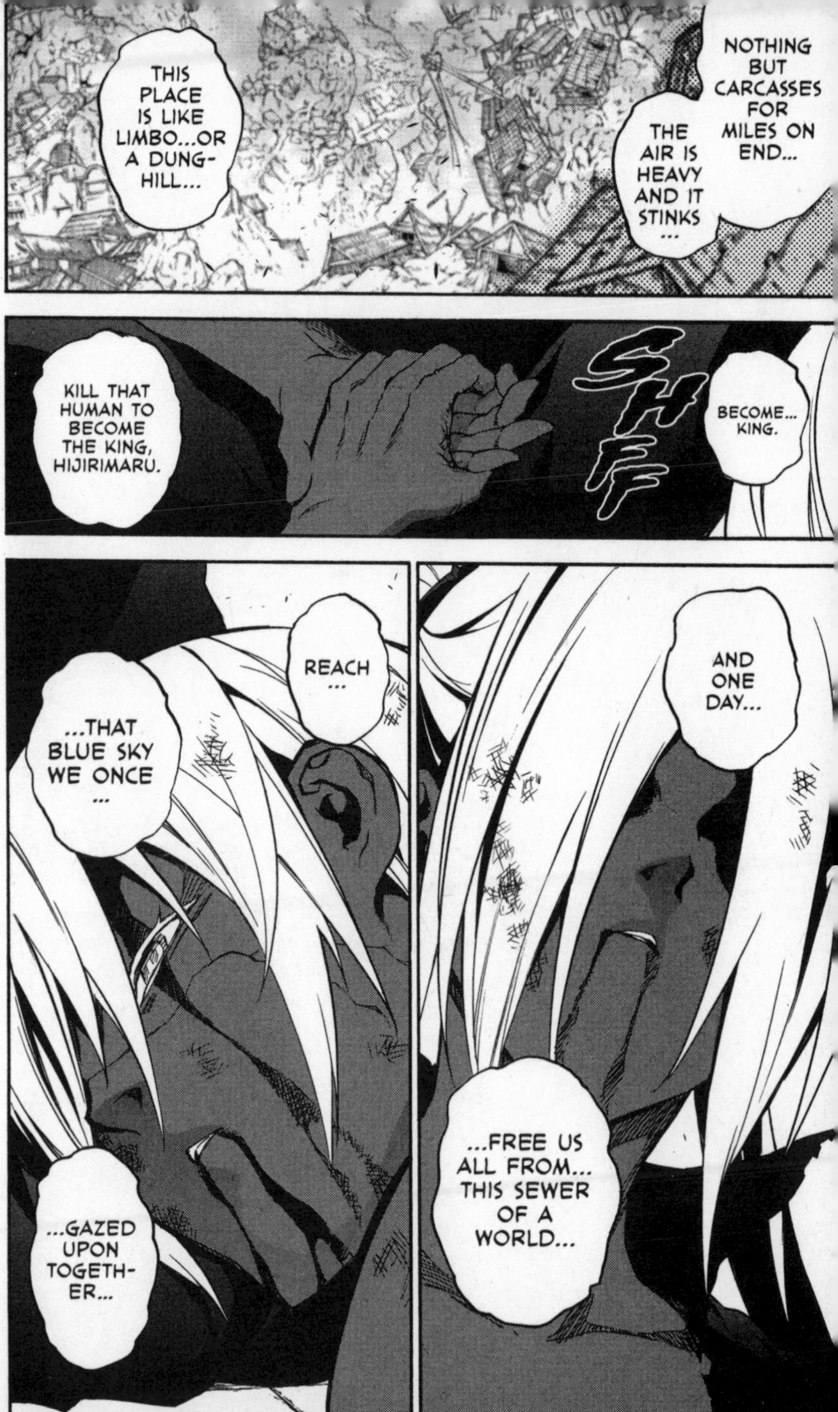
NOTHING BUT CARCASSES FOR MILES ON END...
THE AIR IS HEAVY AND IT STINKS...
THIS PLACE IS LIKE LIMBO...OR A DUNG-HILL...
BECOME... KING.
SHFF
KILL THAT HUMAN TO BECOME THE KING, HIJIRIMARU.
AND ONE DAY...
...FREE US ALL FROM... THIS SEWER OF A WORLD...
REACH...
...THAT BLUE SKY WE ONCE...
...GAZED UPON TOGETH-ER...

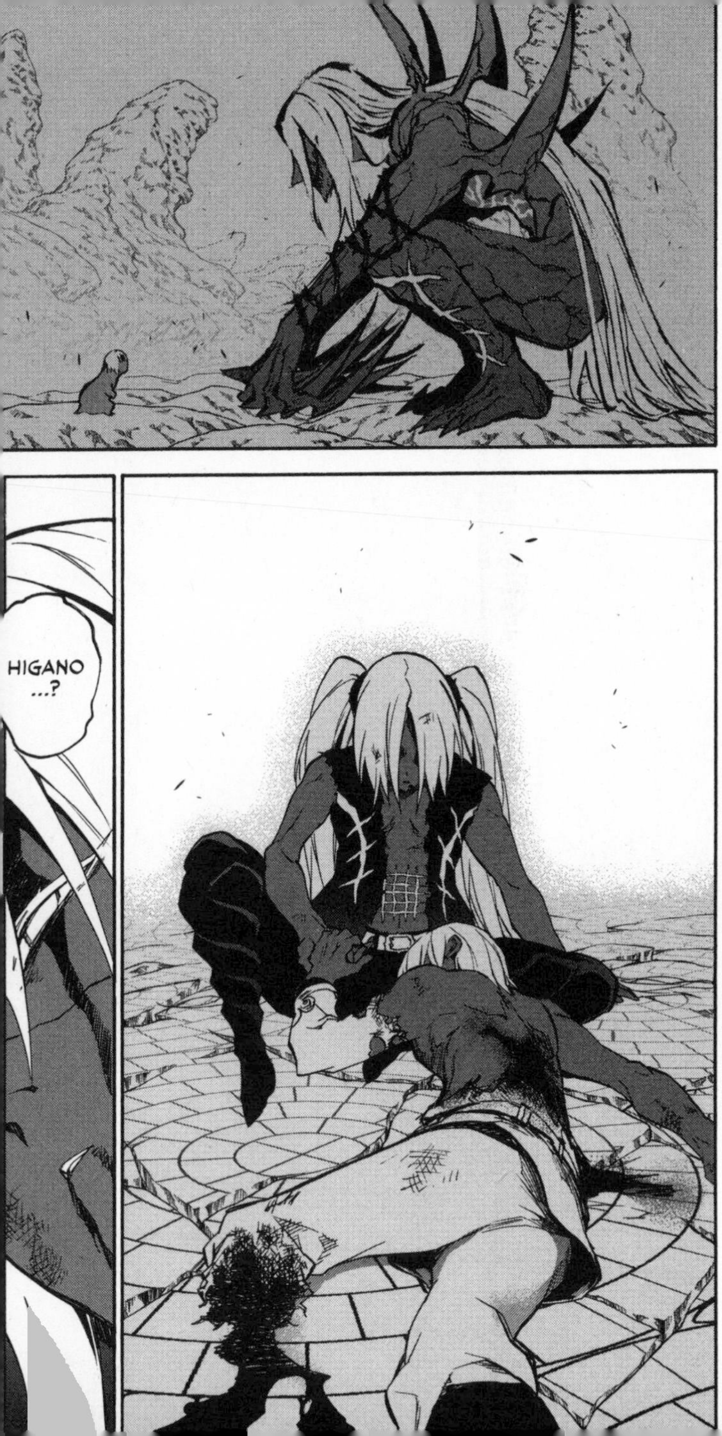
HIGANO ...?

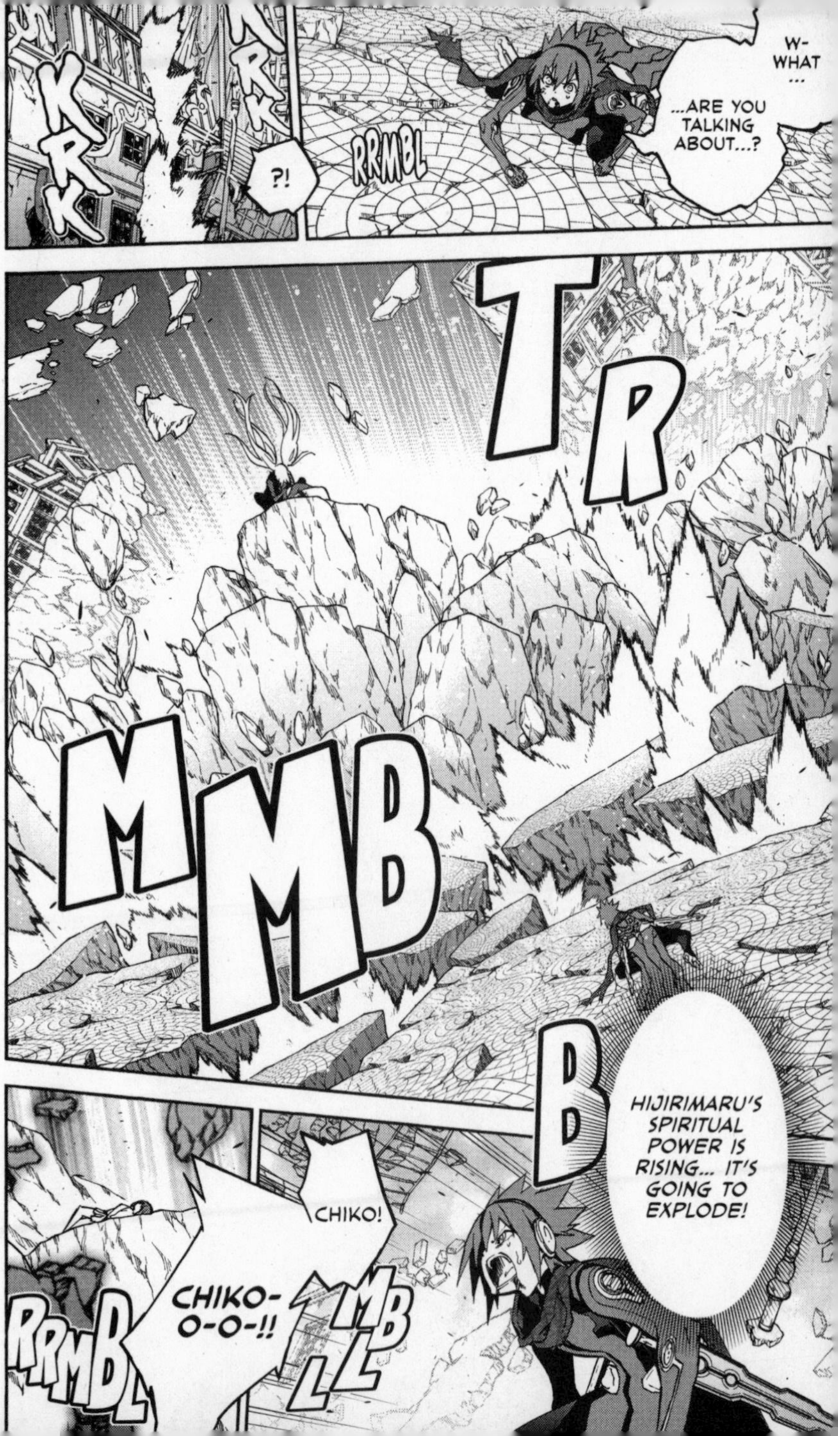
W-WHAT...
...ARE YOU TALKING ABOUT...?
RRMBL
?!
RK
KRK
TR
MMB
B
HIJIRIMARU'S SPIRITUAL POWER IS RISING... IT'S GOING TO EXPLODE!
CHIKO!
MMB
LL
CHIKO-O-O-!!
RRMBL

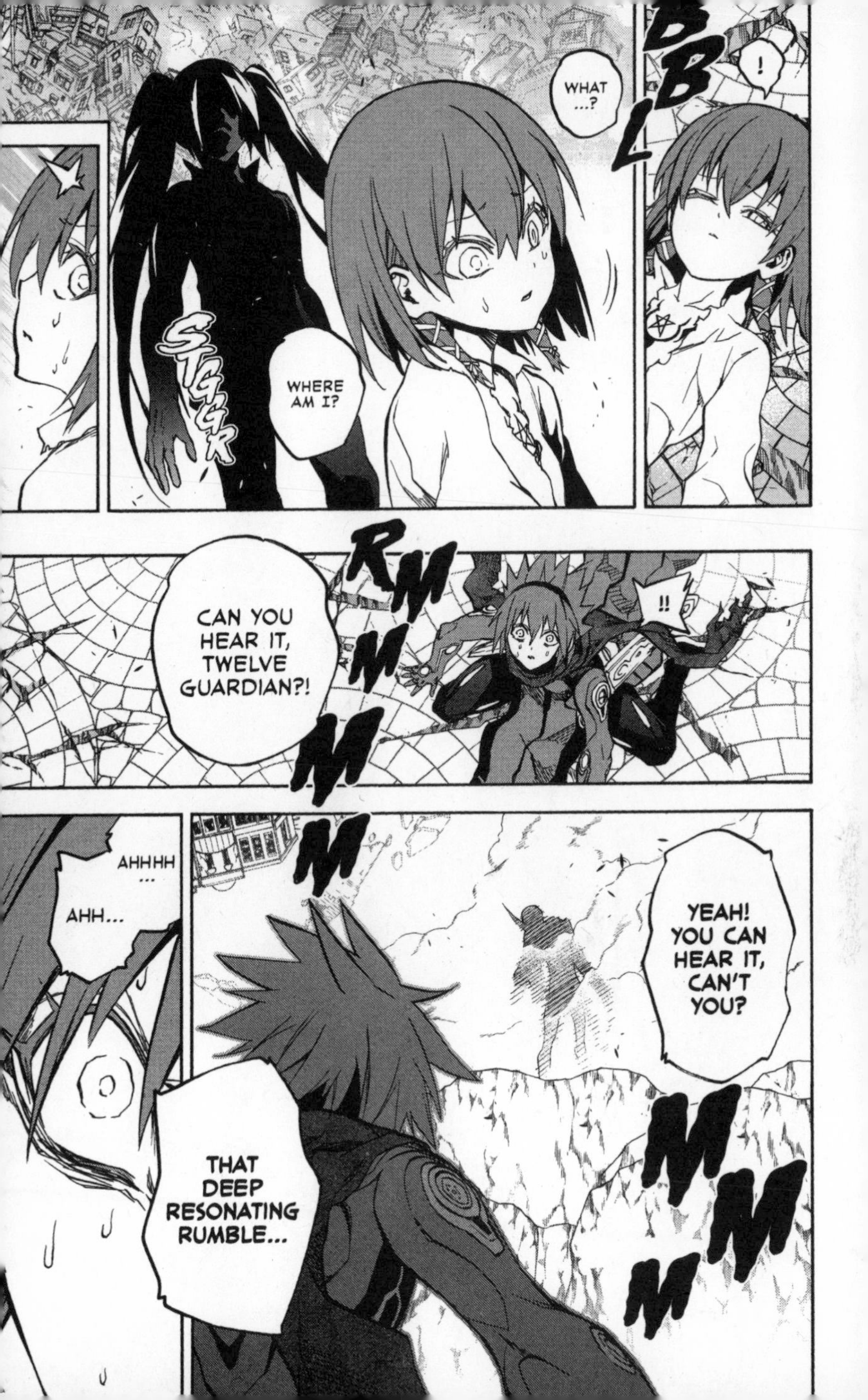
BBL
!
WHAT ...?
WHERE AM I?
STGGR
!!
RMMMMMM
CAN YOU HEAR IT, TWELVE GUARDIAN?!
YEAH! YOU CAN HEAR IT, CAN'T YOU?
THAT DEEP RESONATING RUMBLE...
MMMMM
AHHHH ...
AHH...

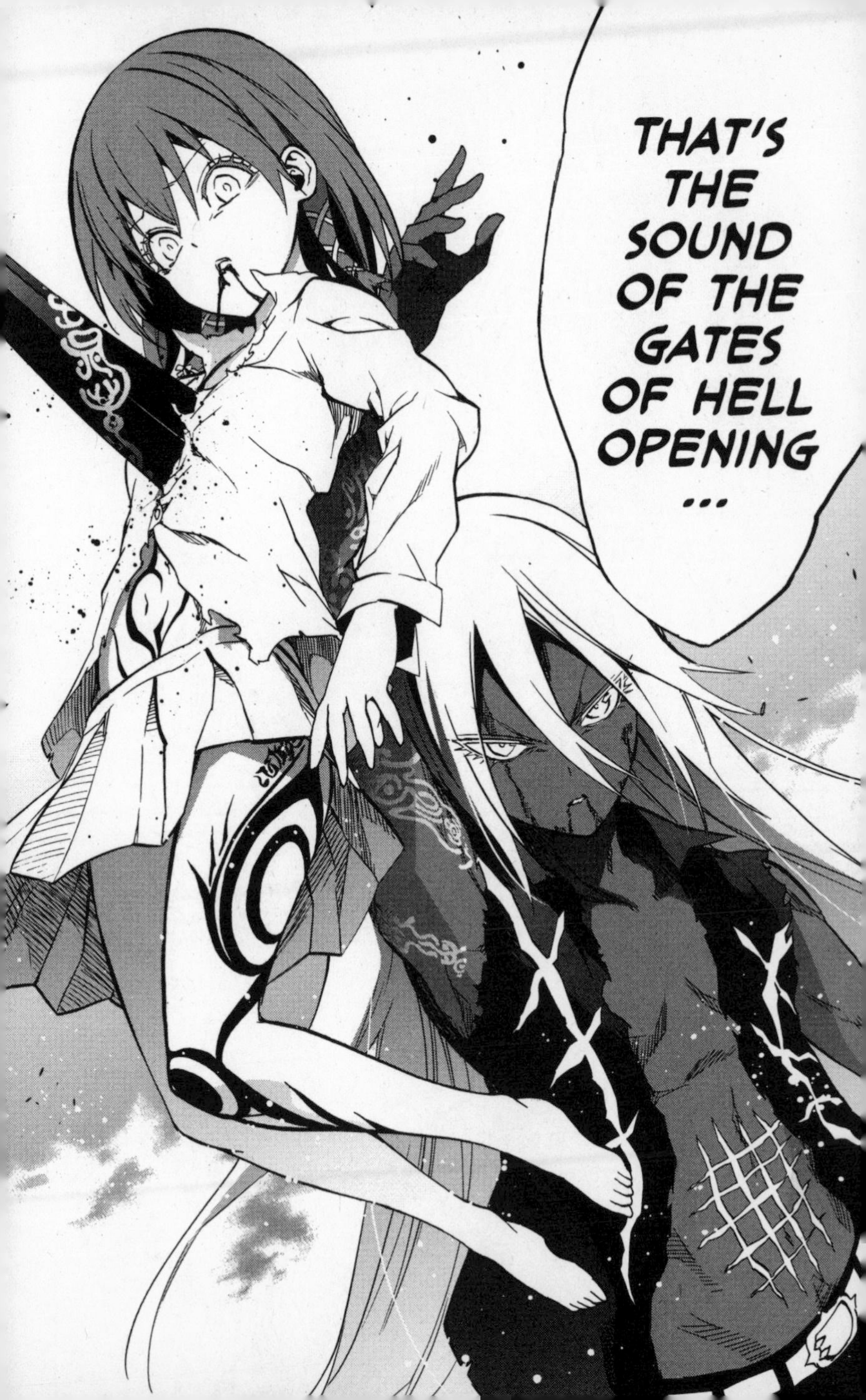
THAT'S THE SOUND OF THE GATES OF HELL OPENING ...

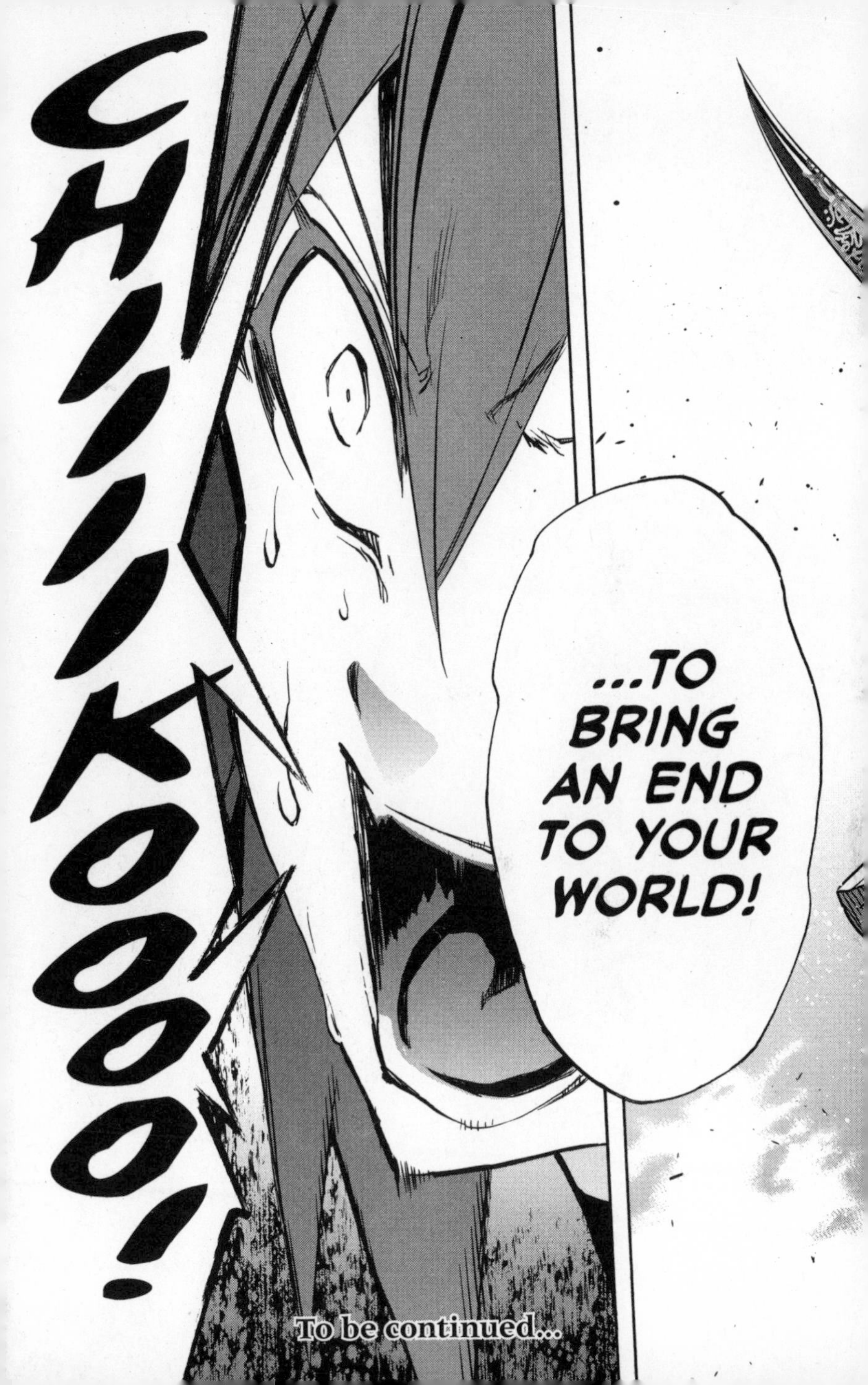
CHIIIKOOOO!
...TO BRING AN END TO YOUR WORLD!
To be continued...

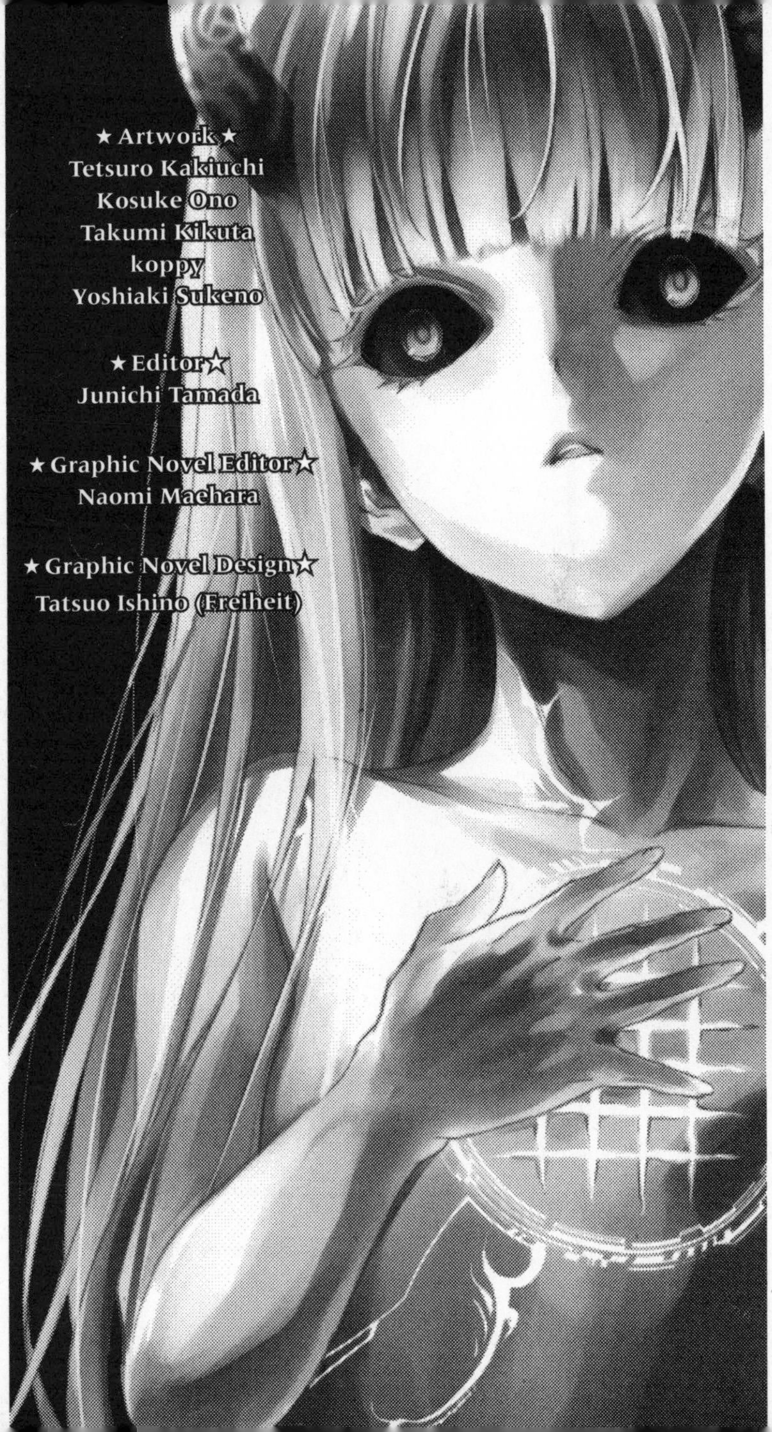

★Artwork★
Tetsuro Kakiuchi
Kosuke Ono
Takumi Kikuta
koppy
Yoshiaki Sukeno

★Editor★
Junichi Tamada

★Graphic Novel Editor★
Naomi Maehara

★Graphic Novel Design★
Tatsuo Ishino (Freiheit)

BY THE WAY, MY HOMETOWN WAS LOCATED IN THE SUPER BOONIES OF WAKAYAMA PREFECTURE. IT WAS A FORTY-MINUTE RIDE BY CAR TO THE CLOSEST CONVENIENCE STORE, AND THERE WERE ONLY FIVE OTHER KIDS WHO GRADUATED MIDDLE SCHOOL WITH ME.

my previous series, *Good Luck Gi*
racters all had names based on fl
l it makes it easier for me to com
th new names when I set a patte

f you may have already noticed,
s, *Twin Star Exorcists*, the family na
o and Adashino are all taken from
d villages in the Kansai region (
n of Arima, whose first name is t
). By the way, the human charac
f locations in the Kansai region,
have names of locations from els

I FAIL TO SEE ANY RESEMBLANCE BETWEEN YOU AND YOUR DAUGHTER.

SHUT UP.

KENO was born July 23, 1981, in Wa
om Kyoto Seika University, where he
the Tezuka Award for Best Newcomer
he began his previous work, the super
ich was adapted into the anime *Good*

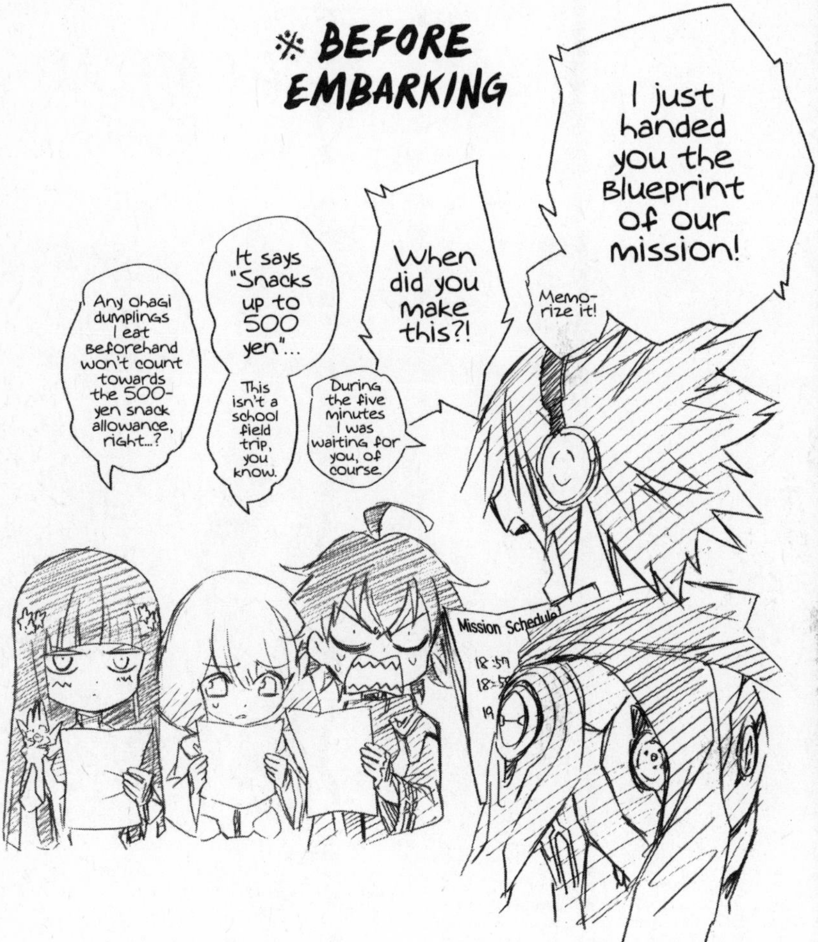
※ BEFORE EMBARKING
I just handed you the Blueprint of our mission!
Memorize it!
When did you make this?!
During the five minutes I was waiting for you, of course.
It says "Snacks up to 500 yen"...
This isn't a school field trip, you know.
Any ohagi dumplings I eat beforehand won't count towards the 500-yen snack allowance, right...?
Mission Schedule

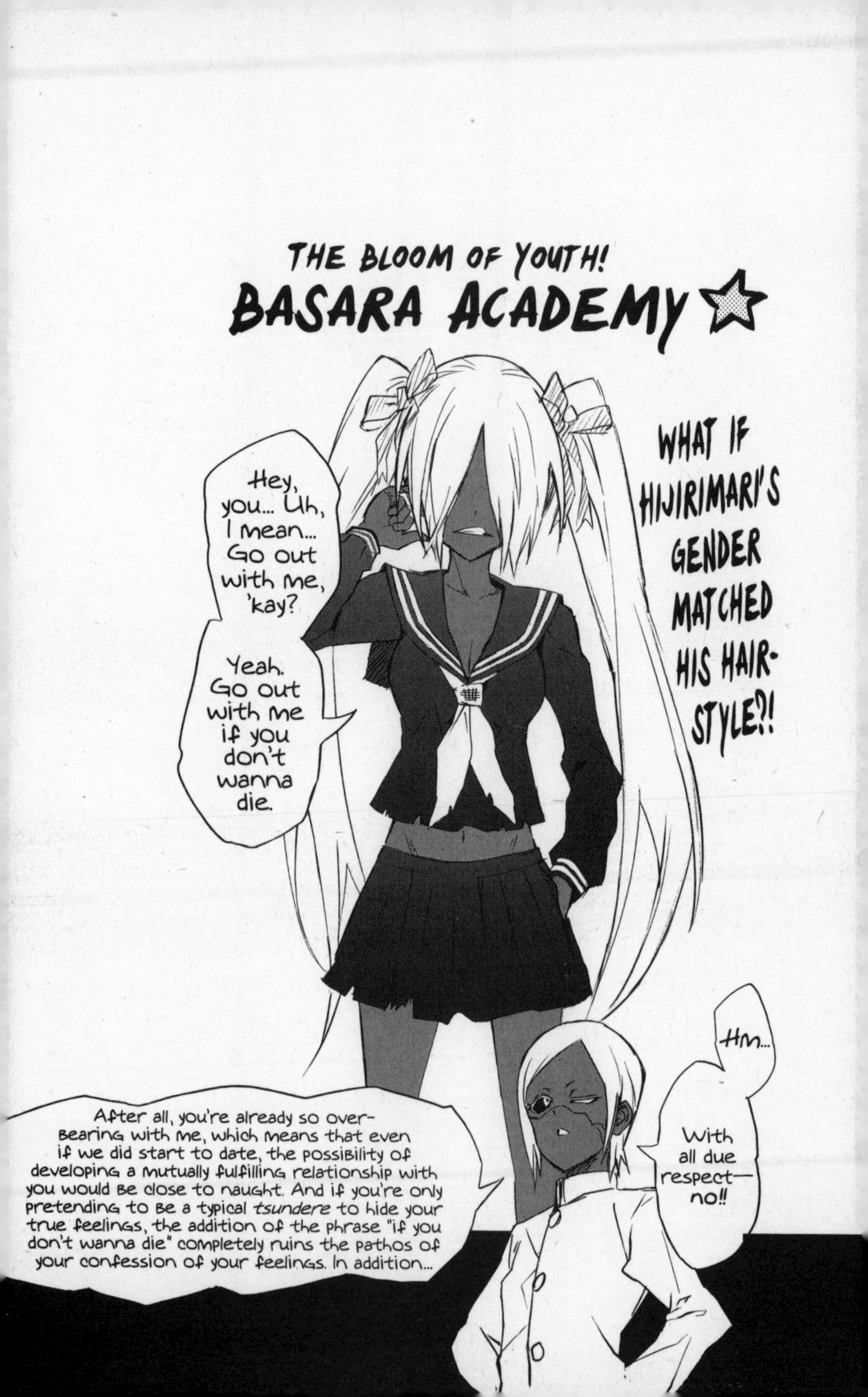
THE BLOOM OF YOUTH!
BASARA ACADEMY☆
WHAT IF HIJIRIMARI'S GENDER MATCHED HIS HAIR-STYLE?!
Hey, you... Uh, I mean... Go out with me, 'kay?
Yeah. Go out with me if you don't wanna die.
Hm...
With all due respect—no!!
After all, you're already so over-bearing with me, which means that even if we did start to date, the possibility of developing a mutually fulfilling relationship with you would be close to naught. And if you're only pretending to be a typical *tsundere* to hide your true feelings, the addition of the phrase "if you don't wanna die" completely ruins the pathos of your confession of your feelings. In addition...

—SHONEN JUMP Manga Edition—

STORY & ART Yoshiaki Sukeno

TRANSLATION **Tetsuichiro Miyaki**
ENGLISH ADAPTATION **Bryant Turnage**
TOUCH-UP ART & LETTERING **Stephen Dutro**
DESIGN **Shawn Carrico**
EDITOR **Annette Roman**

SOUSEI NO ONMYOJI © 2013 by Yoshiaki Sukeno
All rights reserved.
First published in Japan in 2013 by SHUEISHA Inc., Tokyo.
English translation rights arranged by SHUEISHA Inc.

The stories, characters and incidents mentioned in this
publication are entirely fictional.

Printed in the U.S.A.

Published by VIZ Media, LLC
P.O. Box 77010
San Francisco, CA 94107

10 9 8 7 6 5 4 3 2 1
First printing, April 2017

www.viz.com

www.shonenjump.com

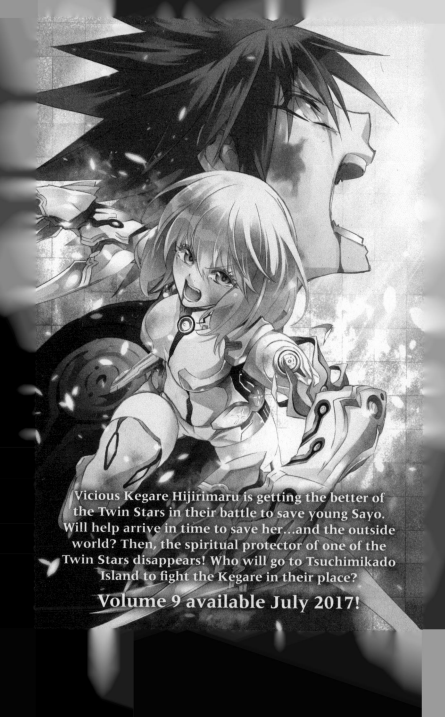

Vicious Kegare Hijirimaru is getting the better of the Twin Stars in their battle to save young Sayo. Will help arrive in time to save her...and the outside world? Then, the spiritual protector of one of the Twin Stars disappears! Who will go to Tsuchimikado Island to fight the Kegare in their place?

Volume 9 available July 2017!

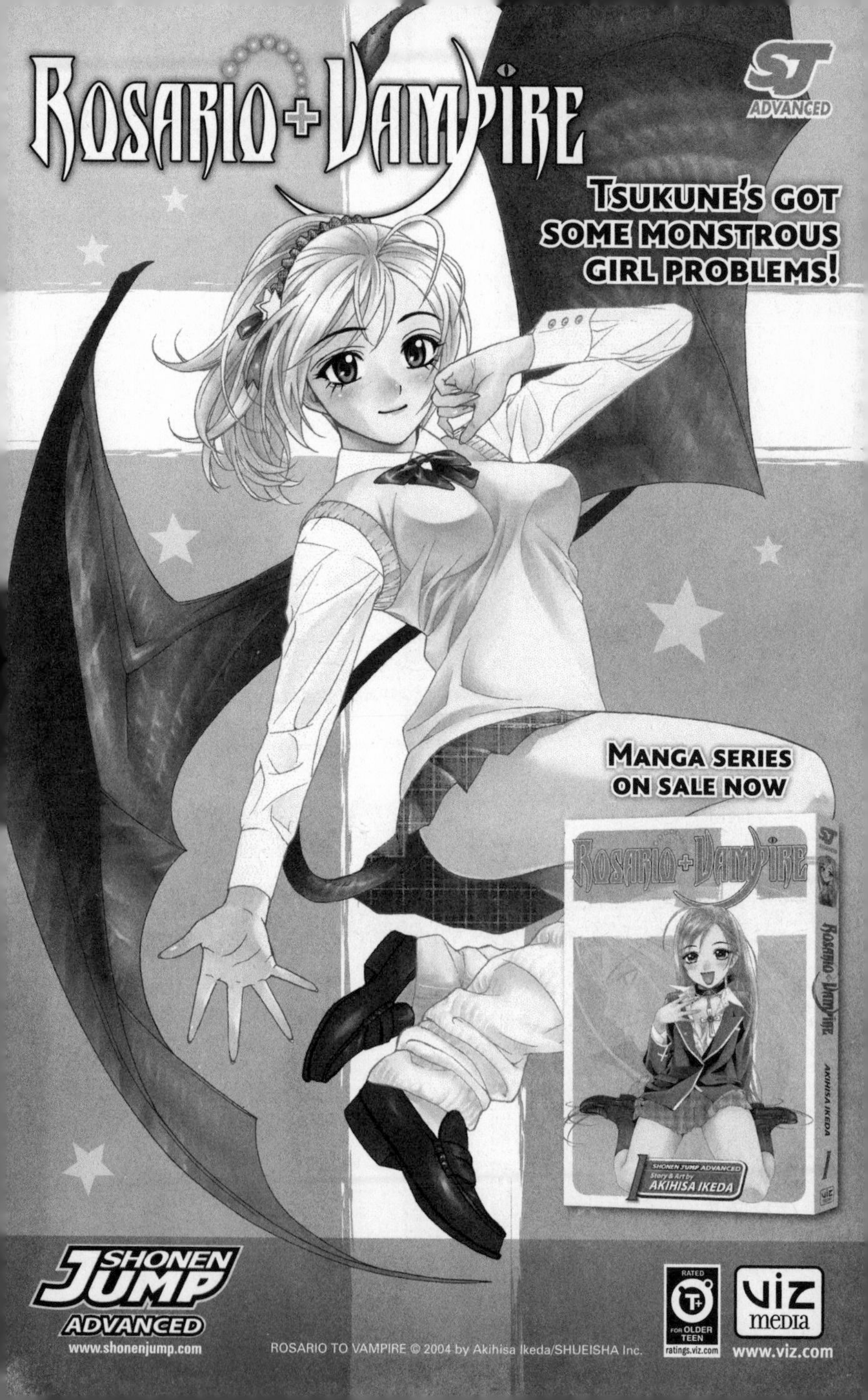
ROSARIO+VAMPIRE
SJ ADVANCED
TSUKUNE'S GOT SOME MONSTROUS GIRL PROBLEMS!
MANGA SERIES ON SALE NOW
ROSARIO+VAMPIRE
SHONEN JUMP ADVANCED
Story & Art by AKIHISA IKEDA
SHONEN JUMP ADVANCED
www.shonenjump.com
ROSARIO TO VAMPIRE © 2004 by Akihisa Ikeda/SHUEISHA Inc.
RATED T+ FOR OLDER TEEN
ratings.viz.com
VIZ media
www.viz.com

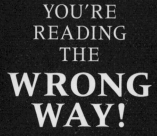

YOU'RE READING THE **WRONG WAY!**

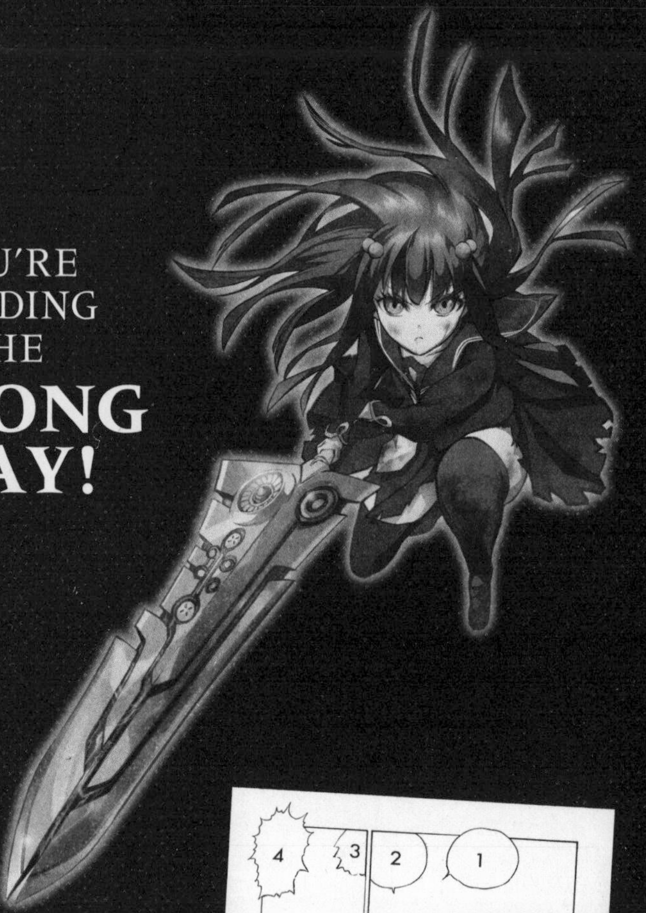

Twin Star Exorcists reads from right to left, starting in the upper-right corner. Japanese is read from right to left, meaning that action, sound effects and word-balloon order are completely reversed from English order.

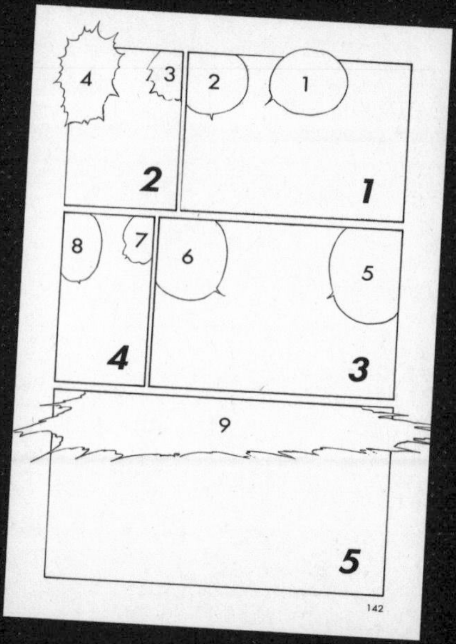

1
2
3
4
1
2
5
6
7
8
3
4
9
5
142